British Diplomacy
and the Armenian Question,
from the 1830s to 1914

British Diplomacy
and the Armenian Question,
from the 1830s to 1914

Arman J. Kirakossian

Gomidas Institute Books

Princeton and London

This Publication was made possible by a generous grant from
The Dolores Zohrab Liebmann Fund

The Gomidas Institute, PO Box 208, Princeton, NJ 08542-0208
The Gomidas Institute (UK), PO Box 32665, London W14 0XT
© 2003 by the Gomidas Institute
All Rights Reserved. Published 2003
Printed in the United States of America
12 11 10 09 08 07 06 05 04 03   7 6 5 4 3 2 1

Originally published in 1999 as *Britanakan divanagitutiune yev
arevmtahayutian khndire (XIX-rd dari 30-akan tt.–1914 t.)* by the Gitutiun
press of the National Academy of Sciences of the Republic of Armenia,
under the auspices of the academy's Institute of History.

Library of Congress Cataloging-in-Publication Data
Kirakosîan, A. Dzh. (Arman Dzhonovich)
    [Britanakan divanagitut'yunĕ ev arevmtahayut'yan khndirĕ]
    British diplomacy and the Armenian question : from the 1830s to 1914 /
Arman John Kirakossian.
        p.   cm.
    Translated from the Armenian.
    Includes bibliographical references and index.
    ISBN 1-884630-06-5 (hardcover) — ISBN 1-884630-07-3 (pbk.)
    1. Armenian question. 2. Armenians—Turkey. 3. Great Britain—Foreign
relations—Turkey. 4. Turkey—Foreign relations—Great Britain.   I. Title.
DS194.K56713 2003
956.6'20154—dc22

                                                                2003014753

To the memory of my parents,
John Kirakossian and Lia Ghazakhetsian

Contents

Acknowledgements

The author is extremely grateful to The Dolores Zohrab Liebmann Fund for making possible the English-language publication of this book. The author thanks Haik Gugarats for translating the Armenian original of the book into English, and Edward Alexander for editing the manuscript. The author also thanks Vincent Lima and the Gomidas Institute. Last but not least, the author owes a debt of gratitude to his family and friends whose love, respect, and devotion helped bring this work to fruition.

Preface

The fate of Western Armenia—commonly referred to as "The Armenian Question"—is a key issue in the modern history of the Armenian people. It emerged as a factor in international politics in the wake of the Russo-Turkish War of 1877–78. As an integral part of the Eastern Question, the Armenian Question became a subject of bilateral and multilateral discussions between the Great European Powers—Great Britain, Russia, Germany, France, Austria-Hungary, and Italy. For the European countries, especially Britain, the issue was viewed through the prism of their interests in the Near East and as a tool to assert influence over the decaying Ottoman Empire, as well as to stake a claim over its dominions. In the years that followed, the term "Armenian Question" would signify the historical challenges to Armenia and as such, come to have a broader ideological meaning and scope. Political Armenology uses the term "Armenian Question" to signify the implementation of reforms in Western Armenia, the establishment of autonomy, liberation of Armenia from foreign domination, unification of two parts of Armenia, reestablishment of an independent Armenian state on the Armenian Plateau, as well as the Armenian national liberation movement, and international efforts to achieve recognition and condemnation of the Armenian Genocide.

In the first half of the nineteenth century, the Ottoman Empire—at the time the largest sovereign state in the Near East—became an object of competition between the major European powers. Guided by their national interests, each of the powers strove for political and economic domination of the empire while defending the principle of its territorial integrity. The preservation of the status quo in Turkey eventually metamorphosed into a senseless, irrelevant principle obscuring the long-term processes of ethnic and religious divisions and administrative decay in the Ottoman Empire.

Britain, as the major power of the nineteenth century, assumed a major role in the international politics of the Near East. From the 1830s until the years before the First World War, the British priorities were consistent and predictable: asserting Britain's economic and political influence over Turkey while protecting its territorial integrity from encroachment by other powers, most notably Russia. While Russia asserted, with equal consistency, its right to protect the Christian subjects of the Ottoman Empire, British policy was to press for internal reforms in Turkey that could strengthen it economically and militarily, achieve equality between, and prosperity for, the Christian and Muslim communities, and suppress the national yearnings of non-Turkish peoples.

The British policy of pressing for reforms from above did not improve the lot of the non-Turkish groups, including the Armenian people, and in fact, the situation in Ottoman provinces populated by the Armenians deteriorated steadily. To remove the threat of potential European intervention that the Armenian Question posed, Abdulhamid II's government in 1894–96 took the radical step of carrying out persecution and large-scale massacres of the Armenian population. Twenty years later, the successors to Abdulhamid, the Young Turks, organized and implemented a policy of genocide that in the process of expelling the native people from its ancestral land exterminated one and a half million Armenians.

The author will attempt to present the development and evolution of British foreign policy making as it impacted on the Ottoman Empire and its Armenian population and other ethnic elements, and he will delineate British diplomatic activities and the British government's role at various stages of the Armenian Question from the 1830s to 1914. British foreign policy is analyzed in the context of international and regional dynamics, against the backdrop of Britain's political system and public opinion, the internal and foreign policy of the Ottoman Government, the state of affairs in Western Armenia, and the Armenian national movement.

This book complements and serves as a prequel to prominent Armenian-Cypriot historian Akaby Nassibian's *Britain and the Armenian Question: 1915–1923* (London, 1984) in documenting the domestic and international policies of the British government related to the Armenian Question in the nineteenth and early twentieth centuries, and makes extensive use of British Foreign Office archival and published materials, and other relevant literature and documents.

The author began his research on the subject in the late 1970s, publishing a monograph in Russian, *Great Britain and the Armenian Question: 1890s* (Yerevan, 1990), and has used the research materials for articles he has contributed to *Encyclopedia of the Armenian Question* (Yerevan, 1992, 1996) and other monographs and academic publications. The first edition of this book was published in Armenian by the Institute of History of the National Academy of Sciences of the Republic of Armenia in 1999.

The author has made extensive use of national libraries and archives in Yerevan, Moscow, London, Athens, and Washington, D.C., and has collected, researched, and analyzed nearly all British diplomatic correspondence from the period covered in the book. The breadth, scope, and straightforward prose of the British Foreign Office documents, telegrams, and dispatches make them an extremely valuable resource for gaining insight into the making of foreign policy in Britain, the rest of Europe, and the Ottoman Empire, and into the process of reforms in the Armenian-populated provinces, the conditions of Western Armenia's population, and the Armenian national movement. Most of these documents appear here as source material for the first time. The author also draws upon memoirs, academic papers, British Foreign Office Blue Books, and contemporary media publications in Britain and the United States.

The book consists of five chapters, a conclusion, notes, a bibliography, and an index. The endnotes refer to archival or other material to allow the reader to ascertain the origin of the information, and include brief biographic data on the most prominent public figures featured in the book.

Chapter 1. British Policies toward the Ottoman Empire and its Christian Minorities, 1830s–1870s

1. The Formation of Great Britain's Near Eastern Policy

At the turn of the eighteenth century, England had become one of the world's leading industrial and trading nations. England's position vis-à-vis other Powers only improved with the demise of Napoleon's France, in the wake of the Congress of Vienna. Great Britain had also become a major colonial Power, and her colonial designs only intensified in India, China, Afghanistan, New Zealand and Australia by mid-century. England sought to solidify and guard its commercial advantage, and it already possessed an advanced economy that none of its Continental rivals could compete with. These developments led to increased tension in its relations with other European Powers, notably France. The latter, though weaker as a Power, was still a viable commercial and colonial competitor of England, which sought to check French expansionism with the help of Prussia and Austria, while simultaneously keeping both out of Russia's reach. Pursuing active balance-of-power politics, England viewed with distrust other Powers' colonial expansion plans. The aim of the balance-of-power system was to prevent the emergence of a strong power that could single-handedly undermine the international system.[1] England would prevent any European nation from accruing too much power and would alternatively ally with or challenge any player in this system to maintain the overall balance.[2]

The relative importance of the Near East and the Balkans in European diplomacy gradually started to increase in the 1830s, parallel to increasing tensions among the European Powers over their attempt to exercise political and economic domination over various parts of the Ottoman Empire. The Ottoman Empire was at the crossroads of major strategic and trade routes, and controlling them was, potentially, the key to an overall domination by any power. These geopolitical developments turned the Ottoman Empire into one of the key elements in the European balance-of-power system.[3]

It is possible to identify two somewhat irreconcilable trends in the Near East policies of the European Powers. On the one hand, the Ottoman Empire's territorial integrity was to be preserved while it was being turned into an economic appendage of the European Powers, that is, a peripheral entity separating Europe from its African and Asian colonies. On the other hand, the European nations would attempt to impose or carve out spheres of influence in the various parts of the Ottoman Empire to prevent their permanent secession as a result of national liberation movements. No matter how conflicting, these two main policies, the second one especially required complete cooperation among all the main players in the European balance-of-powers system, with the commitment to uphold it.[4]

After the end of the Napoleonic wars, Great Britain concentrated on Russia as the greater peril to the European balance of powers. Russian territorial expansion in the wake of the Russo-Turkish wars of the eighteenth century was of serious concern to the British Government, which viewed the newcomer to the European Powers' club with deep suspicion. Although their joint efforts and cooperation in the struggle against Napoleon's France helped mitigate the Russian-British disagreements, the Russian successes in the 1826–28 Russo-Persian War and especially the 1828–29 Russo-Turkish war rekindled the old British mistrust of Russian intentions. The increase in Russia's relative power in the south and its territorial expansion there was viewed as potentially dangerous to the British domination of India.[5] The suppression of the Polish Rebellion in 1830 only galvanized the anti-Russian feelings, but a key turning point was the Egyptian-Turkish disagreement of 1831–33 and the Russian-Ottoman treaty of Unkiar-Skelessi, which was viewed as a major victory for Russian diplomacy, since it was achieved implicitly, as a result of the Russian mediation of the Turkish-Egyptian dispute, rather than on the battlefield. The treaty provided for permanent mutual consultations to ensure "serenity and security" of the contracting parties, as well as for assistance against third party interference. A secret clause in the treaty would require the Turkish authorities to close the Straits to all foreign navy ships should the Russian Government request it to do so.[6]

Russian-Ottoman relations between 1790 and 1850, including the few wars and direct negotiations between the two Powers, achieved a measure of relative equilibrium in the Near East, Southeast Europe, Asia Minor and South Caucasus, with continued commercial and economic ties, and understanding on a number of issues, such as the Balkan insurrections and the status of the Holy Land.

Russian-Turkish relations, nevertheless, were only one element in the mosaic of international relations and competing interests in the region. The quest of the European Powers to gain a foothold in the region and their attempts to impose a degree of control and influence there indirectly contributed to the deterioration in Russian-Turkish relations. The latest Turkish-Russian treaty, consequently, was a cause of major concern among European Powers and British statesmen.

In the eighteenth century, England was virtually indifferent toward the Ottoman Empire. In fact, England supported Russia during its war against Turkey in 1768–74, if only to uphold the English-Russian commercial ties. The new British policy toward the Ottoman Empire was crafted during what became known as the Palmerston era. During his long tenure as Foreign Secretary and then Prime Minister, Lord Henry John Palmerston[7] was a defining figure in the formulation of British foreign policy. It was best described by him in his famous statement that England "has no eternal allies and no permanent enemies. Our interests are eternal, and those interests it is our duty to follow."[8]

The Near Eastern direction of that foreign policy was a major priority for Lord Palmerston. The scope and content of the policy changed frequently in the decades that followed, yet one key factor remained at its core. Since the early 1830s, the British Government had upheld the principle of the territorial integrity of the Ottoman Empire and had opposed any program to divide it. In July 1833, immediately after the Russian-Turkish treaty was signed, Palmerston said that formation of new territorial and national entities out of the Ottoman provinces was an issue of great interest to England. He argued that it did not matter whether the Empire was Christian or Muslim, but that the political considerations, namely, preservation of stability, freedom and balance of power in Europe, required that the territorial integrity of the Ottoman Empire remain intact.[9]

From 1833 to 1839, Palmerston's Turkish policy pursued the following objectives: (a) check Russian interference in Turkish affairs and remove the Russian protectorate over the Empire; b) increase British political and economic influence in the Empire and make it dependent on British support; (c) promote military, economic and legal reforms and improve the position of the Christian minorities of the Empire.

As a proponent of a constitutional system, Lord Palmerston suggested that the Ottoman Empire should be reformed from above—by Sultan's decree. He hoped that the implementation of the reforms would reinvigorate the Ottoman Empire, and help it become a vital and able element in the European balance-of-power system. Palmerston's advocacy of an independent and integral Ottoman Empire was flexible and credible enough to survive intact until 1914.[10]

To neutralize the effects of the 1833 Russo-Turkish Convention, England now pushed for a commercial treaty with the Ottoman Empire that would also promote—under British control—the reforms in the Ottoman government. Acting on Palmerston's instructions, the British Ambassador in Constantinople, Lord Ponsonby, told the Sublime Porte that the British Government and His Majesty the King support the reform process in the Ottoman Empire. The Ambassador pledged to provide new weapons and English instructors to a regular Ottoman Army, invite Turkish cadets to the British academies, and strengthen the Bosphorus defenses. Palmerston worked directly with the Turkish Embassy in London, and, after 1836, with the Sultan's Ambassador, Mustafa Reshid Pasha.[11]

The British diplomatic efforts paid off, as the Turkish statesmen and the Sultan accepted the British proposals, viewing alliance with the strongest Power in the world and implementation of the reforms as a necessary first step to secure the survival, preservation and 'Europeanization' of the Empire. The Sublime Porte was also suspicious of the Russian advances toward France, which supported Egyptian Pasha Mohammad Ali.

Upon expiration of the 1820 English-Turkish commercial treaty in 1834, the Sultan's government petitioned London to review the import lists to allow for greater exports of Ottoman products to Great Britain. Accepting Turkish demands, Palmerston, nevertheless, made it conditional on political demands of his own, such as opening the Straits to British military ships, the exclusive right to supply weapons to Turkey, inviting British military instructors to drill the Ottoman Army, and so on.[12]

The three-year tenure of Mustafa Reshid Pasha in Europe and his role as the Ambassador in London left a mark on his political views and his position on the necessity for reforms in the Ottoman Empire. In his report to Sultan Mahmud II, he not only outlined Palmerston's proposals for the main directions of the reforms, but also presented a detailed program for economic and industrial revival of the Empire. To implement this program, he suggested it was necessary to draw on the experience of the leading European nations, and pull British specialists into the Sultan's service.[13]

The British-Turkish commercial treaty of August 1838 was a turning point for British diplomacy, as well as for the Turkish reforms. The treaty provided for free trade and customs-free maritime navigation through Turkish territorial waters and the Black Sea Straits, as well as an end to monopoly and the forced procurement system. Great Britain was the first European nation that won the right to export agricultural products and natural resources.[14]

While France was the main trading partner of the Ottoman Empire at the turn of the eighteenth century, beginning in the 1820s, Britain became a leading trade partner and source of imports.[15] In 1856, British exports to the Ottoman Empire were 141.3 million francs, and imports 80 million francs (the French exports were 91.9 million and exports, 131.5 million francs).[16] Between 1820 and the 1840s, British trade accounted for 31 percent of the total foreign trade turnover in Turkey, while British exports to the Ottoman empire exceeded those of France by 1.5 times, Austria by 1.9 times, and Russia by nearly 6 times.[17]

Palmerston could not prevent the second Turkish-Egyptian clash, which began in 1840, but he succeeded in having it resolved in favor of the Sultan's government, which eliminated the danger of an exclusive Russian influence over the Ottoman Empire. British diplomacy also resulted in an agreement among the five relevant Powers—and the conclusion of a convention in July 1840—on the use of the Black Sea Straits by Great Britain, Austria, Prussia and Russia, and the Ottoman Empire, followed by another Quintuple Convention in 1841, with France added as another signatory. According to the latter Convention, the Straits were closed to traffic by the military vessels of any country during a non-belligerent period. Thus, the use of the Black Sea

Straits was to be regulated by multilateral treaties, rather than by a mutual understanding between the two concerned parties, Russia and Turkey. Russia was only one of the signatories of the international treaties, with a status equal to others, and consequently lost its right of sole protectorate over the Ottoman Empire.[18]

The Melbourne-Palmerston Whig Ministry was replaced by the Tories' Robert Peel[19] in 1841–46, and George Aberdeen[20] was the new Foreign Secretary. The Russian and Ottoman policies of Great Britain were greatly changed, as Peel was considered a Russophile and Lord Aberdeen was viewed as a sworn enemy of Turkey. Both the Prime Minister and the Foreign Secretary were unhappy with Palmerston's conduct of relations with Russia and Turkey and were anxious to improve British-Russian relations.[21]

As a result, Czar Nicholas I visited England in May 1844. The main issue during negotiations with Peel and Aberdeen was clarification of the two countries' positions on the Ottoman Empire. The parties agreed to have a common position should the Ottoman Empire collapse or be attacked by a third country. They also agreed that Great Britain and Russia would protect the territorial integrity of the Ottoman Empire. Upon returning to Russia, Foreign Minister Karl Nesselrode presented a memorandum to the British government on partition of the Ottoman Empire. The British Government, however, did not accept the Russian Czar's plan, as it did not want to have specific commitments.[22]

In 1846, Peel's government was replaced by the Whig Party's John Russel[23] and Lord Palmerston was once again at the helm of the Foreign Office. His Ottoman policies met serious opposition on a scale far greater than in the 1820s to 1840s. In the decade leading to the Crimean War (1853–56), when Palmerston thought he had secured Liberal support for his foreign policy, an alternative foreign policy-thinking developed in England, which was associated with the ideas and positions of Richard Cobden. Cobden, in an 1835 treatise entitled England, Ireland, and America, had suggested that defense of the Ottoman Empire against the Russians was not in the interests of Great Britain. Another treatise, entitled Russia, published in 1836, criticized the balance-of-power policies of Palmerston, basing his arguments on changing international situation, growing influence of the United States and its policies, collapse of the colonial regime, and the prevalence of the free trade regime.[24]

During the parliamentary debates, he challenged the Foreign Office position on the Ottoman Empire's territorial integrity, calling the Turks an "alien race" unworthy of living next door to European civilization. He called for greater British involvement with the fate of the Christian minorities in the Ottoman Empire, and greater correlation between British foreign policy and the interests of the Christian minorities. Cobden argued that civilization would only gain should Constantinople fall into Russia's hands. The official British objectives were to gain influence in the Ottoman Empire and new markets there, and to promote the reforms. In turn, Cobden and his supporters called for greater emphasis on access to markets in Continental Europe and Russia.[25]

Despite growing opposition in Great Britain, Palmerston's position on the Ottoman Empire continued to dominate in the 1830s and 1840s, and in the decades to come.

The occupation of the Danubian Principalities in 1848 and the Balta-Liman Convention signed by the Ottoman Empire and Russia in April 1849, contributed to a further deterioration of Russian-British relations. The Convention that allowed the Sultan to name the rulers of Principalities, after prior consultations with the Emperor of Russia, was viewed by the European Powers as an extension of the 1833 Russian-Ottoman treaty. The British Government was concerned about the Russian troops' presence in the Ottoman Empire, the Russian interference in the internal affairs of the Sublime Porte, and was mistrustful of Russia's support for the Balkan Slav and Greek nationalists. Lord Palmerston was ready to take measures to prevent an undesirable turn of events, and the opportunity presented itself when Czar Nicholas I demanded extradition of the Polish and Hungarian revolutionaries who had taken refuge in the Ottoman Empire. In an official statement, Lord Palmerston said that extradition of political émigrés would be tantamount to a complete Russian subjugation of Turkey. To prevent this from happening, and in a move calculated at undermining Russian influence and credibility, Great Britain and France staged military maneuvers in the Straits, which was explicitly forbidden by the 1841 London Convention.[26] In his note of October 1, 1849, to Lord Palmerston, the Ottoman Chargé in London, Keberesle Mehmed Pasha expressed hope that Great Britain, as a friendly nation, would be supportive of the Sublime Porte as far as its honor and dignity as an independent state were concerned.[27]

The British navy was eventually removed from the Straits following a demarche by the Russian Ambassador while Russia withdrew its request, thus settling this incident. Nevertheless, the incident highlighted the future trends and directions of Ottoman-British cooperation.

2. The Formation of Great Britain's Policy Toward the Christian Subjects of the Ottoman Empire

By the middle of the 19th century, an important development became apparent in the multi-ethnic Ottoman Empire: non-Turkish peoples began to play a leading role in the economic activities of the Empire. The suppressed minorities showed signs of developing and exercising entrepreneurial skills, but were impeded by the ruling Turkish political and feudal elite, which served to deter the overall development of the country. Growing social and political disparity and revolutionary ideas that penetrated the Ottoman Empire in 1789, 1830, and 1848 laid the foundation for a national liberation ideology and movement among the non-Turkish peoples of the Empire.[28]

From an ethnic perspective, the Ottoman Empire was a composite of over 60 nationalities of different cultural and religious affiliations and of dissimilar levels of social, economic, political, and cultural development. Against this backdrop, the growing economic strength of the Christian minorities, and the reawakening and growing realization of their national identities, increased pressure from the European Powers on the Porte, thereby rendering impossible any attempt by the Sultan's Government to Islamize the Empire.[29]

Recognizing the imminence of problems in the internal life of the Empire, some representatives of the Ottoman elite advocated a new approach to the status of the Christian minorities of the Empire as early as the turn of the 18th century. Reforms were proposed to revive and modernize the economy, strengthen the central government, and prevent the national liberation movements and any possible interventions by the European Powers on behalf, and under the pretext, of defense of their co-religionists.

The national movement among the Slavic peoples in the Balkans and the liberation of Greece in the 1820s were milestones in the development of new approaches to the territorial integrity and governance of the Empire, and Sultan Mahmud II was the first ruler to attempt such reforms in the 1820s and

1830s. The Sultan said that all subjects of the Empire were 'his children' whom he would treat equally and who, in his view, differed only in matters of faith.[30]

The first period (1830–1850s) of Tanzimat—as this reform movement is known—saw an emergence of new ideas on the treatment of the Christian subjects of the empire. The author of the reforms, Reshid Pasha, called for guarantees for life, property and dignity for all the subjects of the Empire, without exclusions, as explicitly defined in the Gülhane-Hatte-Sheriff (Royal Decree of Gülhane).[31] The principle of 'equal treatment' was evident in a number of other legislative acts in the1840s. Reshid Pasha went one step further when he declared the unity of all the Sultan's subjects, a policy in effect until the beginning of the Crimean War. This policy was used as a tool against foreign encroachment, first of all against the perceived Russian threat. In 1848, the Sultan's Foreign Minister, Mehmed Emin Ali Pasha told the Russian envoy, Vladimir Titov, that improvement in the condition of the Christians was the best way to prevent them from making revolution. The European Powers had suppressed revolutions, the Turkish Foreign Minister said, while in the Ottoman Empire, all the subjects were equal, lived in equal conditions, and had similar responsibilities before the Empire.[32]

The British Government, which had already supported the cohesiveness, independence, and integrity of the Ottoman Empire, was supportive of the Ottoman officials' reform efforts, especially in the national question. The British Foreign Office concurred that only serious reforms could check the growing strength of the national liberation movement and the Christian minorities struggle to overthrow the Sultan's control, with the help of Russia. The Christian minorities began to figure prominently in England's Ottoman diplomacy in early 1830s. In his correspondence with Ambassador Ponsonby, Lord Palmerston suggested that increased involvement of the Christian minorities in local government, creation of militias under the control of Turkish officials, and enlistment of Christians in the Ottoman army could be a viable alternative to Russian interference in the Balkans.[33]

These objectives were foremost on the minds of the British envoys stationed in Constantinople—Ponsonby and, later, Stratford Canning (Lord Redcliffe). Always raising the specter of Russian-sponsored activities aimed against the Ottoman Empire's territorial integrity, Canning called on the Sublime Porte to implement reforms to alleviate the tension and put down revolts in the

Danubian Principalities, Bulgaria, Lebanon and other Arab regions. The British diplomats stressed that in the Balkans the Ottoman Empire was threatened by the Russian Czar's Slavophile policies that could spark a rebellion there. At the same time, it was insinuated that the eastern provinces were also endangered, as Russia would attempt a crusade against the Muslim population. The British Foreign Office was not unsympathetic toward the Turkish explanation and propaganda that declared that the national movements in Bulgaria, Herzegovina, Bosnia, Lebanon, Moldavia, Wallachia, and Albania were spearheaded by those rebels who opposed the principles of unity and equality of all the subjects of the Empire.[34]

It was during Aberdeen's tenure that the British position on the Christians of the Ottoman Empire was specified. In his October 1841, correspondence to Ambassador Canning, Aberdeen summarized Lord Palmerston's position on the Ottoman Empire. Along with the economic, military, and police reforms, the Ambassador was authorized to urge the Sublime Porte to develop and implement a greater tolerance policy toward the Christians and improve the conditions of Christians in Syria.[35]

In early 1842, Canning received special instructions from Aberdeen, specifying the official position on the Christian population. The Ambassador was instructed to work to advance the rights guaranteed under the Gülhane Decree. The document stated that the Christians were the most industrious people of the Empire, and, thus, to ignore them would jeopardize the integrity and survival of the Empire. Aberdeen stressed that the British Government would not intervene in the disputes between this or that Christian minority, and would not prefer one to the other.[36]

Unlike France, which had already been the protector of the Catholics since 1740, and Russia, which had been accepted as the Orthodox protecting Power in 1774, Britain did not choose a single religious group to protect, but, rather, defended the commercial interests across a variety of faiths. It was not until 1840s that the British moved to single out Protestants for protection.[37] Due to Canning's intervention, the British and German subjects in Jerusalem were granted the right to build a Protestant Church there.[38] The British Ambassador extended his protection to the Armenian Protestants,[39] and in 1850, succeeded in making the Protestants of the Empire a separate 'millet,' a distinct religious entity.[40]

Since his appointment as the Ambassador, Canning made the case for greater representation of Christians in the public life of the Ottoman Empire, such as their appointment to government offices, public service, the army, and the police, as well as the right to equal testimony before the court.[41]

Canning worked hard to abolish the death penalty for religious conversions. The incident in question concerned an Armenian who had converted to Islam, and had later converted back, and was executed for apostasy. In January 1844, Aberdeen demanded that Canning petition the Sultan's government to abolish, once and for all, the death penalty for religious conversion. If the Porte had any regard for England's friendship or hoped that England's protection could be extended in an hour of peril, the Foreign Secretary wrote, then Turkey should immediately renounce such a 'barbaric' practice.[42] After arduous and lengthy negotiations with the Sultan's government, the Ambassador wrote to Aberdeen that the question of the death penalty for apostasy had been conclusively settled. The Sultan had additionally pledged not to persecute the Christian faith or any Christian for practicing it, Ambassador Canning reported. In an official declaration on March 21, 1844, the Sublime Porte announced that it would take effectual measures to prevent the executions of the apostates.[43] The Sultan, nevertheless, did not abrogate the laws requiring a death penalty for renouncing Islam, and the Ottoman authorities continued to enforce them.

Canning went on temporary leave to London in 1846, but, prior to his departure presented a list of measures that needed to be implemented in the Empire, including a reform of taxation, increased education opportunities, and better regulation of sectarian relations between the Islamic and Christian subjects of the Empire.[44]

In October 1846, Palmerston, who had recently returned to power, sent a telegram to the British Chargé, Embassy Secretary Weresly. He stated that if special reforms were to be undertaken by the Sultan's government, the multi-ethnic and sectarian population would contribute to the general prosperity and development of the country. To achieve such a desirable end, he suggested, it was essential that the respect for life and property rights be practiced and that the privileges and rights be extended to all classes of society. Palmerston, at the same time, expressed concern that such measures might be contrary to Muslim public opinion.[45]

Upon his return to Constantinople in 1848, Canning drafted and presented to the Sublime Porte his "Five Points," a program of relief for the Christian minorities. He suggested that the Sultan's government should undertake to (1) uphold the Christians' right for free practice of their faith, the building of churches, and immunity for the Christian clergy; (2) extend to the Christian population the same rights and privileges exercised by the Muslims; (3) eliminate the special tax on non-Muslim farmers, known as 'kharaj'; (4) allow for enlistment of the Christians in military service, with the right to occupy officers' positions; and (5) uphold a Christian's right to give testimony against a Muslim before the courts.[46] Canning's Five Points were a reflection of those British and European policies aimed at removing the exclusive Russian right to interfere on behalf of the Christian minorities of the Empire.

The Sultan's government created a special commission to study the British Ambassador's proposals. Nevertheless, Canning wrote to Palmerston in late 1849 that his proposals had not been implemented since the commissioners sympathetic to his suggestions comprised a minority, while the only action taken by Grand Vizier Reshid Pasha had been to send circulars to the governors in the provinces.[47] The Ambassador presented another memorandum to the Sultan in 1850, once again arguing for the implementation of reforms. However, the political support of Reshid Pasha and other reformers was already waning, and the Canning program was no longer discussed.[48]

3. Britain and the Near Eastern Crisis of the 1850s

The Eastern Question increased in intensity in the years leading to the Crimean War, and became the focus of the European Powers' policies in the Near East. In the language of diplomacy, the 'Eastern Question' refers to the relations between the Ottoman Empire and the European Powers and Russia, the liberation movement of the oppressed minorities in the Empire and its exploitation by other Powers, as well as the Powers' race to obtain commercial and political concessions from the Empire. The first use of the term occurred at the 1822 Verona Conference, during the discussions on the Greek national liberation movement and the situation in the Balkans.

By the 1850s, the Eastern Question gained in complexity and nuances parallel to the increased tensions in the Near East between the leading European Powers of the day. Despite the inevitable conflict of interests among Britain,

France, and Austria, these Powers shared two main objectives: to secure the political and economic strengthening of the Ottoman Empire by means of reforms, and to prevent the liberation movements of the Christian minorities. The two main objectives of the European Powers should be seen in the context of their efforts to contain the Russian influence in the Near East, and they led to increased polarization in Russian-Turkish relations.

The disagreements between the European Powers over the Ottoman Empire were usually colored by religious differences, as each nation sought to establish its control over the Orthodox, Catholic, and Protestant population. For example, the French diplomatic efforts in the Ottoman Empire took a markedly tougher line in early 1850s. In May 1851, the French envoy to the Porte, Charles La Valette demanded that the Porte make a proclamation listing the rights and privileges of the Catholic clergy and laity in the Empire. Only after La Valette's threats of dispatching the navy into the Bosphorus and the Syrian coastline did the Sublime Porte proclaim in a special declaration, issued on February 8, 1852, the rights and privileges of the Catholic population, as well as on the joint use of the Holy Sites with the Orthodox Christians.[49]

In the early 1850s, the interests of the British Government and the Porte coincided on the suppression of liberation movements. Both Canning and his temporary replacement in 1852–53, Colonel Hugh Rose, demanded that the Porte take measures to suppress anti-Turkish disturbances in various quarters of the Empire, in order to prevent a possible Russian intervention. It was not uncommon for the British Embassy and consular officials to undertake organizing anti-revolutionary expeditions, or to assist the local governor's efforts in this regard. Such activities by British officials were observed during the suppression of revolts in Arabia (in 1850's), Montenegro, Northern Albania, and Herzegovina (in 1852).[50]

In conjunction with the more pro-active British diplomacy in the Near East, the role of the British consuls in the Ottoman Empire gained in prominence. The policy of appointing industrious and able people to these positions allowed them to gain considerable authority and influence, which could be channeled toward promoting reforms locally.

In early 1853, Russia and Great Britain entered into active political discussions on the future of the Ottoman Empire and the condition of its Christian subjects. On January 11, British Ambassador to Russia Hamilton Seymour reported to Foreign Secretary Lord John Russell on his audience with Czar Nicholas I. During this meeting, the Czar said that the affairs of Turkey were in a very disorganized state and that the country itself seemed to be falling apart. In the Czar's opinion, the fall would be a great calamity, and, he observed, it was important that England and Russia should reach understanding upon these affairs and that neither take any decisive step of which the other was not apprised. "We have on our hands a sick man—a very sick man," the Emperor said. "It will be, I tell you frankly, a great misfortune if, one of these days, he should slip away from us, especially before all necessary arrangements were made."

Responding, Seymour remarked, "It is the part of a generous and strong man to treat with gentleness the sick and feeble man." The Ambassador proposed that no decision should be taken by Russia in the affairs of Turkey without the prior agreement of the British Government. In his summary of the minutes of the audience, the Ambassador noted that Britain should "desire a close concert with Russia" to prevent the downfall of Turkey, while "Russia would be well pleased that the concert should apply to the events by which this downfall is to be followed."[51]

In his next audience with the Ambassador, which took place on January 14, the Czar said, "my country is so vast, so happily circumstanced in every way, that it would be unreasonable in me to desire more territory or more power than I possess. On the contrary, I am the first to tell you that our great, perhaps our only danger is that which would arise from an extension given to an Empire already too large.

"Close to us lies Turkey, and in our present condition, nothing better for our interests can be desired. The times have gone by when we had anything to fear from the fanatical spirit or the military enterprise of the Turks, and yet the country is strong enough... to preserve its independence, and to ensure respectful treatment from other countries.

"Well in that Empire there are several millions of Christians whose interests I am called upon to watch over while the right of doing so is secured to me by treaty... Our religion, as established in this country, came to us from the East, and there are feelings, as well as obligations, which never must be lost sight of." The Czar went on to say that the 'sick man' might suddenly "die upon our hands" and it would not be possible to "resuscitate what is dead." He proposed to the British Government to provide beforehand for the contingency, rather than risking chaos, confusion and the certainty of a European war, all of which could occur unexpectedly.

The Czar also said it was of great importance that "we [two countries] understand one another and not allow events to take us by surprise." He stressed that "if England and I arrive at an understanding of this matter... it is indifferent to me what others do or think." The Czar confided, "I tell you plainly that if England thinks of establishing herself one of these days at Constantinople, I will not allow it." The Ambassador's report to the Foreign Secretary noted that two consequences might be anticipated from the appearance of an imperial army on the frontiers of Turkey. "One, the counter-demonstration which might be provoked on the part of France, the other, and the more serious, the rising on the part of the Christian population against the Sultan's authority," the report said. In Seymour's opinion, the concert between two principal governments interested in Turkey's destinies—England and Russia—could prevent Turkey's sudden downfall.[52]

On February 9, Lord Russell wrote to Seymour that Britain would not enter into any agreement providing for the contingent fall of the Ottoman Empire, without prior communication with the Russian Czar. The Foreign Secretary suggested that utmost forbearance must be displayed to Turkey and that any demands by foreign Powers should be made by way of a friendly negotiation rather than peremptory requests. He also cautioned against any coercive military or naval demonstrations and proposed that all differences regarding Turkish matters should be resolved in the concert of Great Powers. Lord Russell wanted to urge the Sultan to treat his Christian subjects in conformity with the principles of equity and religious freedom. Nor was this only a moral consideration, and as if to make himself clearer, the Foreign Secretary concluded his communication with an observation that a more impartial law and equal administration would reduce Russia's leeway in exercising its rights as a protecting Power.[53]

In February 1853, Britain's new Foreign Secretary, George Clarendon,[54] instructed Ambassador Canning to urge upon Sultan Abdul Mejid the necessity of implementing the reforms alleviating the condition of the Christian population. The unequal and destitute condition of the Christians were the main reasons for outside interference in the internal affairs of the Ottoman

Empire, Clarendon noted, adding that improvement in their conditions was an important guarantee of the economic prosperity and stability of the Ottoman Empire. The Ambassador was further instructed to cooperate and consult with his French counterpart. Clarendon mentioned that Britain and France share many common interests and positions on the Eastern issues, including defending the independence and integrity of the Turkish state.[55]

On February 15, Canning communicated to Clarendon that the Sultan had finally heeded his petitions made over the course of the previous four years to consider Christians as being on equal footing with the Muslims in matters of criminal jurisprudence. The Sultan, thus, extended his earlier decree, issued only for Cairo and Alexandria, to be valid throughout the Empire. The Ambassador noted with satisfaction that he had worked for four years to bring this about, and had most recently made a strong demarche in this regard to Reshid Pasha.[56]

In yet another report to the Foreign Office, Ambassador Canning wrote on February 24 that the Sultan's "great act" would be followed by other proofs of the Sultan's comprehensive beneficence, reflecting the improved attitude on the part of the general population.[57] In his reply, Clarendon expressed his satisfaction with the reform act and hoped that the Sultan's subjects would receive it as proof of the Sultan's determination to address their grievances and remove any grounds for complaint.[58]

On February 20 Ambassador Seymour had another audience with Czar Nicholas, noting that the 'sick man' would not pass away immediately, as history had been full of examples that established states did not suddenly die out. Czar Nicholas replied that the British Government was mistaken in its belief that Turkey retained any element of existence, repeating his assertion that the 'sick man was dying,' an event that should not take anyone by surprise. He proposed that the two countries come to some understanding, not a treaty or protocol, but an informal general understanding on the matter of Turkey's future.[59]

The Czar was convinced that the catastrophe would strike at any moment, caused by an external intervention or war, an old or new Turkish insurgency, or a general uprising by the Christian population against Muslim rule. The Czar even said he would not consider a Russian occupation of Constantinople, or a similar action by the British or the French. Nicholas I also made clear he would not tolerate the restoration of Byzantium or an enlargement of the Greek state, or, even worse, breaking-up of the Ottoman Empire into multiple republics, which would then "grant asylum to the Kossuths and Mazzinis of the world." He said Russia would be willing to go to war to prevent such developments. He described the internal Turkish situation as chaotic, noting that he believed the country lacked order and strong governments and was undergoing continuous insurgencies. Seymour told the Czar that the main difference between Britain and Russia was that Russia dwelt on the presumed fall of Turkey and arrangements after the fall, while Britain looked to keep Turkey intact and undertake measures to prevent its condition from becoming worse.[60]

In his February 21 memorandum to the British Government, Czar Nicholas noted that the atrocities committed in Montenegro, Bulgaria, Bosnia and Herzegovina gave too much reason to other Christian-populated areas of the Empire to suspect that a similar fate might befall them. He suggested that the atrocities were calculated to provoke a general uprising by the Christians, which would hasten the Empire's fall.[61]

On March 23, Clarendon wrote to Seymour that the British Government shared the Russian Czar's position on the occupation of Constantinople by any foreign Power, since it would be incompatible with the current balance of power and the principles of maintaining peace in Europe. The Foreign Secretary agreed that Byzantium could not be resurrected, that bad governance on the part of Greece offered no encouragement to extend its territorial dominion, and that as long as there was no provincial or communal government, large tracts of the Empire would be overcome by anarchy. Clarendon contended that England had no desire for territorial aggrandizement and could not be party to an arrangement from which it would derive such benefit. Moreover, England would never be a party to an understanding that would be kept secret from other nations. The British Government was convinced that no arrangement could control events and that no understanding could be kept secret. Moreover, Clarendon suggested that such an arrangement could incite the Christian subjects to rebel against the central government. He suggested that a European congress be called to address the problem, but, as a major pre-condition, that the present order of things in Turkey be maintained. The British Government, he noted, aimed to preserve peace and to uphold the

Turkish Empire. He noted that any problem in the East would cause discord among the Western Powers; conversely, any issue in the West could assume a revolutionary character and cause a revision of the social system in the East.

Clarendon expressed his conviction that the signs of Turkish decay were not more evident or more rapid than before. Turkey still possessed great energy and wealth, he noted, and the existing corruption did not yet threaten the existence of the state. He also suggested that the treatment of the Christians in Turkey was not that harsh, and that the Empire's toleration of its subjects could moderate the views of some governments that beheld Turkey with contempt as a barbarous state.[62]

Thus, the British Government turned down the Russian offer of an informal understanding in the event of a Turkish collapse. At the same time, the British government warned Russia against any excessive demand or show of military or naval force to coerce the Sultan's government.[63]

In his April 21 memorandum to the British Government, the Russian Czar noted that Britain's information on the state of the Ottoman Empire differed widely from his information, which showed that Turkey had not displayed tolerance toward its Christian subjects. The Russian Emperor agreed that constant harassment of the Turkish authorities with overbearing demands in a manner humiliating to Turkey's independence and dignity could not serve any useful purpose. He noted that he was ready to work with England to prolong the existence of the Turkish Empire.[64]

A special Russian mission to the Sultan, headed by Alexander Menshikov, arrived in Constantinople on March 9, and raised the issue of the Orthodox Christians and defense of their rights. In May, Menshikov demanded that the Sublime Porte make a proclamation to uphold and renew the rights and privileges previously granted to the Orthodox Christian subjects of the Empire, equal to those enjoyed by the Muslims and other denominations. Responding to the Russian proposal, Ambassador Canning, who had returned to Turkey in April after an extensive round of talks in Paris and Vienna, met with the French, Austrian, and Prussian envoys to discuss the situation. The envoys made a joint decision to appeal to the Sultan to reject the Russian proposal. The Russian demarche was strongly denounced by the European Powers as incompatible with the 1841 London Convention. The British and French

Governments decided to hold naval demonstrations in the Straits to reinforce the message.[65]

Parallel to the military preparations, the British and Ottoman governments worked to find a legal way to remove the Russian monopoly on protection of the Christian population of the Empire. On June 12, the Porte submitted a memorandum to the British Ambassador, apprising him of the Sultan's decision to grant religious privileges, rights and immunities to the Greek, Armenian, Catholic, Protestant, and Jewish population and their religious groups, as further proof of the Sultan's benevolence[66].

One month later, the Porte submitted another memorandum to Russia and other European Powers informing them of specific measures the Empire would undertake to protect the Orthodox Christians. At the same time, it asked the European Powers to guarantee its obligations before the Russian Empire. Russia, however, turned down the memorandum.[67]

British, French, Austrian, and Prussian representatives attempted to reconcile the Ottoman Empire and Russia, while guarding their own interests. The representatives of these nations met in Vienna, producing on July 31 what became known as the Vienna Memorandum. While addressed to the Sultan, the memorandum's real addressee was Russia, and reiterated the provisions of the Küchük-Kainarji and Adrianople Treaties referring to the Russian protection of the Ottoman Empire's Orthodox minority, as well as provided for extending to the Orthodox Christians the rights and privileges granted by the Porte to other religious denominations. The implementation of these treaties would henceforth be enforced by the Western Powers. The Ottoman Empire rejected the Powers' mediation efforts, and viewed the memorandum as an attempt to establish a protectorate over 12 million Christian subjects of the Empire. The Ottoman Government then declared war on Russia.[68]

The Ottoman defeat at the battle of Sinope caused great concern to the British Government. The British and French Governments used it as a pretext to present a new mediation effort in December 1853, providing for territorial integrity of the Ottoman Empire and the necessary reforms alleviating the condition of the Christian population of the Empire and implemented under the general supervision of the Powers.[69]

The British Embassy in Constantinople continued to press urgently for measures improving the condition of the Christians. Canning reported to

Clarendon on December 6, 1853, that the decree granting privileges to the Protestants had been issued some six months before, that he had tried to confirm its transmission to the local governors, and was given a positive assurance that the local Pashas had indeed received the necessary instructions from the central authority in that regard.[70]

The Crimean War served as a catalyst to the growth of anti-Turkish liberation movements in Christian-populated parts of the Empire. In 1853–54, discontent in Bulgaria and Kurdistan grew in intensity, while the anti-Turkish risings by Greeks in Epirus, Thessalia, and Aegean regions grew substantially in January 1854. Britain dispatched observers and garrisons to these regions, as well as to the islands of Khios, Rhodes, and Samos, to repel the insurgents and prevent possible uprisings. The British attempted to persuade Greece to join the allied forces against Russia.[71] On July 4, 1853, Canning wrote in his report to Clarendon that, in his view, the main threat to the Ottoman Empire would come from a general anti-Turkish uprising, not a strong Russian field army. He advocated an array of measures to prevent such an uprising. The Ambassador wrote that Turkey, with its natural resources and potential, faced the choice of becoming Russian or being saved by Europe.[72]

The British Foreign Office and Military Command planned to create special military units comprised of the Christian minorities, as well as Hungarian, Polish and Italian émigrés. The Rothschild bank group advocated a military unit comprised of Jews, which coincided with British plans to resettle Jewish population in Palestine, under British protectorate. The Sultan's government opposed these proposals, fearing that such units would eventually slip from the control of the central government and become a strong tool in the hands of the British.[73]

Under British diplomatic pressure, on March 8, 1854, four days prior to the signing of the Anglo-French military convention, Reshid Pasha presented a memorandum to the foreign diplomats accredited to Turkey, presenting the Sultan's program to improve the condition of Christians in Turkey. According to the program, the Sultan undertook to (1) remove the special taxes on Christians, kharaj, and introduce a new uniform tax on all subjects of the Empire; (2) guarantee civil equality of all subjects of the Empire, without prejudice, enforcing this with appropriate administrative and legal measures; (3) grant the Christians the right to occupy high-level civil service and military positions; (4) grant property rights to the Christians and foreigners residing in the Empire; (5) provide all the religious denominations with the right to construct and maintain places of worship.[74] This document, which was the main precondition for the military alliance, allowed the British Government to limit Russian influence in the Near East and establish a joint control by the Powers over the internal situation in Turkey.

The logical continuation of this policy was the protocol signed in Vienna on April 9, 1854, by the representatives of Austria, France, Great Britain and Prussia. The protocol provided for a dual objective of maintaining the territorial integrity of the Ottoman Empire, including the Russian evacuation of the Danubian Principalities, and of consolidating civil and religious rights of the Christian subjects of the Empire.[75]

The same provisions were contained in the protocol signed in Vienna on May 23, by the representatives of the same governments. Article 2 of the protocol stated that the territorial integrity of the Ottoman Empire and evacuation of the districts occupied by the Russian Army were among the objectives of the four Powers.[76]

On December 28, 1854, the plenipotentiary representatives of Austria, France, and Britain presented a memorandum to the Russian envoy in Vienna, Prince Alexander Gorchakov, containing the Powers' demands toward Russia. The memorandum demanded that Russia give up the exclusive protectorate it had established over Moldavia, Wallachia, and Serbia, placing them under the joint guarantee of Five Powers. The memorandum also demanded free navigation on the Danube. Another critical provision was to place Turkey in the context of the European power equilibrium and end the Russian domination of the Black Sea. Article 4 required Russia to renounce the "erroneous interpretation" of the Küchük-Kainarji Treaty that allowed Russia to take under its official protectorate the Christian subjects of the Sultan, since such interpretation threatened the sovereignty and integrity of the Ottoman state. The protocol took note of the measures promulgated by the Sultan to respect and equalize the religious rights of the Christians.[77]

On February 22, 1855, Clarendon sent instructions to the British envoy in Vienna, Lord Russell, that contained provisions for securing peace in Europe, thereby underlining the importance of the Ottoman Empire to the European balance of power: evacuation of the Danubian Principalities by the Russian troops, free navigation by the European navies in the Black Sea, strengthening the Turkish army and navy, as well as improving the conditions of the Christian population. According to Clarendon, reconciling the conflicts and creating harmony between Christians and Muslims in the Empire was also an important objective. Clarendon urged restraint and self-control on the part of the European Powers in the dealings on behalf of the Christian subjects of the Ottoman Empire. He noted that internal peace in Turkey would be greatly enhanced if the European Powers renounced all sectarian prejudices and treated all Christian subjects equally, and requested that religious rights should be extended to all the Christians, without prejudice. He noted that it would be desirable to have the Sultan abolish all legal distinctions between his Muslim and Christian subjects and formally communicate to the European Powers the decrees by which it would be done.[78]

On May 13, the Ottoman envoy in Britain, Musurus Pasha, presented to Clarendon Ali Pasha's memorandum on the religious rights of the Christian minorities of the Empire. The memorandum stated that the question of the religious protection of the Christian subjects of the Empire could be used by Russia to deliver a dangerous blow to the sovereign rights and legitimate authority of the Sultan. It accused Russia of planning—under the pretense of protection of the Christian population—to dismember the Ottoman Empire and of waging a religious crusade in the ongoing war. Ali Pasha wrote that Russia had long sought, actively and successfully, to mislead Europe and cover its political objectives with these religious aims. Russia's aim was to destroy the Ottoman Empire, create satellite states and establish protectorates over them, the memorandum contended. Successive Sultans granted privileges to the Christian minorities, although they could have used their unlimited power against them, Ali Pasha wrote. All atrocities that might have taken place were caused by national differences, wars, and invasions. Moreover, under the janissaries, the Muslim domination did assume a lamentable aspect toward the Christians, Ali Pasha readily admitted, yet nowadays Turkey was a different state, and had made significant progress in this regard. The current government renounced forced conversions of non-Muslims, the memorandum noted, and the Porte reiterated its readiness to grant equal rights to the Christians and respect this in practice. The false pretense of the protection of Orthodox Christians covered Russian designs against Ottoman sovereignty, which was more dangerous than loss of any territory. Ali Pasha expressed hope that with the help of the European Powers, the Porte would resist any Russian advances on this issue.[79]

In response to Ali Pasha's memorandum, Clarendon sent a cable to Canning, clarifying the British Government's position on the rights of the Christian population of the Empire. He noted that any demand by the Five Powers on this issue would constitute no less an infringement on Turkish independence than that by a single Power. A better way to settle the issue would be for the Sultan, in his own sovereign power, to do for the Christians all that was required, and then communicate to the allies everything that he had done, Clarendon noted. He also asked Canning to petition the Sultan on the following issues: (1) eligibility of the non-Muslim subjects for any position in the Army; (2) admission of non-Muslim evidence in civil and criminal jurisprudence; (3) establishment of mixed courts of justice for all cases in which Muslims and non-Muslims are parties; (4) appointment of a Christian officer as assessor to every Governor, with a full right to appeal to the central authority against any act of the Governor; (5) eligibility of Christians for all positions in the central and provincial administration; and (6) total abolition of a system of sale of offices. The British Government suggested that the Sultan's government should not only display tolerance toward the non-Muslim faiths, but also institute punishment for forced conversions. By doing so, the Sultan would enlist the favorable public opinion of Europe, Clarendon asserted.[80]

On June 19, the British Foreign Office sent a circular note to the British missions in foreign countries on the results of the Vienna conference on Russian peace proposals. During the conference, Britain and her allies decided (1) to abolish the Russian right to interfere in certain provinces of Turkey; (2) to deprive Russia of exclusive control over the lower Danube, transferring the administration to all Powers, including Russia; (3) to include Turkey in the system of European equilibrium and end Russian domination of the Black Sea; (4) to renounce Russian protection of the Christian population of the Ottoman Empire; instead, the Sultan, by his own sovereign right, would proclaim the necessary privileges and rights.[81]

The same document re-asserted the Foreign Office position on the Christian minorities in the Ottoman Empire. It stated that England and France had taken a uniform interest in the welfare of the Christian population, based on

Article 4 of the Vienna Protocol, i.e., excluding extension of exclusive rights of protection to any single nation, such as Russia. The document contended that despite the war and the end of Russian interference, the Sultan continued to treat his Christian subjects in a wise and benevolent way. The circular pointed out that Russia had misinterpreted the provisions of the Küchük-Kainarji treaty that had required the Sultan to protect the Christian faith, and had used it as a pretext to interfere on behalf of the Christian population if the Sultan violated its rights. Had this practice continued unabated, the circular concluded, the Sultan's power in the Ottoman Empire would have been overthrown by Russian supremacy.[82]

On September 7, 1855, Lord Cowley, Britain's Ambassador in France, reported to Clarendon that he had received a deputation from the Society of Friends of Religious Liberty the previous day. The Society had held a number of meetings headed by Sir Culling Eardley, and had composed a public address to the Queen, which was presented to Lord Cowley. The address, signed by citizens of various European countries, asked the British Government to exercise its powerful influence with the Sultan to obtain full religious liberty in the Ottoman Empire and abolish the death penalty for apostasy.[83]

In the autumn of 1855, British diplomacy redoubled its efforts on this issue. The Foreign Office petitioned the Turkish authorities to improve the condition of the Christian population, abolish discriminatory acts against certain faiths, and introduce freedom of religion and equality of faiths. The British Government wanted to settle all disagreements on the subject of treatment of the Christian population in the Ottoman Empire, in advance of the peace negotiations.

On September 17, Clarendon wrote to Canning that the issue of capital punishment for apostasy must be brought to closure. He noted that the Porte had assured Her Majesty's Ambassador that it would have abolished the law providing for a death penalty in case of a Muslim converting to Christianity.

Clarendon instructed the Ambassador to raise the issue with the Porte, noting that the Turkish authorities should not expect the Great Powers—who were making serious efforts and sacrifices to save the Turkish Empire from ruin and destruction—to tolerate a law that was a source of persecution to their coreligionists. Clarendon demanded that the Ottoman Government immediately abolish the law.[84]

Clarendon sent a similar note to Ambassador Cowley, urging cooperation and joint action by all Powers, including France, to achieve progress. On September 25 Cowley informed the Foreign Secretary that the French concurred with this position.[85]

In response to Clarendon's instructions, Ambassador Canning met with the Ottoman Secretary of State Mehmed Fuad Pasha and Grand Vizier Ali Pasha several times in October, demanding in no uncertain terms to abolish the death penalty for apostasy. Fuad Pasha assured the Ambassador that he had heard nothing of executions in Aleppo and Adrianople, and that the government took all measures to prevent such acts. He disputed the Ambassador's assertion of an unequal treatment of the Protestants, arguing instead that the principles of Protestantism were of much interest and that the Porte found it in its interest to encourage them. Fuad Pasha and Ali Pasha gave assurances that the government was tolerant and had addressed the key complaints about the unequal status of religions. An inefficient system of administration was the principal cause of distress now, both to the Muslim and non-Muslim population. The Ottoman officials contended that the only religion-related criminal offense was for blasphemy, i.e., disparaging the faith or God.[86]

At the initiative of Ambassador Canning, a meeting between Ali Pasha and British, French, and Austrian envoys was held in his house in January 1856. Canning noted that the Ottoman Government would find it to its advantage, both internally and externally, in no longer acting on the predominance of religious or racial exclusiveness but promoting national unity and strength. Noting the administrative malfeasance, resistance of local officials, ethnic and religious disagreements, the Ambassador called on the Turkish authorities to address all outstanding issues in advance of the peace negotiations. In his opinion, it was the only manner in which the Russian exclusive protectorate could be removed.[87]

In his January 14 dispatch to the Foreign Office, the British Ambassador noted that the sovereignty of the Ottoman Sultan was connected with the great European system, and it was the desire of these Powers to heed in advance any danger that might confront it. The progress of war showed, Canning argued, that combined operations would sooner or later result in a peace process, as desired by Europe and required by Turkey. Thus, it was imperative to develop the principles on which to base the peace agreement and take measures to secure a beneficial result for this Empire, which had sacrificed much. In the Ambassador's view, the Empire's revival was contingent upon the removal of differences between Muslims and Christians and the implementation of administrative and national reforms.[88]

With this in mind, the British mission prepared a package of reforms to improve the condition of the Christian minorities in the Empire, which was then discussed at the French Legation on January 16 in the presence of British, French, and Austrian Ambassadors. After making some additions and changes, the Ambassadors presented the program to the Grand Vizier and two Turkish ministers.[89] Incorporating the Ottoman officials' suggestions, the envoys presented the program to the Porte. The document suggested to (1) take effective measures to implement the guarantees under the Imperial Decree of Gülhane and the laws of Tanzimat, without distinction for class or religion; (2) acknowledge and preserve all the rights and privileges previously conferred to the non-Muslim population; (3) ensure that every community bring its immunities and regulations into conformity with the ongoing reforms, the progress of civilization and of the age; (4) allow non-Muslim communities unhindered rights to repair places of worship, schools, hospitals, and cemeteries, with building designs to be approved by the community's Patriarch or head, and the Porte; (5) abolish any designation or distinction of any religion, language or race as inferior to any other; and that (6) no subject, without prejudice to his religious views, should be molested; (7) all subjects shall be eligible for public employment according to their capacity and merit; (8) all subjects shall receive education at civil or military schools; (9) all civil and criminal cases between Muslim and non-Muslim parties are to be heard in mixed courts; (10) the penal, civil, and commercial laws and the rules of procedure for the mixed tribunals shall be drawn and codified, and made available in European languages; (11) the penitentiary system shall be reformed; (12) the police in the capital and provincial towns shall be reformed in conformity with the reforms; (13) equality in taxes and other obligations, including military conscription, shall be enforced; (14) constitutions of provincial and commercial councils shall be reformed, and provide for free voting in the communities; (15) all subjects shall enjoy equal rights in the purchase, sale, and management of property; (16) the fiscal system be reformed, with equality for all subjects in this respect; (17) all patriarchs and community heads, and delegate designated by the Porte shall have the right to take part in deliberations of the Supreme Council of Justice; and finally, (18) the laws against corruption and extortion be enforced.[90]

Due to British diplomatic efforts, on February 21, in advance of the Paris Peace Conference, the Sultan proclaimed a decree on the privileges of the Empire's minority populations, known as Hatte-Gülhane-Humayun. The decree noted that its intent was to augment the well-being and prosperity and ensure the happiness of all the Sultan's subjects, whom he declared to be equal in his sight and equally dear to him, united to each other by cordial ties of patriotism, and to ensure the means of daily increasing the prosperity of the Empire.

The decree declared that the rights and privileges of all the subjects of the Empire, promised under the Gülhane-Hatte-Humayun and promulgated by the Tanzimat, were reiterated and re-granted, and offered concrete steps to ensure their implementation. The decree also confirmed the privileges granted to the non-Muslim population under the previous Sultans. The Porte would from now on accept the building plans submitted by the community heads. All the subjects were guaranteed choice of religion; nobody could be converted by force. All the subjects would henceforth be eligible for public employment, education at civil or military schools, and employment in the sciences, arts, or crafts.

The decree also included provisions for reforms of the police, tax, and justice systems, as well as in finance. It provided for the establishment of banks, construction of new roads and canals.[91]

Thus, the Sultan's decree largely reflected the British Ambassador's memorandum. The main objective of the 1856 Gülhane-Hatte-Humayun decree was to promote consolidation and assimilation of the Empire's many peoples. At the time, the Turkish officials considered assimilation as the only way to guarantee territorial integrity and the suppression of the national liberation movements of the Christian minorities.

The discussions of the condition of the Ottoman Christian population during the Paris peace conference took place according to the British plan. Clarendon stressed the need to protect Turkish interests, suggesting that all proposals on the issue of national minorities must be discussed in conjunction with the program of reforms for the Ottoman Empire. In their turn, the Ottoman diplomats accepted the Vienna Protocol's position on the European

Powers' role in the protection of the Christian minorities, and attempted to remove all references to the Christian subjects from the discussions.[92]

The first protocol of the conference noted that immunities of the Christian subjects of the Porte should be confirmed without prejudice to the independence and dignity of the Sultan. The protocol referred to deliberations between the Porte and Britain, France, and Austria on ensuring the political and religious rights of the Christian subjects of the Empire. During the February 28 session of the conference, Ali Pasha demanded that all references to the Christian subjects of the Empire be removed from the agenda, since the Gülhane-Hatte-Humayun decree had effectively restored the rights of the non-Muslims and proclaimed the reforms. Nevertheless, Russia and Austria insisted on inclusion of a special article in the final draft of the conference protocol, calling for an improvement in the condition of the Christian population.[93] On the same day, Clarendon instructed Canning to congratulate the Porte on its acceptance of wise and effective reforms and expressed hope that the Sultan's government would do all it could to implement the reforms and to ensure the prosperity and immunities of the non-Muslim subjects of the Empire.[94]

On March 25, the Russian representative argued that his government had a special interest in the Christian population of the Ottoman Empire, asking to include an appropriate reference to the Russian interests. The Russian position was countermanded by the British envoy who had successfully argued for the passage of the draft prepared by the Western Powers.[95] According to Article 9 of the Paris Treaty, the Sultan had issued a special decree in order to alleviate the condition of his Christian subjects, and the parties to the treaty acknowledged the importance of the fact, which could in no way be interpreted to allow intervention, jointly or unilaterally, in the Sultan's dealings with his subjects and in the internal affairs of the Empire.[96]

The Treaty of Paris, which concluded the Crimean War, did not contain a reference to Western Armenia, yet it was directly connected with the fate of the Armenians living there. Although defeated in war, the Russian Army was victorious on the Caucasus front, capturing Kars and other Armenian-populated regions. The Russian military advances, however, were nullified by the Paris Treaty, due to the intervention of British diplomacy, and the region occupied by the Russian troops were returned to Turkey.

4. British Diplomacy and the Protection of the Christian Minorities in the Ottoman Empire, 1850s–1870s

One of the results of the Crimean War was the strengthening of British positions in the Ottoman Empire and the significant weakening of Russia, its main rival in the Near East. The Ottoman Empire was nominally one of the victors and became a part of the Concert of Europe, but failed to overcome the enormous political and economic problems at home. The Empire's dependence on the Western Powers increased, just as the government's oppression of the Christian minorities increased, parallel to the rise of national liberation movements.

During the period following the end of the Crimean War, well into 1870's, the Eastern Question remained one of the most complex issues in international relations. The Eastern Question had three major components: (1) the European Powers were trying to uphold and increase their influence in the Ottoman Empire; (2) non-Turkish peoples were fighting the government to topple the Empire's domination; and (3) the Sublime Porte had the dual objective of suppressing domestic revolts and containing the Western Powers' interest and pressure.

Britain was the only western Power that explicitly supported the principle of the territorial integrity of the Ottoman Empire, a position well understood and appreciated by the Tanzimat-era Turkish leaders. Fuad Pasha wrote in his will in 1862 that it was better to lose a few provinces than see England abandon the Porte.[97]

The British Government extended not only political but also financial support to the Sultan's government. The British investments in the Ottoman Empire were nearly 17 millions pounds as of 1857. The Ottoman Bank was founded in Constantinople in 1856, with British charter capital of half a million pounds. The Bank had chapters in Beirut, Smyrna, and Salonica, and was financing British foreign trade in the Ottoman Empire.[98]

British diplomacy was concerned about the precarious financial and economic health of the Empire, as well as the continued oppression of the Christians. From September to December 1858, Ambassador Canning sent innumerable letters to the authorities urging them to carry out the reforms promised in Gülhane-Hatte-Humayun, such as alleviating the position of the non-Turkish peoples, and granting equal rights to Muslim and non-Muslim subjects. The British Ambassador noted that the Ottoman Empire would otherwise fall apart or break into several smaller states that would fall into Russia's sphere of influence.[99] Following the Crimean War Russia focused its efforts on the Christian minorities in the Empire, in an attempt to regain its influence in the Balkans. Unlike Britain, the Russian authorities demanded reforms that would have addressed the concerns of the Christian subjects only.

The Tory government of Lord Edward Derby[100] came briefly to power in 1858. The Tories' foreign policy was more moderate and cautious. Britain drew closer to France, to prevent a possible Russian-French alliance against British interests in case the Ottoman Empire fell apart, which was not an unlikely prospect at the time. The financial support of the Ottoman Empire also diminished and the British Government did not stand by the Sultan's government during the standoff in Serbia and Montenegro.

Britain returned to the previous policy when Lord Parlmerston's party returned to power in 1859. Lord Russell replaced Foreign Secretary Mulmsberry, and Ambassador Canning was replaced by Sir Henry Bulwer. The new Ambassador, like his predecessor, was a supporter of the reform movement in the Ottoman Empire, and was particularly concerned with the financial and economic situation of the Empire. He proposed the idea of forming joint Ottoman-European commissions for financial reforms, as well as of introducing the strictest economy measures throughout the government, including in the Sultan's court.

In his telegrams to Russell, Bulwer described the desperate state of the Christian population of the Empire and emphasized the need for enforcing the provisions of Gülhane-Hatte-Humayun. The Ambassador, however, intervened on behalf of the Christians only on a few, exceptional occasions. Every time Russia attempted to intervene on behalf of the Christian subjects of the Empire, British diplomacy defended the interests of the Sublime Porte and cautioned against infringing on the sovereignty of the Sultan's government. The British Foreign Secretary held the view that the Greek and Slav uprisings would only cause more oppression, deplete the country's finances, and shift the government's attention away from the reforms. Russell believed that even if the Christian people emerged victorious, it would lead to lawlessness, ethnic strife, and a general war in the event of interference by a European Power. The

British position reflected the ideas of the Ottoman ministers, Ali Pasha and Fuad Pasha, who advocated the principle of 'one state with integrated people.' The British Foreign Office concurred with their view that independent Balkan states or an independent Armenia would soon fall into Russia's sphere of influence.

On June 25, 1859, Russell wrote to Bulwer that he had met with the Russian Ambassador, Baron Philip Brunnov. Brunnov stated that the Imperial Russian Government advised the Sultan to maintain law and order in his country and to defend the rights of the Christian subjects. The Foreign Secretary told the Russian Ambassador that such advice would be ill received by the Turkish Government, and furthermore, it was dangerous to make the Sultan's subjects cast their hopes with foreign governments. Brunnov agreed with the Foreign Secretary, and said that the best course of action was coordinated efforts by all European Powers in Turkey.[101]

On July 26, Bulwer sent a detailed assessment of the situation in the Ottoman Empire. He wrote that the inferior status of the Christians was not only on account of their religion but also their location in "not perfectly civilized and well-governed" parts of the Empire. The British envoy suggested that both Muslims and Christians in remote provinces were oppressed and that the lower-class Muslims there suffered even more from bad government than the Christians who enjoyed some degree of protection from foreign governments. He noted that the Turks considered themselves superior even to other Muslim people, like Arabs, as well as to Armenians and Greeks. The Turks were convinced, the British envoy wrote, that the Muslims would lose, and the Christians gain from the enforcement of Hatte Humayun.

Bulwer proposed some measures to diffuse the tension between the Christian and Muslim peoples of the Empire, including, (1) greater responsibility to individual officials and a strengthened system of controls, which would help the Sultan's reforms; (2) creation of honorary positions for the non-Muslims; (3) establishment of Vice-Governor's positions in the provinces predominantly populated by the Christians; (4) employment of European specialists in the government department to improve efficiency. The Ambassador noted that the position of the Christian population was significantly improved and that those 'simple and not too difficult' measures would further alleviate it.[102]

On August 9, Russell instructed Bulwer that in his discussions with the

Porte he should stress that the implementation of the reforms would in no way increase the influence of Britain or any other Power in the Ottoman Empire, but would contribute to Turkey's joining Europe, economic development and stability there, as well as to the alleviation in the condition of all the subjects of the Empire.[103]

In his report dated August 16, the Ambassador noted that no amount of general and rapid reform could transform the whole Ottoman state into a perfectly governed Empire based on European principles, and criticized British press reports that robberies and murders had continued unabated despite the reforms still underway. He called such assertions absurd since similar crimes could and did happen in other countries as well. Bulwer stated his belief that in dealing with the Turkish Government, one should adopt the policy of friendly encouragement, pointing the importance of the implemented reforms and patiently explaining the need for more reforms.[104]

It is perhaps due to Bulwer's energetic efforts that these positions of the Foreign Office were reflected in the Joint Memorandum presented to the Grand Vizier by the diplomatic representatives of six Powers in Constantinople on October 4, 1859. The memorandum stated that the implementation of the reforms should continue, independent of the differences in religion and race. The aim of the reforms should be the establishment of a system of government under which all of the Sultan's subjects would share in the benefits of the country's development.[105]

The Ottoman Cabinet discussed the country's financial situation and the general state of the economy during its October 13 session, in the presence of the Sultan. The Grand Vizier, Ali Pasha, described the country's finances as deplorable and suggested that strict economy measures must be adopted, alongside with the administrative reforms to ensure law and order. The Sultan was not satisfied with Ali Pasha's presentation and dismissed him as the Grand Vizier. In his dispatch to the Foreign Office, Ambassador Bulwer called the dismissal deeply regretful, noting Ali Pasha's role in the planning and implementation of the reforms.[106]

The British Foreign Office started to review its Near East policy in the 1860's, following mass unrest in the Balkans, Syria, Egypt and other parts of the Ottoman Empire which seemed to prove the impossibility of preserving the vast empire's territorial integrity. Sensing an eventual demise of the

Ottoman Empire, Palmerston attempted to turn Greece into a pillar of his Eastern policies, without much success.

The British Government was gravely concerned with the 1860 massacre of the Christian population of Jeddah, Syria, when the French consul and the British Vice Consul also fell victim to the murders. Faced with indisputable facts and a public outcry in Europe, Palmerston told the House of Commons that the authorities were implicated in the massacre, having done nothing to prevent it and even having incited the Muslim mob.[107] On April 24, 1860, Bulwer reported to Russell that general uneasiness and alarm permeated the Empire following the riots in Jeddah and other developments. He noted that the mob had been incited by the dervishes from the eastern vilayets (provinces) and refugees from the European provinces.[108]

On June 7, Russell informed Bulwer of the discussions that took place in St. Petersburg. The European Powers' representatives addressed the issue of massacres of the Christian population in Bulgaria, Bosnia, Herzegovina, and Syria, and proposed that the Sultan, within a certain timeframe, establish a commission to investigate the incidents, punish the perpetrators, improve the administration of the provinces, and carry out new reforms. Russell held that the Treaty of Paris did not allow any single European Power to intervene on behalf of the Sultan's subjects, so that all Powers had to cooperate in presenting proposals agreeable both to the Sultan and to his subjects.[109]

In response to the frequent Russian interventions on behalf of the Christian minorities, Bulwer decided to ask the British consuls for more active work. He sent a circular on June 11 instructing them to examine the economic conditions in the provinces, the conditions in which the Christian population lived, the progress of implementation of the Gülhane-Hatte-Humayun, reasons for the delays, the behavior and actions of the local administrations, instructing the consuls to put forward proposals for addressing these issues. The Ambassador was convinced that the crimes decried by Russia—robberies, looting, and murders—reflected the Ottoman reality but were greatly exaggerated. He reiterated his statement that such crimes were not unheard of in more civilized countries. Like any other Christian nation, Bulwer wrote, the British Government wanted to improve the lot of the Ottoman Christians. Nevertheless, Britain supported the territorial integrity of the Ottoman Empire, in the absence of which stability in the Orient would totally collapse, leading perhaps to a general war. The aim of British diplomacy, therefore, was to work patiently with the Sultan's government and the local authorities to promote the reforms.[110]

In his August 6, 1860 correspondence to Ali Pasha, Bulwer stated that it was evident to him the Ottoman Government could not last without radical reforms. It was possible to maintain the Sultan on his throne and to preserve Turks generally in high positions, he wrote, but it was impossible, as he eloquently stated, to turn the Empire into a farm to be tended by a few Pashas. It was equally impossible to manage the country for the benefit of the Turkish race alone, he said, or to exclude European genius and talent from it. He went on to flatter Ali Pasha by writing that the Turkish people's knowledge of business, in which they enjoyed an ancient supremacy, gave them a position with which other peoples in the Empire could not compete. Yet, he continued, in order to maintain this superiority, Turks must display superior qualities, while corruption, indolence, favoritism and prejudice should not be tolerated. He concluded by urging the use of European talent to address the problems.[111]

In his August 25 and September 13 telegrams to Ambassador Bulwer, Russell specifically addressed the subject of Russian policy on the Ottoman Empire and the Christian population there. He noted that Turkish domestic policies had been constrained by obligations to Russia in the period between the Treaty of Küchük-Kainarji and the Treaty of Paris. By repetitive treaties, military interventions, and demonstrative protectionism, the Ottoman Christians had become the subjects of the Russian Czar as well. Thus, the Foreign Secretary concluded, for almost a century Russian policy had been to implicitly dominate the national minorities of the Ottoman Empire. The Treaty of Paris terminated this arrangement by establishing a joint protectorate over the Christians by the Five Powers, a mechanism more beneficial to the Sultan.[112] The Foreign Secretary wrote that Britain supported the Ottoman state not only out of purely British interest, but also out of concern that its disintegration could lead to clashes and, inevitably, a general European war. Russell stated that of all the peoples of the Empire, including Turks, Slavs, Greeks, Armenians, Arabs, and others, only the Turks were capable of ruling the Empire.[113] He said he believed that the massacres had not been a result of the anti-Christian animosity of Islam or the Muslim people, but, rather, the modus operandi of the Sultan's appointed Pashas and Beys who incited such incidents.[114]

On November 12, 1860 Bulwer reported to Russell that the Porte had been gradually changing its attitudes toward the Christian population, in particular granting them several political positions. The Ambassador considered this important progress, since political power had always been a monopoly of the Turks.[115] He noted that the ethnic differences mattered more than the religious differences, and made some generalizations about Turkish superiority in command of government, Armenian industriousness, Greek acute intelligence, and the commercial and administrative talent of the Jews. Application of these unique national characteristics, according to the Ambassador, combined with the involvement of the Europeans, could transform the Ottoman Empire.[116]

In yet another similar report, dated January 8, 1861, Bulwer wrote of misconceptions in Europe that Turkey was one nation composed of several ethnic elements, each seeing the benefit of being united. In reality, he noted, there is no single Ottoman nation, but, several peoples, with each inhabitant thinking of himself in terms of belonging to a particular people, like the Armenians, Greeks, or Turks. Bulwer suggested that the best course of action on the national minorities was to involve them in the government, which was bound to mitigate the nationalist fervor.[117]

The British Foreign Office attached great hope to the ascension of the new Sultan, Abdul Aziz. Russell wrote to Bulwer on July 4, 1861, that the ascension would create a new opportunity for the British Government to assist the Porte in implementation of the reforms. In a special dispatch dated July 29, 1861, the Foreign Secretary instructed his Ambassador to study the character and actions of the new Sultan, and to try to carefully steer his activities toward positive goals. Russell, nevertheless, noted the enthusiasm with which Abdul Aziz's coronation had been met in the most fundamentalist and extremist classes, who had hoped the new Sultan would annul the privileges granted to the Christians.[118]

The British Government continued to provide political and financial assistance to the Porte in suppression of the national revolts in the Empire, helping the Sultan's government during the rebellions in Herzegovina and Zeytoun in 1862, as well as during the war with Montenegrins. The British Foreign Office made serious efforts to prevent a possible assistance to the Balkan insurgents from the Italian revolutionaries. The liberation of the Christian population of the Balkans was frowned upon since that struggle was supported by Russia.[119] Russian Ambassador to London Brunnov reported to Russian Foreign Minister Gorchakov that since the turn of the eighteenth century the British Government had been overcome by a deep suspicion of the Russian motives in the East. London was convinced, the Russian Ambassador noted, that Russia would either aggrandize its territory at Turkish expense or exercise influence over Turkey's Christian peoples by partitioning the Empire. According to the Ambassador, European Turkey was viewed in London as a natural barrier on the path of Russia's advance toward the Mediterranean, while Asiatic Turkey was likewise shielding the British dominions in India.[120]

In his February 12, 1863, cable to Bulwer, Russell noted that as long as Turkey had permanent and determined enemies, it would have a loyal and impartial ally. He believed that Russia would support every rebellious subject of the Sultan. The French actions in Serbia and Montenegro showed that France was not a staunch ally of Turkey, the way it had been during the Crimean War. Russell noted that Prussia would follow Russia's lead, while Italy would wait for France and Russia to act first, and, therefore, the Ottoman Empire's staunchest allies were Austria and England. The Foreign Secretary instructed his Ambassador to raise a number of issues with the Sultan as a preventive measure against a general uprising. Addressing those issues would guarantee a permanent British support: (1) secure life and property rights for all the subjects of the Empire; (2) put the financial house in order; and (3) improve the army and the navy.[121]

The British envoy was also concerned about the local authorities in Zeytoun and Diyarbakir, which seemingly encouraged the persecution of the Armenians, since such actions might cause interference from the Russians. On August 13, 1863, Bulwer wrote that he was satisfied to have heard of the recall of the Diyarbakir Governor by the Porte, for allowing disturbances and inciting anti-Armenian pogroms. Local British Consul J.C. Taylor reported that the persecution had been so harsh and severe that thousands of Armenians considered converting to Catholicism to claim the protection of the French Consulate, and that more than 1400 families planned to emigrate to

Eastern Armenia. The Foreign Secretary instructed the Ambassador to urge the authorities to restore order and provide for public safety.[122]

The British diplomatic missions would spare no effort to protect the Anglican and other Protestant churches in the Empire, and the rights and interests of the British and American missionaries and the Turkish subjects who converted to Protestantism. A due cause presented itself in July-August 1864, when the Turkish authorities issued a ban on the sale of Bibles in Constantinople, shut down the British Bible Society's store, and arrested a few missionaries and Turkish converts. The situation was addressed only after the personal involvement of the Ambassador. In his July 27 dispatch to Russell, Bulwer said he believed no Turkish or Muslim Government would tolerate what they perceived as a Christian crusade against their people, and that this controversy could cause a religious conflict. Bulwer even suggested that Turks would be no different from other non-Protestant Christian nations who wouldn't like the well-being of their citizens to be jeopardized by the animosity incited by the Protestants. In his reply, dated August 11, the Foreign Secretary stated that missionaries must have the right to sell Bibles and preach Christianity in churches and private houses, and noted that the promise not to punish converts to Christianity had been in effect for a number of years. He also stated that the Embassy should not protect public preaching that could disturb the public peace and incite fanaticism.[123]

The Anglo-French competition in the Near East became more pronounced in the 1860's. Although the Porte exercised nominal suzerainty over Tunisia, Egypt, and Syria, these provinces had become objects of competition for the two European Powers. France dominated in Syria, and Britain in Egypt. A number of developments led to the diminishing of British involvement in the Eastern Question: the approaching completion of the Suez Canal, which would deprive the Ottoman Empire of its importance as the overland route to India; the death of Palmerston on October 16, 1865, who personified the active British interest in Eastern affairs; domestic problems, as well as the complexity of managing a vast colonial empire and putting down several rebellions there. The new Conservative government headed by Lord Derby replaced Bulwer with Lord Richard Lyons. Ambassador Lyons was cautious and balanced, in line with the general policy of the government which attempted to settle its conflicts with France in the Near East.

Although Britain lost, for the moment, its previously acute interest in Near Eastern affairs, the British consuls continued to inform the Embassy of the conditions of the Christian population, and the Embassy kept the Foreign Office apprised of developments. The British Consul in Rustchuk Robert Dalyell, reported to Lyons on March 11, 1867 that the Christian population continued to be oppressed by the Turkish authorities, while Consul Henry Cumberbatch reported from Smyrna on March 29 that, some persecution of the Protestant Armenians notwithstanding, the condition of the Christians in the towns was much better than in the rural areas, where Gülhane-Hatte-Sheriff and Gülhane-Hatte-Humayun remained a dead letter. He noted that government positions and schools were open solely to the Muslims, with only a few exceptions, and that the justice system and taxation was unfair toward the Christians. Vice Consul F.T. Sankey reported from Kustendje on April 1 that the degree of persecution of the Christian population depended on the temper and caprice of the local governor.[124]

Vice Consul Barker reported from Epirus to the Ambassador on April 2. His consular career had started in 1828, and he had served in Egypt, Syria, and Bulgaria and traveled extensively in Mesopotamia and Armenia. He noted that the living conditions of the Christians in the European part of Turkey were worse compared to the Asiatic part, where they held land and house properties. He stated that the Christian population in Asia, including Greeks, Armenians, Syrians, or Maronites, was no worse off than the Muslims, who also complained of bad government.[125] Acting Consul General Rogers reported from Beirut on April 12 that despite great improvements in the situation of the Christian population in the previous two decades, the Christians were far from possessing perfect civil or religious liberty or equality with the Muslims. He conceded that even though the central government was interested in placing the Christians on an equal footing with the Muslims, the massacres in Aleppo in 1853 and in Damascus in 1860 had shown the strength of the Muslim fanatics who were jealous of the increasing rights of the Christian population.[126] In his April 17 dispatch to the Foreign Office, Consul Palgrave, the British consul in Trabzon, reported that startling complaints had been made of Turkish oppression, anti-Christian fanaticism, and threatened massacres. He suggested that foreign interference was the real cause of unrest among the Christians. He went on to state that the Greeks, having obtained equality already, now strove to establish domination over other groups.[127] On January 30, 1868, Consul Palgrave submitted an assessment of the situation in Erzurum, Kars, Ardahan, Amasia, Sivas, and other cities, and concluded that the Muslims in those cities were as likely to suffer from the same injustices as the Greeks, Armenians, Protestants, and Catholics.[128]

In his May 6, 1867 summary of consular reports, Lord Lyons wrote to the Prime Minister, Lord Derby, that the general prosperity of the Christians in the Ottoman Empire had increased recently, and their progress outstripped that of the Muslim population. He noted that the Christians and Muslims suffered equally from bad government, and had similar grievances. He pointed out that the great majority of the Muslims could not look upon the Christians as their equals, which wounded the pride and self-respect of the Christians. All government positions were now nominally open to the Christians but in reality they never had been placed in high offices. The Christians paid a special tax in lieu of conscription, having little desire to join the Army. The Ambassador concluded that the Sultan's government had not made progress in establishing itself as the national government for the Christians as well.[129]

The Liberal Cabinet of William Gladstone[130] (1868–74) set domination of Egypt and the Suez Canal as priorities for the British Government, which ran contrary to the British principle of preserving the territorial integrity of the Ottoman Empire. Consequently, the British Government displayed almost no interest in the internal problems of the Porte, including the reform process and the condition of the Christians.

The British Government chose not to interfere in the Crete crisis of 1866–69, and formulated no position on the issue, other than issuing proposals on establishment of an administrative autonomy for the Cretans, which only irritated the Porte.[131]

British Consul General J.C. Taylor reported from Erzurum on March 19, 1869 that the local Armenian population was disposed positively toward the Russians, viewing Russia as the only Power capable of delivering them from the Sultan's yoke. In this report to Foreign Secretary Clarendon, Taylor suggested that the attempts by the British and French consular agents and missionaries to establish control over the Armenians had been futile. According to him, the vilayets' Armenian population would rather become Russian subjects and would even fight on the Russian side. In Taylor's assessment, the

Armenians occupied an important position in the province by virtue of being the most populous group, and being in the majority in the most important valleys, controlling the commerce and agriculture, and three-fourths of the capital in the cities; thus, their falling under the Russian influence could turn them into an important and dangerous element for anti-government activities.[132] The author's research uncovered this to be the first time such an assessment appeared in the British diplomatic papers, and the sentiments expressed here, in fact, became the justification for the Ottoman Government's anti-Armenian policy in the years to come.

The same report contains some numbers on the population of Erzurum, Diyarbakir, and Kharput Vilayets, which are as follows:

	Erzurum	Diyarbakir	Kharput
Turks	272,500	30,000	140,000
Kurds	357,000	391,000	100,000
Christians	411,000	108,000	130,000
Jews	1,200	1,000	N/A
Yezidis	2,000	8,000	N/A
Kizil-bashis	158,000	12,500	30,000
Arabs	N/A	118,000	N/A
Chechens	N/A	15,000	N/A
Total	1,201,700	683,500	400,000

Of the Christian population in the Erzurum district, 287,700 were Armenians, 110,000 were Nestorians, 8,000 were Armenian Catholics, 4000 were Greek Orthodox, and 1300 were Protestants.[133]

In 1869, the prominent Turkish government officials of the reform period, Ali Pasha and Fuad Pasha, finally succeeded in securing a passage of a "fusion" (or melting pot, in modern terminology) law, based on the principle of Ottoman citizenship. According to the law, all inhabitants of the Empire, irrespective of their national or religious denomination, were declared subjects of the Empire. Superficially, the law was beneficial to the non-Muslims, since it was the first time in history that the Muslims and Christians received equal status before law. At the same time, the law would deprive the national minorities of their national identity since the declared objective was the principle of assimilation or fusion. But the deaths of Fuad Pasha in 1869 and Ali Pasha in 1871 stopped the reform process in its tracks, giving way to the traditional conservative policies that were anti-Christian and against national movements.[134]

The Franco-Prussian War in 1870–71 further shifted Great Britain's attention from the East. This helped Turkey and Russia draw closer, since the Porte felt deprived of the traditional British and French support. The Porte, therefore, reciprocated the Russian efforts to improve relations between two governments. Taking advantage of the instability in Europe, the Russian Government attempted to enlist Turkey's support in the removal of limitations imposed on Russian naval activities in the Black Sea following the Crimean War. The 1871 London Convention, in fact, voided the provisions of the Treaty of Paris on the neutrality of the Black Sea, and allowed Russia to maintain navy and shore fortifications there.

The Sublime Porte continued to be concerned about Russia's activities within the Christian population of the Empire. On November 1, 1870, the new British Ambassador in Constantinople, Sir Henry Elliot reported to Foreign Secretary Lord George Granville[135] that he had met with Ali Pasha, who had been re-appointed as Grand Vizier. Ali Pasha expressed concern about the new Russian efforts to exercise monopoly over protection of the Christian subjects of the Empire. According to the Ambassador, Ali Pasha stated that general protection over the Christians subjects by all European Powers was preferable to the Porte than the sole protectorate by Russia.[136] This principle was adopted by the European Powers during the 1878 Berlin Congress as the policy in Western Armenia.

Meanwhile, the British consuls continued to report on the increasingly frequent persecution of the Christian and, in particular, Armenian population in the eastern provinces of the Empire.[137]

Notes

[1] K. Bourne, *The Foreign Policy of Victorian England, 1830–1902* (Oxford, 1970), p. 10; H. W. V. Temperley, *The Victorian Age in Politics, War and Diplomacy.* (Cambridge, 1928), p. 55.

[2] D. Beales, *From Castlereagh to Gladstone, 1815–1885* (London, 1971), p. 159.

[3] I. L. Fadeeva, *Osmanskaya imperiya i anglo-turetskie otnosheniya v seredine xix v.* (Moscow, 1982) p .29; M. N. Todorova, *Angliya, Rossiya i Tanzimat* (Moscow, 1983), p. 49.

[4] V. I. Sheremet, *Osmanskaya imperiya i Zapadnaya Yevropa. Vtoraya tret' xix v.* (Moscow, 1986), p. 260.

[5] J. H. Gleason, *The Genesis of Russophobia in Great Britain* (London, 1950), p. 12.

[6] *Istoriya diplomatii*, vol. 1 (Moscow, 1959), p. 555.

[7] Lord Palmerston (Palmerston, Henry John Temple, Third Viscount of): British politician and diplomat, notable for his efforts to maintain the balance of power in Europe. He served as war secretary (1809–28), foreign secretary (1830–34, 1835–41, and 1846–51) and prime minister (1855–58 and 1859–65).

[8] Hansard Parliamentary Debates. 3d Series. Vol. 97, London, 1848, p. 123.

[9] House of Commons, 1833, July 11. Opinions and Policy of Palmerston. London, 1852, p. 246.

[10] E. Kedourie, *England and the Middle East: The Destruction of the Ottoman Empire. 1914–1921* (London, 1956), p. 10.

[11] Mustafa Reshid Pasha (1800–1858), an Ottoman statesman and diplomat. He was the initiator and the driving force behind the reforms of the first period of Tanzimat. He was Ambassador to Great Britain in 1836–39, and later served as Grand Vizier (1839–41, 1846–52, with interruptions).

[12] Sheremet, *Osmanskaya imperiya*, p. 89.

[13] Ibid., p. 39.

[14] *Vneshneekonomicheskie svyazi Osmanskoy imperii v novoe vremya (konets xviii–nachalo xx v.)* (Moscow, 1989), p. 44.

[15] Fadeeva, *Osmanskaya imperiya*, p 37.

[16] Sheremet, *Osmanskaya imperiya*, p. 50.

[17] *Vneshneekonomicheskie svyazi*, p. 65.

[18] *Istoriya diplomatii*, vol. 1, pp. 560–61; Todorova, *Angliya, Rossiya i Tanzimat*, p. 58.

[19] Sir Robert Peel (1788–1850), British statesman. He served as Home Office Secretary (1822–27, 1828–30), and Prime Minister (1834–35, 1841–46). Peel headed a moderate faction of the Tories, the so-called Peelites.

[20] George Hamilton-Gordon, Fourth Earl of Aberdeen (1874–60), a British politician and diplomat. He served as Foreign Secretary (1828–30, 1841–46), and Prime Minister (1852–66) as leader of the Conservative Party. A prominent member of the Peelites.

[21] Bourne, *The Foreign Policy of Victorian England*, p. 47.

[22] *Istoriya diplomatii*, vol. 1, pp. 562–63; Todorova, *Angliya, Rossiya i Tanzimat*, pp. 59–60.

[23] John Russel, First Earl Russel (1792–1878), British politician and diplomat. He served as Home Office Secretary (1835–39), Colonial Secretary (1839–41), Foreign Secretary (1852–53, 1859–65), and Prime Minister (1846–52, 1865–66).

[24] W. H. Dawson, *Richard Cobden and Foreign Policy* (London, 1926), pp. 211–12.

[25] Hansard Parliamentary Debates. 3d Series. Vol. CXXIX (London, 1853), pp. 1798–1810.

[26] *Istoriya diplomatii*, vol. 1, pp. 588–89.

[27] Sheremet, *Osmanskaya imperiya*, p. 148.

[28] H. G. Intchikian, *Osmanian kaysrutian ankume* (The fall of the Ottoman Empire) (Yerevan, 1984); R. A. Safrastyan, *Doktrina osmanizma v politicheskoy zhizni Osmanskoy imperii (50–70 gg. xix v.)* (Yerevan, 1985), pp. 18–19; Fadeeva, *Osmanskaya imperiya*, p. 61; Sheremet, *Osmanskaya imperiya*, pp. 82–83.

[29] Safrastyan, *Doktrina osmanizma*, pp. 19–20.

[30] Ibid., p. 26.

[31] A. Palmer, *The Decline and Fall of the Ottoman Empire* (New York, 1992), pp. 106–7.

[32] Russian Federation, Arkhiv vneshney politiki Rossii (AVPR): F. Politicheskiy arkhiv, Kantselyariya, 1848, d. 43, l. 155–73.

[33] C. K. Webster, *The Foreign Policy of Palmerston: Britain, the Liberal Movement and the Eastern Question*, vol. 2 (London, 1951), pp. 540–41.

[34] Sheremet, *Osmanskaya imperiya*, pp. 142–43.

[35] E. F. Malcolm-Smith, *The Life of Stratford Canning* (London, 1933), p. 167.

[36] Todorova, *Angliya, Rossiya i Tanzimat*, p. 77.

[37] Sheremet, *Osmanskaya imperiya*, pp. 85–86.

[38] H. W. V. Temperley, *England and the Near East: The Crimea* (London, 1936), p. 229.

[39] Ibid.

[40] A. Cunningham, *Stratford Canning and the Tanzimat: Beginnings of Modernization in the Middle East* (Chicago, 1968), p. 261.

[41] Malcolm-Smith, *The Life of Stratford Canning*, p. 185.

[42] Eastern Papers. Part XVIII. Correspondence respecting Christian Privileges in Turkey. (London, 1856), p. 15.

[43] Ibid.

[44] Malcolm-Smith, *The Life of Stratford Canning*, p. 212.

[45] Todorova, *Angliya, Rossiya i Tanzimat*, p. 78.

[46] Sheremet, *Osmanskaya imperiya*, p. 136.

[47] Malcolm-Smith, *The Life of Stratford Canning*, p. 222.

[48] Ibid., p. 223.

[49] V. A. Georgiev, N. S. Kinyapina, M. T. Panchenkova, et al., *Vostochnyy vopros vo vneshney politike Rossii (konets xviii–nachalo xx veka)* (Moscow, 1978), pp. 132–33.

[50] Sheremet, *Osmanskaya imperiya*, pp. 158–59.

[51] Eastern Papers. Part V. Communications respecting Turkey made to Her Majesty`s Government by the Emperor of Russia, with the Answers returned to them. January to April 1853. London, 1854, pp. 2–3.

[52] Ibid., pp. 3–6.

[53] Ibid., pp. 7–8.

[54] Clarendon, George William Frederick Villiers, Fourth Earl of (1800–1870), British statesman and diplomat. He served as Lord Lieutenant of Ireland (1847–52), and as Foreign Secretary (1853–58, 1865–66, 1868–70).

[55] Sheremet, *Osmanskaya imperiya*, p. 164.

[56] Correspondence respecting the Condition of Protestants in Turkey. 1853–1854 (In Continuation of Papers presented to both Houses of Parliament in 1851). London, 1854, p. 4.

[57] Ibid., p. 5.

[58] Ibid., p. 11.

[59] Eastern Papers. Part V, pp. 8–9.

[60] Ibid., pp. 9–10.

[61] Ibid., p. 10.

[62] Ibid., pp. 19–20.

[63] Sheremet, *Osmanskaya imperiya*, p. 163.

[64] Eastern Papers. Part V, p. 26.

[65] Georgiev, et al., *Vostochnyy vopros*, pp. 132–34.

[66] Correspondence respecting the Condition of Protestants..., p. 2.

[67] Georgiev, et al., *Vostochnyy vopros*, p. 135.

[68] Ibid., p. 136.

[69] Ibid., p. 137.

[70] Correspondence respecting the Condition of Protestants..., p. 3.

[71] Georgiev, et al., *Vostochnyy vopros*, p. 138.

[72] Sheremet, *Osmanskaya imperiya*, pp. 173–74.

[73] Ibid., pp. 220–21.

[74] Ibid., pp. 205–6.

[75] Eastern Papers. Part VIII. Protocol signed at Vienna on the 8th of April, 1854, by the Representatives of Austria, France, Great Britain and Prussia. London, 1854, p. 2.

[76] Eastern Papers. Part IX. Protocol signed at Vienna on the 23rd of May, 1854 by the Representatives of Austria, France, Great Britain and Prussia. London, 1854, p. 2.

[77] Eastern Papers. Part XIII. Papers relating to the Negotiations at Vienna on the Eastern Question. London, 1855, p. 2.

[78] Eastern Papers. Part XVI. Instructions to Lord John Russell on Proceeding to Vienna. London, 1855, pp. 1–3.

[79] Eastern Papers. Part XVIII, pp. 8–11.

[80] Ibid., pp. 12–13.

[81] Eastern Papers. Part XV. Communications with the Austrian Government. London, 1855, p. 41.

[82] Ibid., p. 44.

[83] Eastern Papers. Part XVIII, p. 19.

[84] Ibid., pp. 23–24.

[85] Ibid., p. 25.

[86] Ibid., pp. 27–28.

[87] Ibid., pp. 32–33.

[88] Ibid., pp. 38–39.

[89] Ibid., p. 42.

[90] Ibid., pp. 49–51.

[91] Eastern Papers. Part XVII. Firman and Hatti-Sherif by the Sultan, relative to Privileges and Reforms in Turkey. London, 1856, pp. 4–7.

[92] Sheremet, *Osmanskaya imperiya*, pp. 244–47.

[93] Protocol of Conferences held at Paris relative to the General Treaty of Peace. London, 1856, p. 8.

[94] Turkey No 17 (1877). Instructions addressed to Her Majesty's Embassy at Constantinople respecting financial and administrative Reforms and the Protection of Christians in Turkey, 1856–1875. London, 1877, Part 1, p. 5.

[95] Ibid., pp. 57–58.

[96] *Shornik dogovorov Rossii s drugimi gosudarstvami. 1856–1917* (Moscow, 1952), pp. 25–26.

[97] Fadeeva, *Osmanskaya imperiya*, p. 85.

[98] Ibid., pp. 95–97.

[99] Papers relating to Administrative and Financial Reforms in Turkey. 1858–1861. London, 1861, pp. 2–13.

[100] Derby, Edward George Geoffrey Smith Stanley, Fourteenth Earl of, (1799–1869), a British statesman. He served as Colonial Secretary (1840–44), and Prime Minister (1852, 1858–59, 1866–68).

[101] Turkey, No 17, Part 2, p. 81.

[102] Papers relating, pp. 15–16.

[103] Turkey, No 17, Part 1, pp. 12–13.

[104] Papers relating, p. 19.

[105] Ibid., p. 21.

[106] Ibid., p. 23.

[107] Fadeeva, *Osmanskaya imperiya*, pp. 102–3.

[108] Papers relating, p. 31.

[109] Turkey, No 17, Part 2, pp. 84–85.

[110] Reports received from Her Majesty`s Consuls relating to the Condition of Christians in Turkey, 1860. London, 1861, pp. 1–3.

[111] Papers relating, p. 47.

[112] Turkey, No 17, Part 2, p. 88.

[113] Ibid., pp. 90–91.

[114] Ibid., pp. 89.

[115] Papers relating, p. 58.

[116] Ibid., pp. 66–67, 70.

[117] Ibid., p. 103.

[118] Turkey, No 17, Part 1, pp. 26–27.

[119] Fadeeva, *Osmanskaya imperiya*, p. 122.

[120] Ibid., pp. 44–45.

[121] Turkey, No 17, Part 1, p. 34.

[122] Turkey, No 17, Part 2, p. 110.

[123] Correspondence respecting Protestant Missionaries and Converts in Turkey. London, 1865, pp. 5–6.

[124] Reports received from Her Majesty`s Ambassador and Consuls relating to the Condition of Christians in Turkey, 1867. London, 1867, pp. 1–4.

[125] Ibid., p. 7.

[126] Ibid., p. 50.

[127] Ibid., p. 74.

[128] Turkey, No 16 (1877). Reports by Her Majesty`s Diplomatic and Consular Agents in Turkey respecting the Condition of the Christian Subjects of the Porte. 1868–1875. London, 1877, pp. 1–3.

[129] Reports received, pp. 77–78.

[130] Gladstone, William Ewart (1809–1898), British statesman. He served as President of the Board of Trade (1843–45), Colonial Secretary (1845–47), Chancellor of the Exchequer (1852–55, 1859–66), and becoming leader of the Liberal Party, he served as Prime Minister (1868–74, 1880–85, 1886, 1892–94).

[131] Fadeeva, *Osmanskaya imperiya*, p. 135.

[132] Turkey, No 16, pp. 17–36.

[133] Ibid., pp. 17–18.

[134] Safrastyan, *Doktrina osmanizma*, pp. 60–62.

[135] Granville, George Leveson-Gower Granville, 2d Earl, (1815–1891), a British Liberal politician. He served as Colonial Secretary (1868–70, 1886), and as Foreign Secretary (1870–74, 1880–85).

[136] Turkey, No 16, pp. 42–43.

[137] Ibid., pp. 72, 75.

Chapter 2. Western Armenia and British Policy During the Middle Eastern Crisis of 1875–78

1. British Diplomacy and the Balkan Question, 1875–77

The Ottoman Empire, once again beset by economic crisis in the 1870s, all but gave up on the reform efforts. The implemented administrative reforms had not resulted in greater economic efficiency and better government, largely because of the vestiges of the old feudal-style economic relations and the continuing ethnic unrest and persecutions. In October 1875, the Sublime Porte declared bankruptcy, being unable to service its external debt; the interest payments had reached the astronomical figure of 6 billion francs. The European Powers further increased their control over the Empire's finances, eliminating competitors in the market. The country's weak industrial base stagnated under the double pressure of the authorities' mismanagement and the foreign competition. A law in 1874 allowed foreign citizens to receive licenses for industrial production, which, coupled with the previously granted concessions to foreign commercial interests, gave them an absolute edge over any local producer.[1]

The European governments took advantage of the growing economic and political weakness of the Ottoman Empire to advance their objectives and interests there. All were eager to control the East-West commercial routes passing through the Empire. The competition between Great Britain and France, in particular, increased after the opening of the Suez Canal in 1869, although the French defeat in the Franco-Prussian War of 1870–71 significantly strengthened the British positions in the Eastern Mediterranean. Russia tried to play one European nation against another as it extended assistance to the Christian peoples in the Ottoman Empire to restore its former positions in the Balkans. Russian-British relations were exacerbated during the crisis of 1873–75 in the Near and Middle East which emerged at the same time as an economic crisis in Western countries.

The British Government was perhaps the more successful among the European Powers vying for control in the Ottoman Empire, not only by its economic power but also due to extensive diplomatic activities in the Empire. In 1870's, the Turkish-British trade volume was 12–13 million pounds annually. Most products transported through the Suez Canal were carried by British ships, and Britain increased its purchases of cotton from the Mesopotamia region from 12 thousand pounds to 199 thousand pounds during the decade.[2]

The Conservative Party led by Benjamin Disraeli (Lord Beaconsfield)[3] led the British Government in 1874–80. This period stands out for the active efforts by the government expansion of the British positions abroad, with the Government waging colonial wars in India, Afghanistan, South Africa, suppressing revolts in Ireland and other places. The British Government solidified its control over Cyprus, the Suez Canal, and Egypt. Without prior consent or consultation with the Parliament, the Disraeli Cabinet purchased 40% of the Suez Canal shares from Ismail Pasha, the previous ruler of Egypt, which set the stage for the British domination of Egypt.

Against the backdrop of the acute economic crisis in the Ottoman Empire and internal instability, the constitutional reform movement gained more supporters. The Porte was now trying to stir up pro-Sultan, nationalist, anti-Christian emotions to distract attention from its ongoing political, social, and economic difficulties and as a substitute for the constitutional reform ideas that had gained a foothold in the military, in the administration, and among the intellectuals. The heavy-handed tactics of the Sultan's government and the political, economic, and ethnic persecutions during the June 1875 anti-Turkish uprising in Bosnia and Herzegovina sparked an international crisis, usually referred to in diplomatic history as the Near Eastern Crisis of 1875–78. The danger of seemingly imminent collapse of the Ottoman Empire and formation of pro-Russian statelets out of the ruins of the Empire became a serious issue in international relations. An object of intense diplomatic discussion and competition among the European Powers, this could have led to a general war. Nineteen years had passed since the 1856 Congress of Paris, and it became clear that none of the Sultan's promises to implement reforms in the Balkans had been implemented. The situation in Bulgaria, Bosnia and Herzegovina, Romania, Wallachia, Serbia, and Montenegro had actually deteriorated in the previous two decades. The collective right of the European Powers to protect the Christian minorities had been exercised only to prevent any Russian interference in the region.

The Russian interests coincided with the national liberation aspirations of the Balkan peoples, but the Russian Government's actions were limited by the restrictions imposed on it by the Treaty of Paris. Russia was also not quite ready for another war with the Ottoman Empire, and it first engaged in frantic diplomatic efforts with the Sultan's Government, enlisting the cooperation of its closest allies, Austria-Hungary and Germany.[4] Multi-ethnic Austria-Hungary defended the principle of the territorial integrity of the Ottoman Empire because it felt the new independent Slav states in the Balkans would threaten the Habsburg's Empire from without. Officially, Germany had declared its neutrality and impartiality in the Eastern Question and was also a close ally of Russia, but Chancellor Bismarck[5] also had a hidden agenda, hoping to kindle a Russian-Turkish military confrontation, as well as tensions in British-Russian and French-Russian relations.

The members of the Three Emperors League – Russia, Germany, and Austria-Hungary - finally decided to engage in common diplomatic efforts, and the envoys of the three countries presented a joint memorandum to Sultan Abdul Aziz in August 1875, with several proposals aimed at satisfying the demands of the Slav population in the provinces. An international commission comprised of the representatives of all European Powers attempted to mediate between the Sultan and the insurgents. In October and December 1875, the Sultan issued decrees unveiling mass-scale reforms in the provinces affected by the insurgency, which however failed to address the grievances and did not therefore contain the rebellion.

On December 30, 1876, the Austro-Hungarian Foreign Minister, Count Gyula Andrassi,[6] acting on behalf of the Three Emperors League, presented a proposal for the peaceful settlement of the Balkan crisis to the Powers. The proposal called on all signatories of the Treaty of Paris to urge the Porte to implement political, economic, and religious reforms in the insurgent provinces. France and Italy accepted the proposal, and the ball was now in the court of the British Government. Prime Minister Disraeli took his time deliberating over the British position, apparently waiting to see how the crisis in Russian-Turkish relations would develop. Preventing a possible military confrontation between those countries was neither a priority for, nor an objective of, British diplomacy.

In the early stages of the insurgency, Foreign Secretary Lord Derby wrote to Ambassador Elliott, in his letters of August 12 and 24, that it would have been better for the Porte to settle the crisis on its own, without any foreign interference.[7] When Andrassi's proposals reached Lord Derby, the Foreign Office looked for ways to join the Powers' initiative but without being bound by any obligations. The peaceful settlement in the Balkans was not a major priority for Disraeli who, nevertheless, had to cope with public opinion in Britain and other European nations, which demanded of their governments that the issue be addressed. At the same time, the Liberal opposition lead by Gladstone never missed a chance to point out the mistakes made by the Conservatives and raised the issue in the Parliament.

In January 1876, the British Government tasked the Ambassador with clarifying the position of the Porte on the Andrassi proposals in the event that Britain endorsed them too. The British Ambassador warned the Sultan's government that the British endorsement of the European Powers' demarche would not create additional difficulties for the Porte. On January 13, the Ottoman Foreign Minister Rashid Pasha told Elliott that the Porte would rather have the British Government join the Austrian Government's demarche, unless it was deemed totally unacceptable to Turkey.[8] Consequently, in his message to the Austro-Hungarian Ambassador in London, Lord Derby endorsed the Austrian proposals, while expressing comments and reservations on all five points. The British Foreign Secretary noted that Sultans Abdul Mejid and Abdul Aziz had already promised to carry out reforms, in addressing the concerns of the Christian population.[9]

On February 3, the Austro-Hungarian Ambassador to the Ottoman Empire, Ambassador Siczi, accompanied by the ambassadors of five other European Powers, verbally presented Andrassi's proposals to Rashid Pasha. The proposal had never been presented to the Porte in writing; further, there were no punitive mechanisms attached to the proposal in case the Sultan rejected the demands of the Powers. Reporting to London on the European Ambassador's meeting with Rashid Pasha, Elliott noted that no pressure had been applied and that the proposal's aim was to encourage the Porte.[10]

In truth, the Sultan's government had no intention of acceding to demands to carry out reforms in the Balkans, and it intensified its military actions against the insurgents. The situation further deteriorated in April 1876, when rebellions broke out in Bulgaria, Serbia, and Montenegro. The Porte started amassing troops near Serbia and Montenegro, and Russia proposed to the governments of Germany and Austria-Hungary to work together to address the crisis. Russian Foreign Minister Count Alexander Gorchakov,[11] Bismarck and Andrassi held a round of negotiations in Berlin in April and early May, signing a memorandum on a joint approach by the three Powers on the Eastern Question. The memorandum, made public on May 13, demanded that the Sultan's government declare a cease-fire for two months, negotiate with the rebels and carry out reforms under the supervision of the consular officers of the European Powers. The memorandum, which was also in compliance with the Treaty of Paris, was presented to other nations as well. France and Italy immediately endorsed it, but the British Government categorically rejected it. Disraeli said publicly that the Berlin Memorandum was an affront to the authority of the Porte, and on May 24, he dispatched a British naval contingent to Constantinople.[12] Queen Victoria was among those who expressed bewilderment at such a move,[13] and Disraeli was quoted as saying that the navy had been sent not to protect the Christians or the Turks but, rather, Her Majesty's Empire. He noted that the Berlin Memorandum would lead to the fall of Constantinople into Russian hands, and the establishment of Russian control over the Ottoman fleet.[14]

The British expressions of support allowed the Sultan to ignore the demands of the other European Powers, and the Ottoman authorities carried out a violent campaign of reprisals in Bulgaria, which resulted in more than 30,000 deaths.[15] This unprecedented cruelty in the suppression of the Bulgarian insurgency caused a wave of public indignation in Britain, and became a hot partisan issue between the supporters of Disraeli and Gladstone. In late July, the Government's foreign policy was criticized severely in the House of Commons and in the press. In his brochure *The Bulgarian Horrors and the Question of the East,* Gladstone called on the British public to demand of the Government to reverse its policy on Turkey and to press, in concert with other European nations, for abolition of Turkish rule in Bulgaria.[16]

Reporting on the Bulgarian developments, Ambassador Elliott remarked cynically to Lord Derby that he believed 10–20,000 Bulgarian victims were a commonplace event in that "semi-civilized Asiatic" country, which should not cause British policy to be changed.[17] Soon, however, under the pressure of public opinion and the opposition, the British Government chose different tactics for dealing with the Bulgarian situation. Elliott was instructed to protest the excesses to the Sultan's government and warn of possible consequences should the violent repression continue. In his dispatches of August 22 and September 5, Lord Derby further instructed his Ambassador to tell the Porte that any British sympathies toward Turkey had largely vanished as a result of the Bulgarian catastrophe. The Ambassador was instructed to say that the agitation of the British public had reached a point that would make it impossible for the British Government from coming to the defense of Turkey in the event of a Russian-Ottoman military conflict.[18]

In June 1876 Serbia and Montenegro signed a defense alliance, and declared war on the Porte. British diplomacy was not taken by surprise, and accepted the developments calmly, although it was clear this would inevitably lead to a Russian-Turkish standoff. The Russian Ambassador in London, Count Pyotr Shuvalov,[19] met with Disraeli to discuss the British position on the Balkan war. Disraeli said that he expected the war to be cruel but short in duration. He said that the insurgent provinces would receive a status similar to that of Romania in event of a Turkish military defeat, an outcome that Europe could intervene to enforce. He also suggested that the European Powers should intervene in case of a military victory for Turkey, to prevent possible repercussions and persecution of the Christians.[20]

The Turkish military defeated the Serbian Army much more easily than it had the insurgents in Bosnia and Herzegovina. On August 26, Serbian Prince Milan appealed to the European consuls in Belgrade to mediate a cease-fire. However, during a palace coup in Constantinople, Sultan Murad V was replaced by his younger brother, Abdul Hamid II.[21] Exercising its influence over the new Sultan, the British Government persuaded the European Powers to propose a cease-fire arrangement to the Sultan, and to call a Convention in Constantinople to address the Eastern Question. All major Powers endorsed the proposal, but the Sultan's government effectively rejected it by setting impossibly tough conditions for the cease-fire.

In his September 4 letter to Lord Derby, Disraeli presented his ideas on possible developments in the Eastern Question. He expressed doubts as to the possibility of a speedy settlement of the Balkan crisis, which, according to him, would last until the spring of the following year when Austria and Russia would move troops to the region for a final settlement of the Eastern Question. The British Prime Minister envisioned a division of the Balkan spoils between Austria-Hungary and Russia, with Britain sharing in the benefits of the settlement. He also suggested that Constantinople should become a neutral city and a free port, under British protectorate.[22] This was in effect a partition plan for the Ottoman Empire, which ran contrary to the declared objective of the Disraeli Cabinet to maintain the territorial integrity of the Ottoman Empire. In yet another letter to Lord Derby, dated September 23, the Prime Minister noted there were no discrepancies between the official British policy and the idea of the partitioning of Turkey, since the ultimate objective of the British Government was to maintain its domination in the East.[23]

The major European Powers, meanwhile, continued to negotiate a peaceful settlement of the Balkan crisis in September-October 1876, without any discernible results. British diplomacy came forward with a program of restoring *status quo belle ante* for Serbia, and local autonomy for Bosnia and Herzegovina and Bulgaria. All Powers agreed to the proposal, but the Russian Government proposed to amend it by placing a joint naval contingent of the Powers in the Sea of Marmara. The British Government rejected the amendment since it ran contrary to Disraeli's secret plans. Abdul Hamid, in the meantime, continued to obstruct the peace process, and hostilities resumed in October after the temporary cease-fire expired. With nationalist and Muslim fundamentalist emotions running high in Turkey, the new Sultan's government did not find it expedient to grant concessions to the Christian population of the insurgent areas, declaring an imminent passage of a Constitution and implementation of the reforms on its basis.[24]

With prior consent of the Russian Government, Disraeli invited all the signatories of the Treaty of Paris to attend a conference in Constantinople to discuss the Eastern Question. Representatives of Great Britain, Russia, France, Italy, Germany, Austria-Hungary, and Romania assembled in Constantinople in early December. The British Government was represented by the then Secretary of State for India, Lord Robert Salisbury,[25] who was instructed by Disraeli to impede any attempts by other Power to impose the terms of settlement on Turkey.[26] The British diplomats worked hard to ensure that the Sultan rejected any proposal by the European Powers, which would have allowed Britain to set aside its obligations before other Powers, as provided for in the Treaty of Paris. This policy was aimed at making a Russian-Turkish military confrontation inevitable, which would then allow Britain to gain greater political and economic influence in the Near East.

Before the conference, scheduled for December 14-23, officially started, the representatives of the European Powers gathered in the Russian Embassy to discuss the Russian proposal for the peaceful settlement of the Balkan crisis. The meeting was chaired by the Russian Ambassador, Count Nikolai Ignatiev,[27] and proceeded with great difficulty since Lord Salisbury took issue with every point made by the Russian representative. The diplomatic representatives finally agreed on a common proposal, which would preserve the autonomy of Serbia, grant minor territorial gains to Montenegro, unite Bosnia and Herzegovina in one province, and divide Bulgaria into an Eastern and Western regions, each with a guaranteed right to self-government and freedom of religion. Reforms addressing the situation of the Christian population in those regions were to be carried out under the supervision of the Europeans. On December 23, the representative of the Sublime Porte was invited to the meeting to be presented with the proposed Constitution – the first in the Ottoman Empire. He rejected the proposal because equal status for the Christians and Muslims and wide-scale reforms were guaranteed.

The European Powers continued to negotiate with the Porte, to persuade it to accept the peace program. Salisbury's efforts toward that goal were also outstanding, although the British were well aware of the Sultan's contemptuous attitude toward the settlement. The British representative met with newly appointed Grand Vizier Midhat Pasha and the Sultan himself, criticized their attitude toward the peace proposal of the European Powers, and threatened to withdraw British political, economic, and financial support. The Ottoman Government, however, did not make a single concession, and on January 20, 1877, the European countries declared the Conference closed and recalled their Ambassadors.[28]

In his personal correspondence with his friends, Salisbury wrote immediately after his return from Constantinople that the traditional British position on the Ottoman Empire's territorial integrity had to be changed to initiate a division of the Sultan's domains.[29] Disraeli also began referring to an impending collapse of the Ottoman Empire. He told Lord Derby that the partition was inevitable, and Britain should not hesitate to seize the parts of Turkey essential for the British Empire's security.[30] In other words, Britain now intended to help itself to the Ottoman territories, including Cyprus, in the aftermath of the Russian-Turkish war. British diplomacy, nevertheless, did not want to sever its relations with the Sultan's Government, which could have driven the Sultan closer to Russia. At the end of December, Midhat Pasha sent a special envoy to London, choosing his close aide Grigor Otian, who had helped him draft the Constitution, for this mission. The latter was charged with clarifying the British position in the event of a Russian military offensive. Otian and the Ottoman Ambassador in London, Musurus Pasha told Lord Derby during their meeting that the Sultan had found it impossible to allow European control over the reforms, which had been the main provision of the international proposal. With passions running high among the Muslim population, the Turkish Government implied that it would rather start a war with Russia. Lord Derby did not give any specific answer, saying that it was the decision of the Porte.[31]

Faced with the indifferent attitude of the British Government, the Sultan decided to adopt a more conciliatory stance. In his next meeting with Lord Derby, which took place on January 29, 1877, Otian read a telegram from Midhat Pasha, which stated that the Porte would, in general, agree to the terms of the international proposals wherever possible, and expressed hope that such a position of the Sultan's Government would be viewed 'amicably and approvingly' by Britain. Lord Derby replied that the international convention had had two main objectives: to ensure peace in Europe and to improve the administration of government in the Ottoman Empire. Expressing what he described as a personal opinion, Lord Derby noted that the conference had failed to reach its objectives due to the Ottoman stance, which would now give certain countries a *casus belli* against the Ottoman Empire. Otian raised the issue of the general amnesty, which was part of the proposal, and said that Midhat Pasha would implement the measure for both the Turks and the Christians. Lord Derby asked if such an amnesty would cover the perpetrators of the Bulgarian massacres as well, and Otian replied that it would be very difficult to exclude them from the amnesty. Derby suggested against applying the amnesty to those jailed for taking part in the massacres.[32]

After the failure of the Constantinople conference, British diplomacy wanted to clarify the Russian position on the Eastern Question. The British Ambassador to Russia, Lord Loftus, met with Foreign Minister Prince Gorchakov on January 22, and was told by him that Russia would not act outside the 'Concert of Europe.' Gorchakov suggested that Europe had been challenged and had to take decisive steps to protect its honor. Gorchakov said that, according to his information from Ambassador Ignatiev, the Porte would soon propose direct negotiations with Russia, but Russia, Gorchakov said, would not join talks with Turkey independently of the European Powers.[33]

On February 15, Lord Derby wrote Loftus that the Russian Ambassador in London had told him Russia had a 500,000-strong army, but would prefer to settle its differences with the Porte peacefully. The Russian Government proposed that the European Powers act jointly to alleviate the conditions of the Christian population of the Ottoman Empire. If Europe were to control and guarantee the reforms process, the Russian Ambassador said, then Russia would not have to act independently.[34]

On February 20, Disraeli indirectly suggested to Count Shuvalov, the Russian Ambassador in London, that Britain and Russia could come to an understanding in the event of the fall of the Ottoman Empire. Disraeli said that it was implausible that Russia could settle the Eastern Question on its own or in concert with the German or Austro-Hungarian Empires. He said that British interests in the Ottoman Empire were too important for Britain to be relegated to a secondary position in the settlement of the Eastern Question. Disraeli told the Russian Ambassador that Britain, "a peace-loving yet strong nation," could work with Russia to address the Eastern Question.[35]

Faced with external threats, Sultan Abdul Hamid resorted to extraordinary measures by establishing an authoritarian regime, and, at the same time, attempting to restore relations with the Great Powers, including Great Britain and Russia. On February 5, Midhat Pasha and his supporters were arrested and subsequently exiled, and on February 28 the Porte signed a peace agreement with Serbia, at terms extremely favorable to the latter.

In early March, Ambassador Ignatiev made a tour of the European capitals to present the Russian peace proposal on the Eastern Question. Germany, France, Austria-Hungary, and Italy immediately accepted the Russian proposals. While in Paris, Ignatiev told the British Ambassador there, Lord Lyons, that the Russian Government wanted to maintain peace jointly with other European Powers, and in a "cordial understanding" with Britain. According to Ignatiev, the Ottoman Empire was on the verge of falling to pieces – a dangerous development for Russia and Europe – and internal conditions were threatening the Christian population of the Empire. The Russian representative suggested signing a Memorandum in London containing the proposals developed earlier in Constantinople, to be presented to the Porte.[36]

On March 13, Lord Derby informed Loftus that Shuvalov had presented to him the draft of the six Powers' Memorandum. The Memorandum stated that the participants of the Constantinople conference, aiming for a peaceful resolution of the Eastern Question, expressed their general interest in the condition of the Christian population of the Ottoman Empire, and appealed to the Porte to implement the necessary reforms. The diplomatic representatives of the Powers in the Ottoman Empire were to establish control over the reforms. If the Powers' appeals were rebuffed and the condition of the Christians deteriorated further, the draft would reserve to the Powers the right to provide for the welfare of the Christians and general peace by all necessary means.[37]

Convinced that Abdul Hamid would reject the Powers' proposal since it would undermine his authority in the eyes of his Muslim subjects, Lord Derby signed the Memorandum on March 31, after a long round of negotiations with Shuvalov and Ignatiev.[38]

At about the same time, Abdul Hamid declared at the opening session of the Ottoman parliament that he would work to improve the welfare of the Empire, continue the Tanzimat reforms and do his utmost to defend the dignity and independence of the Empire.[39] On April 9, the Sultan's government presented a note to the Powers in which, expressing unhappiness over their interference in Turkish internal affairs, it rejected the European demands. In his April 12 letter to the British Charge d'affairés in Constantinople, Lord Derby informed him of his meeting with Musurus Pasha. The Foreign Secretary told his visitor that, given the irreconcilable differences between the positions of the two countries, there was nothing to be negotiated, and expressed his regret that the British Government would be unable to prevent the war.[40]

Russian-Turkish diplomatic contacts were broken off immediately after the Turkish rejection of the London Memorandum, and on April 24, Czar Alexander II signed a decree declaring war on the Ottoman Empire.

2. The Condition of Western Armenians during the Near Eastern Crisis, as relayed in British Foreign Office papers

Parallel to the increasing violence and persecution to which the Armenian population in Western Armenia was subjected in 1875–77, British diplomacy's interest in the condition of the Armenian Christians in those vilayets increased. Prior to this period, the British Foreign Office papers were full of references to the condition of the Lebanese Christians and Slavs and the policies of the Porte and local authorities toward these two groups. In the 1870's, however, the British Foreign Office increasingly directed its attention to the situation in Western Armenia, where the Turkish authorities and the Kurdish feudal elite subjected the local Armenian population to systematic oppression, to the degree that robbery, arson and murder became daily occurrences.

According to the reports of British consular agents, the condition of the Christian population of the eastern vilayets, including the Armenians, had not improved, and the only changes had been for the worse. On July 19, 1875, British Consul Zohrab informed Derby that the vilayet was in a terrible state, Gülhane-Hatte-Hümayun had not been implemented, and that the people sent from the capital city to rule over this "destitute country" appeared to be motivated primarily by anti-Christian fanaticism, brutality, and malfeasance. Zohrab reported also that the murders of Armenians, rapes of young women, and robberies had become commonplace.[41]

Another common tool of oppression against the Armenian population was the arson that targeted the property of the Armenian merchants, disturbing the commerce and trade flow in the provinces. In 1876 alone, arson, as well as looting by Muslim mob and Turkish soldiers, destroyed more than 250 Armenian-owned shops in Van (over 500, according to Armenian sources). The shop-owners presented yet another petition to the Porte, which was ignored.[42]

On December 11, 1876, Vice-Consul Alfred Biliotti reported to Ambassador Elliott from Trabzon on the results of the investigation of tax assessors' excesses in the villages of the province. Although the investigation confirmed the abuses of the tax officials, the governor of the province told the Vice Consul that the Armenians had deliberately exaggerated the situation out of "selfish motives." According to the governor, the Armenians adopted a menacing stance against the already threatened government that would lead to some "regrettable repercussions." Biliotti noted that the governor, while himself exaggerating the threats, had been frank and sincere in his opinions.[43]

On December 26, Zohrab reported to Lord Derby that the condition of the Armenian peasants and businessmen was deteriorating day by day, that the Turkish officials and police did not take any steps to protect them from the assaults and robberies by Muslim mobs, Kurdish tribes, and the abuses of tax collectors, and would frequently even spearhead these attacks themselves.[44]

The national liberation movement of the Balkan peoples and the immediate involvement of the European Powers in the Eastern Question had a powerful effect on the hitherto suppressed national movement among the Armenians of the Ottoman Empire - on the development of a national liberation ideology and a transformation of their national identity. The Armenian population increasingly realized that its liberation from the Ottoman Empire would serve to address their problems, and in 1876, the Armenian National Assembly in Constantinople debated an appeal to the European Powers and Russia with a request to implement reforms in Western Armenia. In December, Patriarch Nerses Varzhapetian appealed to the representatives of the European Powers assembled in Constantinople for the conference. The Armenian Patriarch asked for their nations' help in alleviating the condition of the Armenians and obtaining for the Armenian-populated regions the same privileges that the Powers were pressing the Porte to grant to the Balkan provinces. Ambassador Elliott noted in that regard that the position of the Armenians was no better than that of the Slav insurgents, and suggested that this could spark a rebellion among the Armenians as well. The Ambassador forwarded to Salisbury a copy of *For Turkey's Armenians; the Armenians and the Eastern Question*, a book by Anglican priest Rev. Curtis that was published in London.[45] On January 26, 1877, Lord Derby was informed that the Ambassadorial conference received petitions from the Protestant, Armenian-Catholic and Armenian Gregorian communities, as well as from the British citizens residing in Turkey, with almost identical reports. The petitions thanked Britain for its persistent efforts on behalf of the Christians in the Ottoman Empire.[46] However, the attempts to draw the Conference's focus on the Armenian community as well proved fruitless.

On January 22, Biliotti reported to Lord Derby that the Constantinople Conference and the mediation efforts by the Powers concerning the Eastern

Question had had a profound effect on the attitudes and activities of the population in the eastern provinces. He noted, however, that the Turks had become more earnestly patriotic, and that there were now signs of religious fanaticism. The Vice Consul noted that the Muslim faith was the link that bound many parts of the heterogeneous Turkish people together, although it would be incorrect to say that fanaticism was the only feeling prevalent among the Turks. His conclusion was that religion was the primary force behind Turkish patriotism. As long as one or several European Powers were perceived to be supporters of Turkey, this fanatical patriotism was not harmful, but tended to reach a high point when all the European Powers were perceived to be united against the Turks in some sort of a conspiracy. The Vice Consul reported that he did not believe the Turks were intrinsically vicious and did not harass the Christians only on the basis of their religion but because of their supposed affiliation with the Russians, who were truly hated. The Turks in the provinces were now too preoccupied with the thought of resisting the European pressure on Turkey to express any displeasure with the Christians, according to Biliotti. However, should the European Powers attempt to apply pressure on Turkey, the anger of the Muslim mobs could be expressed in actions against the Christians in ways far more cruel than hitherto observed, the Vice Consul concluded matter-of-factly.[47]

According to the report of the Vice Consul, the Christians believed that their safety would be threatened if all the European Powers turned against Turkey, but they hoped that the British Government would stand by its Ottoman ally. Moreover, according to Biliotti, since the European Powers were preoccupied with the fate of the Slav peoples, the Christians of the eastern provinces had no choice but to be supportive of the Turks. The British diplomat believed that the Christians in his jurisdiction, including the Orthodox, the Armenians, Protestants and Catholics were equally predisposed against Russia. The Armenians, according to Biliotti, had certain hopes of 'rejuvenating' their national identity in the Ottoman Empire, whereas those in Russia could not entertain such hopes. Everyone seemed to prefer even the current Turkish authorities to the Russian administration, the Vice Consul noted.[48]

Other British consular agents were not so optimistic as they continued to report continuing unrest in the eastern vilayets. On January 30, Zohrab told Elliott of the reports of the Kurdish attacks in Bitlis province, accompanied by looting, robberies, rapes and murders. The Consul believed that the Kurds were taking advantage of the weakened and disorganized local government, which was unable to control the situation. Governor Samih Pasha admitted that the country was in grave danger and suggested that the people should take care of their own protection since his powers were so limited.[49]

The failure of the Constantinople Conference and the departure of the European Ambassadors had negatively affected the situation in the eastern provinces. Biliotti reported to Lord Derby on February 7 that the local Turkish Pasha was greatly disconcerted upon hearing the news, admitting to the Vice Consul that the central government would sometimes raise the specter of European interference in an attempt to control the Muslim population, even exaggerating the degree of possible intervention. Now that European disapproval had become a reality, the Government no longer possessed an effective tool of pressure, and the Muslims, with nothing to lose, could become unruly.[50]

The Armenian population of Erzurum province began to suffer even greater abuses in mid-March, when the assaults and robberies by the Kurds were compounded by the looting and murders conducted by Ottoman officers and conscripts. Zohrab reported to Derby on March 15 that the persecution of the Christians in the city of Erzurum increased daily while the local government and the central authorities did nothing to prevent the abuses by the military. The villages were completely at the mercy of the military commanders and their troops.[51] On March 20, Biliotti reported to London that the military committed serious abuses against the Christians in the Gümüshkhane region.[52]

On March 27, the Foreign Secretary sent a circular note to all the consular agents in the Ottoman Empire, instructing the British Consuls to submit prompt, detailed, accurate reports on every instance of an alleged abuse against a Christian, and to visit the places where such abuse was reported to have taken place.[53]

The Russo-Turkish war of 1877-78 and the military activities on the Asia Minor front delivered a severe blow to the Armenians in the Eastern provinces. The Sultan's government and the local authorities did little to stop widespread looting and vindictiveness by the regular troops and the Kurdish irregulars in the Van, Bitlis, Mosul, and Diyarbakir provinces. On June 28, Zohrab reported to the newly appointed British Ambassador, Sir Henry Layard[54] on the situation in Van province. The Kurds assembled in Van to form an infantry battalion, received 800 rifles, and instead of being sent to the frontlines, were dispersed widely over the provinces, looting and burning several villages. The destruction of property was so complete that the population of the affected villages faced starvation and was reduced to collecting seeds and roots from the mountains for food, the consular report stated. Zohrab reported that the famine reached such proportions that the Governor of Van received permission to disburse the wheat stocks earmarked for the army. He noted that the situation in Mush and Bitlis was no different and that a famine was sure to break out in these provinces the following year.[55]

In turn, Layard reported to Lord Derby on July 4 and 10 of the abuses, robberies, and murders in Van province. He reported that the Kurdish irregulars led by Sheikh Jelaleddin of Khizan took advantage of the state of war to wage destruction and rob the entire region. According to information from Armenian Patriarch Nerses, more than 25 Armenian villages in the region were robbed. According to the Ambassador, the Porte was going to send a high-ranking military delegation to Van to stop the Kurdish abuses and to protect the local population.[56]

Patriarch Nerses maintained close contacts with the British Embassy as the events unfolded in Western Armenia. On July 24, he met with Ambassador Layard to discuss the condition of the Armenians in Van. The Patriarch told the Ambassador that the retreating Russian troops burned the Armenian church in Bagavan and detained the local pastor for refusing to call on his parish to rise against the Sultan. Patriarch Nerses believed that this event would affect the pro-Russian sentiments among the Armenians while the Turkish authorities could use this occasion to crack down on the Kurdish attacks on the Armenians.[57] Around the same time, the Patriarch wrote a letter to the Archbishop of Canterbury (chief bishop of the Anglican Church), describing the condition of the Armenian Christians and appealing for the support of the British people and the Anglican Church. The Patriarch informed the Archbishop that he had ordered to include English in the curriculum of the Armenian parochial schools, and asked for the support of the Anglican Church in this endeavor. Forwarding the letter to the addressee, Ambassador Layard wrote to Lord Derby that the appeal should be acceded to, inasmuch as the study of the English language and literature would be beneficial to the Armenians.[58]

In July and August, Zohrab continued to report on the developments in Erzurum province. On August 21, he wrote to Lord Derby that the Kurdish irregulars carried out a massacre in Bayazid, killing 480 people, and abducting 340 young boys and girls.[59] To verify the authenticity of the reports of the atrocities committed by the Kurdish bands, Ambassador Layard sent a member of his staff, a Mr. Ressam, to Diyarbakir, Van, Bitlis, and Mush.[60] The special envoy reported to the Ambassador on September 6 from Diyarbakir that the tension between the Muslim and Christian population was largely a result of flawed and corrupt activities by the local Turkish officials. He wrote that the Christians complained of the constant verbal abuses hurled at them in the streets and markets by the Muslims, who threatened to destroy "the infidels." Ressam reported that the Armenians living in the Slivan region had been driven into the pro-Russian camp due to the persecution and robberies suffered at the hands of the Kurdish bandits.[61]

On October 15, Ressam reported to Ambassador Layard that the previous reports of the robberies committed by the Kurdish bands against the Armenian Christians in Van had been substantiated. According to him, the Armenians living in Diyarbakir, Sert, Bitlis, Mush, and Van had been subjected to repeated robberies and murders. Following on the heels of the retreating Russian troops, the Kurdish irregulars raided the four Armenian-populated regions of Alashkert, Karakilisa, Diadin, and Bayazid, kidnapping between 250 and 300 Armenian women and children. The British diplomat reported that Muslim fanaticism had reached a high point in these areas, and that the Kurdish tribes had justified their actions by declaring a holy war—*jihad*—against the Armenians. Ressam also reported that the local Turkish governors, Abder Rahman in Diyarbakir and Hassan Pasha in Van had done their utmost to stop the massacres.[62]

On November 28, the British Consul in Tiflis (Tbilisi), Mr. Rickets, reported that some 850 Armenian families immigrated from Alashkert and Bayazid when the Army of Russian General Ter-Ghukasov retreated. According to the consul, there were 4250 Armenians among the refugees, of which 23 families were resettled in Surmalu, 270 families in Ejmiatsin, 150 families in Nor Bayazet, 200 families in Sevan, 87 families in Yerevan, and 119 families in

Alexandropol. The refugees reported that of 216 Armenian families living in Bayazid, 80 households emigrated to Russia, and the rest to Persia. The refugees told the Consul they would consider returning home only if the region was re-occupied by the Russian troops.[63]

According to the British diplomatic sources, as the result of the internal displacement during the 1877–78 Russian-Turkish war, the massacres and atrocities committed by the Kurdish irregulars, and the government-sponsored resettlement of the Circassians, Turks, and Lezgins in Eastern Asia Minor, the Armenian population of the six easternmost provinces of the Ottoman Empire was reduced to 35% of the total population there in 1878.[64] As American historian Robert Zeidner pointed out in his book, the changing demographics were enough for the European Powers to press the Armenians to delay their secessionist plans; the Armenians were no longer "more privileged" than other Christian minorities.[65]

3. British Policy during the 1877–78 Russian-Turkish War and the Armenian Question

British neutrality during the 1877–78 Russian-Turkish War was conditional. In his note of May 1, 1877, Lord Derby declared that the British Government disapproved of the Russian actions since they were in violation of the Treaty of Paris (1856) and the London Agreement (1871), which stipulated that the Powers had to respect the territorial integrity and independence of the Ottoman Empire.[66] A day earlier, he had made public a 'Declaration of the British Neutrality,' which, in effect, expressed British support for the Ottoman Empire.[67] Indeed, throughout the war, British diplomats encouraged the Sultan's government to fight on, British military engineers assisted in construction of fortifications in the Balkans and Western Armenia, and British military instructors drilled the Turkish officers and privates in the modern methods of warfare and in the use of newly-arrived British weapons.[68]

The Sultan's government, therefore, hoped that Britain would at some point join in the war against Russia, thus ensuring a victory for the Ottoman Empire. Prime Minister Disraeli, however, had to contend with internal political factors in the exercise of his foreign policy. The opposition Liberal Party criticized the government for supporting Turkey, while jingoist hardliners called on the government to declare war on Russia. Nevertheless, the powerful commercial interest groups were content with neutrality, and, essentially, prevailed on the government to preserve British neutrality. In his letter of May 6, 1877, Lord Derby informed the Russian Ambassador, Count Shuvalov, of the British position. The letter stated that the British Government would continue to abide by its neutrality pledge on the following conditions: (1) the Suez Canal must continue its operations to secure unhindered passage between Europe and Asia; any attempt to blockade the Canal or the Canal area would be tantamount to the blockade of India and therefore a threat to worldwide commerce; (2) Egypt was not to be attacked or even temporarily occupied, since the European financial and commercial interests there would be harmed; (3) Britain would not allow capture of Constantinople or its transfer into "hands other than those of the current possessors"; (4) the British Government would not accept an altering of the current status of the Black Sea Straits or the agreements setting the status; (5) the British Government might find other interests, for example, in the Persian Gulf that it would consider necessary to protect.[69] This note reaffirmed the conditionality of the British neutrality pledge, and was intended as a message to the Sultan that he did not need to worry about the loss of his capital, the Straits, or the departure of the British commercial capital.

The Russian Government summarized its position vis-à-vis the British note in the letter to Shuvalov sent by Foreign Minister Gorchakov on May 18, which was presented to Lord Derby by the Russian Ambassador. The Russian Foreign Minister acknowledged the British conditions, noting that the military hostilities would not be extended beyond what was required by the military needs. It also called on the British government not to disregard the special Russian interests for which Russia was ready to make sacrifices during the conflict. Russian policy aimed at permanently halting the deteriorating condition of the Christians in the Ottoman Empire and the unrest it had caused, Gorchakov wrote. He acknowledged that Europe would be affected by the war and expressed his hope that the Russian Empire would, in cooperation with its allies and friends, achieve a desired outcome in the war.[70]

In the initial period of the war, the British Government was not concerned by the Russian military victories. In mid-May, the Russian army of General Loris-Melikov captured Ardahan and began the siege of Kars. On the Balkan front, the Russian Army crossed the Danube and captured the Shipka Pass in

Bulgaria. Only by committing a significant amount of troops to the eastern and western fronts was the Ottoman Empire able to postpone its military collapse until November.

The British Government sought to reduce negative public opinion in the country. In July, the British navy was ordered to group in the Aegean Sea, and the government requested the Parliament to vote an additional 2.5 million pounds in military funding. A 1,500-man strong contingent was sent to Malta.[71] The militant stance of Britain was intended to prevent a decisive Russian advance and to encourage the Sultan's government. The letters of Prime Minister Disraeli to the Queen and to Ambassador Layard, as well as his public speeches, gave cause to believe that he supported a declaration of war on Russia. During a Cabinet meeting on August 15, Disraeli rebutted Lord Derby's assertion that Britain would not have allies in case of a war with Russia, saying that by having Turkey, Britain needed no more allies. Britain dominated the seas, he declared, and could cross Armenia and threaten the Asian provinces of Russia.[72]. In his August 6 letter to Layard, the Prime Minister stated that he intended to protect the territorial integrity and independence of the Ottoman Empire, if that was possible. The Turks had proved their right to independence, Disraeli wrote, and expressed a hope that post-war Turkey would be a welcome guest, not a shunned visitor in Europe. He said that if the Russian forces advanced too far, Britain would be forced to intervene and stop the destructive war and the partition plans.[73] In reality, the British Government had decided to intervene unless the Ottoman Empire was fully defeated and then requested the British help, so that it could trade British support for territorial gains.

After a series of reversals, in autumn of 1877 the military balance swung in Russia's favor. The Russian armies defeated Mukhtar Pasha's forces in the Balkan front on October 15 and captured Kars on November 18. General Gurkov's army entered Sofia on January 4. On January 15-17, 1878, the Russian Army emerged victorious during the battle of Philipolis, and, after the fall of Adrianople, reached the outskirts of Constantinople. Erzurum was transferred to Russian control on February 10 under the terms of the cease-fire agreement.

The fall of Kars and occupation of parts of Western Armenia were a cause of grave concern to British diplomacy. In his confidential message to Lord Derby, dated December 4, 1877, Ambassador Layard suggested that the capture of parts of Armenia by the advancing Russian forces would affect British interests. The Russian occupation of Armenia would severely undermine British authority in the East, Ambassador Layard suggested, and, therefore, was to be prevented at all costs, and with the help of other European Powers. Layard, specifically, made the following points in his telegram:

1. The fall of Kars and the occupation of Armenia would be construed as proof of Russian military superiority and Britain's inability to stop the Russian advances in the East. It would influence Muslim public opinion throughout Asia, and would threaten British domination of India.

2. The control of Armenia, including Batum, Kars, and Van, would give Russia an advantage in any future war against either Persia or Turkey, and would allow it to control all the routes to the Caucasus, Persia, and Turkey, which would fundamentally alter the nature of political and economic relations between Russia and other European Powers. Even if Trabzon and Erzurum were not in Russia's hands now, the possession of Kars and Batum could allow Russia to capture them later. Possessing Armenia, therefore, would make Russia the master of Asia Minor, and master of the Tigris and Euphrates valleys too. If Russia could not send an army to India via Central Asia or by sea, it could do so through Persia now that it controlled the Caspian Sea and Armenia. The population in Persia and Armenia would be more favorably disposed toward the Russians than the Turkic people of Central Asia. That's why Batum and Armenia were essential for Russia, concluded the Ambassador.

3. The Ambassador admitted that the Suez Canal made the question of an alternative route to India rather moot, since the routes passing through British-controlled Suez were more beneficial than the land routes via Syria and Mesopotamia. He argued that the Russian occupation of Armenia would constitute a serious threat against British control of the Suez, and, thus, it was essential to have an alternative route to India through Armenia and Mesopotamia. Therefore, it was essential to leave those areas under Turkish control. The Ambassador suggested that after a peace treaty was signed, Turkey be encouraged to build a railroad linking Constantinople with the Persian Gulf.

4. The Russian occupation of Armenia would have negative effects on British mercantile interests since British products would now be forced to be transported through Batum, rather than through Trabzon and Erzurum, and be subjected to higher taxation and possibly quotas.[74]

The view of the British Ambassador proved to be decisive in formulating the British position on military developments in the Armenian Question. This position did not at all consider the interests of the Armenian population and other minorities in the Empire. British diplomacy worked hard to press Russia to withdraw troops from Western Armenia in exchange for promises of reforms in those areas under a general supervision of the European Powers. This would have tragic consequences for the Armenian population in the years to come.

After the signing of the ceasefire agreement at Adrianople on January 31, 1878, the British diplomatic machine sought to reverse the Russian military advances, protect the Ottoman interests – in exchange for concessions in the Middle East – and to secure territorial gains for Great Britain. The British Government calculated that both Russia and Turkey were exhausted and that the time had come for Britain to dictate its terms. British diplomacy worked on the above objectives through the end of the Berlin Congress (June – July 1878).

The Parliament convened debates in early February on the question of providing the government with 6 million pounds in additional funding in order, in the words of War Minister Hard, "to save the Ottoman Empire from Russia." The Liberal opposition led by William Gladstone rallied its supporters against the government motion, but in the end, the House of Commons voted for the bill. The British navy was put on military alert, and seven thousands troops were transferred from India to Malta. These steps were meant to show that the British Government was serious in its determination to protect the Ottoman Empire. Disraeli, however, had to proceed quietly since public indignation over the atrocities committed by the Turks in Bulgaria had not yet dissipated. This was the main reason for the British policy, which combined flexible diplomacy with the pressure on Russia.[75]

The Russian-Turkish negotiations were marked by diplomatic pressure from Britain and Austria-Hungary, while a British naval formation was deployed in the Straits. The British Government was opposed to the bilateral format of the negotiations on the grounds that any agreement between the Russian and Ottoman Empires had to be approved by other European Powers, as required by the Treaty of Paris and the London Agreement of 1871. Under the terms of the San-Stefano Peace Treaty, signed on March 3 between Russia and Turkey, the Porte recognized the independence of Romania, Serbia, and Montenegro, the autonomy of Bulgaria, Bosnia and Herzegovina, and was forced to cede to Russia Bessarabia, Kars, Ardahan, Bayazid, Batum, Olti, Ardanush, Ardvin, Alashkert, Kahizman, and Khumar.

Article 16 of the San Stefano Treaty read as follows: "As the evacuation by the Russian troops of the territory which they occupy in Armenia, and which is to be restored to Turkey, might give rise to conflicts and complications detrimental to the maintenance of good relations between the two countries, the Sublime Porte engages to carry into effect, without further delay, the improvements and reforms demanded by local requirements in the provinces inhabited by Armenians, and to guarantee their security from Kurds and Circassians."[76] This was the first instance of Armenia and the Armenians reappearing in an international document in modern history. Nevertheless, it was obvious that the Russian Government was not keen on securing autonomy for Armenia, as happened in the case of the Slav peoples in the Balkans. Russia was satisfied with its status as a protector of the Armenians in the eastern provinces and promises of reforms there under Russian monitoring. By acknowledging the possibility of reprisals against the Armenian population in Western Armenia, the Russian Government turned the Ottoman Government's promise of reforms in Armenia into a subject of international law.

During the Russian-Turkish negotiations, the representatives of the Armenian community in Constantinople met with the Russian and British diplomats to demand autonomy for Western Armenia. On March 18, Ambassador Layard informed Lord Derby of a meeting he had held with Armenian Patriarch Nerses. The Patriarch presented the Ambassador with a letter addressed to the British Foreign Secretary, outlining the Armenian position on the issue. Layard reminded Lord Derby of his meeting with the Patriarch the previous year, when the head of the Armenian community in the Ottoman Empire had told him the Armenians were satisfied with Turkish rule and would have preferred it to Russian rule. The Patriarch had even told the Ambassador that the Armenians would gladly have joined the Army and defended the Empire. The Patriarch, nevertheless, reversed his stance telling the Ambassador that the Russian military victories, occupation of the larger part of Western Armenia, the autonomy granted to the Christians in the European part of the Ottoman Empire, and the promise of reforms in Armenia in the Russian-Turkish Treaty completely altered the situation. The Patriarch told the British Ambassador that the Armenians now detested Muslim domination, which proved unable to defend them against the Kurdish attacks in Van province and the region of Bayazid. If the Armenian demands were not addressed by the European Powers, they would appeal to Russia and fight until the whole of Armenia was annexed by Russia, the Patriarch said, adding that the Armenians would otherwise emigrate to Russia *en masse*. Patriarch Nerses said he was hopeful that the question of Armenian autonomy would be discussed during the peace conference and that the European Powers would support establishment of an autonomous Armenian region. The Patriarch gave Layard a copy of his letter to Chancellor Bismarck. Ambassador Layard inquired as to the makeup of Armenia, and the Patriarch said an autonomous Armenia should be comprised of the provinces of Van, Sivas, and larger parts of the Diyarbakir and Cilicia regions. The British Ambassador wrote that in response to his observation that the Muslims constituted a majority of the population in those regions, the Patriarch had replied that the Muslims had also been dissatisfied with the Sultan's rule and would willingly accept a Christian Government, which would afford them protection for their lives and property. The Patriarch concluded by saying that, if the European Powers failed to address the grievances of the Armenians, then the Armenian population would rise and "annex itself to Russia." He added that those were the prevailing attitudes in his community.

Recounting his meeting with the Patriarch, Ambassador Layard expressed his concern to Lord Derby over the possible partitioning of the Ottoman Empire, and suggested that the British Government should be prepared to counter it. He suggested that creation of an autonomous Armenia bordering Russia and Syria would run contrary to British interests. Such autonomy would end in annexation, according to the Ambassador.[77]

In yet another report to the Foreign Secretary, dated March 20, the British Ambassador recounted a meeting with a Sultan's official of Armenian origin, who had told him that a number of Armenian community leaders had been preparing a charter for "Armenian Autonomy," to be presented to the Congress of Powers. The Ambassador's counterpart discounted any objections to the establishment of the autonomy, admitting though that it was hardly possible to include Cilicia in the new entity, despite its former status as an

Armenian kingdom. The official had warned that rejection of the Armenian demands would only drive them toward the Russians, since the majority of the Armenians, according to him, would prefer annexation by Russia to continuing rule by the Turks. The official had said that the Armenians hoped for British support of their demands. The Ambassador added in his report that he had discouraged his interlocutor from restoring what he termed 'ancient King Tigran's Empire,' nor did he promise to present the draft charter to the Foreign Office.[78]

Ambassador Layard continued to send reports prophesying the repercussions of establishing an autonomous Armenian state. On March 25, he wrote that while it was England's hope that a more orderly government and protection of life and property would be guaranteed for the Muslims, Armenians, and other Christians under Turkish rule, it was necessary to rule out creation of a semi-independent Armenian authority. He predicted that, if established, the Armenian Autonomy would secede from the Ottoman Empire and fall under Russian influence. The Ambassador suggested that the British Government remain concerned with the condition of the Armenians during the conference, focusing on guarantees of a better administration and protection from the Kurdish tribes. Layard described the Armenians as a hard-working people, primarily employed in agriculture, and noted that the Armenians had amicable relations with their Turkish neighbors, who also suffered Kurdish attacks. The Armenians living in Constantinople and other large cities were engaged in commerce and banking, and some of them received important government appointments. He noted that the Armenians living in the capital spoke Turkish and got along with the Turks better than the Greeks. So, concluded the Ambassador, it was in the best interests of the Porte to render support and fair treatment to the Armenians, address their concerns, which would prevent them from turning to Russia for help. According to the Ambassador, granting an autonomous status to a province incapable of self-government would only exacerbate the situation and harm British interests.[79]

Ambassador Layard's position was one of the factors establishing the British position on the issue of Armenian autonomy. During the period following the conclusion of the San-Stefano Treaty, Lord Derby did not send any instructions or guidance to the Ambassador on the Armenian Question, largely because he did not share the tougher position of Prime Minister Disraeli, who was enraged by the terms of the Treaty. On March 28, Lord Derby tendered his resignation and was replaced by Salisbury, who shared both Disraeli's position on the Russo-Turkish conflict and Ambassador Layard's views on the Armenian Question.

4. The Armenian Question in British and European Foreign Policy: From San-Stefano to Berlin

The Eastern Question entered into its final stage after the signing of the San Stefano Treaty. The objective of British diplomacy at this stage was to reverse the Russian military gains in the Balkans and Western Armenia. The Ottoman Empire set out to take advantage of the infighting between the Powers by demanding a reward for its neutrality in the new conflict. Upon receiving the official text of the Russian-Turkish treaty on March 23, a special steering committee was set up by the Government in London to present the British position on the Treaty. On Article 16, the Committee's assessment was that the reforms provided therein should be guaranteed by all Powers, not Russia exclusively, and, likewise, such reforms must be controlled by all the Powers. The committee recommended that the new Russian-Turkish frontier be pushed as far to the east as possible, so as to remove it from the commercial routes connecting the port of Trabzon with Persia.[80]

The British Cabinet discussed the San-Stefano Treaty during a special session on March 27. The Prime Minister proposed to ask the House of Commons to call up reserves, declare Great Britain's readiness to use force, as well as to occupy Cyprus and Alexandretta with the British forces in India to neutralize the Russian military presence in Armenia. The Government position was expressed in a circular sent by Foreign Secretary Salisbury to the British Ambassadors abroad, and forwarded to other nations as well. The note condemned the San-Stefano Treaty for violating the principles of the Treaty of Paris (1856) and the London Agreement, and demanded that it be renegotiated in a European Congress. Noting that establishment of a Greater Bulgaria would turn it into a Russian stronghold in the East, Lord Salisbury wrote that occupation of parts of Armenia would make the population of the region dependent on Russia while the European trade and commerce routes from Trabzon to Persia could be closed by Russia at will by means of trade barriers.[81]

On April 13, Ambassador Shuvalov gave Salisbury the Russian reply to his note, which was drafted by Foreign Minister Gorchakov. The Russian Foreign Minister noted that the Russian gains in Armenia were of a defensive measure as they aimed to provide security at the border; these gains were a natural result of the war, the Minister said. If Great Britain wanted to help Turkey, it should have agreed to the Russian proposals before the war, the Minister noted, and the British Government had no right to ignore Russia, which had paid for its victories with the blood of its soldiers. Gorchakov expressed his surprise over British concerns regarding the commercial routes, citing earlier statements by the members of the British Cabinet who had said the Russian conquest of Erzurum and Trabzon would not harm British interests. The Russian Foreign Minister expressed his readiness to discuss all issues of disagreement during a European congress.[82]

By raising anti-Russian hysteria in the Parliament and threatening war with Russia, the British Government prepared the ground for obtaining territorial concessions for Britain. Cyprus was singled out as appropriate compensation since it could be turned into a springboard for further penetration in the Middle East. By taking charge of the reforms in the Ottoman Empire, the British Government could also advance its own agenda. In April, Ambassador Layard wrote to Salisbury that reforms in and the strengthening of Turkey were in Britain's interest, notwithstanding some "emotional theories" by its ethnic minorities. In his opinion, a better-run and better-governed Turkey would be capable of fielding a strong Army and thwarting the Russian advance across the Armenian Plateau.[83]

In mid-April, Disraeli and Salisbury decided to enter into separate negotiations with the Russians in advance of the Berlin Congress, in order to reach a common ground. The British Government made the following points: (1) the territory of an independent Bulgaria should not extend south of the Balkan mountain chain, (2) if Russia were to keep its Asiatic conquest, Britain must receive equivalent compensation to safeguard its interests in Asia.[84] In his April 21 letter to the Queen, Salisbury wrote that Britain would be content with the Russian conquest of Kars if Russia recognized the northern borders of the Ottoman Empire in the Balkans. However, if Russia also gained Batum, the British Government had to receive an island or a post in the vicinity of Asia Minor to neutralize the Russian presence in Armenia.[85]

In late April, Salisbury informed Shuvalov of the British proposals and presented him with a draft of a Russian-British memorandum. After a preliminary discussion, the Russian Ambassador set off for St. Petersburg to obtain the Government's approval of the project. Meanwhile, Ambassador Layard in Constantinople went to work to persuade the Sultan's government to implement some long-needed reforms in Armenia. On May 11, he reported to Salisbury that, under the circumstances, it was important for the Porte to do anything possible to show the Armenians that it would ensure a fair government for them in the future to prevent Russia from interfering on their behalf or raising the Armenian Question,* which would only cause more problems for Turkey. The Ambassador informed Salisbury that, in his meeting with the Grand Vizier, he urged the latter to take urgent measures to defend the Armenian population in Erzurum and Diyarbakir from the Kurds. According to Layard, the Grand Vizier promised to dispatch one of his aides, Ali Shevfik Pasha, to the province with instructions to order the military commanders to suppress the Kurdish attacks and use force to put down any disorders. The Ambassador also suggested appointing a Consul and a Vice Consul in Diyarbakir to monitor the actions of the Sultan's government there.[86]

Finding itself in an unfavorable international position, and under pressure from Great Britain and Austria-Hungary, the Czarist Government decided to make concessions and negotiate with the British Government. On May 23, Ambassador Shuvalov returned to London to discuss the British proposals with Salisbury, eventually signing a secret Russian-British Protocol on Amendment of the Terms of San-Stefano Treaty. The Protocol played down the Russian military gains and turned the terms of the Russian-Turkish peace treaty into a subject of international mediation. The Russian Government had to agree not to create a Greater Bulgaria and to withdraw from some districts in Western Armenia. Article 7 of the Protocol stipulated that the provisions of the San-Stefano Treaty on the reforms in Western Armenia were to be given on behalf of England, in addition to Russia. Under Article 10, the Alashkert Valley and the fortress city of Bayazid were returned to Turkey in view of their importance as a transit point for commerce with Persia and "because of their significance for Turkey." Russia guaranteed that it would not aggrandize its

---

* This marks the first time this term is used in the British Foreign Office papers.

territory at the expense of Asiatic Turkey.[87] In effect, the Powers gathered in Berlin to endorse the terms of the Russian-English Protocol.

In his letter to Ambassador Layard following the signing of the Protocol, Salisbury noted that the British Government could not remain indifferent to the problems in Asiatic Turkey. According to the Secretary, this region was populated by people of various creeds, who had no desire for autonomy or self-government and who needed only a fair administration by the Sultan; annexation of Kars, Batum, and Ardahan by Russia would allow it to destabilize the country and cause the final collapse of the Ottoman Empire. Salisbury said that Britain would not take military measures to force Russia to return the territories to Turkey because it would be a costly endeavor. To stabilize Turkish rule over Asia Minor, the Foreign Secretary noted, it was necessary to conclude a pact with Russia threatening military action in case of further annexations in Asiatic Turkey. The Ambassador was instructed to tell the Sultan's officials that Britain would not undertake the defense of Asiatic Turkey unless it received solid guarantees of reforms for the Christian and other subjects of the Empire. It was necessary to control the Porte and to station British troops near Asia Minor and Syria, which made Cyprus indispensable for Britain, the Foreign Secretary argued. He said that the Sultan's government must be assured that the British domination of Cyprus would guarantee the territorial integrity of the Ottoman Empire, and forwarded a draft of the British-Turkish agreement on Cyprus for discussion with the Turkish officials.[88]

Upon receiving instructions, Layard went to work to persuade the Sultan and his government, assuring Salisbury in a telegram sent the following day that he was ready to assume responsibility for signing the agreement. The Ambassador suggested taking advantage of the chaotic situation in the country and of Abdul Hamid's depressive state to wring out Turkish acquiescence to the British terms. Following confidential negotiations between the Sultan and Layard, on June 4 the Sultan told his Grand Vizier, Safvet Pasha, to sign the agreement. When the Grand Vizier raised some objections, the Ambassador told him that the British Government was under no obligation to adjust the terms of the San-Stefano Treaty during the Berlin Congress and would simply occupy Cyprus by its naval forces, without permission of the Porte. The Grand Vizier acquiesced and was compelled to sign the Cyprus Convention, or a "Defense Alliance between England and Turkey."[89]

According to Article 1 of the agreement, the British Government would come to the aid of the Sultan "if Russia were to occupy Batum, Ardahan, Kars or any of the Sultan's possessions in Asiatic Turkey that were kept under the Sultan's domination according to the final peace treaty." In return, Turkey would undertake such reforms as agreed upon between the two Governments in order to provide better governance and security for the Christians and other subjects of the Empire. Also, the Sultan had to agree to the British administration of Cyprus.[90]

Thus, the British Government concluded agreements with both Russia and Turkey. Confident that Russia was not going to resume hostilities, Britain, nevertheless, managed to take advantage of the Ottoman Empire's situation to take control of Cyprus that would guarantee its domination in the Eastern Mediterranean while remaining its staunch ally and guarantor of its Asiatic domains. There were no references to Western Armenia in the document, and the reforms were guaranteed to the Christians and other subjects of the Empire in general. British diplomacy supplanted the self-determination demands of the oppressed peoples with the general overhaul of the Ottoman Empire, which would delay their liberation. Layard and the Turkish Constitutionalists pressured the Armenian leaders in Constantinople to drop their demands for secession or autonomy within the Empire.

When it became known that the terms of the San Stefano Treaty would be subject to re-negotiating at the Berlin Congress, the Armenian community leaders appealed to the Powers, sending a delegation to the European capitals. The Armenian delegation was headed by Mkrtich Archbishop Khrimian, who was to present a proposal on establishment of an administrative autonomy in the Armenian-populated regions, under the control of the Powers. Patriarch Nerses was convinced that it was necessary to secure the goodwill of both Russia and Great Britain to implement the national autonomy with the help of Europe. The Armenian national community leadership, however, miscalculated since British diplomacy worked on the Armenian issues only in the context of thwarting Russian designs on Asia Minor. Ambassador Layard's vision of a Western Armenia under Ottoman control prevailed.[91]

The Armenian delegation and Archbishop Khrimian left for Rome and Paris, where it met with the Foreign Ministers of Italy and France, and arrived in London. The small but politically active Armenian community in London secured appointments with the Archbishop of Canterbury, William Gladstone, the leader of the opposition, Lord Salisbury, as well as with the Duke of Edinburgh, several MP's, and reporters. The Prime Minister declined to meet with the Armenian delegates, sending his regrets and suggesting a meeting with the Foreign Secretary instead. Meeting with Salisbury on May 10, Archbishop Khrimian presented him with a message from Patriarch Nerses, dated March 1, who appealed for British help to the Armenian Christians in establishing autonomy for the Armenian-populated regions. Salisbury accepted the appeal, and said that the future of the Armenian Question would be determined during the Congress, and assured the delegation that the Congress would secure an administration providing prosperity, freedom, and peace to the Armenians.[92]

In early June, following the visit of the Armenian delegation and as a result of the Armenian community's activities, the Armenian Question was for the first time discussed in the House of Commons. MPs Carnarvon and Shaftsbury presented the desperate condition of the Armenian Christians in the Ottoman Empire, noting that the San Stefano Treaty had not guaranteed equal rights for all the Christian minorities, and demanded that the Cabinet make an effort at the Berlin Congress to defend the interests of the Armenians and promote the reforms in Western Armenia. In response to the inquiries from the Lords, Salisbury said it was impossible to implement special reforms for the Armenians since they were dispersed and lived next to Muslims who would react negatively to such reforms. The Foreign Secretary stated that the Armenian Question was more difficult to address than the issue of Balkan Slavs, and that the solution was a general reform of the Ottoman Empire.[93]

The Congress of Berlin opened on June 13, with the representatives of Britain, Austria-Hungary, Germany, Russia, France and Italy, under the chairmanship of German Chancellor Bismarck. For over a month, the representatives of the Powers worked to ascertain that the terms of the San Stefano Treaty corresponded to the provisions of the Treaty of Paris and the London Agreement of 1871. Delegations from Serbia, Romania, Greece, Montenegro, Persia, and the Armenian National Assembly of Constantinople were also present, but were not allowed to join the Congress, and had to content themselves with bilateral talks. The Romanian and Greek delegations were later granted a right to speak at some of the sessions.

The Queen was represented by Prime Minister Disraeli, Salisbury, and the British Ambassador in Berlin, Odo Russell.[94] On June 8, Salisbury told Russell in a telegram that the Russian annexation of parts of Asiatic Turkey, while clearly affecting British interests, would not be seriously opposed by other Powers. At the same time, the Foreign Secretary noted, it would not be difficult to press Russia for concessions as far as the commercial routes from Trabzon to Tabriz (Persia) were concerned. Salisbury conceded that Russia was unlikely to make concessions on Batum, Kars, and Ardahan, and it was equally unlikely that other Powers would support Britain on this issue. Nevertheless, he instructed the Ambassador to work with the representatives of other Powers to raise this issue, stressing that the formal annexation of the territories seized during the war might abort the attempts to stabilize the Empire and weaken the Sultan's government.[95]

In his opening remarks at the Congress, Disraeli stated that the British Government came to Berlin to settle the Sultan's affairs and to give him an opportunity to display his authority in the Ottoman Empire. The head of the Russian delegation, Foreign Minister Gorchakov, said in his opening statement that Russia's main objective had been to secure self-government for the Christian peoples of the Ottoman Empire[96].

From June 13 to July 4, the delegates discussed the provisions of the San Stefano Treaty on the Balkans and the Straits. Under British and Austro-Hungarian pressure, Bulgaria was divided into two parts: the northern part, located to the north of the Balkan mountains, became an autonomous state, while the southern part – Eastern Rumelia – remained under Ottoman suzerainty. Russia successfully defended the independence of Serbia, Montenegro, and Romania, while Bosnia and Herzegovina were placed under the mandate of the Austrian Emperor.[97] The British Government supported Austria-Hungary on this issue.

The Powers decided to offer their good offices and mediation if Greece and Turkey failed to settle their boundary disputes in bilateral talks.[98] The British position on the Balkan and, in particular, on the Greek-Turkish dispute caused indignation in the Sultan's government. Layard wrote to Disraeli and Salisbury that the Ottoman Government officials had viewed the British diplomatic moves at the Congress with deep distrust, suspecting the English of complicity in some conspiracy to divide the Ottoman Empire. Layard reported that the Porte had decided to postpone the transfer of sovereignty over Cyprus to Great Britain until after the conclusion of the Congress, on the grounds that it would cause Russia to refuse to leave the Sultan's Asiatic possessions while other Powers might present the Sultan with territorial demands of their own.[99]

Disraeli and Salisbury were enraged by the Ottoman Government's posturing. Two days prior to the discussion of the Asiatic provinces of Turkey, Salisbury wrote to Layard that the British Government viewed the Porte's position as "a flagrant betrayal and deep ingratitude" for the British efforts to save the Empire. Britain would not undertake any actions on Turkey unless the Sultan signed the proclamation on Cyprus, Salisbury wrote, instructing the Ambassador to inform the Sultan of this position and to spare no effort to secure the Sultan's signature on the proclamation.[100]

It was essential to the British delegation that the existence of the Anglo-Turkish Convention not be revealed until the status of Batum and the Armenian provinces was discussed and decided upon. This would have allowed the British Government to secure greater concessions from Russia and to present itself as the chief defender of the territorial integrity of the Ottoman Empire.

On July 4, during the twelfth plenary session, Article 16 of the San Stefano Treaty that addressed the Armenian Question was discussed by the Congress. Agreeing with the language of the Article on granting "reforms and improvements to the Armenians," Salisbury demanded that the terms providing for the presence of Russian troops to enforce the aforementioned reforms be dropped, threatening, otherwise, to introduce a new, amended article. In response, Ambassador Shuvalov said that he was not ready to discuss the article but expressed his concern that, should the Russian forces withdraw from those provinces at that time, serious disturbances could arise. He proposed to postpone the discussion in order to address the issue comprehensively at some other point.[101]

The British press unexpectedly published the secret Anglo-Russian protocol in early July. The press and the opposition accused the Government of double-dealing and caving in to the Russian demands. During a meeting of the Russian and British delegations at the Congress, the British delegates demanded that Russia return not only the Alashkert Valley, Bayazid, and

Erzurum, as provided in the Protocol, but also Kars, Ardahan, and Batum. Salisbury claimed that the loss of these provinces would negatively affect the Sultan's authority in Asia, and said he was ready to tender his resignation since he had signed the protocol in the first place. Such resignation, he explained, would invalidate the Protocol and Russia would then have to withdraw from Batum as well. On July 6, during the discussion of Article 19 of the San Stefano Treaty, the British delegation declared that England would be forced to defend its interests and influence by all means it saw fit in the event of the Russian annexation of Kars and Ardahan.[102]

Salisbury's posturing and statements, in effect, prepared the ground for reconciling the European Powers with the British acquisition of Cyprus. The Russian delegates viewed the British Foreign Secretary's position as blackmail, and Shuvalov appealed to Bismarck for mediation. After studying the Anglo-Russian protocol, Bismarck advised Disraeli to diffuse the tensions. During the fourteenth plenary session, Shuvalov declared that the Russian Government had decided to withdraw from Bayazid and Alashkert Valley, which had been acquired by Russia under the terms of the San Stefano Treaty, and to declare Batum a free port. In response, Disraeli said that he was completely satisfied with the proposal, although his government's preference had been to keep Batum under the Sultan's sovereignty.[103]

The plenary session continued, turning to Article 16, addressing the Armenian Question. Salisbury distributed to the delegates a British version of the article, which substituted the provision for the Russian troops enforcing the reforms with a general European supervision of the process. He announced that the interests of the Armenians should be protected and the aim of the British proposal was to give them hopes of imminent improvements and future progress. In his argument with Shuvalov, Salisbury stressed the necessity of joint European control of the reforms. France supported the Russian version, but the British draft eventually prevailed.

The head of the Ottoman delegation, Karatheodori Pasha, agreed that the ungovernable tribes had carried out atrocities during the war but added that the Porte had taken practical measures to stop them. He asked for the Powers' confidence in the measures undertaken by the Porte, and offered the following amendment to the British draft: "The Sublime Porte shall report to the six Powers on its actions toward that objective." Shuvalov suggested that the

Article remain intact. Bismarck expressed reservations about the effectiveness of the article, and suggested that the Turkish and British delegates work on a new draft and present it during the next session.[104]

The final draft of the Article addressing the Armenian Question was presented on behalf of the Ottoman and British delegations by Salisbury on July 8, during the fifteenth plenary session.[105] It ran as follows: "The Sublime Porte undertakes to carry out, without further delay, the improvements and reforms demanded by local requirements in the provinces inhabited by the Armenians, and to guarantee their security against the Circassians and Kurds. It will periodically make known the steps taken to this effect to the Powers, who will superintend their application."[106]

Thus, British diplomacy succeeded in replacing Article 16 of the San Stefano Treaty with Article 61 of the Berlin Treaty, and removing the Russian monopoly over Western Armenian affairs. In the period between the San Stefano Treaty and the Congress of Berlin, British diplomacy managed to weaken the Russian military gains of the 1877-78 Russo-Turkish War, maintain its influence in the Ottoman Empire, and even secured acquisition of Cyprus, the important isle in the Eastern Mediterranean. While, under the provisions of Article 16 of San Stefano Treaty, the withdrawal of the Russian troops was an incentive to carry out the reforms in Western Armenia, it was not clear how the Powers would "superintend the application of the reforms" under the terms of Article 61. The San Stefano Treaty referred to Armenia as a place name, while the Treaty of Berlin mentions "provinces inhabited by the Armenians." The issue was not merely semantic, since British diplomacy avoided using the geographical place name "Armenia" to preclude even the possibility of establishing autonomy there in the future. The Armenian Question became an issue of international relations at San Stefano and Berlin, yet it also continued to be viewed as an internal issue of the Ottoman Empire.

Having benefited from his agreement with the British Government, and taken advantage of the indifference by the European Powers toward the fate of the Christian minorities residing in mainland Asia Minor, including the Armenians, and abusing the unclear and ineffective language of Article 61 of the Berlin Treaty, Sultan Abdul Hamid set out to redraw his administrative units and intensified the campaign to annihilate the Armenian population so that the term "provinces inhabited by the Armenians" would cease to exist.

Notes

[1] *Vneshneekonomicheskie svyazi*, pp. 78–90.

[2] Ibid., pp. 94–96.

[3] Disraeli, Benjamin, First Earl of Beaconsfield, (1804–1881), British statesman and leader of the Conservative party (1848–81). He was a member of the House of Commons from 1837 to 1876, and of the House of Lords from 1876 until his death. He served as Chancellor of the Exchequer (1852, 1858–59, 1866–68) and Prime Minister (1868, 1874–80).

[4] Three Emperors' League, an informal alliance concluded in 1873 between Austria-Hungary, Germany, and Russia, with secret provisions for mutual military assistance. The Russian-British tensions in Central Asia motivated Russia to cooperate with Germany. With France as a permanent adversary, Germany was interested in improvement of Russian-German relations in order to avoid a two-front war in a potential war. In turn, Austria-Hungary was trying to both secure an alliance with Germany in case of a military conflict with Russia over the Balkans, and, simultaneously, attempted to find an understanding with Russia for delimitation of spheres of influence in that region. Prolongation treaties to extend the League were signed in 1881 and 1884 but a flare-up of tensions between the Powers ended the alliance in 1885.

[5] Bismarck, Prince Otto Eduard Leopold von, (1815–1898), German statesman and diplomat. He served as Prussia's representative to the German Diet in Frankfurt (1851–59), Prussian Ambassador to Russia (1859–62) and France (1862), becoming Prussia's Premier (1862–67), Chancellor of the North German Confederation (1867–71), and Reich Chancellor (1871–90).

[6] Andrassy, Count Gyula (Julius) Sr., (1823–1890), Hungarian statesman and diplomat. An active participant of the 1848–49 Hungarian Revolution, he returned to Hungary in 1866 and helped forge the compromise forming the dual Monarchy of Austria-Hungary in 1867. He served as Prime Minister of Hungary (1867–71), and Foreign Minister of Austria-Hungary (1871–79).

[7] Eastern Papers. Part LXVII (1875–1876). London, 1883, pp. 74–75.

[8] Turkey No. 2 (1876). Correspondence respecting Affairs in Bosnia and Herzegovina (1875–1876). London, 1876, p. 95.

[9] Ibid., p. 106.

[10] Eastern Papers. Part LXVII, pp. 92–96.

[11] Gorchakov, Alexander Mikhailovich, Prince (1798–1883), Russian diplomat and statesman. He was in Foreign Service since 1824 on diplomatic assignments to Great Britain, Italy, Prussia, Austria, German Bund, and served as Foreign Minister from 1856 to 1882.

[12] R. W. Seton-Watson, *Disraeli, Gladstone and the Eastern Question: A Study in Diplomacy and Party Politics* (New York, 1962), p. 33.

[13] Queen Victoria, *Letters*, vol. 2 (London, 1926), p. 453.

[14] Seton-Watson, *Disraeli, Gladstone and the Eastern Question*, p. 35.

[15] *Istoriya diplomatii*, vol. 2 (Moscow, 1963), p. 92.

[16] W. E. Gladstone, *Bulgarian Horrors and the Question of the East* (London, 1876), pp. 31–32.

[17] Seton-Watson, *Disraeli, Gladstone and the Eastern Question*, p. 63.

[18] Turkey No. 1 (1876–1877). Correspondence respecting the Conference in Constantinople and the Affairs in Turkey. London, 1877, p. 159.

[19] Shuvalov, Pyotr Andreevich, Count (1827–1889), Russian statesman and diplomat. He served as Chief of Gendarmerie and Imperial Chancellery's Third Department (secret police) (1866–74), and as Russian Ambassador to Britain (1874–79).

[20] O. B. Shparo, *Zakhvat Kipra Angliey* (Moscow, 1974), p. 57.

[21] Abdul Hamid II (1842–1918), Ottoman Turkish Sultan in 1876–1909. Presenting himself as proponent of reforms and constitutional order in his early reign, he promulgated the Constitution of 1876. However, he dismissed the parliament in 1878, instituting a cruel regime (*zulum*), and brutally suppressed the liberation movements by the Bulgarians, Macedonians, Arabs, and Armenians. He directed the Armenian Massacres of 1894–96, earning himself the epithet 'Red Sultan.' During the 1908 Young Turk revolution he was forced to restore the Constitution, and, after an unsuccessful coup attempt in 1909, was dethroned and exiled.

[22] W. F. Monypenny and G. Buckle, *The Life of Disraeli*, vol. 6, p. 52.

[23] Seton-Watson, *Disraeli, Gladstone and the Eastern Question*, p. 88.

[24] *Istoriya diplomatii*, vol. 2, pp. 99–104.

[25] Salisbury, Robert Arthur Talbot Gascoyne, Third Marquis of (1830–1903), British statesman and Conservative politician. He served as Secretary of State for India (1866–67, 1874–78), Foreign Secretary (1878–80). A member of the House of Lords, he assumed the leadership of the Conservative party in 1881 and served as

Prime Minister in 1885–86, 1886–92, 1895–1902, and, concurrently until 1900, as Foreign Secretary.

[26] Shparo, *Zakhvat Kipra Angliey*, p. 79.

[27] Ignatiev, Nikolai Pavlovich, Count, General (1832–1908), Russian diplomat and statesman. He served on diplomatic assignments to Great Britain and China (1856–61), as Director of Asia Department at the Foreign Ministry (1861–64), and then as Minister to, and later, Ambassador to the Ottoman Empire (1864–77). He became Interior Minister (1881–82), and a member of the State Council (1882–1908).

[28] Shparo, *Zakhvat Kipra Angliey*, pp. 84–89; Georgiev, et al., *Vostochnyy vopros*, pp. 210–13; *Istoriya diplomatii*, vol. 2 pp. 106–8.

[29] G. Cecil, *Life of Robert Marquis of Salisbury* (London, 1921), p. 132.

[30] Seton-Watson, *Disraeli, Gladstone and the Eastern Question*, p. 139.

[31] Eastern Papers. Part LXVIII (1876–1877). London, 1884, pp. 1094–96.

[32] Turkey No. 15 (1877). Further Correspondence respecting the Affairs of Turkey. London, 1877, pp. 23–24.

[33] Ibid., p. 22.

[34] Ibid., pp. 139–40.

[35] Shparo, *Zakhvat Kipra Angliey*, pp. 105–6.

[36] Turkey No 15 (1877), pp. 172–73.

[37] Ibid., pp. 194–95.

[38] Ibid., pp. 297–98.

[39] Ibid., p. 286.

[40] Ibid., p. 355.

[41] Turkey No. 16 (1877). Reports by Her Majesty's Diplomatic and Consular Agents in Turkey respecting the Condition of the Christian Subjects of the Porte. 1865–1875. London, 1877, pp. 142–45.

[42] Turkey No. 15 (1877), p. 3.

[43] Ibid., pp. 5–6.

[44] Ibid., p. 8.

[45] John Kirakossian, *Burzhuakan divanagitutiune yev Hayastane (19-rd dari 70-akan tt.)* (Bourgeois diplomacy and Armenia, 1870s), (Yerevan, 1978), pp. 54–55, 60–61.

[46] Turkey No. 15 (1877), p. 67.

[47] Ibid., p. 65.

[48] Ibid., p. 65–66.

[49] Ibid., pp. 146–47.

[50] Ibid., p. 147.

[51] Ibid., p. 306.

[52] Ibid., pp. 308–9.

[53] Ibid., p. 270.

[54] Sir Austen Henry Layard (1817–1894), a British diplomat and archeologist, who achieved fame by excavating the remains of Nineveh in 1849–51. He served in the House of Commons (1860–69), and later as Ambassador to Spain (1869–77) and Ottoman Empire (1877–80). An experienced diplomat, Layard enjoyed unlimited confidence of Prime Minister Disraeli. He was tasked with strengthening the British influence with the Sultan's government, since Layard was a colleague and disciple of former Ambassador Canning, a self-described 'great friend of the Turks.'

[55] Turkey No. 1 (1878). Further Correspondence respecting the Affairs of Turkey. London, 1878, pp. 72, 150.

[56] Ibid., pp. 43, 64.

[57] Ibid., p. 101.

[58] Ibid., p. 85.

[59] Ibid., p. 287.

[60] Ibid., p. 137–38.

[61] Ibid., p. 399.

[62] FO 424/62, No 245/1, pp. 142–45.

[63] Turkey No. 1 (1878), pp. 533–34.

[64] Robert F. Zeidner, "Britain and the Launching of the Armenian Question," *International Journal of Middle East Studies* 1976, no. 7, p. 468.

[65] Ibid., pp. 468–69.

[66] Eastern Papers. Part LXVIII (1876–1877), pp. 840–41.

[67] Ibid., pp. 857–63.

[68] Shparo, *Zakhvat Kipra Angliey*, p. 118.

[69] Russia No. 2 (1877). Correspondence respecting the War between Russia and Turkey. London, 1877, pp. 1–2.

[70] Ibid., pp. 3–4.

[71] Shparo, *Zakhvat Kipra Angliey*, pp. 130–31.

[72] Seton-Watson, *Disraeli, Gladstone and the Eastern Question*, p. 218.

[73] Ibid., pp. 218–19.

[74] FO 424/63/124, pp. 86–89.

[75] John Kirakossian, "San-Stefanoyi hashtutian paymanagire yev angliakan divanagitutiune" (The San Stefano peace treaty and English diplomacy), *Banber Yerevani Hamalsarani* 1978, no. 1., p. 88.

[76] J. S. Kirakosyan, ed., *Hayastane mijazgayin divanagitutian yev sovetakan artakin kaghakakanutian pastatghterum (1828–1923)* (Armenia in the documents of international diplomacy and Soviet foreign policy, 1828–1923) (Yerevan, 1972), p. 92.

[77] FO 424/68/639, pp. 346–48.

[78] FO 424/68/644, p. 354.

[79] FO 424/69/107, pp. 54–55.

[80] H. W. V. Temperley and L. M. Penson, *Foundations of British Foreign Policy from Pitt (1792) to Salisbury (1902)* (Cambridge, 1938), pp. 369–70.

[81] Christopher J. Walker, *Armenia: The Survival of a Nation* (New York, 1980), p. 112. According to 1876 data, the amount of British commerce transiting on Trabzon-Bayazid road was a significant amount. The British imports from Persia comprised £104,081 while the British exports to Persia were £754,764. Charles Williams, *The Armenian Campaign: A Diary of the Campaign of 1878 in Armenia and Koordistan* (London, 1878), p. 361.

[82] Turkey No. 27 (1878). Further Correspondence respecting the preliminary Treaty of Peace between Russia and Turkey signed at San-Stefano. London, 1878, pp. 8–9.

[83] Kirakossian, *Bourgeois Diplomacy and Armenia (1870s)*, p. 176.

[84] Cecil, *Life of Robert Marquis of Salisbury* p. 242.

[85] Seton-Watson, *Disraeli, Gladstone and the Eastern Question*, p. 410.

[86] FO 424/70/587, pp. 360–61.

[87] *Armenia in International Diplomacy and Soviet Foreign Policy Documents (1828–1923)*, p. 100.

[88] Turkey No. 36 (1878). Correspondence respecting the Convention between Great Britain and Turkey of June 4, 1878. London, 1878, pp. 1–2.

[89] Shparo, *Zakhvat Kipra Angliey*, pp. 194–95.

[90] *Armenia in International Diplomacy and Soviet Foreign Policy Documents (1828–1923)*, p. 104.

[91] Kirakossian, John, *Bourgeois Diplomacy and Armenia (1870s)*, pp. 220–21.

[92] Sarkissian, A. O., *History of the Armenian Question to 1885* (Urbana, 1938), pp. 78–79; Kirakossian, John, *Bourgeois Diplomacy and Armenia (1870s)*, pp. 98–104.

[93] Hansard`s Parliamentary Debates, 1878. Vol. 240, pp. 1242–46.

[94] Turkey No. 39 (1878). Correspondence relating to the Congress of Berlin with the Protocol of the Congress. London, 1878, p. 1.

[95] Ibid., pp. 2–3.

[96] Ibid., p. 13.

[97] Kirakosyan, ed., *Hayastane mijazgayin divanagitutian*, pp. 106–26.

[98] Ibid., p. 116.

[99] Dwight E. Lee, *Great Britain and the Cyprus Convention Policy of 1878* (Cambridge, 1934), pp. 97–98.

[100] Ibid., p. 98.

[101] Turkey No. 39 (1878), p. 186.

[102] Ibid., p. 207.

[103] Ibid., pp. 208–9.

[104] Ibid., p. 210.

[105] Ibid., p. 225.

[106] Kirakosyan, ed., *Hayastane mijazgayin divanagitutian*, p. 128.

Chapter 3. The Issue of the Armenian Reforms and British Government Policies, 1878–92

1. The Policy of the Conservative Government on the Armenian Question, 1878–80

The decisions of the Berlin Congress created fundamental changes in the political life of the European nations, and were crucial in securing the liberation of the Balkan peoples from Ottoman rule. Serbia, Montenegro, and Romania achieved independence, Bulgaria and Eastern Rumelia were granted autonomy; Russia received Bessarabia, Kars, Ardahan, and Batum, while Austria-Hungary established control over Bosnia and Herzegovina. These territorial changes had not, however, addressed the core problems of the Eastern Question and did not decrease the tensions in international relations. The crisis and the Berlin Congress further aggravated the existing disagreements between the Powers. Moreover, the creation of the German-Austrian alliance on October 7, 1879, eventually resulted in closer ties between France and the Russian Empire. The two distinct military alliances that were formed as a result of these developments would later clash in World War I.

Immediately after the conclusion of the Berlin Congress, Russian-British negotiations commenced on the simultaneous removal of the Russian troops from the vicinity of Constantinople and the British naval contingent in the Sea of Marmara. Nevertheless, the relations between the two Powers remained strained. The British Government took advantage of post-war Russia's financial and military weakness to improve its position in the Near East.

Enforcement of Article 61 of the Berlin Treaty that required the Sultan's government to implement reforms for the Armenian-populated provinces became a priority for the Disraeli Cabinet. British consuls were posted to several cities in Western Armenia, and their reports on the conditions of the Armenian population and the activities of the local administration became a constant source of pressure for the British Government in its dealings with the Sublime Porte, as well as an important tool for extracting more concessions from the Sultan. Most British Consuls and Vice Consuls had intelligence or engineering backgrounds, and were tasked with studying the local topography, geography, populations, and customs. The two main objectives of British diplomacy were to prevent the spread of Russian influence in the Near East, and to achieve a peaceful separation of Egypt from the Ottoman Empire, and it is in this context that the Armenian Question was addressed.

Only a day after the Congress was officially closed, Ambassador Layard reported to Salisbury that Russian agents continued to agitate the Armenian population of Asiatic Turkey against the Sultan's government. According to the Ambassador, a pro-Russian organization had been formed in the capital comprised of influential Armenians. A week before the letter, the Armenian Patriarch Nerses informed the Ambassador that he would not be able to lead the Patriarchate much longer if the Berlin Congress failed to address the Armenian grievances or if Britain did not assume a protectorate over the Armenians. The Patriarch had said that he would call on his flock to ignore the Russian agitation and to remain loyal to the Sultan. According to Layard, it was due to the current Patriarch's efforts that the Armenians did not rebel against the Sultan, but he noted the widespread feelings among the Armenian community that the Slav people were on the verge of achieving independence or autonomy only because they had raised arms in support of the Russian troops. During his conversation with the Patriarch, the British Ambassador disclosed to him the clauses of the Cyprus Convention, persuading him that the Armenian reforms were guaranteed under the Convention.[1]

The Ambassador reported to Foreign Secretary Salisbury that he had reliable information about the Russian plans to create a pro-Russian party comprised of Armenians,[2] and that there were plans to restore the newly captured ancient city of Ani and turn it into a capital of Armenia. According to the report, the Tsarist government planned to populate the city of Ani with 10,000 Armenians; Russian agents were said to be persuading the Armenian population in Turkey to resettle for that purpose.[3]

On August 8, Lord Salisbury instructed the Ambassador in Constantinople to implore the Sultan's government to implement reforms in the Armenian-populated regions of Asiatic Turkey, as provided for in Article 61 and the

Cyprus Convention. The Foreign Secretary wrote that timely implementation was essential for the success of the reforms, since the Christian population was spread unevenly among several provinces where the Muslims comprised the majority of the population. He also suggested that the reforms might have negative repercussions. Salisbury proposed to establish an effective gendarmerie in the Asiatic provinces, led by the European officers, and to establish regional central courts in key cities in Asia, such as Smyrna, Erzurum, Diyarbakir, Aleppo, Damascus, and Baghdad, with appellate jurisdiction over local courts. A European jurist would be assigned to each regional central court, with veto rights over every decision. Salisbury cited the precedence of India in arguing for the success of such a system. Salisbury further proposed to appoint European tax assessors in every vilayet (province) to collect government revenue and abolish the tithes. Salisbury argued that the governors, tax assessors, and judges must be appointed for a specific term only.[4]

On August 21, Layard informed the Foreign Office that he had sent a note to the Porte urging the implementation of the reforms and discussed it with Grand Vizier Safvet Pasha, who promised to present the proposals to the Sultan and the Cabinet for immediate consideration.

Safvet Pasha told the Ambassador that the proposal to establish a gendarmerie under leadership of European officers would definitely be rejected. The Grand Vizier also pointed out that courts already existed in those cities, and thus, it was only necessary to find knowledgeable and qualified jurists to appoint to those courts. He said that any European appointee must be able to speak Turkish, otherwise the people might be enraged by the appointments of foreigners and view it as meddling in Turkish affairs. Safvet Pasha suggested that the abolition of the tithes would not be acceptable to the population, who found it easier to pay the tax in kind rather than in monetary form. He had said that there had been no objections to term limits for officials although the main challenge was to find qualified candidates. Ambassador Layard added that in his opinion the objections came essentially from the Cabinet, which was hostile to the idea of the reforms altogether and viewed it as a means for establishing control over the Empire by the European Powers. Ambassador Layard, nevertheless, described Safvet Pasha as a progressive, liberal-minded person.[5]

Ambassador Layard presented the British proposals to Sultan Abdul

Hamid personally a few days later. The latter asked to convey his gratitude to the British Government for its interest in his country. The Sultan told the Ambassador that he planned to establish a special law school to provide skilled specialists for the implementation of the reforms. The Sultan also requested a loan from Britain, and thanked the Prime Minister and the Foreign Secretary for making favorable references to him in their public statements. The Sultan concluded by saying that Britain was a real ally of Turkey.[6]

On September 14, Layard reported to Salisbury that, according to a message from British Vice Consul Biliotti, the Armenian population of Erzurum province was deeply concerned and verging on panic because of rumors of impending massacres once the Russian troops would be withdrawn.[7] Salisbury had also received a report from Consul Layalle in Tiflis informing him that several thousand Armenians had crossed the border from Alashkert and Karakilisa regions and resettled near Yerevan.[8] The Ambassador immediately requested a meeting with the Sultan and cautioned him about the threat of massacres of the Christians following the withdrawal of the Russian troops. The Ambassador informed the Sultan that the panic-stricken Armenians were preparing to leave with the Russians. Layard urged the Sultan to take immediate steps to protect the Armenians and to appoint an Armenian governor. Abdul Hamid promised the British Ambassador to address the situation and, in his presence, issued an appropriate order to Safvet Pasha. The Sultan, however, dismissed the demand to appoint an ethnic Armenian as governor, pointing out that the current governor was an ethnic Kurd who was well respected by the Kurdish community.[9]

Two days later, Layard reported to Salisbury that the expected massacres of the Armenians had, in fact, been exaggerated and spread by Russian agents. He, nevertheless, suggested that the time was ripe to pressure the Sultan's government to implement reforms before public opinion in Europe turned against the Ottoman government. Layard was convinced that in the face of negative public opinion in the European nations, the British Government would be forced to withdraw its support from the Porte, and had told so to Safvet Pasha, who, in turn, assured him that the Porte was concerned about possible developments and would do its best to prevent any problems. Layard suggested that Salisbury sent Consul Zohrab to Armenia, noting that the latter had always been good at finding common ground with the local authorities.[10]

On September 19, Layard reported to the Foreign Office that after their last meeting, the Sultan had ordered Governor Ismail Hakki Pasha to take measures to ensure the safety of the Armenian population. The governor gave assurances that the rumors of imminent massacres were groundless, and that he was personally responsible for the safety of the Armenians. The Ambassador expressed the opinion that Russia was trying to undermine Europe's role in the Armenian Question, incite the Armenians against the Turkish authorities, and generate an atmosphere of fear.[11]

On the same day, Ambassador Layard met with Patriarch Nerses and briefed him on the measures undertaken by the Sultan's government. The Patriarch was dismissive of the Sultan's assurances and noted that appointment of an ethnic Armenian governor was the only viable solution. The British Ambassador replied that the time was not yet ripe for such an appointment, and stressed the need for restoring law and order, collecting weapons from and establishing control over the Kurdish tribes.[12]

On September 25, Salisbury was informed by the Russian Embassy in London that the Russian Government was taking steps to stem the immigration of the Armenian population from the Ottoman Empire into Eastern Armenia. In particular, General Lazarev published an article in the magazine, *Saint Petersburg*, urging the people of Western Armenia not to abandon their native land and assuring them that Russia and other European signatories of the Berlin Treaty would do their utmost to protect the Armenians.[13]

Soon after the Berlin Treaty was signed it became obvious that not only would the Powers be unable to enforce the provisions of Article 61 but also that they could not ensure the safety of the Armenian population or stem its emigration. Biliotti reported to Salisbury that on September 15, a 65-man strong Muslim band ransacked Khoterjur village, with 150 out of 800 houses and the local church burned down and part of the Armenian population massacred.[14] Biliotti met with the Governor of Trebizond, Yusuf Pasha to demand swift retribution against the perpetrators.[15] Biliotti always forwarded to the Foreign Office the petitions from the Armenian population to the Consulate.[16]

On October 12, Layard informed Salisbury that he had discussed the massacre of the Armenian population of Khoterjur with Safvet Pasha, who had thanked the Ambassador for alerting him to the situation and had asked that

Biliotti continue sending complete reports on the developments so that he could order the local authorities to arrest the perpetrators and bring them to justice.[17]

On October 11, Consul Henderson reported to Layard from Aleppo that more than 70 Armenians had been murdered there while the local government took no action to arrest or otherwise punish the murderers.[18] In his next report, Henderson informed the Embassy that Aleppo Governor Kiamil Pasha had arrested 19 Armenian women and children during his visit to the Zeytoun region and taken them back with him, causing an outcry from the Armenian and Arab communities.[19]

Salisbury apparently chose to ignore or discount the alarming reports arriving from the Ottoman Empire when he informed British Ambassador in Russia Loftus on October 16 that the British officers dispatched to monitor rumors of the massacres of the Christian population in the wake of the Russian troops' withdrawal had reported that the local authorities took "effective" measures against such developments, and that the country was peaceful. The Foreign Secretary instructed the Ambassador to demand that the Russians begin the withdrawal of the troops immediately since there were no grounds for them to stay.[20]

In October, Captain Henry Trotter was posted to Erzurum as the new Consul and would gradually begin to be referred to as the Consul in Kurdistan. Trotter came from Army Intelligence, having served in the Colonial troops in Bombay and Bengal, and was well acquainted with Armenia and its customs. On October 22, Layard instructed him to report fully to the Embassy and the Foreign Office on local developments, the Russian adherence to the provisions of the Berlin Treaty, and the situation of the Armenian population in the wake of the Russian Army withdrawal. Should there loom any danger to the safety of the Armenian population, Trotter was to inform the Embassy immediately and meet with the local authorities to urge them to defuse the situation and to punish the perpetrators of the disorder.[21]

In his reports of October 24 and 30 to the Foreign Office, Layard presented and analyzed Safvet Pasha's answer to the British proposals on the implementation of the reforms. His overall assessment was that the reaction of the Porte was not helpful although he conceded that, in the view of the internal political difficulties, there were positive signs as well. According to Layard, the majority in the Cabinet as well as influential elites throughout the country opposed what was perceived as foreign interference, and viewed the British proposals as encroachment on the powers of the Sultan and the country's sovereignty. These officials viewed the British proposals as the first step toward establishment of British control and a direct protectorate over Asiatic Turkey, with subsequent annexation.

In its official reply, the Porte agreed to establish a gendarmerie but specified that the Europeans could assist in its formation, but not as commanders. Conceding the need to reform the courts, the Sultan's government refused the idea of appointing European jurists as judges on the grounds that such jurists would not know the language, customs, and laws of the country. The Sultan's Government suggested that European marshals instead be appointed to monitor the activities of the courts. The Porte consented to the reform of the tax system but pointed out that the new system be tested in one or two regions first. Layard noted with satisfaction that the Porte agreed to term limits for all officials, and that the Sultan himself suggested five years for a regular term of appointment.[22]

On November 8, Vice Consul Biliotti reported from Erzurum to the Foreign Office that the local Armenian population had been inquiring as to the possibility of the appointment of an ethnic Armenian governor. The Vice Consul commented that such an appointment or establishment of Armenian autonomy would not be desirable since the Armenians comprised a minority in the larger Anatolia region, adding that such demands were caused by Russian agitation. He suggested that the reforms could be implemented under strong British pressure, preferably with British troops present there. He went on to note that an Armenia administered by British officers would be a magnet for Armenians from other regions, as well as from Russia and Persia, so that the Armenians would finally become a majority of the population.[23]

Upon arrival in Erzurum, Trotter reported to Salisbury, on November 13, that there had been positive changes since the previous year: the houses demolished during the hostilities had been restored and the commerce thrived due to the Armenian merchants. Nevertheless, Kurdish bands continued to terrorize the neighboring villages while the local administration was unwilling or unable to take measures against it. According to Trotter, some two to three thousand Armenian families were evacuated by Russian troops from the Alashkert Valley, and only 250 families returned. The Consul noted that ethnic Armenian officers in the Russian Army—General Lazarev stationed in Kars, Major Kamsarakan (who was Assistant Military Governor of Erzurum), Lieutenant Nikoghosov and Alaskhert Governor Arakelov—were cherished by the Armenian population.[24]

On December 2, Layard reported to Salisbury that, acting upon his information, Grand Vizier Safvet Pasha instructed the local governor to take measures to protect the Armenian population of the Kegh region. Osman Effendi was sent as a central government plenipotentiary to oversee the effort to rein in the Kurdish tribal leaders. However, an American missionary reported that Osman was bribed by the Kurdish leaders and took no action to alleviate the conditions of the Christians. The Ambassador also received a credible report of the detention of the Muslim elder, Suleyman Agha, a prominent advocate of rights for the Armenians, who was transferred to Erzinjan and died there. Layard presented these facts to Safvet Pasha, warning him that the Porte would be faced with a serious change in the position of the British Government and hostile public opinion if these developments continued.[25]

Per Ambassador Layard's instructions, the consuls continued to send reports on the condition of the Armenians in the provinces. On December 2, Henderson reported from Aintab that the local population was approximately 40,000, of whom 15,000 were Christian, including 5,000 Protestants. The Consul noted that the American missionaries had built a college, seminary, and a girl's school. There were seven active Protestant churches in the city—one Anglican and six Presbyterian. According to Henderson, the local Armenian population, which was mostly preoccupied in cotton, soap, wine, and tobacco sales, was thriving.[26] Trotter, on the other hand, reported from Diyarbakir on December 21 that the Armenian population there was under constant attack from the Kurdish bandits, and was not doing well. Trotter proposed that Vice Consuls be posted to Diyarbakir, Erzurum, Kharput, Van, Bitlis, and Mush.[27]

On December 21, Layard met with Sultan Abdul Hamid to discuss the British reform proposals, noting that the implementation of reforms was necessary to placate British public opinion. The Sultan agreed with the envoy and asked for a loan to facilitate the implementation of the reforms. The Ambassador stated that the British Government and public would be sympathetic to that request once they were convinced of the genuine interest on the part of the Porte to implement the reforms, since it would also serve the goal of restoring law and order in the country. Abdul Hamid gave Layard his word of honor that he would spare no effort in that direction.[28]

Yet, neither British diplomatic activities nor the promises of the Sultan and his government yielded significant changes. The condition of the Armenian population deteriorated further in 1879. On January 5, Trotter reported to Salisbury on his field trip to the neighboring villages. The Consul reported the prevailing state of lawlessness for the previous two years, and noted that there existed virtually no guarantees or protection for the Armenians or their property. He described the miserable conditions of two Armenian-populated villages, Timar (50 households) and Dher (400 households), ransacked by a Kurdish gang led by Hussein Bey.[29]

On January 6, Henderson reported to the British Ambassador from Aleppo that the condition of the Armenians in Zeytoun and Marash regions had degenerated and that more than 200 Armenians were arbitrarily detained in Marash, where 30% of the population was Armenian, and some 300 Armenian homes destroyed. Henderson noted that there had been no trace of Russian agitation,[30] yet Governor Kiamil Pasha told the visiting First Secretary of the British Embassy, Edward Mallet, that the Armenians had been punished for sedition and organizing rebellion against the Sultan.[31] Layard made three written demarches (on January 4, 20, and 22) to Foreign Minister Karatheodori Pasha, noting that it was difficult to find more appalling behavior than that exhibited by the Turkish government officials, and their subordinates in Zeytoun and Marash. The Ambassador demanded that urgent measures be taken to punish Kiamil Pasha and his subordinates.[32] In his instructions to Layard, on January 23 Salisbury thanked him for submitting a strongly worded demarche to the Porte and told him to continue to demand punishment for the officials persecuting the Christian population.[33]

On February 3, Layard informed Salisbury that the Porte decided to send two commissions to Eastern Asia Minor to study the conditions of the local population and investigate the attacks. The commissions would include Turkish and Armenian officials, and one of them would visit Erzurum and Van, and the other Diyarbakir and Aleppo. The Ambassador asked Grand Vizier Haireddin Pasha and Foreign Minister Karatheodori Pasha to include British consuls in the commissions but the request was denied so as not to allow representatives of certain other Powers to be included in the commissions as well. The Foreign Secretary informed Layard that Russia would raise the Armenian Question in the same manner it had raised the question of Bulgaria. Russian Ambassador Alexei Lobanov-Rostovski[34] had already made a demarche to the Porte on the implementation of Article 61.[35]

In their reports to the Embassy sent, respectively, on February 23 and February 22, Consul Henderson and the Vice Consul Henry Mardin in Marash found the situation in Zeytoun appalling. The compactly living Armenian population of Zeytoun, numbering 10,000, was surrounded by Muslim-populated villages, and lived in constant danger of robberies and murders, rendering their situation untenable. The Governor refused to send the kaymakam* there on the pretext that his life could be endangered. Henderson further reported that Governor Kiamil Pasha was preparing to send troops there, ostensibly to restore "the authority of the government." Henderson expressed his concern that he could not do anything to improve the lot of the Armenian prisoners, since the Governor had announced he would do everything to keep them in detention and had supposedly reached an understanding in this regard with the Grand Vizier and the Justice and Interior Ministers. The Governor accused the Armenian Patriarch in Constantinople of inciting the Armenian population of Zeytoun against the government.[36]

In early March, the Porte informed British Chargé Mallet that the government would remove the Governor of Aleppo if the commission could confirm the atrocities committed by him. Mallet appealed to the Grand Vizier with the request to release the innocent Armenians detained in Marash and Aleppo but was told that the detainees had been charged with having murdered Turkish officials, which was currently being investigated by the commission. During the discussion, Mallet proposed to separate the developments in Zeytoun from the issue of the reforms.[37] In his letters of March 18 and March 27 to Chargé Mallet, Patriarch Nerses requested assistance for the Armenians by enforcing the provisions of the Berlin Treaty, expressing his hope that the Christian Powers of Europe would assist the Christian population in the Ottoman Empire.[38] Mallet assured His Eminence that the British Government continued to adhere to its obligations under the Treaty of Berlin and the

---

* Governor of a territorial subunit, *caza.*

June 4 Convention, as well as to the obligations "any Christian government had before mankind."[39]

On March 19, Mallet informed Salisbury that the Porte had finally removed Kiamil Pasha as Governor of Aleppo and appointed the city's commandant, Omer Pasha, as acting governor.[40] According to Henderson, the Armenian population of the region was thankful to the British Government for its support.[41] In his reply, Salisbury instructed him to push for speedy investigation of the Zeytoun events.[42]

On April 3, Mallet informed Salisbury that the newly appointed Governor of Aleppo, Ghalib Pasha, accompanied by members of the commission investigating the Zeytoun events, Mahzar Pasha and Nourian Pasha, were en route to Aleppo on board a French postal ship. The British Embassy sent a British naval officer, Lieutenant Herbert Chermside to accompany the delegation.[43]

In April, the British Government appointed Lieutenant-Colonel Charles Wilson as Consul General in Anatolia. In his April 24 instructions to the newly appointed Consul General, Salisbury noted that the Cyprus Convention had provided a great opportunity to the Ottoman Empire to improve its internal administration and alleviate the conditions of the peoples in the Empire. The Foreign Secretary instructed Wilson to investigate the condition of all ethnic groups, assist the local Turkish authorities, keep the British government and Embassy informed of the progress being made in establishing law and order and the implementation of reforms in the Armenian-populated areas.[44]

On May 3, the British Embassy sent a note to the Porte expressing its satisfaction with the measures authorities had taken to restore order in the Zeytoun and Marash regions. The note stated that the removal of Kiamil Pasha, the appointment of Ghalib Pasha, and the impartial investigation by the commission had restored the confidence of the Christian population toward the authorities and had checked the spread of the conflict. The investigation revealed that the events had been caused by the ineffectiveness and corruption of Kiamil Pasha's administration.[45]

On May 6, Sultan Abdul Hamid invited Layard to a dinner and informed him that the draft program of reforms had been completed and would soon be presented to the Council of Ministers. The Ottoman sovereign suggested that a major difficulty was the opposition to the program from the Ministers.[46]

A week later the Porte established a special commission to investigate the conditions of the Armenian population in and around Erzurum province, which included Yusuf Pasha and Sarkis Effendi. The British Government instructed Trotter to accompany them, with the prior consent of the Sultan's government, as Layard informed him on May 12. The Ambassador authorized him to discuss the findings with other members of the commission, investigate the local conditions and listen to and record the grievances from the Christians. As Layard noted, the main objective of the commission would be to prepare a draft program of reforms, and Trotter was to use his influence to help prepare a comprehensive document reflecting the interests of all concerned parties and ethnic groups in the region. The Ambassador instructed the Consul to keep in mind the official British policy, which was to achieve a cohesion of all the strata in the Empire under the Sultan's rule and to secure just, fair, and equal conditions for all peoples.[47]

The official British position was also formulated in the May 21 letter Layard sent to Salisbury that stated the British Government would spare no effort to achieve better governance for the peoples inhabiting Asiatic Turkey.[48]

Before assuming his post of Consul General, Wilson presented a list of names as nominees for Consulship: Captain Stuart of the Hussars' 11th Regiment in Konya, Captain Harry Cooper of the 47th Regiment in Kayseri and Adana, Colonel Williers of the Grenadiers Guard in Kastamuni, and Lieutenant Chermside of the Royal Engineers in Bursa.[49]

On May 21, Layard received a letter from Patriarch Nerses asking for the British intercession to kick-start the implementation of the reforms. The Patriarch urged the British Government to establish an Armenian autonomy similar to the one created in Eastern Rumelia.[50]

On June 5, acting on Salisbury's instructions,[51] the British Embassy sent a note to the Porte protesting the inaction of the Commission investigating the events in Zeytoun. The Embassy pointed out that, despite preliminary positive impressions, the Commission returned to Aleppo without having taken any measures to address the situation, which only aggravated the fears of the Christian populations and further predisposed the Muslims against the Christians. The Commission had decided to station a garrison in Zeytoun, but the Embassy had protested this decision suggesting instead to take real steps to defuse the tensions.[52]

In a confidential message to Salisbury, Layard reported that according to credible information received from the British consuls and the Armenian Patriarch, the situation in the eastern provinces of Asiatic Turkey remained unchanged, and that general lawlessness, assaults on lives and property, and harassment of Christians continued unabated. Moreover, as Layard pointed out, the commissions created by the Porte only exacerbated the situation. The Ambassador was convinced that the Armenian Question had become a real issue in the Ottoman Empire, like the Bulgarian Question before it. He noted that the aim of agitation in Asia Minor was the establishment of an Armenian nation, unleashing a predictable sequence of consequences: negative reaction by the Muslims, the protests of Christians, and eventually, European intervention. The Ambassador noted that he had repeatedly urged the Turkish ministers to take steps to implement the provisions of the Berlin Treaty and the June 4 Convention relating to Armenia, as well as to protect the Christians and improve the government of Asiatic Turkey, and that the loss of some territories was a real possibility should the reforms stall.[53]

On June 20, Layard met with Patriarch Nerses and assured him of his readiness to do everything he could to defend the rights of the Armenians and other Christian subjects of the Empire and to secure better administration for them. The Ambassador warned the Patriarch that he would not play along with plans to destabilize the Empire or diminish the authority of the Sultan, and that such agitation could only damage the condition of the Armenian community. He urged the Patriarch to take only legal steps to address the concerns of the community. Forwarding his minutes to Salisbury, Layard added that there were some influential members of the community who had attempted to involve the Patriarch in their agitation campaign.[54]

In June and July the Armenian Question was a subject of debate in the House of Lords. During a debate on June 27, Lord Carnarvon criticized Disraeli's position on the Armenian Question, stating that the Porte had been deceiving the British Government, that Article 61 had not been implemented while the government commissions sent to the Armenian-populated regions failed to disclose the real situation, i.e., harassment and persecutions perpetrated by the local authorities and the Kurds. In the Government's reply, Salisbury said he shared Lord Carnarvon's concern for the Armenian people but he rejected his criticism of the Government. Salisbury pledged to continue pressuring the Sultan to grant reform measures to the Armenians.[55]

In his July 1, telegram to Salisbury, Layard reported another letter from Patriarch Nerses expressing regret that Trotter was designated Consul General in Kurdistan, not Armenia. The Ambassador noted that this was another indication of designs to establish an Armenian entity in Asiatic Turkey that, some people hoped, would achieve autonomy, and later, independence with European or Russian help. The Ambassador added that, in the light of the developments in its European territory, the Ottoman Government would resist any attempts to do so and would not even agree to designate any region or province by the name 'Armenia.' The Ambassador noted that the Porte would refuse to accept the diplomat's credentials should the British Government accept the Patriarch's proposal and designate him as the Consul General to Armenia. As the Ambassador put it, it would be tantamount to appointing a Consul to 'Judea.' The Ambassador concluded by saying that he had repeatedly urged the Porte to start implementing the reforms in the Asiatic domains of the Sultan and provide for protection, and fair and equal government for all the peoples in the region, and warned that otherwise the Armenian and other ethnic questions would diminish the Sultan's authority and reduce his territories.[56]

On July 7, Layard met with Karatheodori Pasha and proposed to release the detainees from Zeytoun on their own recognizance and start negotiations with the leader of the rebels, Prince Papik Yenitunian, to satisfy the demands of the Christian population of Zeytoun and to prevent the armed assaults of the Muslims on that region. The Ambassador warned that bloodshed was inevitable and would affect European public opinion, as had happened in the case of Bulgaria, with repercussions for Turkey.[57] Layard drew Karatheodori Pasha's attention to the debate in the House of Lords initiated by Lord Carnarvon, which reflected the great interest in Great Britain concerning Ottoman policy toward the Armenians. With that in mind, the Ambassador urged his counterpart to begin the reforms immediately. The Foreign Minister replied that the Porte had been discussing the reforms in earnest and would soon be approved by the Sultan and implemented.[58]

Two days later, Ambassador Layard received new reports from the field describing the still difficult plight of the Armenian population, and sent another stern note to the Sublime Porte. The note invited the attention of the Porte to the "unbearable persecution" suffered by the Armenians and urged the Sultan's Government to abide by its pledges of equal treatment and guarantees of life and property for all its subjects, regardless of their ethnic or religious affiliation. The Embassy note stated that the only authority prevailing in the eastern provinces seemed to be that of the Kurdish warlords and chieftains, whose main preoccupation was robbery and persecution of the Christian population.[59]

In his telegram to Layard, Salisbury noted that the delays in implementation of reforms in the Eastern provinces of the Ottoman Empire were of great concern to the British Government. The Foreign Secretary thanked Layard for his efforts on this issue.[60] In his reply, the Ambassador expressed his belief that the Porte had become convinced of the absolute necessity to do something for the Armenians, and said he hoped they would implement the reforms. He pledged to do his best to achieve this outcome.[61]

The British consuls continued to report to the Ambassador and the Foreign Office on the activities of the government commissions sent to Erzurum and Zeytoun. On July 7, Trotter reported that the commission had arrived in Erzurum and selected an advisory panel, drawn proportionally to represent the local population (totaling 252,811, of which 197,768 were Muslim and 55,043 Christian). Thus, the commission included 10 Christians (7 Armenian Apostolic, one Armenian Catholic, and one Greek Orthodox), and 28 Muslims. According to Trotter, reforms would be implemented based on the new charter of the province that the central government had prepared, with input from the local residents and the governor. The reforms that would contradict the charter of the province would be left to the central government's jurisdiction. Trotter reported his meeting with a delegation representing the Armenian community that presented their proposals for reforms, providing for: equal representation for Muslims and Christians in the administrative organs, appointment of a European head and officers for the newly created gendarmerie, official use of the Armenian language, and abolition of the tithe.[62]

On July 17, the British Embassy sent another note to the Porte urging the implementation of the reforms and, in particular, suggesting to include European officers in the gendarmerie under creation in Erzurum province. The document noted that the British Government considered the creation of an effective gendarmerie in Erzurum province of particular importance in light of the unstable situation there and the persecution of the Christian population by some Muslim chieftains. The British Government hoped that the Porte would honor its pledge to use experienced European officers in formation of the gendarmerie.[63]

In his next report, dated July 25, Trotter said that the more he had acquainted himself with the activities of the government commission, the less hope it had inspired for the prompt implementation of the reforms. According to the Consul, the commission members had been authorized to nominate deputy chief judges and alternates for the newly established criminal and civil courts, but the Governor made his appointment without having consulted with the commission. Next, the commission had had specific instructions to dissolve the old Council of the Province and organize elections of new members, based on the new charter, yet the instruction had been invalidated and the governor regained the right to control the elections, i.e. the corrupt members of the old council would regain their positions. Trotter noted that the commission had been authorized to replace any corrupt or ineffective official of the local government, but the only dismissals had been conducted by the governor, without prior consultation with the commission. Finally, the commission had been ordered to study the efficiency of the taxation system, and make necessary improvements within the existing legal framework, but the governor had recently been ordered by the central government to revert to the old system of taxation. Trotter reported that the recent instructions from the Porte had deliberately narrowed the scope of the commission and aimed at preserving the status quo in the province.[64]

Meanwhile, on July 12 Henderson and Chermside reported to Layard from Aleppo that the activities of a member of the commission investigating the Zeytoun incident, Mahzar Pasha, had agitated the Muslim mob against the Christians; such activities reflected the fundamentalist beliefs of extremist circles in Constantinople and contributed to the deteriorating situation in the province.[65] The Ambassador sent a British diplomat, Alfred Mendison, to the Grand Vizier's office to report on these developments. The latter lamented that the Porte always found itself in a bind because of the constant complaints of the British diplomats, since no Ottoman official was now free to conduct his business unimpeded. He added that the charges against the Turkish official needed to be confirmed since they had been leveled from such a distance. Nevertheless, after consulting with the Foreign Minister, the Grand Vizier proposed to call a session of the Council of Ministers immediately to discuss the appointment of a High Commissioner with extraordinary Powers in order to stabilize the situation in Zeytoun, including an authorization to punish Mahzar Pasha or any other official found incompetent in the Zeytoun matter.[66]

In his telegram to Salisbury, dated July 25, Trotter noted that his official designation as Consul to Kurdistan had been received negatively by the Armenian population, and cited newspaper articles from Constantinople to back his case. He suggested taking into account the interests of the Armenians, and suggested that the British Government should collaborate more closely with them. He cited official Turkish statistics, which gave the following breakdown of the population of the Erzurum and Van provinces, respectively: 197,768 Muslims and 55,043 non-Muslims, and 126,208 Muslims and 97,555 non-Muslims. Trotter noted that, in his opinion, the Christian population was underreported by at least 40%. According to Taylor's estimates, the combined population of Erzurum and Van provinces was 442,500 Turks, 848,000 Kurds, 200,500 kizilbashis, and 649,000 Christians. Noting the statistics, and the active participation of the Armenian population in the public life of the regions, Trotter proposed to change the designation of the consulate to "Consul in Turkish Armenia and Kurdistan," or, should that prove impossible, as "Eastern Asiatic Turkey." He also suggested dividing the consular jurisdictions into Eastern and Western Anatolian districts and cooperating with the Armenians on implementation of the reforms.[67] Significantly, Trotter did not sign his letter with his title of Consul in Kurdistan, attaching instead a personal signature only.

In reference to Trotter's proposal, Layard reported to Salisbury that it would have been undesirable to request the agreement of the Porte to the appointment of a 'Consul to Armenia' since there was no such name in the political division of Turkey. The Ambassador noted that the ultimate objective of the "agitation related to the Armenian Question" was the establishment of an Armenian autonomy under European auspices. He noted that the term 'Kurdistan' could be removed from the Consul's title should it prove too offensive to the Armenians, but added that the term Kurdistan was in use to designate the Kurdish-populated areas without anybody attempting to establish an autonomy for them. The Ambassador advised against any changes in the official designation under the existing circumstances.[68]

In his letter to Vice Consul Clayton in Van, dated July 24, Trotter urged him to collect accurate data on the number of nomad and settled Kurds as well as the Armenians. Trotter described the official Turkish statistics as incomplete and not credible. For example, the official statistics listed 48,000 Armenian men in the Mush region, while, according to the local Armenian bishop, the correct figure was 120,000. Trotter instructed Clayton to cooperate with Russian Consul Kamsarakan in the collection of vital statistics and the issue of the reforms.[69]

On July 29, Layard had a three-hour meeting with Sultan Abdul Hamid. During the meeting, the Ambassador told the Sultan that the Porte had not fulfilled the conditions of the Cyprus Convention signed more than a year before. On behalf of the British Government, he expressed regret that the Ottoman government's "specific pledges" had not been implemented. The Sultan once again promised Layard to begin the reforms in the near future, adding that the financial, economic, and international issues that had arisen after the war prevented him from concentrating on the reforms. He gave his 'word of honor' to Layard that the reforms promised to the British Government would soon be implemented and said he had given orders to his ministers to that effect. His only objection was on the issue of the tithe, and the Sultan pointed out that the British Government itself had not abolished the tax in Cyprus.

Layard met with the Grand Vizier the following day, and the latter assured the British Ambassador that he had received instructions from the Sultan and that certain measures would soon be promulgated to implement reforms.[70]

Convinced that the Sultan's pledges had been insincere, Layard instructed Admiral Hornby's Mediterranean fleet to sail off from Malta toward Lemnos Island and wait there until further notice. On July 31, Layard sent a confidential telegram to Salisbury asking for an authorization to order the fleet to approach Constantinople if the Sultan did not honor his pledges.[71] Salisbury sent the necessary authorization.[72]

On June 27, Salisbury told the House of Lords that a special commission comprised of Turkish Government officials was discussing the issue of reforms to be implemented in Asia Minor. On August 1, however, Consul Trotter reported from Erzurum that, in his assessment, despite the earnestness and sincerity of the commission members and their good intentions, their report would hardly mark a progress in the reforms process because of the narrow scope of their authorization from the central government. According to the consul, his knowledge of the Turkish officials and the prevailing conditions in the country convinced him that it would be impossible to implement reforms in that country without the presence of honest and efficient European officials.[73]

Trotter's assessment was indirectly confirmed by a telegram from Vice Consul Clayton, sent on August 2 from Mush. Clayton described the horrid conditions of the Armenian villages in the Mush region that had been continuously attacked, ransacked, robbed, and massacred not only by the Kurdish tribes but also by the Turkish regular troops. Clayton reported that he had seen no evidence of foreign agitation but added that the Armenians had recently become more aware of the conditions in Europe and of the ideas of freedom and equality, and were more likely to consider their conditions untenable.[74]

In his report to Salisbury, dated August 8, Trotter noted that the Armenian community submitted a reform draft to the commission that would have allotted half of the administrative positions in the province to the Armenians, on the grounds that nomadic Kurds could not be represented in the provincial administration. The Consul reported the population data provided by the Armenians, which differed from the official statistics. According to the Armenian data, there were 195,500 Christians, 185,000 Turks, 112,500 nomadic and settled Kurds, and 3,000 Yezidis in the province. Trotter reported that the Armenians had begun to boycott the sessions of the commissions since they were dissatisfied with its proceedings.[75]

On August 10, Layard sent another note to the Porte addressing the activities of the commission sent to Erzurum and Van. The British Embassy complained that, despite an auspicious beginning, the members of the commission encountered serious resistance on the part of the local authorities, and, possessing limited powers and not quite absolute support from Constantinople, were now in despair and unable to implement "the good will of the Sultan to improve the conditions of his Christian subjects."[76]

On July 31, Clayton reported from Mush that the local Armenians were unhappy over the plans to resettle some three to four thousand Muslim migrants from the Kars and Batum regions mostly in the villages, rather than cities, since the Armenians were concerned it might affect the local villages.[77]

On September 10, the Armenian population of Bayazid presented a petition to the commission describing conditions before and after the war. According to the petition, in the prewar period the population included some 200 Christian households and 400 to 500 Muslim households, and the Armenians and Muslims lived peacefully and prosperously next to each other. During the war, prior to the Russian occupation, the local residents formed a council and decided to protect each other's community if such a need arose. Consequently, during the Russian occupation many Muslims had found refuge in the Armenians homes before they were convinced of the peaceful intentions of the Russians and returned to their homes. However, after the Russian troops had been withdrawn, the Armenian population began to be harassed by the Turks and Kurds, who looted their property. As a result of the massacre, some 800 people were killed or wounded, and most Armenian families immigrated to Persia. The petition stated that the Armenians were threatened with a complete elimination of their race, and expressed hope that the Sultan would show compassion toward the Armenians and alleviate their concerns.[78]

On the same day, Clayton reported to Trotter from Van that he had met with two Russian Armenians from Tiflis who had arrived in the region with the intention to train teachers and establish agricultural schools. The visitors told Clayton that the Armenians villagers in the neighboring regions hoped that Russia would rescue the Armenian population from its dire straits, not unlike the way it helped the Bulgarians. According to Clayton, the visiting Armenians from Russia realized that there was no hope for Russian intervention, and that the local educated elites had abandoned their campaign for autonomy, concentrating instead on protecting the population of Western Armenia from robberies and massacres and achieving equal status with the Muslims. In Clayton's opinion, "the Armenians in Turkey have intellectual and moral freedom but are oppressed physically, while the Armenians in Russia live prosperously, but are deprived morally and intellectually."[79]

On September 23, the Armenians in Hadjin presented a petition to the commission enumerating their grievances. According to the petition, more than 10 Armenians had been murdered and 55 wounded in the last five years, and 6,000 Turkish liras worth of cattle and products had been stolen; the roads outside the city were not secure, and the Christians were continuously harassed by Turkish officials who referred to them as *giaour*s (infidels) and refused to accept their testimony in courts. Although out of the general population of 8,500 people, some 8,000 were Armenians,* only one city official— the Treasurer—was Armenian. For the same reason, the Armenians requested that the local mayor be an Armenian. The local government confiscated the watermill and three stores belonging to the Armenians, the revenues from which had been used to finance the local church and school. The petition also listed lack of a doctor, post office, and telegraph, and made the case for reducing taxes since the soil in the area was infertile.[80]

On September 26, the Armenian population of Kharput also submitted a petition, describing the miserable conditions in the region. However, the Commission Chairman, Haberdin Pasha, refused to accept the petition since he viewed it as a personal affront to him.[81]

Despite the constant flow of telegrams from the British consular officers describing the deteriorating condition of the Armenian population, and increasing persecution by the local governments, regular troops, and Kurdish irregulars, on September 29, Salisbury sent a confidential circular to the consuls asserting that there was a clandestine movement among the Armenians in Turkey working to establish Armenian autonomy, and asking the consuls to report the attitudes of their Armenian communities and their position vis-à-vis Russia.[82]

On October 1, Trotter reported to Salisbury that the central government had used the pretext of the reforms to get rid of certain Kurdish chieftains who flouted the authorities. The Consul reported that the government decreed to exile them to Albania, but the chieftains were successfully arguing with the Porte to remain at large. Trotter noted that the Kurdish tribes whose chiefs fell out of favor with the government threatened to retaliate against the Armenians. The report added that the Armenians in the Palu and Kharput regions were especially threatened since the local government took no steps to protect them from arbitrary murders and robberies.[83]

In his next report to Salisbury, dated October 7, Trotter reported that some

---

* Most likely, this is the number of the male population, since the 1915 statistics listed 25 –30,000 Armenians living in Hadjin out of the general population of 35,000.

10,000 Muslim families living in the Kars, Ardahan, and Kahizman regions wanted to move to Turkey, and the Russian government wanted to resettle the vacated areas with Russians and Cossacks to prevent the Armenians from moving into those areas. Trotter noted, in explanation, that some 2,000 Armenian families who had resettled in Russia after the 1828–29 War wanted to return to their abandoned settlements in the Alashkert Valley, but the Tsarist government was denying them permission.[84]

In September, Trotter asked Captain William Everett to visit Alashkert, Karakilisa, Diadin, and Bayazid to study the condition of the Armenian population in those localities. On October 7, Everett reported to the Consul that the regions had changed hands five times during the Russian-Turkish war, and both armies confiscated provisions from the civilians. Both Armenian and Turkish communities were subjected to looting and murder by the Kurdish irregulars and bandits, as well as the local authorities. According to Everett, the region was currently under the control of the bandits and looters who continued to harass the Armenian population with impunity. Everett was convinced that the reforms would be impossible to implement without the presence and participation of the European officials since any reform measure could cause new pressures.[85] Based on Everett's report, the British Embassy presented another note to the Sublime Porte protesting the "unacceptable" attitude of the Turkish officials and Kurds toward the Armenians. The note expressed surprise at the ease with each the Porte tolerated actions aimed against its authority.[86]

On October 23, Layard called on newly appointed Grand Vizier Said Pasha. Noting that the Prime Minister had been installed at an extremely critical juncture, the Ambassador urged him to rein in the anarchy prevalent in all parts of the Empire, to implement promptly the reforms promised to Europe, and to provide for the protection of the Armenian subjects of the Empire, otherwise the Government, Sultan's throne and the existence of the Empire would be threatened. Layard warned Said Pasha that the British Government could no longer tolerate the persecution and harassment of the Christian population of Asiatic Turkey and the violations of the Turkish-British convention. The Ambassador made the same presentation to the newly appointed Foreign Minister, Sawas Pasha. Both officials assured Layard that the promises made to the British Government would be honored.[87]

The day after the meetings took place, Layard sent a note to the Porte referring to the continuing reports from the consular officers about the persecution of Armenians residing in Armenia and Kurdistan. The note argued that such reports would affect the British Government, Parliament, and public opinion in their attitudes toward Turkey. The note urged the Porte to promptly take measures to address the situation, protect the Christian population, and provide for equal rights for them and the Muslim subjects.[88]

On October 25, Layard met with the Interior Minister, Nadim Pasha, to once again urge a prompt implementation of the reforms. On this occasion, however, the British Ambassador demanded that an Englishman, Baker Pasha, be appointed High Commissioner in Armenia, threatening to order the British Fleet to approach Constantinople if this demand were not met. In fact, Layard had already sent the order to Admiral Hornby to sail from Malta on November 5. Prodded by this threat, the Turkish minister promised to use his influence with the Sultan to ask him to implement the necessary measures.[89] Abdul Hamid immediately dispatched one of his officials, Munir Bey, to meet with the Ambassador asking him to reconsider the decision. Through his envoy, the Sultan told the British Ambassador that he had thought the Cyprus Convention would honor his sovereign rights, and if the British Government insisted on appointing Baker Pasha as High Commissioner, the Sultan would take the necessary steps to defend his Empire.[90] On November 1, Layard advised Salisbury to extend the deadline for the Sultan to take some steps to implement the reforms, and to postpone the fleet's departure from Malta by 15–20 days.[91]

On November 4, the Ottoman Ambassador in London, Musurus Pasha called on Salisbury, and promised that there would be no changes in the Ottoman Government's position and that reforms would be implemented promptly. The Porte agreed to appoint Baker Pasha as independent commander of the gendarmerie in Kurdistan if the British Fleet did not enter Turkish waters. Salisbury told the Ambassador that the British Fleet would stay in Malta if the Sultan honored his promises.[92] The same day, Layard reported to Salisbury that the Russian and French envoys met with the Ottoman foreign minister and advised him to disregard the British show of force.[93]

On November 6, Salisbury wrote to Layard that the British Government considered appointment of a European officer to independent command of the gendarmerie in Asia Minor as an indispensable condition of the reforms process and instructed the Ambassador to work in that direction.[94] In another telegram, dated November 8, Salisbury noted that if other Powers did not agree to appoint Baker Pasha, he would agree to appoint an Austrian, German, or French officer in that position.[95]

On November 10, Layard had a lengthy meeting with Sultan Abdul Hamid, who told him that while Great Britain remained a staunch friend and ally of the Ottoman Empire, the decision to move the fleet "had saddened him" and caused delays in final approval of the reform draft, since it would have been a forced decision. The Sultan suggested that the British Government publicly disavow its threat to stage a naval demonstration. In turn, the Ambassador noted that the British Government would not be satisfied unless Baker Pasha was appointed to an independent command of the gendarmerie in Armenia or another troubled region.[96] On November 12, Salisbury noted in his telegram to Layard that the Ambassador could make a public statement [requested by the Sultan] only after the Sultan had presented to him the decree appointing Baker as independent commander of at least a 5000-man strong gendarmerie in Asia Minor. Salisbury was convinced that without such precaution the Sultan would ridicule the British demands.[97]

On November 12, Nadim Pasha sent the Secretary General of the Interior Ministry, Artin Dadyan, who was an ethnic Armenian, to meet with Ambassador Layard and present to him the main points of the reform draft submitted to the government for discussion. Layard told the envoy that he would be satisfied only if the draft was promulgated in a decree by the Sultan and the first steps were taken to implement it. The Ambassador told Dadyan that recent anti-British articles in the Turkish press were in his opinion an indication of Russian-Ottoman talks to restore normal relations between two countries. Layard warned that if that indeed were the case, the Porte would become involved in the Russian sphere of influence, and Nadim Pasha's presence in the Cabinet would be perceived to be behind these developments—with repercussions for Nadim Pasha. Asserting that he was authorized to speak on behalf of Nadim Pasha, Dadyan assured the Ambassador that he would resist any attempts by the Sultan, the Porte or a third party to conclude an alliance with Russia. Layard inquired if Nadim Pasha had any information about the meeting between the Sultan and the Russian Ambassador, and Dadyan revealed that the Russian envoy had advised the Sultan to disregard the British naval threats.[98]

Two days later, Sultan Abdul Hamid sent Munir Bey to meet with Layard and assure him that his decree on implementation of the reforms guaranteed by the government was in process and would be published soon. Munir Bey added that the Sultan would send Baker to study the local conditions and lead the gendarmerie in Asia Minor.[99]

On November 21, Layard was invited to a dinner with Abdul Hamid, and had a lengthy discussion with the Sultan who assured him that he would not make an alliance with Russia. The Sultan promised to send Baker to Diyarbakir with an appropriate authorization. He announced his decision to appoint Rustem Pasha as Governor of Erzurum. Layard reported to Salisbury that he had a good impression about the meeting and the progress in relations with the Porte.[100]

Meanwhile, the British Embassy continued to receive information about the deteriorating plight of the Armenian population. On November 17, Consul Henderson forwarded from Aleppo a petition signed by 1520 Armenian Christians displaced from Mush, Van, and other regions, which was addressed to Layard. The petition described the conditions of the Armenians in those regions who were suffering persecution by the local governments and the Kurdish bandits.[101]

On November 22, Clayton reported from Van that the upheavals in the Armenian community of Van had been caused by the famine, robberies, and the local government's actions rather than by Russian agitation. In his assessment, the Armenian community had lost its faith in the British ability to promote the reforms, and considered appealing for Russian help the following year, which was not an indication of any special regard for Russia, but rather was caused by their destitute conditions. If the commissions' activities yielded no results and British mediation did not change the situation, the Armenian community would consider the British efforts a failure while the Turks and Kurds would conclude they could operate with impunity, the Vice Consul noted. In his opinion, if Great Britain did not intervene, the conditions of the Christian population would further deteriorate and Russia would step in to assume the mantle of the defense of the Christians, with that community's acquiescence.[102]

The Armenian community of Vaspurakan presented a petition to Clayton that the destitute conditions of the Armenian community worked in the interests of the Sultan's government while the Kurds were only a "successful tool for the government to obstruct the reform process." The petition stated that the Armenians were harassed by the central government, the local authorities, and the Kurds. The authorities incited the Kurdish tribes against the Armenian population, and when the European Powers demand to restore law and order in the provinces, the government's response was to complain of lack of funds and resources. According to the petition, the Armenians did not resort to the use of arms only because the British were intent to resolve the Armenian Question without loss of life, yet the Armenians were losing patience and there was a 'dangerous movement' among the Armenians in Van to turn to Russia for help. The petition was concluded with another request for assistance from the British Government.[103]

Summarizing the consular officers' reports, Layard sent a long note to the Porte, dated November 23, referring to the harassment of the Armenian Christians by the Kurds and in some instances, "regrettably," by Turkish officials as well. According to the note the commissions were ineffective while the intercessions by the British consuls had been obstructed. Drawing the attention of the Porte to the matter, the note urged the government to implement fair reforms to remedy the conditions of its Christian subjects and end their sufferings.[104]

During the winter of 1879–80, the conditions of the Armenian population continued to worsen. Vice Consul Clayton reported from Van on December 17 that the instances of famine-related deaths had become commonplace in the region. Clayton informed Trotter that the former Armenian patriarch, Archbishop Khrimian, who was then head of the Van diocese, toured the local parishes urging patience and moderation, peaceful relations with neighboring peoples, and not to appeal to the Russians or British for help. According to the Vice Consul, Archbishop Khrimian's sermons greatly affected the urban population but he doubted they would be well received among the rural communities, which he claimed were awaiting the arrival of the Russians.[105] On February 2, 1880, Clayton sent a confidential report to Layard arguing that the local population was increasingly more disposed toward Russia. The Vice Consul had been told many times by his local interlocutors that the Armenians would prefer British support and assistance but saw the Russians as more interested with the fate of the Christian population of the Ottoman Empire than the British. According to Clayton, the Armenians could not ignore the fact that Bulgaria had been liberated by Russian arms while Great Britain had not done anything to improve the plight of the Christians.[106]

In his January 31 confidential telegram to Salisbury, Layard informed him that a member of the Russian-Turkish commission delineating the border, Yahya Pasha, had returned to the capital recently, and had presented the activities of the British consular officers in an unfavorable light. According to the report, the British consuls were accused of actions undermining the Turkish government's sovereignty and inciting the Christian population against the Sultan's authority. The Turkish official warned of dire consequences of such actions, and argued that the Russian position was more beneficial to Turkish interests than to those of Great Britain.[107]

A special commission charged with studying the local conditions in the eastern provinces, and the state of the local government, gendarmerie, and police in those regions, was sent to Erzurum on January 19. The commission was appointed by the Sultan and included Baker Pasha and Said Pasha.[108] In a letter dated February 1, Baker reported to Layard that he had encountered "ambitious plans for the future" among the Armenian leaders, and noted that those designs were largely impractical and even dangerous for the interests of the Armenian community. He dismissed as unreasonable the demands for Armenian autonomy since the Armenian population was in the minority in all the provinces. Baker added that the agitation among the Armenians had turned the Turkish officials against them, and that the demands for autonomy would surely misfire because the Armenians would then be left alone to the mercy of the Kurdish chieftains.[109]

An American missionary, Robert Chambers, told Vice Consul Everett in Erzurum that the rural Armenian population had recently become more pro-Russian, increasingly so in the previous two or three months when the British inability to accelerate the implementation of the reforms and to improve the state of the Armenian community had become apparent. The American missionary was convinced that the Armenians would have preferred to have the British resolve their situation but they were nevertheless prepared to appeal to the Russians or some other Power since the British had done nothing for them.[110]

On February 17, Layard reported to Salisbury that, in his assessment, the Porte would never agree to appoint an Armenian as governor in Erzurum since that would be viewed as the first step toward the establishment of Armenian autonomy. The Ambassador noted that it was in the best interests of the Armenian community not to press the idea of autonomy similar to that in Eastern Rumelia since it would only incite the Muslim mob, and lead to bloodshed if not a general massacre of the Armenians, which could only be stopped by Russian military intervention. The Russian action, Layard argued, would incorporate the Armenians into the Russian Empire and lead to loss of their identity. Layard noted that to raise the question of Armenian autonomy would only confirm the suspicions of the Porte, lead to new problems, and undermine the British and German efforts to carry out practical and effective measures to protect the Armenians and to secure their fair representation in the administration of the provinces where they lived.[111]

In February 1880, Patriarch Nerses Varzhapetian met with the representatives of the British and German embassies. According to the British Embassy officer, the Patriarch had presented a number of proposals such as appointment of a British, German, or Armenian as Governor, creation of an international European commission, and establishment of Armenian autonomy in the manner of Eastern Rumelia. The Patriarch suggested Nubar Pasha, Grigor Otian, Stepan Pasha or Kostand Pasha as candidates for Governor. On behalf of their governments, the British and German representatives dismissed the Patriarch's demands as unacceptable. The German diplomat stated that Armenian autonomy would be accepted neither by the Sultan nor the European Powers, and added that Germany had no direct interests in the Ottoman Empire and would only act to defend the rights of the Empire's Christian subjects.[112]

The reports of the British consular officers sent to the Embassy and Foreign Office in March and April continued to reflect the desperate state of the Armenian communities in the country. On April 3, Everett reported to Layard from Erzurum that more than 100 Armenians died of famine in the Alashkert region.[113] Consul Wilson reported from Sivas that the region was on the brink of serious disorder since the local Turkish officials had done nothing to resettle the Muslims displaced from Bulgaria and Eastern Rumelia. In many regions, the Circassian refugees seized the land plots from the local villagers. Wilson estimated that there were 15 to 20,000 Circassian refugees in Ada Bazar alone.[114]

By the spring of 1880, it became evident that Disraeli's and Salisbury's policies of "peaceful penetration" into the region stretching from the Aegean Sea to India had been largely ineffective. Tsarist Russia checked the Conservative government's designs on Afghanistan and in the Ottoman Empire. The British Government's proposals to introduce troops in Eastern Rumelia or conclude a secret treaty against the Slav states had been rejected by the Sultan, and the British appeals and threats of a naval intervention failed to persuade the Sultan to carry out the provisions of Article 61 of the Berlin Treaty. By engaging in negotiations with Germany and Austria-Hungary to revive the 'Three Emperors League,' Russia managed to counter the anti-Russian policies of Britain. Internal political blunders, the tax increases and a poor harvest in 1879 contributed to the decline in fortunes of the Conservative party. On March 6, Prime Minister Disraeli was forced to call new elections.

2. The Gladstone Cabinet and the Issue of Reforms in 1880–85

The Liberal Party won the general elections in April 1880, and William Gladstone assumed the office of Prime Minister once again. Earl Granville became the new Foreign Secretary. Disraeli died in the same month, and the leadership of the Conservative Party passed to Lord Salisbury. During the election campaign, Gladstone made the Conservative Government's colonial policy a major target of criticism, and promised to the electorate that he would pursue peaceful policies based on principles of the 'Concert of Europe,' i.e., joint and coordinated actions by six major European Powers to promote peace. Disraeli's position on the Armenian Question had been subjected to criticism from this perspective as well. Gladstone made a major foreign policy speech in Edinburgh on November 25, 1879. He noted that England had acquired Cyprus, assumed control of Egypt together with France, and would soon push the frontiers of its colonies in South Africa to the southern borders of the Portuguese domains there. England had also assumed the responsibility to improve the administration of the Turkish provinces in Asia Minor and the rest of Asiatic Turkey, including Arabia, Gladstone said. He noted that

England had also pledged to defend the Turkish frontier in Armenia against a Russian attack, a responsibility that would require troops to cross hundreds of miles of mountainous terrain or cross thousands of miles by sea. Gladstone concluded by pledging to reduce the "confusion" of the British obligations.[115] As far as the Armenian Question was concerned, it meant joint and coordinated actions by the European Powers to force the Sultan's government to carry out its obligations under Article 61 of the Berlin Treaty.

On April 27, 1880, Layard presented a special report to the Foreign Office summarizing the British-Turkish relations as well as the current state of the Ottoman Empire. He noted that the Sultan had recently began to express reservations about the British Government's position, dating to the 1878 British proposal for the Austrian occupation of Bosnia and Herzegovina; the Sultan was also unhappy about the British threats of sending a fleet into Turkish territorial waters in November 1879. Nevertheless, the Ambassador noted that, out of his own interests, the Sultan was disposed to maintain friendly relations with Great Britain. Layard noted that the friendly attitudes toward the British Government used to be shared by the Christian subjects of the Empire, who, under the terms of the Cyprus Convention, should have been the beneficiaries of the Ottoman reforms to be carried out under the British supervision. The Ambassador, however, cited the reports of the British consuls in Erzurum, Van, and Diyarbakir to argue that the Armenian community had largely lost faith in the British support for the reforms process. The disappointment was exploited by Russia which intended to use the Armenians as a tool to gain new territories in Asiatic Turkey, the report concluded.[116]

According to the special report, the British Government sent a note signed by Salisbury on August 8, 1878, asking the Porte to carry out reforms in the Armenian-populated areas, and the Ottoman assurances to do so were communicated by Safvet Pasha on October 24, 1878. The program provided for a gendarmerie staffed by European officers, the appointment of a financial and legal European agent in the provinces, a five-term limit for governors, and so on. None of these items had been carried out, while the activities of the government commissions comprised of both Christian and Muslim officials, who had been sent to the regions to investigate the local conditions, had not yielded positive results. In fact, these commissions in many cases contributed to further tension and deterioration in the plight of the local Christians.

Despite the promise of the Sultan to appoint Baker Pasha as Commander of the gendarmerie in Kurdistan and Erzurum, he was instead appointed chairman of the commission sent to Asia Minor, Mesopotamia, and Syria to reconnoiter the regions and make proposals for establishment of gendarmerie.[117]

The Ambassador noted that he had used all resources at his disposal, including threats of the use of force, to compel the Sultan to carry out his obligations. He had constantly issued warnings of corruption among officials and raised the appalling conditions of the Christian population, noting that these developments could lead to the partition of the Empire. The Sultan issued a number of promises yet nothing had been accomplished. Layard suggested that if Great Britain was serious about saving the Ottoman Empire, it should go beyond issuing threats of action. He was convinced that since the end of the Turkish-Russian War the Sultan had been under the influence of an extremist and anti-European circle that convinced him that reforms and the Europeanization of the country would lead it to disaster.[118]

According to Layard, the conditions of the Armenian community had only deteriorated in the previous two years. While the Armenians had initially been hopeful for the success of the British policy, they had been disappointed and were now entertaining hopes to establish an autonomous, if not semi-independent, Armenia. There were ad-hoc committees and Armenian media that were working to promote that idea in Constantinople and Europe, he noted. The Ambassador expressed his belief that such a program was seriously flawed and would have serious repercussions since the Armenian population was in the minority in most regions. It was insane to ignore the Kurdish factor, the Ambassador argued, especially now that the news of treatment accorded to the Muslim population in [newly liberated] Christian autonomies in the European part of the Ottoman Empire had reached the Muslims in Asia Minor. The Armenian demands for autonomy would spark a general massacre and lead to Russian intervention, Layard argued.[119]

After he familiarized himself with, and acquiesced to, the foreign policy positions of the new government, Layard noted that the British Government should cooperate or coordinate its policy on the Ottoman Empire with other European nations. He argued that only prompt implementation of the reforms could save the Empire from disaster, and that it was best carried out under European supervision.[120]

The Gladstone Cabinet's new foreign policy was reflected in a circular sent by Granville to the British Ambassadors in the Five European Powers on May 4. The new head of the Foreign Office noted that it was in the interests of Europe to end the delays in implementing several provisions of the Berlin Treaty, and that the coordinated efforts of all the Powers were the best means to achieve that objective. The British Government proposed that all European Powers submit, through their envoys in Constantinople, collective notes to the Turkish Government to force it to carry out its obligations on the issues of Greece, Montenegro, and Armenia. The British Government concluded that the Porte had not carried out its obligations on the Armenian Questions as per Article 61 and had not made efforts to secure the supervision of the European Powers over the reforms. According to Granville, in the view of the continuing appalling state of the Armenian community, the provisions of the article could not remain a dead letter but needed to be enforced by a coordinated effort of the Powers.[121]

This was the first serious indication that the new government disavowed the Disraeli policy of a unilateral defense of the Ottoman Empire and drew closer to the positions of Russia and the other European Powers.

On May 6, Granville informed Layard that the Government was replacing him with MP George Goschen.[122] Granville assured Layard that the Government had appreciated his abilities and steadfast work and the Ambassador to use the occasion of the farewell call on the Sultan to inform him and the Porte of the gravity of the current state of the Ottoman Empire. The Ambassador was also instructed to tell the Sultan about the decision to present a joint petition on behalf of the Powers demanding of him an immediate implementation of the provisions of the Berlin Treaty concerning Greece, Montenegro, and Armenia.[123]

In a May 18 letter, Granville informed Goschen that the government's decision to appoint him Ambassador was because of the events taking place in Armenia, and the difficult situation in Turkey, and instructed him to work in conjunction with the envoys of other European Powers on a set of measures to address the issues of Greece, Montenegro, and Armenia. Granville laid out in great detail the Armenian Question, the provisions of Article 61, the Disraeli government's attempts to redress the situation, the ineffective and counterproductive actions of the Porte, and the miserable state of the

Armenian population. According to the Secretary, the British Government was well aware of the difficulties that could accompany the implementation of the reforms in the provinces. He noted that the reforms would be easier to implement in the provinces populated by Christians under the influence of European civilization, and practically impossible to carry out in the mountainous areas populated by Muslim tribes. Granville stated the government's position that the coordinated efforts of all the Powers could promote the reforms, restore law and order, and provide for the protection of life and the property of Christians and Muslims alike. Towards these ends, it was necessary to establish a gendarmerie, abolish arbitrary taxation, and modernize the appointment of officials. Although the British Government had decided to act in concert with the other Powers, Granville wanted the newly appointed Ambassador to assure the Sultan and the Porte that the recommendations of the British Government were of a friendly nature and would coincide with Turkish interests.[124]

On June 1, Granville informed Goschen that the signatories of the Berlin Treaty agreed to present collective notes to the Porte urging an immediate implementation of the Turkish obligations on Greece, Montenegro, and the Armenian-populated regions. The Foreign Secretary instructed him to consult with other envoys and present the note to the Sultan's government.[125]

The European ambassadors presented such a note to the Porte on June 18. In his note to Turkish Foreign Minister Abeddin Pasha, Goschen informed him that delays in the implementation of certain articles of the Berlin Treaty by Turkey had become a subject of consultations among the Powers. The Powers agreed that European interests required an end to delays in execution of the conditions spelled out in the Treaty on July 13, 1878.

In addition to the issues related to the demarcation of Turkish-Greek and Turkish-Montenegrin borders, the note raised the issue of reforms in the Armenian-populated regions, as provided for in Article 61, since the Sultan's Government had not done anything in this area. It was mentioned that Article 61 had been rendered dead while the situation in the Armenian-populated areas continued to be unbearable. The Powers concluded that only joint and coordinated efforts by them could force the Porte to carry out the reforms, the note claimed. The British Government, therefore, demanded of the Porte to promptly carry out the reforms, and inform the Powers in minute detail of the measures it intended to take toward that goal.[126]

On June 17, Goschen called on Abeddin Pasha to discuss the Armenian Question. The Ambassador noted that his activities as Governor of Sivas displayed his ability and skills. Abeddin Pasha admitted to administrative deficiencies and the inefficiency of the police, and said the reforms were a necessity. He presented a draft program that would soon be submitted to the Cabinet. It provided for dividing the districts of a province into small communities comprised of 7–8 villages, each of which would elect its head and establish municipal police. The Minister proposed to create juries in every province, including two Christians and two Muslims. Abeddin Pasha said it was necessary to involve the European officers in establishing the gendarmerie. Immediately after the meeting, Goschen met with the Armenian Patriarch, who said the only solution to the crisis was establishment of a large province with a Christian Governor-General appointed for a term of five years. The Armenian region would be placed under European, or preferably, British protectorate. The Ambassador countered that the Armenians were not in the majority of the province in question, but the Patriarch noted that the nomadic Kurds should not be taken into account since they spent only six months in the province each year.[127]

The British consulates in Western Armenia continued to report local developments and political affiliations, as well as provide ethnographic data on the customs of the Armenians. Their reports on the conditions of the Armenians are of particular interest, and they are summarized briefly here for the reader.

On June 16, Consul General Wilson submitted a report "On Anatolia and Necessary Reforms." According to the report, the Armenians were divided into Apostolic, Catholic, and Protestant groups, which "were usually at variance with one another, rarely combined for any common object." The Apostolic Armenians were "rarely if ever united among themselves on any question of local politics." According to the Consul, the Armenian character was complex and difficult to understand; the rural population was 'sober, intelligent, frugal, and hard-working, and greedy for gain,' yet 'entirely without education, immoral, fanatic, bigoted, and completely under the influence of an illiterate, ignorant, and sensual clergy' who opposed education and advancement. The urbanized Armenians were 'shrewd, intelligent, egotistical and proud, and with slight superficial education.' There was a small group of well-educated people in every city who occupied positions of prominence.

According to Wilson, geographic proximity, old traditions, and religious links inclined the Armenians toward Russia. The Armenians "dreamed of Loris-Melikov, their mythical kings, and of revenge on the Muslim" but some reforms common to everyone would contend them. "Let the Armenian have a career, let him work, engage in trade, and earn money, and he will cease to be politically troublesome," the Consul concluded, adding that the Armenians were excitable and litigious but possessed an aptitude for commerce and a spirit of nationality.

According to Wilson, the Armenian movement was dangerous in that it was aimed against the Turkish authorities with an objective to supplant them. He noted that the Porte should be aware of that in realizing the need for quick reforms. The Armenians were disappointed with the British because the conditions of the Cyprus Convention were unfulfilled, but it was not a deeply rooted feeling; they would welcome anybody who would put an end to their constant harassment. According to the Consul, the country could not overcome the crisis or carry out reforms without strong outside pressure.[128]

In a secret report to Major Trotter, dated June 25, Vice Consul Everett divided the Armenian population into three main groups. The first group, to which the largely uneducated peasantry belonged, longed for freedom but was tightly controlled by the priests and unable to carry arms. Yet they all believed that the hour of freedom was near and were waiting for a sign, confining themselves to sending petitions to the clergy and the foreign consuls. The second group, that included the Catholics and government officials, was opposed to extremism and pushed strongly for implementation of the reforms. Finally, the third group, drawn largely from the educated Apostolic Armenian (Gregorian) community, had the intention of liberating their countrymen from oppression, out of patriotic or ambitious motives. Their objective was to arouse the peasant class, and they were allegedly in communication with a 'committee' in Constantinople, and 'committees' in all other regions.

According to Everett, the Armenians were now awaiting some action by Great Britain or other major Powers concerning Armenia's future. They had hopes that autonomy could save the Armenians from oppression and secure the flow of British commerce. At the same time, Armenian activists were preparing the people in the event that European help would not materialize. Everett noted a movement to educate the rural population, with instructors being imported from Constantinople. He maintained that the instructors were in reality political agents of the Central Committee whose objectives were propagation of their ideas, instilling a stronger feeling of patriotism, and formation of alliances with Kurdish chieftains who were equally interested in throwing off the Turkish yoke. Everett noted that the Armenians were likely to provoke disturbances if the European Powers failed to address the Armenian Question in a practical way, so that Russia or another Power intervened. Everett estimated that the Armenian organizations would be ready for this mode of struggle in two years' time.[129]

On June 28, Goschen met with Abeddin Pasha to discuss the Armenian Question and the issue of reforms. The Foreign Minister told Goschen that the Council of Ministers was discussing the demarche of the European Powers, and was studying the demographics of the eastern provinces. Abeddin said that the official Turkish statistics would differ from the numbers provided by the Armenian Patriarch, and proposed forming a commission comprised of two English officers and two Turkish officials to ascertain the exact statistics. Goschen suggested including an Armenian in the commission, but the Foreign Minister objected to the idea, adding that he would prefer to leave out the Turks from the commission too. The Turkish official assured the envoy that the reforms would continue in conjunction with the inquiry, but reiterated the official objection to the idea of an Armenian autonomy since the Armenians were not in a majority in any of the districts.[130]

On June 30, Earl Granville sent a confidential message to Ambassador Goschen informing him of the government's decision not to practice the special supervisory powers reserved to the British consuls under the Cyprus Convention, since they would be in contradiction to Article 61 of the Berlin Treaty. Although the provision of the Cyprus Convention requiring British help in defense of the Asiatic provinces of Turkey against Russia was still acceptable to the new government, the British envoy was instructed to bring pressure on the Sultan with regard to the execution of the conditions of the Berlin Treaty.[131]

On July 1, the acting Vice Consul in Diyarbakir, Thomas Boyadjian presented his draft program of the Armenian reforms in a confidential dispatch to Granville. He noted that the present division of the provinces in Asia Minor was such that none contained a majority Christian population. The nomadic Kurds lived in the mountainous areas while the Armenians lived mostly in the plains. Boyadjian proposed to carve out a new province from the Armenian-populated plains of Erzerum, Van, Bitlis, and Diyarbakir, so that they comprised a majority population. He suggested that a Christian Governor-General should be appointed to the newly created province for a fixed term, with a Muslim Vice Governor; the sub-Governors would be appointed based on the local demographics. Boyadjian noted that the first Governor General should preferably be European since a native Christian might be resented. The Turkish Civil Law should be kept since it was overall acceptable, but a few changes concerning the collection of taxes and tithes were warranted. A strong gendarmerie staffed by Europeans should be established to protect the province from the Kurds and Circassians. The judges should be selected from the Turks and Christians. No more than 15–20% of the tax revenues should be sent to the Sultan's Treasury, with the balance kept for local expenses, public works, and education. Some 50,000 breech-loading rifles distributed by the government to the Kurds should be recalled or confiscated. Boyadjian concluded that strict European supervision was essential for the carrying out of the reforms.[132]

Goschen received the Turkish reply to the collective note from Abeddin Pasha on the morning of July 6. The Porte had apparently concluded that because of dissension among the Powers they represented no serious threat or danger, and essentially submitted a list of empty promises. According to Goschen, the reply was unsatisfactory to the British Government since it had clearly been influenced by the reactionary party at the court and contained no concrete measures. The Porte had established a commission to draft a program of reforms and protection of the Armenian population. The Turkish note contained official statistics on the number of the Armenians in the provinces of Van, Diyarbakir, Bitlis, Erzurum, and Sivas, according to which the Armenians comprised only 17% of the population. But according to the Armenian Patriarchate, the Armenians comprised 42.5% of the population, the Turks 17.4%, and the Kurds 20.7%; Goschen was inclined to dismiss both sets of statistics as unreliable.[133]

Not satisfied with the official reply from the Porte, the British Government continued consultations with the other Powers seeking joint action to pressure the Sultan. On July 15, Goschen presented to Granville a draft of another collective note that was countersigned by the French Ambassador. The Ambassador expressed his concern that without exact population numbers, the Powers would be averse to agreeing on a set of measures since with the Armenians in the minority it would be dangerous to grant them liberties and a charter.[134]

On July 24, Granville communicated to Goschen the Government's approval of the draft collective note. The Foreign Secretary instructed the Ambassador to remove the language protesting delays in execution of the Cyprus Convention conditions, which called for reforms in exchange for security to the Empire, suggesting instead that the subject should be raised during a meeting with the Ottoman officials.[135] On July 29, Granville noted that the demand to hold a census within three months would only delay the beginning of the reforms and suggested that the numbers of Muslim conscripts and the Christians paying a conscription tax should be sufficient for the purpose.[136]

With Granville's suggestions incorporated into the text, Goschen presented his draft to the European envoys. On August 10, Goshen reported to London that the Ambassadors had largely endorsed his draft and guaranteed its approval by their respective capitals. Russian Ambassador Novikov made some suggestions which were accepted by Goschen. The British Ambassador noted that the new note would be a blueprint for the reforms that the Powers found essential for the Porte to carry out. Goschen considered lack of guarantees to be the weak point of the document, and submitted to the Foreign Office a proposal by Consul Wilson for the establishment of a European supervisory commission to assist in the reforms.[137] The Ambassador reported to the Foreign Office on August 31 that this proposal had been endorsed by all the British consuls.[138]

On September 4, Prime Minister Gladstone spoke before the House of Commons on the subject of Turkey, and argued that the times had changed and the Ottoman Empire had to carry out administrative reforms in order to survive intact. The Foreign Secretary told the Members of Parliament that 'for Turkey to continue to exist and justify itself, that country had to honor its international obligations and be able to improve the state of its subject races by just and good laws.'[139] In days following, Gladstone made a number of statements decrying the Sultan's actions, which, nevertheless, failed to make a dent in the policies of the Porte.

Having received the approval of their governments, the Ambassadors of Great Britain, Germany, Russia, Italy, France, and Austria-Hungary presented a collective note to the Porte on September 7. The document stated that the assurances given in the Turkish note of July 5 did not abide by the spirit and letter of Article 61 of the Berlin Treaty; that the commissions sent to the regions to investigate local conditions produced no tangible results; that the consular officers' reports had indicated no reforms in the judiciary nor progress in the establishment of a gendarmerie or improvement in the police. "The language which the Sublime Porte uses in speaking of the crimes alleged to have been committed in the provinces inhabited by the Armenians shows that it refuses to recognize the degree of anarchy which exists in those provinces," the document charged. The European Powers warned of the gravity of a situation that could lead to wholesale destruction of the Christian population in many districts and noted that no serious proposal had been made for stopping the excesses of the Kurdish and Circassian bandits, who could not be restrained by ordinary laws. The Powers urged strong and 'exceptionally rigorous' measures to put an end to the harassment that was a continuing source of danger to the property, honor, and life of the Armenians.[140]

The note admitted the need for reforms in all parts of the Empire but specified the need for immediate action in the Armenian-populated provinces, as provided for in Article 61. If predominance of the Christian population in the provinces was not taken into account, no real reform would be effected. While the Porte argued that the reforms should be made both for the Kurdish and Armenian communities, the collective note suggested that distinctions had to be made between the two ethnic groups, in the view of the settled nature of one and the seminomadic state of the other. The Powers noted "with satisfaction" that the Mayor of each homogenous commune to be established in the provinces was to belong to the religion of the majority, but decried the absence of a similar provision for higher officials as not congruent with the "local requirements" clause of Article 61. The Powers concluded that the Ottoman proposals did not address the existing situation, did not satisfy the needs of that region's inhabitants, and were not based on the two most important principles of equality and decentralization. The Powers urged the organization of census by an independent commission, carrying out prompt reforms to secure the life and property of the Armenians, taking immediate measures against the incursions of the Kurds, implement the proposed system of finance, and give to Governors-General greater security of office and a more extended responsibility. The Powers also urged that the reforms be carried out under their supervision.[141]

The British Government's new position on greater coordination between the Powers on the Armenian Question, it would appear, should have yielded positive results and forced the Sultan's government to implement the reforms in the face of European solidarity. In fact, the Porte submitted a reply to the envoys on October 3 giving vague promises without specific proposals or guarantees, and showed irritation in the language of the note. It contained the following points: (1) the courts in Erzurum, Van, Bitlis, and Diyarbakir provinces would be reformed to provide for the security of the population and law and for order; (2) the government decided to restructure the police and gendarmerie; (3) the gendarmerie commanders would be appointed by the War Ministry and recalled at the suggestion of the local authorities; (4) the rules on formation of communes would have to adhere to the interests of the state, and be promulgated within four months; (5) part of the locally collected tax revenues could be used for local expenses; (6) the judicial appointments in the provinces would follow the existing procedure while the administrative positions would be filled by the Sultan at the suggestion of the Governor; the governors would have the right to dismiss officials with the exception of police and finance officers; and (7) the courts of assizes would be guided by the Imperial criminal law and existing legislation.[142]

The disagreements among the Powers on the one hand and the lack of practical control mechanisms on the other placed British diplomacy in an ambiguous position. On October 21, Goschen requested that Granville advise him on the steps to be taken to further the reforms in Armenia in view of the fact that the Sultan's government was not carrying out its obligations under the Berlin Treaty. Goschen suggested that the Powers had to develop a new political course regarding Turkey.[143]

On October 18, Wilson presented his thoughts on the subject of reforms to the Embassy. Since the British Government found any form of direct control over the Armenian-populated provinces by an outside Power undesirable,

Wilson suggested finding out how far the other Powers were willing to go in demanding a specific set of reforms from the Porte. If the Powers were willing to demand a reform program, it was necessary to draft a law or a statute and present it to the Porte. Wilson noted that the draft could be prepared by either a mixed European-Turkish commission, or, if the situation warranted, solely by a council of European Powers. He proposed basing the draft on the Basic Statute (Réglement Organique) granted to Lebanon, rather than its equivalents in Eastern Rumelia or Crete that defined a different status for those regions. The Lebanese Statute had eighteen articles, which could apply to Armenia. If, on the other hand, the Powers were not ready to demand a specific set of reforms from Turkey, implementing any reform measure would be unlikely, he argued. And the need for reforms that could save the country from anarchy grew by day.[144]

Endorsing the Wilson plan, Trotter noted that the Turkish Government would not tolerate the existence of a semi-independent state in the neighborhood of Russia, its traditional enemy. In his dispatch to the Ambassador, dated October 19, he noted that it was in the interests of humanity to provide, in an expedient manner, for the protection of life and property of the population. The perpetuation of widespread misrule and anarchy would eventually lead to the destruction of the country and inevitably invite Russian intervention, he argued.[145]

On November 9, Clayton reported to Trotter from Van that, according to American missionaries, the Armenian population, 'encouraged and assisted by the Russian Tsar,' had been getting arms and preparing to rise up in revolt against the Turks, while the Kurdish tribes would stage disturbances on the Persian border to divert the attention of the Turkish authorities. Clayton disbelieved the scheme to have gone so far, and he thought the notion of the Kurdish-Armenian collusion to be absurd. He nevertheless wrote that something was definitely going on: the hot-headed young leaders of the Armenian party had been making inflammatory speeches and the people despaired at the delays in the reform process. Clayton was convinced that the Armenians had lost all faith in European help, particularly in British mediation, and pinned their hopes on Russia. He cited reports from the Alashkert region suggesting that Russian-Armenians had been moving ammunition there and forming units among the peasants.[146] Similar reports were cited in Everett's dispatch from Erzurum, dated November 24. He reported that the eastern and southern districts of the province had been affected by a conspiracy to arm the peasants, while the instructors and political agents had been agitating the people to revolt.[147]

Concerned with these reports, Goschen appealed to Granville on November 16, asking him again to take measures addressing the Armenian Question. He suggested that it was the time to ask the Powers to make another attempt to push the reforms forward. If the European nations did not jump on the wagon or limited their participation to 'indifferent support,' the British Government should not hesitate to assume responsibility.[148]

On December 13, Clayton informed Trotter of his meeting with a representative of a recently formed Armenian organization, who had told him that the subject nations of the Ottoman Empire were increasingly convinced that Europe would not do anything for the minorities who did not resort to the use of arms to liberate themselves, and in the event of a Greek-Turkish war would revolt against the Turkish authorities. The Russians, Clayton's interlocutor noted, were willing to assist the Armenians as a buffer against the Muslims, to reunite the two parts of Armenia, grant autonomy to the new entity and defend its borders. Clayton added that similar sentiments had become widespread in the Armenian community, which was now convinced that the European Powers, and Great Britain in particular would not come to its aide. The Armenian representative noted that if Russia were indeed to establish such an autonomous entity, it would be well endowed with natural resources and shrewd people. Yet Clayton warned his visitor to wait and see if Britain and Europe achieved an improvement of their fortunes, but even if it did not happen, the Armenians would be better off preserving the status quo rather than risking everything on such a gamble.[149]

On December 27, Clayton met with Kamsarakan who had recently visited Bitlis, Diyarbakir, Kharput, Erzinjan, Erzurum, and Mush. During their conversation, Kamsarakan denied the allegations that he had stirred up trouble among the Armenian population, and said that on the contrary, he had always urged the Armenians not to revolt since they had no arms or organization and had no chances of success. According to Kamsarakan, the Porte trusted neither the British nor Russian Governments, and instructed the local authorities to report on the activities of the Russian and British consular officers.

Clayton informed Trotter that Russian-Armenians had supposedly infiltrated the region while some 50 thousand volunteers were preparing to cross the frontier in the future. He noted that it was important to pressure the Ottoman Government to implement reforms to address the Armenian grievances and prevent the spread of Russia's influence.[150] He added that he had repeatedly urged the Armenians not to drive themselves into the hands of Russia because Great Britain would soon improve their conditions by ensuring the carrying out of reforms.[151]

In 1881, the British Government made a fresh initiative on the Armenian Question. On January 12, Earl Granville sent a circular to the British Ambassadors asking them to draw the attention of the Powers to the Armenian Question and proposing to submit another collective note protesting the treatment of the Armenian population and non-execution of the provisions of the Berlin Treaty in this regard.[152] The British proposal was rejected out of hand by the French and German Governments on the pretext that it was not appropriate to raise the Armenian Question while the Greek-Turkish boundary issue remained unresolved.[153] Conversely, the Italian and Russian Governments instructed their envoys in the Ottoman Empire to work jointly with other ambassadors and issue a statement on the implementation of reforms for the Armenian population.[154] On February 14, Granville instructed the British Ambassador in Russia to inform the Russian Government of England's intention to accommodate the position of Germany and France and postpone the joint statement.[155]

On February 9, Goschen received a letter from Granville conveying the concern of the British Government over the prevailing state of the Ottoman Empire and the situation of the Christian population, which was seriously threatening the authority of the Sultan. According to the letter, the British Government was convinced that the Sultan had been misinformed of the real state of things in the Eastern provinces. The Ambassador was charged with informing the Sultan of the existing reality and warning the sovereign that his Christian subjects were being driven to extreme steps by their despair. If the Christians had been treated with respect, they would patiently have waited for the Porte to carry out the grand program of reforms but the Christians complained of being scorned and neglected, Granville noted. The Foreign Secretary suggested that real disturbances damaging the authority of the

Sultan were due to occur in the spring of the coming year if the Porte delays its decision to commence real reforms.[156]

In a confidential report to Trotter, dated February 15, Clayton informed the latter he had 'reliable' information that the agents of the Tiflis-based Armenian committees had arrived in Van to carry out agitation among the Armenian population to revolt against the Sultan's government. They had allegedly spread rumors of an imminent crossing of the border by a 150,000-strong Armenian army, with Russian backing. The Russians were said to have sold weapons to the Armenians and would come to their rescue in case of an emergency. The uprising was supposed to start in the autumn, following a pogrom of the Christian subjects by the Kurdish Sheikh Abeydulla.[157] In his report of February 23, Clayton noted that the leaders of the Armenian community did not approve of the idea since they were convinced the Russian Armenians would abandon them in the event of a serious military resistance, and leave the country. The Vice Consul was convinced that the urbanized Armenians would not support the revolt and the rural population would not join the uprising without the leadership of the cities. He, nevertheless, noted that it was difficult to provide for the contingency of a Kurdish revolt in the spring.[158]

On March 5, Biliotti informed Goschen from Trabzon of the alleged activities by the agents of the Russian Armenian societies. He noted that Russian Consul Obermuller had confessed on one occasion that Vice Consul Kamsarakan waged agitation among his Armenian compatriots in Van urging them to revolt against the Sultan. The Russian Consul had supposedly protested such activities, but had been recalled as a result. The new Russian Consul in Trabzon, Belotserkovets, had, according to Biliotti, been noted for his efforts to stir up the Bulgarian revolt during his earlier posting to Rustchuk.

The British Consul was convinced that the Russian Government had been preparing ground for seizing the lands adjacent to its Caucasus province, since the pretexts would be forthcoming. According to Biliotti, the sympathies of the Armenian and Greek communities lay with Russia. Conversely, the Muslims were opposed to Russian domination and would cooperate with the British to establish control over these regions of Anatolia.[159] This ostensibly private observation of a British Consul had in fact served as the de facto British policy guide for decades. Unfairly labeled as having pro-Russian orientation, the Armenian population of Western Armenia in reality desired nothing more than peace, security, and self-governance for itself, as well as a future free of harassment and persecution. Although British public opinion supported the Christian Armenians and criticized the foreign policies of Conservative and Liberal governments toward Turkey, their needs and concerns did not rank high on the priority list of British diplomacy. Thus, the dissolution and gradual elimination of the Armenian presence from the regions adjacent to the Russian border would, indirectly, be in the interests of British policy, as it existed at the time.

Informed of the consular reports of alleged Russian agitation in Western Armenia, Granville instructed Goschen on April 8 to draw the Sultan's attention to the events in those regions and warn, again, of the possibility of revolts in the country with the Armenians appealing for Russian support.[160]

Unhappy over Goschen's ineffective leadership on the Armenian Question, Granville replaced him with Her Majesty's Ambassador in Russia, Lord Frederick Dufferin in late May.[161] Addressing the House of Commons on the anniversary of the 1878 Cyprus Convention, Gladstone said on June 24 that he expected the new Ambassador in Constantinople to use his authority and spare no efforts to solve the Armenian Question, which he said was of paramount importance. A few days after Dufferin's appointment, the representatives of the Armenian community in England wrote a letter to Granville commending Dufferin on his role in establishing a new administration for Lebanon and expressing hope that he would use his experience in creating a similar administrative model for Armenia to address the local needs and provide for the inviolability of life and property, as envisaged by the Treaty of Berlin.[162]

On June 28, the new Ambassador sent a report of his first meeting with the Sultan to Granville. Abdul Hamid expressed an interest in reestablishing amicable relations with Great Britain, Dufferin reported. The British envoy, in turn, asked the Sultan to honor the Treaty of Berlin by effective measures improving the conditions of the Armenian population; a first step of which could be the appointment of non-corrupt and effective governors who could ensure carrying out of reforms. The Turkish sovereign assured Dufferin that he shared this position of the British Government.[163]

On August 1, Dufferin reported to Granville on his meetings with the Sultan and the Grand Vizier, Said Pasha, during which he had raised the

Armenian Question and emphasized the necessity of carrying out the reforms. He admitted his concern that the representations he had made could only be regarded as a tentative effort toward the accomplishment of a very arduous task that would require the conjunction of many favorable circumstances as well as the strenuous assistance of his colleagues. According to the Ambassador, the ongoing trial of Midhat Pasha* and his supporters preoccupied the Sultan to such a degree that it had become an obstacle for the reforms. Also, the envoys of other Powers urged patience until the evacuation of the ceded territory in Greece and the delimitation of the Montenegrin frontier had been completed. The month of Ramadan was on, which prevented serious business from occurring, he observed. Meanwhile, he suggested raising the issue of removing the governors of Diyarbakir and Bayazid at that time.[164]

During his August 22, meeting with Said Pasha, Dufferin raised the issues of the Armenian reforms and the removal of the corrupt, brutal, and inefficient Turkish officials who brought suffering to the Christian and Muslim communities alike. The Ambassador submitted a list compiled by the British consular agents. The Ambassador assured the Grand Vizier that the 'wretched condition' of the Muslim population was of as much concern to the British Government as that of the Christians. He said he had been instructed to urge those reforms upon the Porte in the general interests of the Sultan and of Turkey, not from a desire to expand privileges granted to one of the ecclesiastic factions. The usage of the term 'Armenia,' Dufferin told the Grand Vizier, indicated a geographic not ethnic entity, and he sought to dispel the Turkish misapprehension of British or European plans to establish an Armenian state in the midst of the Ottoman Empire. He noted that unlike the Greeks of Thessalia and the Bulgarians of Eastern Rumelia, the Armenians were not homogeneously agglomerated in one locality but, rather, were disseminated in scattered groups. He added that it would be 'the sheerest folly' for the Porte to refuse them good government and the benefit of equal laws on account of jealousy or fear of Armenian political pretensions of nationhood. Dufferin noted that it was in the interests of the Ottoman Empire to improve the

---

* Midhat Pasha was viewed with suspicion by the Sultan for his role in the 1876 Constitution, and was exiled to Italy. Lured back to Turkey, he was put on trial and sentenced to death. Under Western pressure, the Sultan commuted the death sentence and exiled Midhat Pasha to Arabia, only to have him murdered in 1884.

condition of the Armenians and use their natural intelligence and aptitude for public employment. The British envoy was convinced of a natural affinity between the Turkish and Armenian races, something he did not think existed between the Turks, Slavs, and Greeks. 'If the dominant Turkish race shed the vestiges of religious fanaticism, the Armenians would prove the most potent bulwark of the Sultan's eastern dominions,' Dufferin predicted, adding that if developments progressed in the opposite direction, Great Britain would become 'an indifferent spectator to the rescue of a suffering population from the corrupt and tyrannical rule of the Pashas by a liberating Power,' i.e. Russia. The Ambassador asked Said Pasha to persuade the Sultan to appoint someone of character and distinction as a High Commissioner for Armenia.[165]

Meanwhile, the British Government asked the Powers to clarify their position on the Armenian Question. On August 24, the British Chargé in Russia, Hugh Wyndham informed Granville of his meeting with Russian Foreign Minister Nikolai Giers.[166] The Minister told Wyndham he was convinced the Turks would only yield a point if pressure had been brought upon them by all Powers, whereas they would evade the issue if they determined that even one single Power was hesitant or lukewarm toward a common course of action. The Ambassador was told that Russia would support the British initiative on the Armenian Question.[167]

Two days later, the British Ambassador in Berlin, Lord Ampthill, submitted a report on his meeting with Acting Foreign Minister Busch, who had told him the German Government would not take the initiative in pressing the Armenian Question on the Porte but would instruct its envoy in Turkey to render all possible assistance to the Russian and British initiatives.[168]

On August 29, Dufferin organized a meeting of foreign envoys in Constantinople, where he presented the British position on the Armenian Question, his representations to the Sultan, the Grand Vizier, and the Foreign Minister, and urged working out common approaches and actions in this area. He proposed to convene another ambassadorial meeting to draft another collective note to the Porte. Meanwhile, he suggested that the Powers refrain from raising the Armenian Question while the Greek and Montenegrin problems remained unresolved. He proposed that the Powers insist on an immediate appointment of a High Commissioner, authorized to dismiss Governors and oversee the reforms process and urge the prompt dismissal of the most notorious governors and officials. He promised to furnish to the other envoys a summary of the cruelties, crimes, robberies, and murders committed in the Armenian villages within the previous two years, and the program for reforms prepared by Colonel Wilson and Major Trotter, for subsequent presentation to the Porte.[169]

On August 23, Wilson and Trotter submitted a memorandum to Dufferin, which consisted of the following points:

1.   Introduction of reforms in the Armenian-populated region;

2.   The Armenian-populated region—the country inhabited by the Armenians, in Wilson's parlance—was to include Erzurum, Van, Bitlis, Hakkiari, Kharput, Dersim, and Diyarbakir (minus Malatia district) provinces, as well as Sivas, Kara-Hisar, Tokat districts of the Sivas Province, Marash district of the Aleppo Province, and part of the Sis district of the Adana province;

3.   Appointment of two commissioners for a term of three years to oversee the reforms process, with full executive powers. One of the commissioners should have power over Erzurum, Van, Bitlis, and Hakkiari, and the other over the rest;

4.   Preservation of the existing administrative division (vilayets, sanjaks, cazas, nahies, caries, mahalles);* readjustment of boundaries by the Commissioners in consultation with the Governors and Consul-Generals;

5.   Urging the Sultan to exercise greatest care as to personal character in appointment of the governors; the Sultan's rights to appoint them was unchallenged;

6.   Abolition of the existing Administrative Councils of the provinces and their replacement by Councils-General, comprised of 18 paid members and granted control over the local budget;

7.   Fixed percentage of the collected tax revenue to be submitted to the Imperial Treasury, the rest to be retained for local expenditures under the control of Councils-General;

8.   Abolition of the Administrative Councils of the districts but their retention on the sub-district (caza) level, comprised of 4–6 members;

9.   Reform in the Courts of Law and law procedures, granting magisterial powers to the sub-district mayors and county administrators, establishment of a traveling Courts of Assize, reduction in number of courts and judges,

---

* Turkish terms for the units of administrative division in Anatolia.

simplification of law procedure and reduction of court fees, and employment of a certain number of Christians as officers, clerks, etc.;

10.   Equality of all Ottoman subjects in the eyes of the law, and fair and proportional employment of Christians in the public offices;

11.   Maintaining public order by a police or gendarmerie comprised in proportional numbers of Muslims and Christians;

12.   Prohibition of quartering government officials, soldiers, and officers of police on the villagers, under severe penalty;

13.   Reassessment of land and house property in every village and town by a local official in concert with the village councils;

14.   Appointment of a high-ranking liaison with the nomad Kurds, vested with full magisterial powers of arrest and punishment.[170]

On September 9, Granville informed Dufferin that he had briefed the Queen on the British Embassy's efforts on the Armenian Question, and that she had asked to convey her appreciation of the Mission's work on that issue. The Foreign Secretary added that two issues were to be given priority: first, appointment of an able and honest High Commissioner or Governor with full powers; and second, development of a set scheme for tax revenue disbursement. Granville noted that it would be advisable to appoint a Muslim as High Commissioner, with Christian subordinates and advisers working for him.[171] Also on September 9, the second meeting of the Powers' envoys convened in Constantinople under the auspices of the British Ambassador. Dufferin opened the conference and noted that the previous collective note, dated September 7, 1880, had not been answered by the Porte, which had not taken any steps toward carrying out its obligations under the Treaty of Berlin. He proposed to send another collective note to the Porte, reiterating the demands set forth in the earlier demarche. The British envoy suggested demanding the Sultan to immediately end the anarchy prevalent in the eastern provinces of the Empire and taking steps toward securing the life and property of the Christian subjects. Dufferin proposed that an appointment of an able administrator with full powers in those regions could guarantee the reforms, not unlike the appointment of Fuad Pasha in Syria in 1861. He suggested nominating Mukhtar Pasha or Rauf Pasha to that position, two officials enjoying the respect of both the Porte and the Powers.

The British envoy proceeded to present the memorandum drawn by Wilson and Trotter, as well as an aide-memoir on the crimes committed in Armenia and abuses by the Turkish officials. Dufferin noted the importance of protecting not only the rights of the Armenians and other Christians but also upholding the interests of the Porte; autonomy or semi-independence for those regions should therefore be omitted from the text.

Dufferin's proposals were generally accepted, but Russian Ambassador Novikov and French Ambassador Tissot took exception to the idea of a collective note, suggesting instead conveying the essence of the conference to the Porte verbally. Dufferin argued for presenting his memorandum intact, but his European counterparts disagreed, noting that the time was not 'appropriate.' Based on Dufferin's presentation, a protocol was drawn to assist the Ambassadors in their individual notes-verbale to the Sultan.[172]

On September 15, Dufferin presented the proposal agreed upon with his colleagues to Sultan Abdul Hamid. The Sultan expressed his concern over the conditions in the eastern provinces, admitted the unfortunate "dearth of capable administrators" in Turkey, and promised to carry out the proposals. He thought the idea of appointing a High Commissioner to the eastern vilayets was an 'excellent' one, and assured the Ambassador he would make an appointment within a month, unless distracted by the financial difficulties of the Empire or the events in Egypt.[173]

On October 1, Dufferin organized another conference of the foreign envoys to discuss the Wilson-Trotter memorandum. Russian Ambassador Novikov raised an objection on the ground that pressing for appointment of a High Commissioner might actually weaken the common action, proposing instead to place their hopes upon the administrator himself reorganizing the region under his command. The British Ambassador insisted that no functionary would be invested by the Sultan with the Powers of drafting a constitution for the Armenian provinces; all that could be expected was an appointment of 'an intelligent and humane administrator' who would check corruption and dismiss incompetent officials.

Dufferin's next proposal to be considered was the appointment of two commissioners, on the grounds that the region to be reformed was simply too large for one commissioner to cover, especially in the winter months. Other Ambassadors pointed out the difficulties of finding two capable and trustworthy officials enjoying the confidence of the international community, the Sultan, and his Ministers, as well as the dangers of antipathy occurring between the two. The British Ambassador then proposed moving to a different subject. In the view of the special interests of the British and Russian Governments in the Armenian Question and the presence of their consular officers in the Armenian provinces, the other envoys suggested that Novikov and Dufferin consider the proposals presented at the conference and amend the draft.[174]

A few days later, Novikov told Dufferin during their private meeting that he was concerned that if the meetings of the European Ambassadors on the Armenian question had become known, it might have created an excitement among the Armenian population, leading to a general insurrection. In such an event, Novikov noted, Russia would have to intervene with its troops for the purpose of restoring order and of preventing the Muslim population from taking the advantage of the occasion to "martyrize the Christian population." Dufferin discounted the possibility of an insurrection, adding that the Armenian Patriarch had assured him that the community would preserve a "reserved and orderly" attitude.[175]

Following his conversation with the Sultan, the British Ambassador pressed for another audience with the sovereign to follow up on the issue of a High Commissioner, but the Sultan did not agree to a meeting. On November 9, Dufferin received a written communication from the Sultan without even a reference to his earlier pledge. The message informed the envoy that the Council of Ministers had presented a draft reform program to the Sultan, who had sent it back to the Porte for further modifications; it was to be presented to the Sultan again shortly. As the letter noted, it was essential for the Sultan to think of the future of the country and consider the interests of all his subjects, and so, it was necessary for him to examine the draft program in great detail.[176]

British diplomacy was engaged then in the issue of Zeytoun. On November 15, Dufferin met with Said Pasha to express the British Government's concern over the situation in Zeytoun and presented a memorandum drafted by Consul General Wilson. Said Pasha promised to have the Governor of Marash fired, to appoint the local military commander to that position, and to take steps to relieve the tensions in that region.[177] The Wilson memorandum pointed out that the reforms promised by the Sultan's government since 1879 failed to have materialized, and that it had effectively left the affairs in

Zeytoun to manage themselves. Zeytoun, according to the British Consul, had consequently evolved into a "semi-barbarous and utterly lawless community" with deep factional divisions that fought one another. Wilson urged the necessity of restoring order in the region, calling it a hotbed of Armenian political activity that could spread to other regions as well. He presented a twelve-point program to address the situation.[178]

On November 22, Turkish Foreign Minister Assim Pasha received Novikov and Dufferin, at the latter's initiative. The foreign envoys expressed their concern over the deteriorating conditions of the Armenian population of the empire and demanded that a High Commissioner's appointment be carried out promptly, as promised by the Sultan. The Minister said he would convey the diplomats' message to his sovereign.[179]

Having received no reply from the Sultan, Dufferin sent another note to the Porte on December 3. In this document, he stated the British position and recommendations on the resolution of the Armenian Question, implementation of the reforms, and appointment of a High Commissioner. The note pointed out that the Porte had not carried out its promises of reforms, and the conditions of the Christian population had in fact grown worse. Dufferin asked the Foreign Minister to organize an audience with the Sultan, so that he could remind him of his promises.[180] Enclosing a copy of the note, Dufferin informed Granville that the great difficulty of his task was the 'absolute indifference' of the European nations, and consequently their representatives, to the conditions of Asia Minor. He added that his colleagues in Constantinople, acting out of courtesy, had never refused to make the demarches agreed upon jointly, but the Porte was well aware that none of them had done it in earnest, and never gave more than a passing thought to the subject.[181]

On December 6, Dufferin received a confidential message from Assistant Foreign Minister Artin Dadyan informing him that the Sultan and the Porte were determined to do nothing about the Armenian reforms until after they clarified the German position on the issue. To that purpose, the Sultan had sent one of his confidantes, the young Reshid Bey, as an emissary to Berlin. Dufferin consequently proposed to induce Germany to join with Great Britain in 'honestly pressing' the appointment of a High Commissioner upon the Sultan.[182] Granville immediately instructed the British Ambassador in Berlin,

Lord Ampthill, to lose no opportunity to secure the German Government's cooperation in pressing the Sultan to act.[183]

Ambassador Ampthill, in turn, asked the German Foreign Minister, Count von Hatzfeldt,[184] to raise the question in his discussions with the Turkish emissaries, Reshid Pasha and Ali Nizami, whose official business in Berlin had been to present Kaiser William I with the Turkish Order of Nishani Imtiyaz. On December 8, Hatzfeldt told Ampthill that neither Turkish dignitary had expressed a clear opinion on the Armenian Question. Reshid had said that the Sultan would soon appoint Mukhtar Pasha as High Commissioner while Ali Nizami said that the appointment would not be made as long as British diplomacy was pressuring the Sultan. Hatzfeldt agreed that the Sultan would not concede under the pressure of the European Powers, and should be given more time to make the appointment and carry out reforms on his own.[185] Chancellor Bismarck reiterated this position to the British Ambassador on December 19. He said he agreed with the British goals of a prosperous and progressive Turkey, but he doubted the usefulness of external pressure in trying to reach those objectives, since such pressure would only infuriate the Sultan and make him delay the reforms. Bismarck called for giving the Sultan more time to reflect on the proposals already presented by the European Powers.[186]

British diplomacy, nevertheless, continued to engage the German Government on the Armenian Question. On January 7, 1882, Chancellor Bismarck's son Herbert,[187] who was a high-ranking official in the German Embassy in London, reported to his father on his meeting with Granville. The two discussed the Armenian Question, and Granville said that the Ottoman Empire would inevitably face a sudden and premature collapse if it did not carry out reforms in the Armenian provinces. He proposed that their respective governments cooperate to put off such an unwelcome development. Granville said that the British demands on the Armenian Question were not too substantial: his government was pressing for an appointment of a High Commissioner to investigate the local conditions and right the wrongs, not to advocate autonomy. As long as nothing had been done to address the situation, Granville said, the Russians might be tempted to take advantage of the dissatisfaction of the Christian population of Armenia to promote their own interests in the region.

In turn, Herbert Bismarck replied that the Sultan, incited by his coterie, had clearly displayed 'insurmountable fear' toward the very term "reforms," since he was afraid the reforms in the Armenian-populated provinces would be followed by similar measures in other parts of Asia Minor, as well as Macedonia and Albania, which would amount to the loss of his authority and absolute power.

Granville apparently ignored this remark, since he referred to Bismarck Sr.'s statement that Germany had no direct interests in the Eastern Question. He called on Germany to use its prestige and authority in Constantinople, which he said was great, added to the small pressure that England applied to the Sultan, after which, Granville said, a High Commissioner would undoubtedly be appointed.

Bismarck replied that his father believed it was in the best interests of Great Britain to avoid altogether pressuring the Sultan since it would alienate him and weaken Turkey. If the external pressure led to the Sultan's dethronement or his assassination by a Muslim fanatic, the collapse of the Ottoman Empire, with its undesirable consequences for Great Britain, would be greatly hastened.[188]

Per Granville's instructions, the British Ambassador to Austria-Hungary, Henry Elliot, met with Austro-Hungarian Foreign Minister Count Gustav Kalnoky[189] on December 27, 1881, to clarify the Austrian position on the Armenian Question. Elliot reported that the Austro-Hungarian Government was not interested in getting involved in this issue, was against any form of pressure on the Porte, and shared the German position. The Austro-Hungarian Minister suggested that Russia would not extend a 'warm welcome' to such efforts since Article 61 was in fact aimed against Russia while the proposed measures to alleviate the conditions of the Armenian population did not correspond to its interests. Kalnoky suggested that the real improvements in Armenia depended on appointing capable administrators.[190]

Dufferin, meanwhile, continued his meetings in Constantinople. On December 25 he met with the Ottoman Foreign Minister who assured him that the Porte had neglected the Armenian issue solely on account of postwar frontier and financial difficulties, but was finally in a position to 'double its efforts' to carry out reforms. The Foreign Minister denied that the Sultan had promised to appoint a High Commissioner on the grounds that similar appointments in the Ottoman Empire had historically proved inefficient and, secondly, the winter weather would prevent such an official from traveling in his region. The Minister said the Sultan would announce the appointment only after the reform draft had been prepared. Dufferin expressed his deep disappointment over the news, since the Sultan had promised six months earlier to appoint a High Commissioner within a month, even as the murders and abuses continued unabated.[191]

Four days later, the British Ambassador received the personal Chamberlain to the Sultan, Munir Bey, who carried a message from Abdul Hamid. Reiterating Foreign Minister Assim Pasha's message, Munir Bey added that the Sultan intended to form an Executive Council for Reforms, comprised of high-ranking Turkish officials, to make the decisions to be carried out by the Commissioner and his deputies. Munir Bey also broached the Sultan's idea of carrying out the reforms in all provinces of Anatolia, rather than only to the Armenian-populated provinces. The British Ambassador pointed out that while the desire of the Sultan to secure prosperity and equal conditions for all of his subjects was commendable, the main issue was the difficult conditions of the Armenian population of the eastern provinces, which had been addressed in Article 61.

Munir then accused the British Government of a hostile attitude toward the Porte and the Sultan personally, which he said was revealed by the British position on the Greek, Montenegrin, and Egyptian issues. The Porte was also concerned about the unilateral British position on the Armenian Question, Munir said, since Great Britain had been the only Power pressuring the Porte without giving it the time to seriously work on reform measures. In his note containing the minutes of this meeting, Dufferin concluded that the Porte intended to frustrate, by a policy of delays and procrastination, the benevolent intentions of Article 61 to improve the conditions of the Armenian population.[192]

On January 8, Granville met with the Ottoman Ambassador to Great Britain to discuss the issue of Armenian reforms. Granville pointed out that the British Government had refrained from pressing too hard on the Porte while it had been preoccupied with the issues of Greek and Montenegrin borders but now that the Porte was finally free to work on other issues, the British Government would demand an immediate implementation of the reforms, which were of vital importance to the Empire. At the same time, the British

Government would in no way act to restrict the authority of the Sultan or press a particular package of reform measures, Granville said, and would only recommend, as a first step, appointing a special Commissioner with wide authority in the provinces in question. The Foreign Secretary expressed his dismay and disappointment over the fact that this proposal, agreed upon by the Turkish sovereign several months before that during his meeting with the British envoy, had not been carried out.[193]

Abdul Hamid finally granted an audience to Lord Dufferin on January 14, 1882. The Sultan complained that the Treaty of Berlin had forced him to constitute autonomies and cede territories, and he had had to comply with those painful provisions since the results had been 'definite, simple, and readily appreciated,' unlike the potential consequences of Article 61. The administrative reorganization of the eastern provinces, as provided for in Article 61, called for serious deliberations since the consequences of a wrong decision could be both disastrous and irrevocable. He admitted to having promised an appointment within a month, but had been unable do so because of the difficulty in finding an appropriate candidate. He assured the British envoy that his ministers had been working on a draft program, and a High Commissioner would be appointed after the program had been approved.

Dufferin said British public opinion and Parliament had been much interested in the welfare of the Christian and Armenian subjects of the Porte, and therefore, the Government would appreciate an indication of a definite time frame for the proposed reforms. In fact, he expressed his concern that the existing uncertainty concerning the Sultan's intentions might influence relations between the two countries. The Sultan replied angrily: "As the Sovereign of Turkey I am telling you that it is my intention to implement that program that was submitted to Europe in the Turkish note of October 3. Let the British Government have patience and show confidence in me."

By transmitting this message, Dufferin proposed to give the Porte two to three months, in order to give the Turkish authorities an ample opportunity to show their true intentions. If satisfactory results would not have been obtained by springtime, it would become necessary for Great Britain to devise some effectual means for compelling the Sultan and his advisers to execute the Treaty obligations to protect the Christian and Armenian population.[194]

Meanwhile, Dufferin continued to work with Novikov to advance the

Wilson-Trotter memorandum on reforms measures. On February 9, the reworked and modified draft program was approved by the conference of foreign envoys in Constantinople. According to Dufferin, the program was not a radical one, but would nevertheless lead to marked amelioration in the living conditions of the [Christian] population, by providing for protection of life and property, proper administration of justice, and economic development.[195]

Following approval by the foreign Powers' representatives, the draft was presented to their respective governments. British diplomacy, however, received no replies in February and March from either other Powers or the Porte, and, consequently, sprang to action. In late March, Dufferin asked his colleagues to join in a common action and present the draft to the Sultan's government. However, the foreign envoys, most notably Austro-Hungarian and German representatives, refused to join in on the grounds of having received no specific instructions from their governments.[196]

On April 21, Granville had another meeting with Herbert Bismarck to discuss the Armenian Question. He told Bismarck that the British Government had given ample opportunity to the Sultan to carry out the reforms in Armenia, yet no initiative had been forthcoming. The Sultan had even reneged on his pledge to appoint a Muslim Governor-General for that region. British diplomacy still believed that the implementation of obligations under the Treaty of Berlin would first of all serve to prevent collapse of the Turkish Empire. The Foreign Secretary asked for the cooperation of the German Government and its representative in Constantinople.

Herbert Bismarck replied that the German Government could only try to convince the Sultan that the British counsel on that matter favored the interests of Turkey itself. While admitting a certain degree of German influence in Constantinople, which was useful in preserving the 'general peace,' Bismarck argued that the German Government would be loath to risk losing that influence, which could happen easily and be undesirable.[197]

On May 2, Dufferin informed Granville of local press reports on the appointment of Said Pasha as the Minister for Reforms in European and Asiatic Turkey. Dufferin noted that Said Pasha had served with distinction as Governor of Varna, Larissa, and of the [Aegean] Archipelago, as well as on Baker Pasha's commission in 1880 and, later, as Vizier. The Ambassador, nevertheless, expressed doubts as to the character and abilities of Said Pasha, and said his appointment was an indication of a lack of real and serious intention on the part of the Sultan to embark upon a thorough system of reforms.[198]

The British consuls continued to send dispatches of the difficult conditions of the Armenian population in Western Armenia and the nascent national movement. On April 29, Trotter reported to Dufferin that the Turkish officials' attitude toward the Christian population in the frontier provinces had only hardened after the signing of the Treaty of Berlin because it had given the European Powers a pretext to interfere in Turkish affairs, and the Christians had openly began to appeal for external support.[199] On June 5, Everett sent a dispatch to Trotter informing him of some activities by the Armenian activists in Erzurum, Mush, and Van, laying ground for awakening national feelings in the Armenian community. This movement was reported to be directed from Russian-held Armenia and to enjoy the tacit support of the Russian Government. He added that the idea of liberation from the Turkish yoke with the help of Russia was by that time widespread in Western Armenia, and the appropriate campaign had allegedly been spearheaded by Vice Consul Kamsarakan in Van. Also, the Russian Consul General in Erzurum, Colonel Dennet, was alleged to have told the Armenian community not to count on British support, because the only Power that could assist Armenia was Russia.[200]

The British Government took over Egypt completely in June–September 1882, under the pretext of protecting British lives and investments in the wake of the Egyptian national movement. While formally still a part of the Ottoman Empire, Egypt became a de facto British colony. Consequently, the British Government focused its attention on the Egyptian problem and in an effort to avoid additional points of conflict with the Porte, altogether refrained from any action on the Armenian Question.

On November 13, the British Chargé d'affairés in Constantinople, Hugh Wyndham, reported to Granville that the Sultan had established three commissions to draft programs for the financial, judicial, and administrative reforms. State Council President Akif Pasha chaired the first commission; the second was to be headed by the cleric, Sheikh-Ul-Islam, and the third by Minister for Public Works Hasan Fehmi Pasha. The British envoy reported that a French and three German officials in the employ of the Porte were included in the commissions preparing the financial and administrative reforms. The commissions were to present their drafts to the Council of Ministers, and then to the Sultan for approval.[201]

According to the British Consul in Erzurum, the local Turkish authorities had discovered an Armenian revolutionary group and some 40 Armenians had been arrested by the troops called into the city.* The Consul reported that the arrests continued and almost 700 Armenians were under suspicion.[202] Upon being informed, Wyndham immediately called on the Grand Vizier who confirmed the Consul's reports and said 'certain hostile misdemeanors' had taken place in Erzurum that had been instigated by the Russians. The Chargé noted that the incendiary activities would continue as long as there was no improvement in the conditions of the Christian community. Wyndham said the British Government pursued no gain and had a sincere interest in the welfare of the Empire by constantly urging the implementation of the reforms for its subjects. He said the reforms continued to be ignored by the Sultan's Government. Said Pasha said he did not doubt the sincerity of British intentions and added that only 'internal impediments' had prevented the Government from implementing the reforms. Wyndham interpreted the remark as a reference to the opposition from the Palace to the reforms.[203]

On December 29, Wyndham met with Patriarch Nerses, who assured him of the intentions of the Armenian community to remain under the rule of the Sultan and of his personal determination not to allow the autocratic rule of Russia over the Turkish Armenians. The Patriarch had said he had done everything in his power to persuade the people to remain patient and peaceful and not to give in to revolutionary sentiments. He noted that the current developments were a matter of life or death for the Armenian community, and that compared to the conditions of Western Armenians, the Russian Armenians appeared to be prosperous and free.[204] The Patriarch denied the existence of an insurgency in Erzurum, pointing out that the authorities had been suspicious of the fundraising drive to benefit the Armenian Monastery in Jerusalem.[205] On January 12, 1883, the British Consul in Erzurum reported to the Chargé that the Porte had ordered Governor Mustafa Pasha not to prosecute the detained Armenians and to release them shortly.[206]

On April 5, Granville instructed Dufferin, who had been on vacation, to

---

* The persons arrested by the military belonged to an Armenian clandestine group called "Defenders of the Homeland."

meet with the Sultan upon his return to Constantinople and to raise the issue of Armenian reforms.[207] The Ambassador met with Abdul Hamid on May 10, and had a lengthy discussion on the developments in Armenia and the reform process. Abdul Hamid said granting special privileges to his Armenian subjects had been ruled out, but Dufferin countered by pointing out that no special powers or regions for a particular community had been requested, and the issue was providing for proper and equal conditions for all the peoples and denominations in the Asiatic provinces. The Ambassador said the Armenians would remain loyal to the Sultan if their living conditions were satisfactory and they were granted an opportunity to uphold their national identity, and their historical and cultural legacy. Otherwise, unwelcome developments might occur in that region, and like Bulgaria, Rumelia, Serbia, Bosnia, and Egypt it would fall under Russian influence. The Ambassador reminded Abdul Hamid that under the terms of the 1878 Anglo-Turkish Convention Great Britain was obligated to come to the defense of the Sultan's Asiatic domains from foreign aggression, in return for a guarantee of reforms by the Porte. Dufferin noted that Great Britain might be forced to disavow its guarantee if the situation did not improve. The British Ambassador noted in his dispatch that his warning had caused great discomfort to the Sultan who had said, with some intensity, that he had already ceded the "beautiful province of Cyprus" to England. Dufferin again called for appointment of a High Commissioner arguing that even a slight change of the form of government would be considered a positive development.[208]

On May 16, Ampthill reported from Berlin on his meeting with Prince Bismarck on the Armenian Question. Bismarck had told the Ambassador that Germany would be ready to cooperate with the British Government on a range of international issues, as well as on the Treaty of Berlin, with the exception of the Armenian Question. Bismarck suggested that the Treaty of Berlin had taken 'too much blood' from the Sultan and the constant pressure by the Powers diminished his authority in the eyes of his subjects and weakened his rule. Bismarck argued that in the interests of European peace it was necessary to refrain from revisiting the Eastern Question for some time and not to complicate the situation by raising 'minor issues.' He said the national aspirations of the Armenians could stir the Russian Government into action and even lead to the liberation of Armenia by Russia, after which it would be impossible for any Power to force her to leave Armenia. Ampthill argued that the British Government had not merely pressed the Sultan but, acting in the interests of both the Armenian population and the Porte, worked to improve the conditions in the Armenian-populated provinces for fear that the unbearable situation in that region might induce the Armenians to appeal for Russia's help. Bismarck said he hated humane element in politics, especially if it concerned foreign subjects, and informed Ampthill of the official instructions to the German Ambassador in Turkey to maintain neutrality in the Armenian Question.[209]

According to a report from the British Ambassador in Vienna, dated May 22, the Austro-Hungarian Government followed the German lead on the Armenian Question. Foreign Minister Kalnoky told Ambassador Henry Elliot he did not think it advisable and expedient to irritate the Sultan on the matter of internal administration and endanger the 'returning confidence' in the friendly disposition of Turkey toward Austria-Hungary.[210]

Despite the German and Austro-Hungarian positions, British diplomacy continued to raise the Armenian Question. At the end of June, Chargé Wyndham was informed that a committee comprised of the Grand Vizier, State Council President, Interior and Justice Ministers had presented a draft memorandum on reforms to the Sultan. The draft had the following main provisions: (1) making municipal officials an elected post throughout the Empire; (2) redrawing of provinces in Asia Minor, with each province to be divided into three or four smaller units; and (3) reforming the police and gendarmerie.[211]

On June 28, the Acting Consul in Erzurum, H. C. A. Eyres reported to Wyndham that a number of Armenians had been arrested and charged with sedition and sentenced to various terms of imprisonment, while sixteen had been set free.[212] Forwarding the dispatch to Granville, Wyndham proposed not to intervene in that case in order to avoid prejudicing the Porte against the general issue of the reforms.[213]

Receiving reports of disturbances in Van allegedly caused by the Armenians, Wyndham sent the British Embassy's Dragoman (interpreter) Marinitch to meet with Armenian Patriarch Nerses who said that the local authorities in Van had forced 13 prominent Armenians to sign a petition to the Sultan, demanding, in the name of the whole Armenian community, amelioration of their conditions, equal rights for Christians and Muslims, improvement in police activity, and finding the reform process purposeless. The petition had subsequently been published in the Constantinople newspapers, and caused an outcry from the Armenian community in Van. The information was later confirmed by Acting Consul Eyres on August 26.[214] The Patriarch suggested that the situation in Armenia had begun to deteriorate further since England became actively involved in the Armenian Question and the issue of reforms. Reporting on this comment by the Patriarch, Wyndham suggested to Granville that Great Britain would be unable to exert necessary pressure on the Porte to improve the conditions in the eastern provinces now that not only Germany and Austria-Hungary, but also Russia and France were unwilling to irritate the Sultan.[215]

Dufferin raised the issue of reforms again at the end of November in what would be his last representation on that topic. The pretext was given by the Grand Vizier and the Foreign Minister, who had informed him of Russia's secret military preparation in Tiflis. Ambassador Dufferin told the Turkish officials that as long as the Christian population of the eastern provinces had been a victim of 'horrible misgovernment and injustice' that depopulated their villages, rendered the roads impassable, and impoverished whole provinces, the righteous discontent and disaffection of the Armenian population would afford a temptation and an excuse for Russian aggression.[216]

In 1884–85, the Liberal Government mostly concerned itself with, and was distracted by, the colonial issues in Africa, Central Asia, and Far East, and consequently abandoned the Armenian Question. The Gladstone Ministry's use of the Armenian Question as a pretext for colonial aggrandizement, particularly in Egypt, failed to secure implementation of Article 61 of the Treaty of Berlin in improving the conditions of the Armenian population and carrying out reforms in the Armenian-populated regions under European supervision. The initial British attempts to cooperate and act jointly with other Powers on the Armenian Question were increasingly not reciprocated, while the constant verbal protests to the Porte not only did not help the Armenian community, but also, on the contrary, seemed to have had the opposite effect.

3. British Diplomacy and the Armenian Question in 1885–92

The Conservative Party led by Salisbury returned to power from June 1885 to February 1886, with Salisbury assuming the Foreign Office portfolio. The British Embassy in Constantinople was headed by Minister Plenipotentiary William White.

A chain of events in the Balkans during the mid-1880's shifted the attention of British diplomacy away from the Asian and African colonies. On September 18, 1885, an uprising broke out in Plovdiv, the capital of Eastern Rumelia, which culminated in the recovery of Bulgaria's independence and unification of the two Bulgarian entities, which ran contrary to the provisions of the Treaty of Berlin. Ironically, the Russian Government that had originally supported a unified Bulgaria at the Congress of Berlin not only did not welcome the developments, but it also sent a note of protest to the other Powers. A convention of the envoys of the great Powers met in Constantinople to discuss the Bulgarian crisis. In the face of Russian Tsar Alexander III's unusual (for Russia) stance on Bulgaria, Salisbury did his best to persuade the Sultan not to send troops to Rumelia and conclude a peace treaty with the Prince of Bulgaria. The Turkish-Bulgarian Treaty provided for a nominally divided Bulgaria, with both parts ruled by the same government.[217]

Seeing a good opportunity in the international discussions of the Bulgarian crisis, the London-based Armenian Patriotic Union Chairman, Karapet Hagopian, and thirty-eight prominent members of the British Armenian community lodged an appeal with Salisbury. The letter, dated November 4, asked Salisbury to raise the status of Article 61 at the Ambassador's conference in Constantinople. The Armenian community hoped that the British Government that had "constantly expressed concern and warm sympathy" with the difficult conditions of the Armenian Christians would work in concert with other Powers to secure implementation of the Treaty of Berlin provisions in Armenia. It was noted that a similar appeal was presented to the French authorities by the Armenian community in France.[218]

On November 18, the Foreign Office informed Hagopian that his appeal had been forwarded to the British diplomatic mission in Constantinople for its information, and that the British Government considered it inappropriate to raise the Armenian Question at the conference inasmuch as it had been convened to discuss the situation in Eastern Rumelia only.[219] At the same time, Salisbury instructed White to present proposals on ways to meet the demands of the Armenian subjects of the Sultan if he expected a "practical outcome."[220] On November 26, White replied that the chances for meaning-ful discussions of the Armenian Question were small since the other envoys had indicated they would like to stay focused on the Rumelia crisis.[221]

The Salisbury Cabinet continued until February 1886, followed by Glad-stone who returned to the Prime Minister's Office in July. The Foreign Office portfolio went to Lord Archibald Rosebery,[222] and Edward Thornton was appointed as Ambassador to the Porte.

The only document relating to the reforms in Western Armenia during that period is a dispatch, dated July 6, from the Foreign Office to the British Embassy. Rosebery noted that at that point the Porte was no longer threat-ened by the developments in Eastern Rumelia and the possibility of hostile Greek action. The time was right to draw the attention of the Sultan and his ministers to the necessity of internal reforms, the Foreign Secretary argued, since it was no longer possible to ignore the need to improve the conditions in Turkey's Asiatic domains. According to Rosebery, the Christian popula-tion of those provinces had not created a problem for the government for the duration of the crisis and thus had proven their allegiance to the Sultan, who would be doing right by removing the many administrative shortcomings in those provinces. Rosebery stressed the need to press the reforms in tax-collection and the legal system, appointment of civil officials, protecting the life and property of individuals, and defending the peaceful and industrious population from arbitrary attacks.

On the subject of British-Turkish relations, Lord Rosebery noted that in return for the British support for peace and tranquility of the Ottoman Empire during the last crisis, the Porte should honor its obligations under Article 61 of the Treaty of Berlin. Absence of any serious attempts to carry out reforms, he added, could turn out be a source of real danger to the integrity of the Ottoman Empire, and in times of crises affect the goodwill of the Euro-pean Powers toward Turkey.

The British Government, nonetheless, refrained from presenting a specific program or set of demands to the Porte, or intervening on behalf of a particu-lar region, creed, or minority group. Rosebery noted the British Government's oft-voiced support for the Sultan's pledges to provide equal conditions for the population of the European and Asiatic parts of Turkey.

Rosebery observed that, given the wide interest in Article 61 existing in the

British parliament, the British Government would refrain from publicizing the diplomatic correspondence on that subject on the grounds that it could possibly stir up negative public opinion.. According to the Foreign Secretary, the British public's discontent and dissatisfaction over the issue could be of great assistance to 'a foreign aggression' threatening the territorial integrity of the Ottoman Empire. Preserving those provinces as an integral part of the Ottoman Empire was an important priority for British foreign policy, Rosebery stated.[223]

Meanwhile, Salisbury returned to the Prime Minister's office in July, and on August 24, Thornton reported to the new Foreign Secretary, Stafford Iddesleigh,[224] that following Rosebery's instructions, he had presented a special note to the Porte raising the issue of carrying out the reforms. Said Pasha had expressed his discontent over the note and complained of 'very erroneous policies' adopted by Great Britain that discounted the great difficulty in carrying out the reforms and the steps already taken by the authorities. He had also argued that the British consuls had only reported the shortcomings in the administrative process, omitting the positive developments.

Thornton said he had replied that the recommendations submitted in the note were of a friendly nature and had been meant to spur the strengthening and development of the Ottoman Empire by improvement of internal administration and the full disposal of resources. The British Ambassador urged Said Pasha to study the note in earnest and discuss it at a subsequent meeting. According to Thornton, his sources, including the German Ambassador to the Porte, the Sultan and the Porte had expressed displeasure and concern over the note, and consequently, it was his recommendation, in view of the agitated state of the government, to avoid raising the reforms issue, focusing instead on specific negative cases.[225]

Three days later, Thornton was received by Grand Vizier Kiamil Pasha who informed him that the Sultan had been greatly affected by the "unduly harsh" style of the note. Kiamil Pasha argued that while Turkey was obligated to carry out reforms in the Armenian-populated provinces under Article 61, the Turkish representatives had agreed to do so under duress since the Porte had then been in such dire straits that its representatives would certainly have signed anything presented to them.

Despite this revisionist attitude, the Grand Vizier listed the steps taken by the Ottoman Government since the Berlin Congress: establishment of regular courts throughout the Empire, opening of schools, setting up a police system and crackdown on banditry. Kiamil Pasha assured the British envoy that more measures were in progress. The Grand Vizier then admitted that the Porte had broken its obligation of periodic reports to the Powers on the process of reforms—a mere formality that had to be forgiven, he insisted. He expressed surprise at the fact that, alone among the signatories of the Treaty of Berlin, Great Britain found it necessary to make comments on the reform issues, while other Powers had been content with it.

In turn, Thornton assured Kiamil Pasha that the British Government had had no intent to insult the Sultan, and the note was based on genuine friendly feelings toward Turkey, and would promote the strengthening and development of the Empire. He also expressed satisfaction with the measures taken by the Porte toward the reform process.[226]

During his meeting with Iddesleigh on August 30, the Ottoman envoy in London, Rustem Pasha, denounced Thornton's note presented to the Porte, and the Foreign Secretary effectively disavowed the note saying it had been based on the 'shallow observations' of the previous Ambassador and was presented without the British Government's authorization.[227]

After a long break, British diplomacy returned to the Armenian Question again in early 1888. On February 4, the newly appointed British Ambassador to the Porte, William White[228] informed Salisbury (who had again assumed the Foreign Office portfolio) that during the last two months the Sultan's government had been carrying out a full-fledged campaign to eradicate the perceived threat of Armenian radicalism and to reveal facts of the Armenian conspiracy. In particular, several Armenian suspects had been arrested in Constantinople while the Sultan was said to be contemplating imposing martial law in the Armenian populated provinces. According to the Ambassador, the 'Armenian conspiracy' was pure supposition, taken seriously by certain people inside the Sultan's court.[229] Ambassador White referred to a dispatch he had received from Vice Consul Russel in Van, reporting that the local Armenian population had been terrorized by the Governor; some twenty Armenians had been arrested and houses had been searched without result in search of seditious documents and literature. Russell was convinced that the Turkish Governor's diligence had not been backed by any serious evidence, since he believed the Armenian population had not acted disloyally toward the Ottoman Government or conspired with a 'third country' to liberate itself. The Vice Consul reported he was sure the Armenians still hoped for an implementation of the Berlin Treaty and that many people had counseled patience to the Armenians, but he completely dismissed reports of an Armenian insurgency brewing in Van.[230]

On March 15, Hagopian sent another appeal to Salisbury, noting that the Porte's total and inexplicable disregard for Article 61 of the Treaty of Berlin had created a highly unfavorable situation in Armenia. He described the anti-Armenian policies of the Sultan carried out in recent years, asked that the British Ambassador and Consuls be instructed not to let down Armenian hopes and demand implementation of the reforms of the Porte. The appeal was accompanied by an aide memoire on the arrests of the Armenians in the Ottoman Empire in 1885–88.[231] Forwarding the documents received from the Armenian community in London, Salisbury instructed the Ambassador to prepare a memorandum on this issue and present proposals in a demarche to the Porte.[232]

White replied (in a confidential message dated March 30) that Abdul Hamid's mind linked Armenia with England, and thus, he had become convinced that any Turkish misfortune was due to British intrigues. As the Ambassador put it, there was a group of courtiers close to the Sultan who would jump at any opportunity to poison's his mind against Britain.[233] Acting British Consul A. C. Wratislow from Erzurum reported to White that the Muslim hatred and envy of the Christian population was increasing rather than declining over time, and the opinion that the Christians were engaged in an anti-government insurgency was widespread among the Muslims. In an effort to combat the "conspiracy," even the slightest suspicion sufficed, and a discovery of an historical map, literature, or national songs was usually sufficient ground for an immediate arrest and political charges.[234] Wratislow said he was convinced that the charges had been groundless, and he had not detected any signs of an organized movement among the local Armenians.[235]

On April 30, Ambassador White had an audience with the Sultan and raised the Armenian Question during their discussion. The Sultan referred to the actions of unruly and evil-minded individuals who received proper punishment, and said that the Armenian nation as a whole displayed nobility and could not be viewed with suspicion or be accused or disloyalty. He assured the Ambassador that he loathed only atheists and that he equally respected all creeds, naming the Armenians occupying positions of prominence under him. The Sultan said the Armenian community was divided into three groups: the members of the first wanted to establish an independent nation but were in the minority, the second group, which was larger in numbers, wanted to join Russia, while the majority was merely loyal.[236]

On April 26, Hagopian sent an appeal on behalf of the Armenian Patriotic Union to the Archbishop of Canterbury, the Very Rev. Edward White Benson, asking him to convey the 'Appeal of the Armenians' to Her Majesty the Queen and Her Government. The appeal listed the desperate conditions of the Ottoman-ruled Armenians, called for carrying out the provisions of Article 61 of the Treaty of Berlin. The Archbishop forwarded the petition to Salisbury, adding in his cover letter that the facts were not unfounded and could generate sympathy among the Christian communities in England and overseas.[237] Salisbury wrote back to the Archbishop of Canterbury to inform him Hagopian's letter had been sent to Ambassador White with an instruction to investigate them. He, nevertheless, added that the British efforts to enforce Article 61 would be futile unless the other signatories of the Treaty joined in. Salisbury cautioned that it was not in the interests of the Armenians to raise the issue then, given the situation in the East. He also advised the Archbishop to be sensitive in his reply to Hagopian because the latter had in the past publicized his correspondence with the British officials.[238]

In his May 28, confidential report to Salisbury, White noted that the Armenian Question might at any time lead to an unfortunate turn of events since there had been and continued to be clandestine propaganda and oppressive countermeasures, such as house searches, arrests and exile. The Ambassador wrote that it was impossible to discern the cause and effect relationship and determine if the latter caused the former or vice versa, but it was obvious to him that the propaganda carried out by some Armenians in London and Paris did nothing to quell the existing tensions between the Armenian population and their Muslim rulers and only upset the existing status quo. There were signs of discontent in the Armenian population of Constantinople, even among those occupying positions of prominence, which the Ambassador considered to be truly catastrophic. Conversely, there was a great concern among some patriotic Pashas about the regions near the Russian frontier, and the Ambassador said he had constantly stressed to them the danger of driving the Armenian population to desperation and the need to improve the condition of the Armenian people ruled by the Sultan. White was concerned with the alleged improvement in the living conditions of Russian Armenia, with a marked rise in liberties, education, and other fields—something he feared would affect the sympathies and allegiances of the Turkish-ruled Armenians.[239]

The British public and parliamentarians kept a close watch on Armenian Question-related developments. In July, Sir James Bryce[240] presented a parliamentary inquiry to the House of Commons about the Sultan's government-sponsored plans to resettled Circassians in the Van region. According to an August 2 dispatch from White to Salisbury, the Grand Vizier and the Foreign Minister had explained to him that some 400 Muslim families, whom the Russians had referred to as Daghestanis, voluntarily migrated from Russia and asked to be resettled in the Ottoman Empire. The Sultan's Government decided to resettle them in the provinces of Sivas, Trabzon, and Erzurum.[241] Vice Consul Russell reported to the Ambassador from Van that he had seen no evidence of Muslims being resettled in that province, and the only information he possessed came from the July 23 issue of the Armenian "Arevelk" newspaper.[242]

On September 24, the Archbishop of Canterbury appealed to Salisbury to prevent the Kurdish reprisals against the Christian population of the Ottoman Empire. The American missionaries McLean and Brown reported that since summer of 1887, the Kurdish tribes had waged armed attacks on the Armenian-populated villages near the Ottoman-Persian frontier. According to the missionaries, some 15,000 armed bandits operated in that area, while the Ottoman authorities had completely sealed off the region to prevent any information from reaching Europe.[243] In response to a British inquiry about the incidents, Ambassador Rustem Pasha submitted a memorandum denying the allegations, calling the missionaries charlatans and promising to take measures to have them expelled.[244] Rejecting the Turkish Ambassador's letter, the Archbishop sent another letter to Salisbury on November 19, presenting new facts about the activities of the Kurdish irregulars and asking to instruct the Embassy and the consuls in the field to investigate the reports.[245]

Another wave of public outcry followed the publication of a public appeal by the Armenian Protestants to the Grand Vizier, listing their grievances, including oppression by the Turkish authorities and arrests of community members.[246] The London Missionary Society presented an appeal to the Government on that issue, demanding that the British Government work with the United States and Germany to secure the rights of the Protestant Christians in the Ottoman Empire.[247] On December 10, Salisbury informed Rustem Pasha that the reports by the American missionaries had been confirmed by the British Consul General in Tabriz (Persia), and by two British travelers, and demanded that the Porte should take immediate measures to protect the Armenian Protestants living in that region. He also considered unacceptable the Turkish threats to expel the missionaries from the Empire.[248]

On November 27, Rustem Pasha appealed to Salisbury on behalf of the Ottoman Government to suspend the publication of the Armenian newspaper *Hayastan*, published in London, for provoking dissatisfaction and discontent among the Armenian subjects of the Sultan. The Prime Minister explained that the Government had no right to ban publication of any newspaper for any political reason.[249] Concerned with the potentially negative effects on the Sultan's attitudes toward the Armenians over the actions of the London-based Armenians, the Armenian Patriarch in Constantinople, Khoren Ashikian presented a similar request to Ambassador White in December. While sympathizing with the Patriarch's concerns, Ambassador White explained to him the disposition toward the press existing in Britain, and called on His Eminence to use his influence with the British Armenians to exercise restraint.[250]

As custom required relative to New Year, the British Embassy's Dragoman, Marinitch, called on the Armenian Patriarch on January 13, 1889. The Patriarch said that the Armenian clergy had always been loyal to the Ottoman Government and he would be delighted if the Porte ordered the local authorities in the regions bordering on Russia displayed a conciliatory approach toward the Armenians. Salisbury instructed White to use the private means at his disposal to assist the Armenians and their Patriarch, without resorting to official representations.[251] Nevertheless, having been informed by British Vice Consul George Pollard Devey of the repeated harassment of the Armenian population in Van, Ambassador White instructed one of his staff members, Mr. Sandyson, to draft a memorandum to the Sultan's First Secretary, Sureya Pasha, about the events in Van. The memorandum referred also to anti-Armenian activities by the Police Commission established in Van four years earlier.[252]

On March 29, Salisbury wrote to White informing him of the meeting between Ambassador Rustem Pasha and Foreign Office Undersecretary James Ferguson. The Ambassador again complained about the libelous reports published in Hayastan, as well as about the proceedings in the House of Commons about the Armenian Question. According to Rustem Pasha, the newspaper had claimed that the Sultan's Government had planned to exterminate the Armenian population, and had called for the legalization of polygamy. Rustem Pasha said the Sultan wanted to treat his Armenian subjects fairly but that articles of that nature were damaging to the interests of the Armenians. He added that the Sultan's government had taken concrete steps to curb the Kurdish attacks on the Armenian regions, and the situation there had manifestly improved.

Ferguson said that the British Government refrained from pressuring the Porte too hard on that issue, understanding the Turkish difficulties, although it continued to receive credible reports from those regions indicating that the situation of the Armenian population continued to be precarious. He said that he did not believe that all the reports were accurate but he was afraid that the Armenians did indeed receive unequal treatment, as well as undergoing unnecessary hardship. Ferguson said he was for the establishment of a truly allied relationship between Turkey and England, but the Porte's continuing unwillingness to implement administrative reforms was a major obstacle. The Undersecretary said it was impossible to halt the proceedings in the House as long as the situation of the Armenian population remained unchanged.[253]

On May 25, White informed Salisbury that some unconfirmed reports had reached him about massacres of the Armenian population in the Mush region. According to Dragoman Marinitch, a group of Armenians from the capital and from the regions staged a rally in front of the Patriarchal Residence to protest the anti-Armenian actions of Kurdish tribal leader Musa Bey. According to Marinitch's field reports, Musa Bey was jailed for having oppressed the Armenians, then was released and subsequently sought to exact his revenge on the Armenians by attacking the Armenian villages, stealing their property, raping women, and harassing the Armenian villagers. The Ambassador requested that Salisbury authorize Colonel Chermside to visit the region to investigate the reports.[254] Replying to White's message on May 29, Salisbury said the Government was concerned with the reports and instructed the Ambassador to verify the information, and to present a demarche to the Porte, demanding an improvement in the situation and the taking of steps to protect the population.[255]

On June 15, the Ottoman Foreign Minister met with the British Ambassador and denied the authenticity of the reports. Moreover, he defended the conduct of the local authorities and Musa Bey, and said that the latter was expected to arrive in Constantinople soon.[256] Meanwhile, the Turkish Ambassador in London wrote to Salisbury on June 26 that the reports were nothing but hearsay spread intentionally for political reasons.. He rejected the possibility of according Armenia the same status as Bulgaria since the Armenians were in the minority in the region.[257]

In early August, Ambassador Rustem Pasha handed to Salisbury a telegram signed by more than 131 Armenian residents of Van, who stated that the local Armenian population did not share the same views of the foreign-based Armenian revolutionary organizations because, historically, the Armenians lived better under the Sultan's rule, preserved their language, national identity, and religion, and continued to remain the loyal subjects of the Empire.[258] Vice Consul Devey reported from Van that the telegram was prepared by one Karapet Natanian and his supporters, and was not representative of the general sentiment of the Armenian population of Van. Moreover, some of the people listed as signatories did not in fact sign the proclamation, while some 40 surnames on the list were not local residents at all.[259]

On August 29, the British Consul in Erzurum, Colonel Chermside, reported to White on the results of his fact-finding trip in Van, Bitlis, and Mush. Compared to his previous journey of ten years before, he found the country to be more peaceful, with road safety ensured, and the number of crimes and level of brutality significantly down, excluding the carnage committed by Musa Bey's forces. The Consul noted that the signs of economic crisis, Kurdish attacks, inequality of the Christian and Muslim population, and mismanagement by the local authorities were unmistakable, but, nevertheless, he found the recent newspaper accounts in the European press about the oppression of the Armenian population to be greatly exaggerated and generally unverifiable. Chermside noted that Turkey had not taken any measure to adhere to the demands of the Treaty of Berlin to improve the situation in the Asiatic provinces and to curb the Muslim fanaticism and envy toward the Christians, who enjoyed better living conditions.

As far as the prevailing attitudes of the Armenian population were concerned, Chermside noted that the educated Armenians leaned toward the West and considered themselves alien to Oriental civilization. As for the uneducated part of the population, while they remained nominally loyal to the Ottoman Government, they would support any Christian Power pursuing anti-Turkish policies. Chermside also reported that there were deep-seated historic animosities toward the Muslims and Kurds. Establishment of clandestine groups in Erzurum and other regions, calls for armed struggle, as well as the recent developments in Van and elsewhere showed the extent of the discontent among the Armenian population. Chermside noted with interest that the Armenians treated him like a representative of their own government, did not refrain from meeting with him and spoke of a common enemy, and were consequently puzzled at his discouraging remarks. Chermside concluded that the situation in the eastern provinces was far from the basic requirements for decent living conditions, yet there had been progress in the areas of civil administration and police in the last decade.[260]

On September 14 Chermside noted in his report to White that the proceedings in the House of Commons were based on exaggerated facts, and that Bryce's statement about an all-out Kurdish attack was far from reality. In the opinion of his Armenian deputy, Mr. Boyadjian, the number of armed assaults had decreased significantly compared to the past, and the victims tended to be mostly Muslim Kurds. According to the Consul, the reports of some plans to exterminate the Armenians were untrue, and he singled out the Hayastan newspaper for spreading the rumors.[261]

The British mission followed the trial of Musa Bey that began in Constantinople in November, and reported to the Government periodically. The reports noted several procedural mistakes, the great respect and courtesy accorded to Musa Bey who was released pending trial, and the harassment received by the Armenian victims who had arrived from the provinces. On November 21, the Embassy sent the Porte a strongly worded note listing the mistakes committed during the trial and requesting that the Armenian victims' families be compensated and their safety guaranteed. Despite the British protests, the court cleared Musa Bey of all the charges.[262]

At Salisbury's request, on December 17 Foreign Office Undersecretary Ferguson met with Minas Cheraz, a prominent Armenian community and political activist and editor of L'Arménie, a London-based newspaper. Described by Ferguson as an intelligent and pleasant individual, Cheraz said the Armenians considered Ambassador Rustem Pasha an acceptable candidate for the office of Governor of Erzurum, and said he wanted to meet with him. Cheraz was quoted as saying Rustem Pasha had proved to be a decisive and impartial administrator during his service in Lebanon, and had reportedly attempted to persuade the Grand Vizier to try Musa Bey in earnest since it was of great importance to, and in the interests of, Turkey. As a member of the Armenian delegation at the Treaty of Berlin, Cheraz could claim to speak on behalf of the Armenian people, and said it would have been a mistake to think the Armenians wanted independence or Russian rule. The former would be impossible because of Armenia's weakness while Russian domination would bring misfortune since that country oppressed national identity and religion. While it was natural for the Slavic peoples to look up to Russia, there were no national or religious affinities between the Armenians and the Russians. To prove his point, he referred to the conversion of an Armenian Apostolic church in Kars to Russian Orthodox. According to Cheraz, the Armenians living in Eastern Armenia resented and opposed the Russian authorities. He hoped that in the future, if the Turks left Europe altogether, they would form an Armenian-Turkish joint state in Asia Minor, and said it was unfortunate the Ottoman Government did not want to benefit from the loyalty of the Armenians. He added that the Sultan's blind and fanatic coterie viewed any reform draft as treason and informed the Russian Embassy of any British request or recommendation, since the Russians had always opposed any program to reform the Ottoman Empire.[263]

In February 1890, the newly appointed Consul in Erzurum, Clifford Lloyd, reported to White that the local authorities had recently strengthened the censorship against the Armenian population. Some 30 Armenians had been arrested and charged with possession of unauthorized literature, including Armenian history textbooks published in Venice, a French map listing a geographic entry for Armenia, and even national song scores.[264]

Trying to escape the results of Turkish central government policies, the attacks of the Kurdish gangs, poverty and deprivation, many Armenian households in Alashkert Valley petitioned the government for permission to immigrate to Persia. According to reports sent to White from Erzurum, the number of the Armenian households wishing to immigrate reached 600 in early March, i.e., some 4,500 Armenians intended to leave for Persia. The Persian authorities in the border regions allowed the influx of the Armenians, but the Turkish police prevented the villagers from moving. The Porte sent a commission to investigate the incident, comprised of two Muslims and one Christian, but the Consul had been unable to find out their findings or the instructions sent to the Governor from Constantinople. In late April, after some 200 villagers had left their settlements in Alashkert and moved toward the border, they were intercepted at Bayazid by the Turkish troops and returned forcibly to their native land.[265] On April 6, the Governor of Erzurum told Consul Lloyd that the safety of the Armenians could be guaranteed if the central government put the Turkish troops stationed in various regions of the countries at the disposal of regional governors, to be used against the Kurdish irregulars and gangs. The Consul concluded that only direct orders from the Porte and coordinated actions of the governors could restore law and order in Kurdistan.[266]

According to periodic reports sent by White to the Foreign Office, the Russian Muslims continued to migrate to the Ottoman Empire and were resettled primarily in the central and eastern provinces of Asia Minor. On March 14, White reported that some 50,000 Circassians received the permission of the Tsar's government to move to Turkey, and the Porte made plans for them to resettle in Konya and Adana regions.[267]

The British Government continued to research the ethnic composition of the eastern provinces of Asia Minor. On May 26, White submitted a report on the population of Erzurum, Bitlis, Van, Diyarbakir, and Kharput provinces, based on the data received from the Justice Ministry and Consul Lloyd. The official statistics put the Muslim population at 1,432,075 (the British consular data was 1,233,402), while the number for the Christians was 512,372 (or 566,297 according to the Consul). According to the official statistics, the Muslims comprised the majority in all the vilayets, while Lloyd's data showed that the Christians comprised the majority of the population in Van (155,988 Christians vs. 115,000 Muslims).[268]

On June 20, Lloyd reported to Chargé d'affairés Fane that there had been clashes between the Muslims and Christians in Erzurum. The cause of the incident was the search of the Sanasarian School and St. Mary Armenian Church in the presence of the Governor and government troops. To protest the government actions, the local Armenians closed their shops and schools and cabled an appeal to the Sultan, while several youths resorted to armed self-defense. Consequently, a Muslim mob armed with firearms, sticks, and stones attacked the Armenian district, killing 10 to 12 people and wounding some 300 Armenians. The American and Persian Consulates that were in close proximity to the Armenian district sheltered many town residents, and only after an intervention by the British Consul did the local authorities station troops in the Armenian district. According to Lloyd, the Armenian population of Erzurum was terrorized, and arrests had been made among the Armenians only while the Muslim mob escaped punishment.[269]

On June 27, Rustem Pasha presented to Salisbury an official paper from the Porte, which blamed the Armenian pogrom on the Armenians themselves.[270]

After prior coordination with the French Ambassador, Chargé Fane called on the Grand Vizier to discuss the Erzurum incident. Fane said the situation in Erzurum was seriously dangerous, and could potentially lead to Muslim-Christian clashes all over the Empire. He then presented a set of recommendations worked out by the British, Russian, and French Consuls in Erzurum aimed at restoring order and preventing negative developments. The Consuls proposed to augment the local garrison in Erzurum by a battalion of troops from Erzinjan, release the Armenian detainees and suspend the trials, and organize mounted patrols in Erzurum and surrounding areas to prevent the rumors from reaching other parts of the Empire. Approving of the proposals, the Grand Vizier promised to take measures immediately.[271]

On July 26 Fane reported to Salisbury that despite the promise given by the Grand Vizier, no Armenians had been released from detention yet. The Charge d'affairés asked the Grand Vizier to honor his promise, which he said would help to stabilize the situation. The latter responded that he had not promised to release the Armenians charged with serious offenses but had ordered a halt in the investigation to calm the situation. He had assured the

British envoy that equal punishment would be received by the Muslims as well in connection with the Erzurum events.[272]

Twenty-eight Armenian detainees were released only at the end of September, while the Attorney General was fired for 'prosecution of innocent people.'[273]

Ambassador White who had returned to Constantinople informed the Foreign Office on August 1 that the Armenian Huntchak Party had held a rally in the Kum Kapu district of Constantinople on July 15. He noted that the Armenian population of the capital had been greatly agitated and concerned with the reports flowing in from the eastern provinces, the results of Musa Bey's trial, and the inaction of Patriarch Ashikian. A group of Armenians interrupted the Sunday service at the Church and read a political statement calling on the Patriarch to petition the Sultan on behalf of the Armenians. Patriarch Ashikian was forced to join the demonstration on July 15 and march with the protesters from Kum Kapu toward the Sultan's palace. The police and troops clashed with the protesters, and casualties had been reported from both sides. According to the Ambassador, the authorities had arrested a number of Armenians, stationed troops near the Patriarchal residence, and restored order in Kum Kapu. White noted that this was the first instance of the Christians taking on the Turkish troops in Constantinople since its capture by the Sultan in 1453.[274] In his next dispatch, dated August 21, Ambassador White advised the Foreign Office against intervening on behalf of the arrested Armenians since he had learned from his sources that Sultan Abdul Hamid was leaning against the death penalty in this case and was holding consultations with prominent Armenians in Constantinople.[275]

According to Lloyd, the sufferings of the Armenian population were caused mainly by lack of protection for their lives and property, lack of freedom, and their inequality vis-à-vis the Muslim population. He also noted that some false or unfounded information sometimes published in the West had had the effect of actually worsening the conditions of the Armenian population and neutralizing any gains by Western diplomats toward establishing justice and better government.[276]

Meanwhile, the British public's interest in the Armenian Question continued to remain high, and the number of parliamentary inquiries to the Prime Minister, the Foreign Office, and the British Embassy was also high. In early

August, Undersecretary of State for Foreign Affairs Ferguson told Viscount Bryce that the British Government had never been more concerned with the developments in the Ottoman Empire than it was then. Bryce countered that the British Government viewed the disturbances in Turkey with marked indifference, and predicted that the protests by the Armenian community could potentially lead to bloody persecution, with subsequent Russian intervention in Western Armenia that would be detrimental to the British interests. Bryce noted that the Government should inform the Porte it considered the 1878 Anglo-Turkish Convention as having lapsed owing to the neglect of Turkey in introducing reforms undertaken in that document. Ferguson dismissed the criticism and the proposal, saying the Government made representations when it was sure they would have a positive effect and was taking all the necessary measures to improve the situation in the Ottoman Empire.[277]

On September 8, Colonel Stuart reported to Salisbury from Tabriz that the local Armenian community, which he estimated at 28,000 people, was agitated at the developments in Erzurum and Constantinople. He claimed that the local Armenians were debating formation of an Armenian kingdom comprised of the Russian, Turkish, and Persian Armenian regions. The British Colonel rushed to dispel the chimera of the Armenian state, noting that it was impossible to establish as long as Russia continued to exist. He also noted the dispersion of the Armenian population over a number of regions where they did not comprise a majority. He claimed from his personal travels in the wake of the Russo-Turkish War that the Armenians were in the minority in most Eastern Anatolian provinces with the exception of Kharput.[278]

On October 25, Lloyd reported to White some instances of armed Armenian groups crossing the Russian-Turkish border with intent to defend the Armenian population from bandit attacks. He added that the Russian government confiscated weapons and made arrests in a bid to prevent border infiltration. The Consul met with the Governor of Erzurum, expressing his Government's concern about the incidents, and proposed one more time that the local authorities take measures to protect the Armenian population from the armed incursions by the Kurds and to ensure greater equality between the Muslim and Christian population. The Governor replied that the Turkish authorities had strengthened border controls in the province, and he welcomed the Russian attempts to seal the border.[279]

On January 6, 1891, Salisbury met with Garegin Yesayan, a personal representative of the Catholicos of the Great House of Cilicia, who had arrived in London to transmit the Catholicos's personal appeal to the Archbishop of Canterbury. Yesayan told the Prime Minister that the Turkish authorities' stance toward the Armenian population had worsened and that the Armenians now hoped for Britain's intercession to prevent them from annihilation. Yesayan stressed that the Armenians did not request independence, but merely freedom of religion and good and orderly government. Yesayan said that the Bishop of Zeytoun had been jailed in Marash, government troops had been quartered in his church and Armenian homes, doctors had administered poisonous medicines to children, Armenians had undergone forcible religious conversion, and the Catholicos had been forced to move to Alexandretta to escape by sea in case of imminent danger. Yesayan asked Salisbury to distrust the official Turkish reports and to conduct an independent investigation to verify his facts. Following the meeting, Salisbury, in fact, instructed the British Consul in Aleppo, Thomas Jago, to conduct an inquiry in Zeytoun.[280]

On January 19, White reported to the Foreign Office that due to mediation by the Armenian Patriarch, the Armenian Catholic Legate, and himself, the Sultan had released 76 Armenian prisoners on the occasion of Armenian Christmas. The Ambassador said he had discussed the amnesty with the Grand Vizier on several occasions. The released prisoners gave an oath of fealty to the Patriarch who urged them to be loyal and obedient to the Sultan.[281]

Devey's January 12 memorandum carefully analyzed the publications in the British press about the Armenian Question. He considered the article entitled "Anarchy, Emotion and Disorder in Armenia" in the Daily News to be largely incorrect and misleading. He considered the reports from Igdir published in the September 16 issue of the newspaper, as well as the letter from Minas Cheraz to Gladstone, to be fraudulent. Devey also dismissed as unfounded the newspaper's reports, in its issues of August 20 and December 3, about the desecration of the Armenian Church in Mush, the Armenian pogroms, distribution of arms to the Kurds by the Ottoman authorities, as well as the claims that the "the Turks have decided to completely annihilate the Armenians."[282]

In his reports to Acting Consul Charles S. Hampson in Erzurum (dated January 14 and 31 and February 9), Devey noted that Armenian agitation in the region had reached new levels, and cited instances of attempted extortion from prominent rich Armenians for 'national needs.' The Vice Consul included a list of the Armenians who had received anonymous letters with such demands. Two weeks later, the city authorities arrested several young Armenians who had supposedly been sending those letters. On February 4, more than 100 Armenians, mostly relatives of those detained, staged a rally in Van, which led to more arrests among the Armenian population.[283]

In the winter months of 1891, the Sultan's government began to organize mounted militia, drafted almost exclusively from the Kurdish tribes and dubbed Hamidiye. Some 30 regiments of Hamidiye had been set up, with 33,000 members.[284] The formation of the Kurdish militia by the Sultan's government meant to stem the Armenian national liberation movement,[285] dramatically alter the balance of power and wherever possible, the ethnic composition in the provinces where the reforms had been scheduled to take place, and to serve as a bulwark against the Russian Army in case of renewal of hostilities in the East.

On January 30, Hampson reported to White from Erzurum that the local authorities had been forming mounted militia regiments modeled on the Russian Cossacks and drawn from the Kurdish tribal elements and that the city authorities had interviewed nearly all the tribal chiefs toward that end. According to the report, the arrangement provided for the Kurds to use their own horses while the government would provide them with arms, uniforms, provisions and ammunition. The militia was to hold semi-annual training exercises, and the tribal chiefs would receive military credentials and ranks below that of colonel.[286]

In March, the Sultan invited all the Kurdish tribal chiefs to Constantinople for the celebration of the Selanlik holiday. He received the militia regiment commanders with great honors and ceremonies, presented them with the imperial insignia and regimental banners that carried the number of the regiment and quotations from the Koran.[287] On May 23, British Consul H. Z. Longworth in Trabzon reported to the Ambassador that the Kurdish tribal leaders who had returned from Constantinople aboard the Austrian ship Helios traveled to Erzurum where the Turkish Fourth Army was stationed, to undergo officer training.[288]

The Armenian population's misapprehension about the developments was reported by Hampson in his dispatch to White on February 28. The local

Armenian population saw correctly that the measures had been targeted against the Armenians and provisions of Article 61 because many of the Kurdish militiamen had stated publicly that their purpose was to suppress the Armenians and that they had received assurances from the government that their reprisals against the Armenians would not be prosecuted.[289] Vice Consul Boyadjian reported similar information from Diyarbakir.[290]

On January 31, White reported to Salisbury that he had instructed the Embassy Dragoman to call on the Grand Vizier and present him Hampson's report about the predicament of the Armenian population. The British Embassy official told the Grand Vizier that the Porte had to take positive steps to alleviate the conditions of the Armenian population and appoint able governors and jurists in the Armenian-populated regions.[291]

On February 21, Hampson reported to the Ambassador that despite the Sultan's decree granting amnesty to the Armenian prisoners, the authorities in Erzurum refused to release them and denied the existence of the amnesty.[292] Jago reported from Aleppo on March 20 that 101 Armenian political prisoners were in jail in Adana and Aleppo.[293] According to Hampson, a Hussein Agha achieved notoriety in the Alashkert Valley by robbing, murdering, and jailing innocent Armenians. On March 23, Salisbury instructed the Ambassador to present to the Grand Vizier facts on Hussein Agha's actions and demand an investigation and, if the facts were confirmed, his immediate expulsion from Alashkert.[294] Despite the Grand Vizier's promise to investigate the evidence, Hussein Agha went to Constantinople together with other tribal leaders, met with the Sultan, and returned to Alashkert without hindrance.[295]

On April 13, Boyadjian reported from Trabzon that notions of armed struggle and fighting for freedom gained ground among the local Armenian population. According to the Vice Consul, the Armenians were convinced that Russia, Britain, and France would come to their assistance. Rumors were spread that a 100,000-strong Armenian army would soon come to the rescue of Western Armenia. Boyadjian noted with concern that such rumors spread mostly by young Armenians could lead to dangerous repercussions.[296]

On May 2, Hampson reported that some Armenian families in Erzurum had begun to migrate toward the Russian border while others moved to Constantinople.[297] The reasons for migration were the unjust policies of the authorities and their inequality compared with the Muslim population. For example, the 1875 charter granted the Christians equal rights in appointments to the government offices, courts, police, and public institutions. Nevertheless, the charter was effectively ignored since only three police officers and only two government officials in Erzurum were Christian. The ratio of the Muslim and Christian population in Erzurum was roughly two to one, while the amount of tax revenue from each segment was approximately equal. The law provided for five percent of the tax revenue to be earmarked for school financing but the Christian-run schools did not receive a penny and the Christians were prohibited from attending Muslim schools. According to Hampson, the travel documents were previously issued by the head of the respective community but in practice, the travel documents of the Christians had to be countersigned by the Muslim community leader as well. Hampson cautioned against writing off these practices as minor concerns since the Armenians were extremely sensitive about government injustice and could no longer tolerate persecution. Hampson said he was convinced the Governor was competent enough to prevent disturbances but the situation was close to critical.[298] He reported to the Ambassador on May 23 that despite the reports of an Armenian uprising, he considered such a turn of events highly unlikely and the reports to be unfounded since the Armenians were largely a peaceful people who possessed no arms or able military leaders. Moreover, he said such reports sounded ridiculous to anybody with knowledge of the region, yet the Turkish authorities chose to treat the rumors as highly plausible.[299]

On July 11, Hagopian sent another appeal to Salisbury about the situation in Armenia. Since the German Kaiser was scheduled to visit London soon, Hagopian noted lack of progress on the Sultan's commitments under the Treaty of Berlin and proposed to discuss the situation and possible joint measures with the Kaiser.[300]

The Salisbury Government did not discuss the Armenian Question with the Kaiser and for the remainder of its term did not take any independent steps to alleviate the conditions of the Armenian population. Throughout 1891, Consuls Jago in Aleppo, Hampson in Erzurum, Vice Consuls Boyadjian in Kharput and Devey in Van continued to supply valuable facts and evidence to the Foreign Office on the troubling developments and disturbances in the eastern provinces of the Ottoman Empire, including open harassment, murders, robberies and arrests of the Armenians by the local authorities and Kurdish militia.[301]

On February 24, 1892, the Archbishop of Canterbury addressed a letter to Salisbury asking the British Government to conduct an investigation and press for the release of the jailed Bishop of Zeytoun, Garegin Yesayan, as well as for the reinstatement to office of Archbishop Khoren Nar Bey, who had been charged by the Sultan's government with sedition for his correspondence with a relative in France. Three days later, the Prime Minister instructed Francis Clair Ford,[302] who had just been appointed as Ambassador to the Porte, to investigate the facts cited in the Archbishop's letter.[303]

On March 5, Hampson reported to the Embassy that a number of Armenians had been arrested in Mush for drafting a petition to the Tsar and collecting more than 2,000 signatures. According to Hampson, the arrests led to serious disturbances and casualties, including deaths.[304]

On March 17, Salisbury sent a special circular to Ambassador Ford concerning the situation in the Asiatic provinces. Faced with the unwillingness of its partners in the Treaty of Berlin to take joint measures, the British Government had refrained in recent years from demanding of the Porte to carry out the reforms under Article 61, Salisbury noted. The British Embassy merely drew the attention of the Grand Vizier and the Sultan's ministers to the facts of bad governance and abuses. The Prime Minister instructed the Ambassador to continue this policy and to use every occasion to demand the restoration of the legal rights of the Sultan's Christian subjects, protection for their life and property, and protection from Kurdish attacks, which, he said, were in the best interests of the Turkish Empire and of humanity. Salisbury also noted that the discontent and resentment of the Christian population had a negative effect on the welfare and stability of the Ottoman Empire.[305]

In April-June the British consular agents continued to report on the Armenian political prisoners in various parts of the country. On April 22, Consul Jago reported to Ford that the Armenian Bishop of Zeytoun had received a life sentence, the school instructor a five year sentence, while 23 others were given prison terms. The parish priest was sentenced to death. According to the Consul, the case was to be reviewed by the Constantinople High Court. Informed of the report, Salisbury instructed the Ambassador to follow the case and to send an Embassy official to the court hearing[306]. On June 6, Ford reported to the Foreign Office that the Turkish authorities refused the Embassy official access to the court hearings. The Ambassador met with Foreign Minister Said Pasha to protest the ban and handed him a paper listing the many irregularities that had taken place during the original trial in Aleppo, as reported by the British consular officials. The paper noted that the case was in the focus of the public and the British Government, and expressed the hope for a just review of the case on appeal.[307]

The Armenian Patriotic Union presented another appeal to the Prime Minister on June 10, shortly before the Cabinet resigned. The appeal stated that the British Blue Books (Foreign Office correspondence) and the information supplied to the Union showed that no real reforms had taken place in Armenia, and the Sultan's government did not honor its commitments before its Armenian subjects, Britain, and the European Powers. The appeal stated that it was impossible to imagine the legal or plausible bases such for mass-scale arrests, detention, exiles or other punishment for unfounded charges of conspiracy and high treason. The Armenians wished for a Lebanon-style administrative arrangement guaranteeing their equality, freedom, and security, which would correspond not only to the provisions of the 1878 Treaty of Berlin, the Anglo-Turkish Convention, the 1880 Joint Memorandum of the Ambassadors, but also the Gülhane-Hatte-Sheriff (1839) and Gülhane-Hatte-Hümayun (1856) decrees of the previous Sultans. The appeal noted it was the duty of Britain to solve the Armenian Question since the British Government had in the past saved the Ottoman Empire from hopeless situations on many occasions. The British Government should prevail upon the Porte to change its position and treatment of the Armenian subjects prevalent since 1878 and to carry out the reforms proposed in 1880 by the European envoys in their memorandum. The petition charged that if the Armenians had indeed comprised a minority in the provinces they inhabited, there were no reasons for the Porte to fear an Armenian 'insurgency,' or ban and burn any books on Armenia for carrying words like 'Armenian kingdom or nation,' as well as historical and religious books, and to arrest them for singing folk or patriotic songs, and for describing their plight in correspondence. The only solution for the Armenian Question could be appointment of a Governor General in the Armenian-populated provinces by the European Powers, the authors of the letter noted.[308]

The Patriotic Union never received a reply from the Foreign Office inasmuch as shortly thereafter the Salisbury Government fell and was replaced by the Liberal Party under William Gladstone. During its term in power, 1886–92, the Conservative Government had taken no effective steps to enforce the reforms under the Treaty of Berlin and the Anglo-Turkish Convention although both documents had been created by Salisbury's direct participation. The major factors for British inaction on this issue, as explained by British diplomatic papers, was the unwillingness of other signatories of the Treaty of Berlin to take collective action, and the indifference and exist-ing disagreements among the European Powers, as well as the concern over possible repercussions for the sovereignty and independence of the Sultan. British diplomacy merely collected the facts from its consular agents and only interceded with the Porte on notorious cases. The British Government did not protest the formation of the Hamidiye mounted militia but it realized that besides its primary function of harassing the Armenian population, it also served as a bulwark against possible Russian intervention—a goal shared by England since the Anglo-Turkish convention.

Notes

[1] FO 424 / 72, No. 211, pp. 160–61.

[2] Ibid., p. 161.

[3] FO 424 / 73, No 394, p. 247.

[4] Turkey, No. 51 (1878). Correspondence Respecting Reforms in Asiatic Turkey. London, 1878, pp. 1–4.

[5] Ibid., pp. 4–5.

[6] FO 424 / 73, No. 453, p. 273.

[7] Turkey, No. 53 (1878). Further Correspondence Respecting the Affairs of Turkey. London, 1878, p. 165.

[8] Turkey, No. 54 (1878). Further Correspondence Respecting the Affairs of Turkey. London, 1878, p. 49.

[9] FO 424 / 74, No 281, p. 175.

[10] Turkey, No. 53 (1878). Further Correspondence Respecting the Affairs of Turkey. London, 1878, pp. 201–2.

[11] FO 424 / 74, No. 388, p. 246.

[12] FO 424 / 74, No. 503, p. 322.

[13] Turkey, No. 53 (1878), p. 222.

[14] Turkey, No. 54 (1878), p. 45.

[15] Ibid., p. 124.

[16] Ibid., pp. 187–88.

[17] Ibid., p. 88.

[18] Turkey, No 1 (1880). Correspondence Respecting the Commission sent by the Porte to Inquire into the Condition of the Vilajet of Aleppo. London, 1880, p. 1.

[19] Ibid., p. 4.

[20] Turkey, No. 54 (1878), p. 68.

[21] FO 424 / 76, No. 20, pp. 28–29.

[22] Turkey, No. 51 (1878), pp. 7–8, 12–16.

[23] FO 424 / 76, No 554, pp. 405–7.

[24] Turkey, No. 10 (1879). Correspondence Respecting the Condition of the Population in Asia Minor and Syria. London, 1879, pp. 1–3.

[25] FO 424 / 77, No. 249, pp. 210–11.

[26] Turkey, No. 1 (1880), pp. 6–7.

[27] FO 424 / 79, No. 546 / 1, pp. 474–76.

[28] FO 424 / 79, No. 48, pp. 45–47.

[29] Turkey, No. 10 (1879), pp. 15–17.

[30] Turkey, No. 1 (1880), p. 11.

[31] Ibid., pp. 19–20.

[32] Ibid., pp. 9–10, 20–21.

[33] Ibid., p. 10.

[34] Lobanov-Rostovski, Alexei Borisovich, Prince (1824–1896), Russian diplomat. He served as Counselor (1856–59) and chargé d'affairés at the Russian Embassy in Constantinople (1859–63), Assistant Interior Minister (1867–68), and was appointed Ambassador to the Ottoman Empire (1878–79), to Great Britain (1879–82), to Austria-Hungary (1882–95), to Germany (1895), and Foreign Minister (1895–96).

[35] FO 424 / 80, No. 317, pp. 265–66.

[36] Turkey, No. 1 (1880), pp. 32–34.

[37] Ibid., pp. 28–29.

[38] FO 424 / 82, No. 36 / 1, p. 29; Turkey, No. 10 (1879), pp. 69–70.

[39] FO 424 / 82, No. 36 / 2, p. 30.

[40] FO 424 / 81, No. 520, p. 375.

[41] Turkey, No. 1 (1880), p. 48.

[42] Ibid., p. 30.

[43] Ibid., p. 42.

[44] Turkey, No. 10 (1879), p. 63.

[45] Turkey, No. 1 (1880), pp. 56–57.

[46] FO 424 / 83, No. 399 / 1, pp. 283–84.

[47] FO 424 / 83, No. 527 / 1, p. 390.

[48] FO 424 / 83, No. 660, p. 498.

[49] Turkey, No. 10 (1879), p. 63.

[50] Ibid., pp. 91–93.

[51] Turkey, No. 1 (1880), p. 65.

[52] FO 424 / 84, No. 216 / 1, pp. 282–83.

[53] FO 424 / 84, No. 287, p. 241.

[54] FO 424 / 84, No. 486, pp. 387–88.

[55] Kirakosyan, ed., *Hayastane mijazgayin divanagitutian*, p. 103.

[56] Turkey, No. 10 (1879), p. 105.

[57] The Zeytoun Rebellion of 1877–78 was caused by the increasing tax burden and harassment of the Turkish authorities. Preceding the rebellion were disturbances in Zeytoun in 1872 and again in 1875, during which the residents expelled gendarmerie police from the city and declared themselves independent. The ongoing war with Russia prevented the Porte to suppress the rebellion, but as soon as the war was concluded, the Porte dispatched a large contingent of troops and seized the city quickly. Some 400 rebels led by Prince Papik Enitunian retreated to the nearby mountains to continue to fight. To avoid giving a pretext to an intervention by the European Powers, the Sultan's government began talks with Papik, which resulted in his appointment as Mayor, reduction of the tax burden on the Armenian residents, and release of the Armenian detainees in Zeytoun.

[58] FO 424 / 85, No. 210, p. 116.

[59] Turkey, No. 10 (1879), pp. 106–7.

[60] Ibid., p. 103.

[61] FO 424 / 85, No. 172, p. 95.

[62] Turkey, No. 4 (1880). Correspondence respecting the Condition of the Populations in Asia Minor and Syria. London, 1880, pp. 1–2.

[63] Turkey, No. 10 (1879), p. 118.

[64] Turkey, No. 4, (1880), pp. 3–4.

[65] FO 424 / 85, No. 365 / 1, pp. 206–7.
[66] FO 424 / 85, No. 365 / 4, pp. 208–9.
[67] Turkey, No. 10 (1879), p. 123.
[68] FO 424 / 86, No. 198, pp. 147–48.
[69] Turkey, No. 10 (1879), pp. 124–25.
[70] FO 424 / 86, No. 197, pp. 144–47.
[71] FO 424 / 86, No. 2, p. 1.
[72] FO 424 / 86, No. 11, p. 3.
[73] Turkey, No. 4 (1880), p. 8.
[74] Ibid., p. 28.
[75] Ibid., pp. 15–16.
[76] Ibid., p. 15.
[77] Ibid., p. 27.
[78] Ibid., pp. 107–9.
[79] Ibid., pp. 78–79.
[80] Ibid., p. 100.
[81] Ibid., p. 97.
[82] FO 424 / 87, No. 393, p. 337.
[83] Turkey, No. 4 (1880), p. 85.
[84] Ibid., pp. 90–91.
[85] Ibid., pp. 105–7.
[86] Ibid., p. 120.
[87] Ibid., pp. 118–19.
[88] Ibid., p. 118.
[89] FO 424 / 88, No. 340, p. 253.
[90] FO 424 / 88, No. 427, p. 314.
[91] FO 424 / 89, No. 17, p. 13.
[92] FO 424 / 89, No. 60, p. 56.
[93] FO 424 / 89, No. 71, p. 62.
[94] FO 424 / 89, No. 77, p. 62; No. 99, p. 69.
[95] FO 424 / 89, No. 100, p. 69.
[96] FO 424 / 89, No. 117, p. 80.
[97] FO 424 / 89, No. 133, p. 133.
[98] FO 424 / 89, No. 310, pp. 253–54.
[99] FO 424 / 89, No. 188, pp. 139–40.
[100] FO 424 / 89, No. 268, p. 224.
[101] Turkey, No. 4 (1880), pp. 150–51.
[102] FO 424 / 106, No. 13 / 2, pp. 28–29.
[103] FO 424 / 106, No. 13 / 4, pp. 29–31.
[104] Turkey, No. 4 (1880), pp. 158–60.
[105] FO 424 / 106, No. 47 / 6, p. 90.
[106] FO 424 / 106, No. 123 / 1, p. 247–48.
[107] FO 424 / 106, No. 58, p. 112.
[108] FO 424 / 106, No. 87, p. 203.
[109] FO 424 / 106, No. 94 / 1, pp. 201–2.
[110] FO 424 / 106, No. 91 / 1, p. 195.
[111] FO 424 / 106, No. 81, pp. 174–75.
[112] FO 424 / 106, No. 81 / 1, pp. 175–77.
[113] Turkey, No. 23 (1880). Further Correspondence Respecting the Condition of the Populations in Asia Minor and Syria. London, 1880, pp. 145–46.
[114] Ibid., pp. 146–48.
[115] J. H. Park, British Prime Ministers of the Nine-

teenth Century: Policies and Speeches (New York and London, 1950), p. 286.
[116] Turkey, No. 7 (1880). Correspondence Respecting the Affairs of Turkey. London, 1880, pp. 2–3
[117] Ibid., pp. 4–5.
[118] Ibid., pp. 5–6.
[119] Ibid., p. 7.
[120] Ibid., p. 8.
[121] Ibid., pp. 1–2.
[122] Goschen, George Joachim, later 1st Viscount Goschen (1831–1907), British financier, politician, and diplomat. He was elected to the House of Commons in 1863, and served as First Lord of the Admiralty (1871–74, 1895–1900), Ambassador to the Ottoman Empire (1880–81), and Chancellor of the Exchequer (1886–92).
[123] Turkey, No. 7 (1880). Correspondence Respecting the Affairs of Turkey. London, 1880, pp. 8.
[124] Ibid., pp. 8–12.
[125] Ibid., p. 12.
[126] FO 424 / 99, No. 449 / 2, pp. 231–32.
[127] Turkey, No. 23 (1880), pp. 227–28.
[128] FO 424 / 106, No. 246 / 1, pp. 497–510.
[129] FO 424 / 107, No. 2, pp. 2–4.
[130] Turkey, No. 23 (1880), pp. 248–49.
[131] FO 424 / 106, No. 248, p. 512.
[132] FO 424 / 106, No. 254, pp. 514–15.
[133] FO 424 / 106, No. 273, pp. 549–50.
[134] Turkey, No. 6 (1881). Further Correspondence Respecting the Condition of the Populations in Asia Minor and Syria. London, 1881, pp. 16–17.
[135] FO 424 / 107, No. 14, p. 11.
[136] Turkey, No. 6 (1880), pp. 19–20.
[137] Ibid., pp. 40–41.
[138] Ibid., p. 90.
[139] John Kirakossian, Burzhuakan divanagitutiune yev Hayastane (19-rd dari 80-akan tt.) (Bourgeois diplomacy and Armenia, 1880s)(Yerevan, 1980), pp. 128–29.
[140] Turkey, No. 23 (1880), pp. 279–80.
[141] Ibid., pp. 280–82.
[142] Turkey, No. 6 (1881), pp. 179–80.
[143] FO 424 / 107, No. 167, pp. 292–93.
[144] CAB 37 / 3, No. 858, pp. 16–17.
[145] CAB 37 / 3, No. 866, p. 21.
[146] FO 424 / 107, No. 212, p. 385.
[147] FO 424 / 107, No. 213, pp. 385–86.
[148] CAB 37 / 4, No. 895, p. 23.
[149] FO 424 / 122, No. 32 / 1, pp. 55–56.
[150] FO 424 / 122, No. 35 / 1, pp. 58–59.
[151] FO 424 / 122, No. 35 / 2, pp. 59–60.
[152] FO 424 / 122, No. 5, p. 7.

[153] FO 424 / 122, No. 23, p. 46.

[154] FO 424 / 122, No. 27, 28, p. 52.

[155] FO 424 / 122, No. 33, p. 56.

[156] FO 424 / 122, No. 29, p. 53.

[157] FO 424 / 122, No. 53 / 1, pp. 84–85.

[158] FO 424 / 122, No. 63 / 1, pp. 95–96.

[159] FO 424 / 122, No. 54 / 1, pp. 85–86.

[160] FO 424 / 122, No. 67, p. 100.

[161] Walker, *Armenia*, p. 124; Dufferin, Frederick Temple Hamilton Blackwood, 1st Marquis of Dufferin and Ava, (1826–1902), British politician and diplomat. He served as Governor General of Canada (1872–78), Ambassador to Russia (1879–81), Ambassador to the Ottoman Empire (1881–84), Viceroy of India (1884–88), Ambassador to Italy (1888–91), and Ambassador to France (1891–96).

[162] FO 424 / 123, No. 13 / 1, pp. 17–18.

[163] FO 424 / 123, No. 6, p. 11.

[164] FO 424 / 123, No. 40, p. 66.

[165] FO 424 / 123, No. 75, pp. 119–21.

[166] Giers, Nikolai Karlovich, (1820–1895), Russian diplomat. He received assignments as Minister to Persia (1863), Switzerland (1869), and Sweden (1872), before becoming Assistant Foreign Minister and Chief of Asian Department at the Foreign Ministry. He succeeded Gorchakov as Foreign Minister in 1882 and served until 1895.

[167] FO 424 / 123, No. 77, pp. 124–25.

[168] FO 424/ 123, No. 78, p. 125.

[169] FO 424 / 123, No. 96, p. 142.

[170] FO 424 / 123, No. 105 / 2, pp. 151–53.

[171] FO 424 / 123, No. 101, pp. 144–45.

[172] FO 424 / 123, No. 113, pp. 160–63.

[173] FO 424/ 123, No. 126, p. 176.

[174] FO 424 / 123, No. 151, pp. 203–5.

[175] FO 424 / 123, No. 152, p. 205.

[176] FO 424 / 123, No. 180, pp. 239–40.

[177] FO 424 / 123, No. 195, p. 248.

[178] FO 424 / 123, No. 195 / 1, pp. 248–49.

[179] FO 424 / 123, No. 203, p. 259.

[180] FO 424 / 123, No. 213 / 1, pp. 263–64.

[181] FO 424 / 123, No. 213, pp. 262–63.

[182] FO 424 / 123, No. 215, pp. 264–65.

[183] FO 424 / 123, No. 207, p. 260.

[184] Hatzfeldt-Wildenburg, Paul Melchior, Count (1831–1901), German diplomat. He served as Ambassador to the Ottoman Empire (1879–81), Foreign Minister (1881–85), Ambassador to Great Britain (1885–1901).

[185] FO 424 / 123, No. 218, p. 266.

[186] FO 424 / 123, No. 235, p. 286.

[187] Bismarck, Herbert von, Prince (1849–1904), German diplomat and son of Chancellor Bismarck. He served as State Secretary at the German Foreign Office in 1886–90.

[188] German Diplomatic Documents, 1871–1914, vol. 1 (London, 1928), pp. 157–58.

[189] Kalnoky, Gustav Sigmund, Count (1832–1989), Austro-Hungarian statesman and diplomat. He served as Minister to the Holy See (1871–74), Denmark (1874–80), Russia (1880–81), and Foreign Minister (1881–95).

[190] FO 424 / 132, No. 6, p. 9.

[191] FO 424 / 132, No. 12, pp. 11–12.

[192] Ibid., pp. 12–14.

[193] FO 424 / 132, No. 7, pp. 9–10.

[194] FO 424 / 132, No. 22, pp. 39–41.

[195] FO 424 / 132, No. 37, pp. 50–51.

[196] FO 424 / 132, No. 75, pp. 101–2.

[197] FO 424 / 132, No. 81, p. 115.

[198] FO 424 / 132, No. 89, p. 123.

[199] FO 424 / 132, No. 88 / 3, pp. 121–22.

[200] FO 424 / 132, No. 101 / 1, p. 134.

[201] FO 424 / 132, No. 135, p. 213.

[202] FO 424 / 132, No. 143, p. 219.

[203] FO 424 / 132, No. 147, p. 200.

[204] FO 424 / 140, No. 1, p. 1.

[205] FO 424 / 140, No. 2, p. 2.

[206] FO 424 / 140, No. 9 / 1, p. 9.

[207] FO 424 / 140, No. 17, p. 15.

[208] FO 424 / 140, No. 31, pp. 25–26.

[209] FO 424 / 140, No. 28, pp. 23–24.

[210] FO 424 / 140, No. 36, pp. 29–30.

[211] FO 424 / 140, No. 55, p. 47.

[212] FO 424 / 140, No. 58 / 1, pp. 48–49.

[213] FO 424 / 140, No. 60, pp. 49–50.

[214] FO 424 / 140, No. 68 / 1, p. 62.

[215] FO 424 / 140, No. 62, pp. 54–55.

[216] FO 424 / 140, No. 99, p. 89.

[217] F. A. Rotshteyn, *Mezhdunarodnye otnosheniya v kontse xix veka* (Moscow and Leningrad, 1960), pp. 124–26; *Istoriya diplomatii*, vol. 2, pp. 236–40.

[218] FO 424 / 142, No. 34 / 1, pp. 42–43.

[219] FO 424 / 142, No. 35, p. 43.

[220] FO 424 / 142, No. 36, pp. 43–44.

[221] FO 424 / 142, No. 37, p. 44.

[222] Rosebery, Archibald Philip Primrose, Fifth Earl of, (1847–1929), British Liberal politician and statesman. He served as Lord Privy Seal (1885–86), Foreign Secretary (1886, 1892–94), Prime Minister (1894–95), and Leader of the Liberal Party (1894–95).

[223] FO 424 / 143, No. 13, pp. 16–17.

[224] Iddesleigh, Stafford Henry Northcote, 1st Earl of, (1818–1887), British politician. He served as

President of the Board of Trade (1866), Secretary of State for India (1867), Chancellor of the Exchequer (1874–80), and Foreign Secretary (1886–87).

225 FO 424 / 143, No. 31, pp. 26–27.

226 FO 424 / 143, No. 32, pp. 27–28.

227 FO 424 / 143, No. 29, p. 25.

228 White, William Arthur, Sir (1824–1891), British diplomat. As Minister Plenipotentiary of the British Embassy in Constantinople, he served as chargé d'affairés in 1885–86, and was later appointed Ambassador (1887–91).

229 FO 424 / 145, No. 7, pp. 6–7.

230 FO 424 / 145, No. 7 / 2, p. 8.

231 Turkey, No. 1 (1889). Correspondence Respecting the Condition of the Populations in Asiatic Turkey. 1888–1889. London, 1889, pp. 1–2.

232 Ibid., pp. 4–5.

233 FO 424 / 145, No. 40, p. 37.

234 FO 424 / 145, No. 40 / 1, p. 38; No. 48 / 1, pp. 42–43.

235 Turkey, No. 1 (1889), p. 11.

236 Ibid., p. 10.

237 Ibid., pp. 10–11.

238 Ibid., p. 13.

239 Ibid., p. 15.

240 Bryce, James, 1st Viscount (1838–1922), British statesman, lawyer, and historian. He was a member of Parliament since 1874, and became a Liberal party leader in 1880. He served as Undersecretary of State for Foreign Affairs (1886), President of the Board of Trade (1894–95), Chief Secretary for Ireland (1905–06), Ambassador to the United States (1907–13). He founded the Anglo-Armenian Society in 1876, and Armenian Association of England in 1893, and traveled extensively in Armenia, Caucasus, Smyrna, and Constantinople. Bryce was also a prominent author, and published *Transcaucasia and Ararat* in 1877. He is best known in the United States for his treatise *The American Commonwealth* (1888). Bryce was one of the first Western politicians to respond to the 1915 Armenian Genocide, and was active in forming British-Armenian Red Cross Society and Fund for Relief. In 1916, he published a collection of documents entitled *The Conditions of the Armenians in the Ottoman Empire, 1915–1916*.

241 Turkey, No. 1 (1889), pp. 18–19.

242 Ibid., pp. 22–23.

243 Ibid., pp. 25–26.

244 Ibid., p. 35.

245 FO 424 / 145, No. 102, p. 101.

246 Turkey, No. 1 (1889), pp. 32–33.

247 Ibid., pp. 36–38.

248 Ibid., p. 42.

249 FO 424 / 145, No. 107, p. 106.

250 FO 424 / 145, No. 108, p. 108.

251 FO 424 / 162, No. 11, p. 8.

252 Turkey, No. 1 (1889), pp. 55–56.

253 Ibid., p. 57.

254 Ibid., pp. 64–65.

255 Ibid., p. 63.

256 Ibid., pp. 77–78.

257 Ibid., p. 77.

258 Turkey, No. 1 (1890). Correspondence Respecting the Condition of the Populations in Asiatic Turkey and the Trial of Moussa Bey. London, 1890, pp. 1–2.

259 Ibid., p. 3.

260 Ibid., pp. 17–21.

261 Ibid., pp. 22–23.

262 Ibid., pp. 33–34, 55, 80, 100–104.

263 FO 424 / 162, No. 103, pp. 133–34.

264 Turkey, No. 1 (1890–1891). Correspondence Respecting the Condition of the Population in Asiatic Turkey and the Proceedings in the Case of Moussa Bey. London, 1891, pp. 17, 24.

265 Ibid., pp. 21, 23–25, 36.

266 Ibid., p. 29.

267 Ibid., p. 24.

268 Ibid., pp. 38–40.

269 Ibid., pp. 45–48, 51–53.

270 Ibid., pp. 50–51.

271 Ibid., p. 53.

272 Ibid., pp. 60–61.

273 Ibid., p. 79.

274 Ibid., pp. 62–64.

275 Ibid., p. 66.

276 Ibid., pp. 73, 81.

277 "A Vanishing Treaty," *The Spectator*, 1890, vol. 65, August 9, p. 172.

278 Turkey, No. 1 (1890–1891), pp. 78–79.

279 Ibid., pp. 99–100.

280 FO 424 / 169, No3, p. 4.

281 Turkey, No. 1 (1892). Further Correspondence Respecting the Condition of the Populations in Asiatic Turkey. London, 1892, p. 2.

282 Ibid., pp. 10–12.

283 Ibid., pp. 12–14, 18.

284 Ya. D. Lazarev, *Prichiny bedstviy armyan v Turtsii i otvetstvennost' za razorenie Sasuna* (Tiflis, 1895), p. 27.

285 As Turkish official Ismail Kemal noted in 1920, the Armenian population was the only people of the Empire that promoted the spread of liberal and, in the view of the Sultan, destructive ideas, and therefore constituted a viper that

needed to be crashed in the head. *The Memoirs of Ismail Kemal* (London, 1920), p. 256.

[286] Turkey, No. 1 (1892), p. 16.

[287] Ibid., pp. 19, 37.

[288] Ibid., p. 56.

[289] Ibid., p. 23.

[290] Ibid., p.36.

[291] Ibid., pp. 3–4.

[292] Ibid., pp. 39–40.

[293] Ibid., p. 42.

[294] Ibid., p. 25.

[295] Ibid., p. 37.

[296] Ibid., p. 47.

[297] Ibid., p. 45.

[298] Ibid., pp. 46–47.

[299] Ibid., pp. 56–57.

[300] FO 424 / 169, No. 71, p. 82.

[301] Turkey, No. 1 (1892), pp. 61–62, 65, 67, 68–69, 75–76, 78–81, 107–8, 109–11.

[302] Ford, Francis Claire, British diplomat. He served as Minister to Spain (1887–1892), Ambassador to the Ottoman Empire (1892–93), and Ambassador to Italy (1893–98).

[303] Turkey, No. 3 (1896). Correspondence Relating to the Asiatic Provinces of Turkey. 1892–1893. London, 1896, p. 6.

[304] Ibid., p. 9.

[305] Ibid., p. 8.

[306] Ibid., p. 19.

[307] FO 424 / 172, No. 52 / 1, pp. 37–38.

[308] FO 424 / 172, No. 54, pp. 41–43.

Chapter 4. The British Government's Policies before and during the Near Eastern Crisis of the 1890s

1. The Gladstone Cabinet and the Armenian Question, 1892–94

The liberal circles in Great Britain and in other European nations regard William Gladstone as a great statesman who defended and sympathized with small and oppressed peoples around the world. This is also the view, by and large, of the British historians. The reality is that Gladstone certainly espoused these causes when he was in the Loyal Opposition but was constrained in his actions while in power. In 1890, he called on the ruling Conservative Government to warn the Porte that failure to adhere to the terms of the Anglo-Turkish Convention could give rise to a dire situation and serious consequences.[1] A well-known researcher and public figure, Emil Dillon,[2] noted that the Liberal leader demanded to allow the Russian Government to resolve the Armenian Question in the interests of Christianity, morality, and humanity, based on that country's geographic position, amicable disposition and civilizing mission.[3]

In his speeches, Gladstone constantly referred to the Treaty of Paris by which the signatory powers had undertaken to protect the territorial integrity of the Ottoman Empire while assuming a responsibility for its internal affairs. A biographer of Gladstone, Paul Knapland, argued that Gladstone was following closely, and was concerned with, the situation in Armenia in the early 1890's, and believed that only joint action by the Powers could improve the conditions of the Armenians. Gladstone's position on the Turkish reforms was to push for local autonomy and the appointment of "honest and able" governors.[4]

Gladstone's final tenure in office coincided with the period during which the ground was prepared by the Sultan's authorities for the massacres of the Armenian population. In 1892, the Porte officially banned the operation of all schools it had not authorized. Another decision limited civil service appointment only to those Empire subjects who had graduated from state-sponsored, i.e., Muslim, schools. After declaring a war on the Christian schools, the Sultan's government proceeded to 'destroy and exterminate' all non-Muslim literature. Banned were such English classics as Shakespeare, Byron, Milton, Scott, while entire passages from the Holy Scriptures that referred to persecutions, courage, freedom, rights, unity, equality, arms, heroism, massacres, and oppression, and other similar terms were completely excised. Two books entitled *Defence* and *Hamidyie Leaders* were published in Constantinople in 1886 and 1892 respectively, that attacked Christianity and the Christian population of the Empire. These books, as well as other anti-Christian literature were given widespread distribution and, combined with the venomous articles in the Turkish-language press in the capital, played an important role in inciting Muslim fundamentalism to radicalism and in preparation for the Armenian massacres.[5]

Thus, it became clear that instead of tackling the deep political, socioeconomic, and ethnic issues accounting for the difficult state of the Armenian population, the Sultan's government had instead decided to foment religious hatred and incite Muslim fundamentalism against the Armenian Christians.

On June 22, the new British Consul in Erzurum, R. W. Graves, informed Ambassador Ford of the swearing-in ceremony of the newly conscripted members of the Hamidiye Kurdish Cavalry, led by the 4th Army Commander, General Zeki Pasha. According to the Consul, Abdul Hamid's special decree had been read to the troops, and followed by a military parade, with the regular troops followed by 1500 Kurdish cavalrymen armed with Martini and Berdan rifles. Zeki Pasha had received a similar parade in Van on June 10. He announced that the government had formed 40 Kurdish military units comprised of 20,000 cavalrymen, to be officered by 40 colonels and 150 captains from the Turkish regular armed forces.[6]

The Gladstone government continued the Conservative Party's policies toward the Ottoman Empire, neglecting the radical changes taking place in the Ottoman Empire and the increasingly intense anti-Armenian actions of the Sultan's government. In response to Minas Cherazi's letter to the Foreign Secretary, dated October 17, Undersecretary Philip Currie[7] wrote that Rosebery did not find it expedient to take joint action with other signatories of the Berlin Treaty to press for its implementation. According to Currie, the British

Embassy and the Ambassador had been instructed to ask the Porte to intervene immediately in case of the persecution or harassment of the Armenian population by the local authorities. Rosebery was convinced that under the circumstances, this policy would be more effective than empty formal declarations.[8]

On November 11, Sultan Abdul Hamid invited Ambassador Ford for an audience and announced an upcoming program of reforms in the Empire's Asiatic provinces. The Sultan told the Ambassador he had sent trusted officials to the Armenian-populated provinces more than one year before who had made a thorough study of the country and presented a comprehensive report on their findings; the reforms would be based on this report. The Sultan said he intended to send a special commission to the regions empowered to reform the gendarmerie and judiciary and remove all legal obstacles promoting injustice. Abdul Hamid assured Ford of his sincere desire to provide for the "welfare and happiness" of all his subjects and thus rid himself of the foreign criticism of his internal policies.[9] On November 16, Rosebery instructed Ford to convey to the Sultan the congratulations of the British Government on his decision to carry out reforms that would 'strengthen the Empire and provide for the welfare of all his subjects.'[10]

Abdul Hamid not only reneged on this solemn promise to the British Government, but he also took advantage of the events taking place in 1893 to further implement his anti-Armenian program. On January 19, 1893, posters and banners containing criticism of the Sultan were found posted on the walls of official buildings and in public places in such cities as Amasia, Marzvan, Chorum, Tokat, Yuzgat, Angora, Diyarbakir, and Sivas. One of the posters called for the abdication of the Sultan on the grounds of his inability to rule the Empire and solve the problems of the country. The incident was immediately used as a pretext by the authorities to escalate the campaign against the Armenian population. In all those cities, Armenian houses were searched and mass arrests made. According to British Consul Longworth in Trabzon, the local government arrested more than 300 Armenians in Amasia on one day alone.[11]

Even at this juncture it would have obvious to a careful observer that the incident had been prepared and carried out by government agents to incite anti-Armenian feelings among the Muslim population and to damage the image of the Armenian population—allegedly caught plotting against the central authority—in the eyes of the European nations and public opinion.[12]

On February 26, Ford reported to Rosebery that the Governor of Sivas had accused the administration of the American College of Marzvan of complicity in distributing the anti-government flyers and had ordered arrests of the Armenian instructors there, Messrs. Thoumayan and Kayayan; another 2,000 Armenians had been detained in the province already. A few days later, the building housing the young women's school was burned to the ground.[13] Consul Longworth reported that the arson had been committed by the Deputy Commander of the Sivas gendarmerie.[14]

Meanwhile, the British Vice-Consul in Angora reported to Acting Consul General Wrench that some 50 to 60 Armenians had been detained in the city following widespread house searches,[15] while Acting Consul General Fitzmaurice reported from Erzurum that Italian Joseppe Goliti had been arrested in Erzinjan and charged with abetting Armenian revolutionaries. The Governor of Erzurum explained that the central government in Constantinople had issued instructions to detain any foreigner with possible ties to the revolutionary movement. Fitzmaurice noted that such government actions clearly violated the recognized rights of foreign citizens under the international treaties.[16]

On March 26 Ford met with Foreign Minister Said Pasha to discuss the 'inadequate' conditions of the Armenian-populated regions of the Empire. The Ambassador quoted various sources in noting that there had been numerous instances of inhuman and unjust treatment of the Christian communities of Asia Minor, and warned the Minister of dire consequences for Turkey if appropriate measures were not taken to curb the oppressive policies. Ford told Said Pasha the recent developments left a dismal impression on the British public and the members of the Parliament who had presented petitions to the Government.

Said Pasha challenged the authenticity of the British newspaper reports but did not deny that arrests had been made in the Armenian community which he said reflected the government's policy of swift response to those developments. The Minister promised to submit to the British Embassy an English language version of the comprehensive report by Angora's Governor.

Ambassador Ford then proposed that British Military Attaché Colonel

Chermside, who was well acquainted with the country and spoke Turkish, be sent to the eastern provinces with the mission of presenting an unbiased report on the local conditions there, which Ford said could be useful to the Sultan's government. Said Pasha promised to raise the issue with the Grand Vizier but was apprehensive of the proposal that he said could inspire the Armenians to hope anew for a foreign intervention and consequently assist the "insurrection." Ford disputed the Foreign Minister's assessment, noting that, as he had said, the Military Attaché would only investigate and report the developments and facts rather than deal with the issues relating to the status of the Armenian population. Ford also reminded the Foreign Minister of the Sultan's earlier promise to send a plenipotentiary commission to the eastern provinces to carry out reforms.

In his report to Rosebery, Ford concluded that the Turkish Government, while realizing the severity of the conditions of the Armenian population, also wanted to take measures to prevent the spread of the de facto existing revolutionary movement.[17]

On March 31, Ford informed Rosebery that American College of Marzvan instructors Thoumayan and Kayayan, as well as 800 other Armenians charged with sedition, had been transferred to Angora for their trial. A few days later, Said Pasha told Ford that the Sultan pardoned most Armenian detainees from Kayseri, Yuzgat, and Marzvan but the main organizers of the conspiracy would have to stand trial.[18]

Of particular importance is Ford's secret dispatch to Rosebery, dated April 7, which confirmed the Sultan's determination not to carry out reforms and resolve the situation by brutal and oppressive methods, notwithstanding the opposition of the Great Powers. Citing a confidential and trusted source, the Ambassador reported on the April 5 meeting between Abdul Hamid II and his Deputy Foreign Minister Artin Dadyan Pasha. The Sultan accused prominent Armenians, including government officials in Constantinople, of fomenting disorder and raising the Armenian Question in the British Parliament through the foreign-based Armenian committees. Artin Dadyan Pasha categorically denied the culpability of the capital's Armenian community and told the Sultan the only recipe for solving the crisis was the formation of a mixed commission to investigate the situation in the country and carry out necessary reforms. The Sultan was quoted as replying he had not the slightest intention of empowering such a commission since it would only complicate the situation and give pretext to the foreign Powers to intervene. Abdul Hamid said he wanted to govern the country on his own and would not stand any Power's intervention even if disorder and massacres broke out. He told Artin Dadyan Pasha to warn other prominent Armenians that he would hold them responsible if the situation deteriorated. Artin Dadyan Pasha, recognizing the possible consequences of the Sultan's fanatical diatribes, asked him to show mercy to his Christian subjects.[19]

On April 10, Ford suggested to Rosebery that Chermside's trip be delayed since the proposal had already achieved a positive result in having the Sultan pardon the Armenians arrested in connection with the Marzvan incident. The Ambassador asked for permission to authorize Consul Graves of Erzurum, who had been visiting in Constantinople, to visit several cities on his trip back, including Angora, Yuzgat, Kayseri, Sivas, Kharput, Diyarbakir, and present a comprehensive report on the 'Armenian movement and the Turkish methods of oppression.'[20]

The arson of the Marzvan College building and arrest of the college instructors led to consultations between British and American diplomatic officials. The American political establishment and public followed the Armenian developments with great interest, and American diplomacy viewed the Armenian Question as a means of applying pressure on the Sultan to improve the conditions of the Christian population in the Empire. During that period, the White House and the Senate spent more time debating the Armenian Question than they did on the Venezuelan affair.[21] Although the Near East was far from the focus of U.S. foreign policy in the latter half of the 19th century, the presence of American missionaries[22] in that region was significant and guaranteed the attention of the Christian Churches and affiliated organizations on the Armenian Question and the conditions of the Christian communities in the Ottoman Empire. The American missionaries worked with the Christian communities primarily, proselytizing, distributing literature, founding churches, schools, and hospitals,[23] and cultivating cultural, charitable, and commercial relations with the Christian subjects of the Empire. The Christian population viewed the United States as a distant great country that sent teachers, benefactors, and doctors to their communities. Some 12,500 Armenians immigrated to the United States in 1891–98, mostly under the auspices of the American missionary organizations.[24]

While recognizing the importance of the United States as one of its main trading partners, the Sultan's Government viewed the missionary activities with suspicion. U.S. exports to Turkey included industrial and agricultural equipment, machines, etc., including more than 2000 ploughs annually.[25] Turkish exports to the U.S. reached 7 million dollars in 1900, and included leather, fur, rugs, fruits, plants, etc.[26]

In his 1893 Annual Message to the Congress, President S. Grover Cleveland addressed U.S.–Turkish relations, including the Marzvan College arson incident. He decried "…the apparent indifference of the Turkish Government to the outrage, notwithstanding the complicity of some of its officials," demanded to punish the perpetrators, and compensate the colleges for the damages sustained. The U.S. President informed the Congress that he had instructed the U.S. Ambassador in Turkey to demand of the Porte that U.S. citizens of Armenian descent residing in Turkey be treated with proper respect.[27]

In early April, the British Embassy sent numerous dispatches to the Foreign Office reporting on the U.S.–Ottoman negotiations concerning the Marzvan College arson. Finally, the Turkish Government agreed to compensate for the damages to the building and provide security to the college, as well as to prosecute the perpetrators.[28] As for the Armenian instructors of the school, Turkish Ambassador Rustem Pasha told Rosebery that the investigation had found Thoumayan to be the main author of the anti-government flyers and that he would soon be prosecuted, a reality that was accepted by the U.S. diplomatic mission and the College, according to Rustem Pasha.[29] On May 6, Vice Consul T. Newton reported to Ford from Angora that all the necessary documentation for the trial had already been brought from Marzvan. According to Newton, the investigation allegedly concluded that Thoumayan had engaged in seditious activities and visited 15 villages on behalf of his cause.[30] The court panel—comprised of two Turkish Muslims, an Armenian Apostolic and an Armenian Catholic—would soon take up the case of Thoumayan, Kayayan, and 51 other Armenians charged with sedition. Newton, who maintained he had established a close relationship with the Governor of Angora, said he would be allowed to monitor the progress of the court hearings, and had already met with one of the defendants. Interviewed by the Vice Consul, the defendant told him unequivocally he was a socialist and had traveled from Athens to Mersin to Kayseri where he had been arrested. The accused said he did not recognize the Ottoman Government or its laws. According to Newton, the defendant's behavior was frank and calm, and he did not hide his socialist views, which, he said, were shared by the majority of the detainees. The British Vice Consul concluded that those defendants would constitute a danger to the country if they were released.[31]

Arriving in Angora in early May, Graves met with Governor Abeddin Pasha and sent the minutes of his meeting to Ambassador Ford. He said there was undoubtedly a generally widespread feeling of discontent among the Armenian population, centered in Marzvan. The arrested Armenians had supposedly testified that the movement had been financed and led by the Armenian committees based in Athens, Geneva, Marseilles, and London, which had sent a number of 'paid agitators' to Central Anatolia who in turn had recruited numerous young hot-headed 'individuals of lower classes.' The Turkish authorities became aware of the existence of the conspiracy from the rumor mill, and got the names of those involved from Armenian informers. The Angora Governor told Graves the Armenian insurgents committed a number of violent crimes, including attacks on telegraph posts, murders of the Armenian informers, and the authorities moved in to crack down on the conspiracy after the flyers had been distributed. Graves reported that it was not unlikely that many innocent people had been among those detained, but they had by then been released under the terms of the Sultan's amnesty. Graves concluded that Abeddin Pasha did not exaggerate the scope of the conspiracy and spoke against the unnecessarily brutal methods of suppressing it, but said that it was an important lesson for the future. The Governor ridiculed the conspirators who "played revolution like a group of schoolchildren" while their leaders watched from the safety of their foreign exile.

Graves then met with one of the defendants, the Huntchak Party activist Anton Rshtuni, who told him that the intention of his comrades had been to create disorders and draw the attention of the world to their problem, with the subsequent intervention by the foreign Powers. Thoumayan, meanwhile, told Consul Graves that the authorities had falsely charged him, mistaking him for his cousin Artin Thoumayan, who he said was a leader of a clandestine group.

On behalf of the British Government, Graves asked Abeddin Pasha to treat the defendant with justice and impartiality since the public in Britain and other European nations paid close attention to the Ottoman developments.[32]

On May 24, Graves reported to Ford about his meeting with Khalil Bey, Governor of Sivas. The Governor assured the British envoy that the Armenians had indeed engaged in seditious activity that, while not directly dangerous to the state, could potentially contribute to the development of animosity toward the Armenian community. The Governor said that the community would suffer the most from Armenian insurgency, although the enemies of Turkey would use it against the Porte. The Turkish official said that the ringleaders of the insurgency, i.e., the American college instructors, must be punished more severely than their followers, who had been misled. He said that despite the appeals from the foreign Powers, Thoumayan and Kayayan would be punished severely. Graves replied that the British Government did not take a position on the trial other than urging that the trial be conducted fairly and impartially. The Governor complained about the U.S. Consul in Sivas, saying that on this issue, he did not wish to cooperate with the Turkish authorities.

Graves's report concluded by saying there had been a real sense of danger among the Armenian population while the recent murders of the government-paid Armenian informers indicated that the authorities had been largely unable to control the situation and combat 'a well-organized and strong clandestine movement.' According to the Consul, rather than expressing nationalist or patriotic motivations, the actions of the Armenian revolutionaries were more of a nihilist and destructive nature.[33]

On June 16, British Chargé Arthur Nicolson[34] informed Rosebery that Thoumayan, Kayayan and thirteen other co-conspirators had been found guilty and sentenced to death, 29 more had been sentenced to various terms ranging from 2 to 15 years, and the rest had been released. The British Chargé asked for instructions on whether to request an amnesty for the prisoners. Rosebery replied that the British Government was concerned with the developments that he said had left a dismal impression on British public opinion, and suggested studying thoroughly the court's findings and the judicial process prior to submitting a request for amnesty to the Porte. The Chargé d'affaires reported the following day that normally, regional courts' death sentences were subject to review by the Constantinople Court of Appeals, but in the case of the Angora Special court the regular procedure would not apply.

Rosebery noted that some reports indicated that the testimony given by the defendants contradicted the court's finding and the verdict. If the review of the trial resulted in such a conclusion, it was the duty of the British mission to demand that the defendants be set free, Rosebery suggested. He instructed Nicolson to inform the Porte of the strong reaction the trial had generated in Britain and ask for a judicial review of the trial by the Court of Appeals.[35]

On June 20, Nicolson met with the Grand Vizier to discuss the British position on the Angora trial and request that the defendants be pardoned. He told the Ottoman official that the trial had generated huge negative publicity in Britain, European countries, and the United States, and could contribute to the development of even deeper anti-Turkish opinion if the Sultan did not retract the action. The Grand Vizier said the final decision belonged to the Constantinople Court of Appeals, and the British Chargé said he hoped that the American College instructors would be pardoned which would serve Turkey's interests.

Nicolson also met with Foreign Minister Said Pasha who promised to do everything possible to maintain the 'best of relations' between the Ottoman and British Empires. He said that the Sultan could issue a special decree in case the Court of Appeals upholds the Angora court's verdict. Consequently, the British Chargé recommended to the Foreign Office that no written demarche be presented to the Porte pending the decision of the Court of Appeals.[36]

Artin Dadyan Pasha, whom Nicolson met the same day, was more forthcoming than the Grand Vizier and the Foreign Minister on the issue of the Angora trial. He could hardly contain his dissatisfaction with the court's verdict and said some among the Sultan's advisers pressed for carrying out the death penalty and ignoring the European Powers' demands. Artin Dadyan Pasha said he was convinced the Sultan would ultimately pardon the convicted instructors but said it would be best if he made the decision on his own rather than under the pressure from without. Nicolson asked Artin Dadyan Pasha to urge the Sultan to reverse the death sentence, noting that the main British political parties were unanimous on this issue.[37]

Having studied the Angora court proceedings forwarded to him by Vice Consul Newton, Rosebery cabled Nicolson on June 27 that in view of the lack of any incriminating evidence against Thoumayan and Kayayan presented during the trial, the British Government would demand their pardon by the Sultan. The British Government, the Foreign Secretary noted, was disappointed with the course and outcome of the trial and could not try to contain the general discontent it generated in Britain.[38] Reiterating this view during his meeting with Rustem Pasha two days later, Rosebery urged that the Porte waste no time in pardoning and releasing the college instructors.[39]

On June 29, Nicolson met with the Foreign Minister and Grand Vizier to present the British position on the Angora trial. The Foreign Minister said it would take the Court of Appeals several days to review the lower court's proceedings, which had arrived only recently, and protested what he labeled religious intolerance in Britain over the recent developments. Nicolson said the existing 'intolerance' was for injustice and urged the Turkish officials to take swift measures to pacify the situation.

Responding to the Grand Vizier's question about the causes for the British public's interest in Turkey's internal affairs, Nicolson said it flowed out of the obligations toward the Ottoman Christian subjects, as spelled out in the Treaty of Berlin. When the Grand Vizier suggested that the Court of Appeals could uphold the Angora court verdict, Nicolson said it would then fall to the Sultan to pardon the defendants whose guilt had not been proven during the unfair trial. The Grand Vizier protested that it would be impossible to release the defendants and offered as an alternative reducing their sentence, but Nicolson continued to insist that the British Government and public would not be content with a mere reduction in their sentences.[40]

On June 30, Nicolson sent a confidential dispatch to Rosebery conveying Said Pasha's 'friendly request' that the British government curb the anti-Turkish propaganda in Britain since the Sultan intended to pardon the defendants but could not be perceived to have done so under external pressure.[41] A few days later the Grand Vizier and the Foreign Minister informed the British Embassy that the Court of Appeals had upheld the Angora court verdict but the Sultan nevertheless intended to issue a pardon and exile Thoumayan and Kayayan from the Ottoman Empire. Expressing his relief, Nicolson said in a report to Rosebery that he hoped the Porte would reduce the sentences of other defendants as well.[42]

Under pressure from the British Embassy, the Sultan's government did indeed reduce the sentences for many of the defendants, but five of them, who had been charged with complicity in murders, were hanged in Angora on August 1.[43]

On August 2, members of the House of Commons rose to protest what they labeled the 'criminal policy' of the Ottoman authorities toward their Armenian subjects. Several MP's requested information from the Foreign Office on the condition of the Armenian detainees. In his official reply to the MP's inquiries, Undersecretary Edward Grey[44] noted that despite interventions by the British diplomatic mission, five defendants had been hanged, while the rest had had their sentences reduced and their condition was, overall, satisfactory.[45]

On September 5, the Grand Vizier told Nicolson during their meeting that he was concerned with what he described as a marked change in British attitudes toward Turkey. He cited the attacks on the Sultan in the press and the prevailing public opinion, which he said should have no interest in Turkish internal affairs. Nicolson responded that the attitudes were shared by all major political parties in Britain, and the recipe for addressing the situation was in the hands of the Porte; the Sultan's government had had only to carry out real and serious reforms in the provinces and clean the local governments of corrupt officials. The British public, in the absence of such measures, would remain convinced that the rights of the Christians in the Empire were being violated.

The Grand Vizier agreed with the view that the situation in Kurdistan was to a certain degree ungovernable but added that the reforms could not be carried out overnight. He said that there had been significant progress in the previous two years, and it was unfair for civilized Western nations to judge the Oriental ones by their own standards.

In turn, Nicolson pointed out that the British public was incensed because when in the past Muslim or Kurdish gangs had carried out killings of the Christians nobody had been punished while now the Turkish authorities summarily penalized 'an Armenian uttering a hot-headed word' or a group of Armenians gathered to discuss possible reforms. He added that the Armenian revolutionary movement was 'childish and irrelevant' and suggested releasing and exiling the remaining convicts.[46]

Upon his return to Constantinople, Ambassador Ford had an audience with Abdul Hamid on October 13. The discussion was limited almost exclusively to the Armenian Question. The Sultan charged the British Government with assisting the Anglo-Armenian Association in London. Rejecting the Sultan's accusations, Ambassador Ford said that the welfare of the Armenian Christian population was not a matter that could fail to interest the British people, since the Christians did not always receive a fair and proper treatment in the Ottoman Empire. He also denied that Britain sought to establish preferential conditions for the Christians vis-à-vis Turks in Asia Minor, since that was impossible, given the demographics in the region: 13 million Turks and 1 million Christians, according to the Ambassador. Therefore, the solution to the Armenian Question was good government and equal justice for Christians and Muslims alike.

The Sultan said that the discontent among the Armenian population was not widespread or general, and indeed there were many Armenians occupying positions of eminence in the capital. He said that discontented Armenian émigrés incited their ethnic brethren against him.

The Ambassador urged the Sultan to appoint new reform-minded governors, like Angoran Governor Abeddin Pasha, to prevent new disorders from breaking out. The Sultan promised to consult with the British Government on the Armenian Question if it, in its turn, would not encourage Armenian political agents 'to discredit him and his Government.'[47]

Consul Cumberbatch reported from Angora in November 1893–February 1894 about the months of disorders in the wake of the 'Armenian movement' trials there. The Consul's reports were based on information furnished by the local authorities about the disturbances by the Armenian population, but Cumberbatch pointed out in one of his reports that given the ethnic composition in the region (ten Turks for one Armenian) the motives of the Armenian rebels could be explained by the oppressive government methods. The disturbances in question concerned incidents in widely different areas—unrelated murders and the distribution of leaflets containing anti-Sultan propaganda. The leaflets claimed that the movement was aimed against the Government rather than the Muslim population because the Government oppressed the Muslims and Christians equally. The most serious events occurred in Yuzgat in December 1893 and February 1894, when, following the public gathering at the Armenian Church and the murder of a policeman at an Armenian house, the local population clashed with the police. Eventually, the Government introduced martial law in Yuzgat province to suppress the rebellion and formed a government commission to investigate the events there.[48]

On February 14, 1894, the newly appointed British Ambassador, Sir Philip Currie, met with Russian Ambassador Alexander Nelidov[49] to discuss the Armenian Question. Nelidov said the Armenian Question was a very serious issue and of importance to Russia in view of the fact that Armenians lived in his country. He said the Armenian movement was split into two parts: some were demanding to implement reforms, while others were preparing to revolt. Nelidov added that the Russian Embassy had recently appealed to the Porte to carry out reforms, but had expressed no sympathy for the cause of revolution. Currie said that the British Embassy had also made numerous representations to the Porte and had found it nearly impossible to achieve any results, adding that the most important part was to secure the appointment of good governors. Ambassador Nelidov agreed to cooperate with his British counterpart in pressuring the Sultan's government on this issue.[50]

On March 7 Ambassador Currie had a lengthy—and in his opinion cordial—discussion with the Grand Vizier. Currie told the Vizier that Anglo-Turkish relations, that had been intimate and friendly for so long, had lately become less so and the distrust could deepen. He proposed a frank exchange of opinions to address the problem and added that while both sides had their faults 'the British Government's policies and actions had not been treated with the same consideration than those of other nations,' and that the British actions and motives had been deliberately misrepresented and misunderstood.

The Grand Vizier said he was satisfied with economic and commercial ties between Turkey and Britain. He then raised three issues of contention in their bilateral relations: the Egyptian Question, the British media position, and the Armenian Question.

Currie told the Vizier that the British takeover of Egypt was not detrimental to the Porte's interest and could have positive consequences for the Ottoman Empire, since the Arab movement in that country was distinctly anti-Turkish and separatist. Once the British troops were removed from Egypt, that province would secede and be irrevocably lost to Turkey. The Grand Vizier said only that such a position was not illogical. As far as the British press was concerned, Currie said the Government was really unable to exert influence over it and that a solution could be for the Porte to take actions favorably perceived by the press and affecting the overall attitude toward the Porte.

The Grand Vizier said that some segments of the British public exerted a bad influence by clearly encouraging the Armenian movement, which he said greatly saddened the Sultan's government. The positive resolution of all three issues, he continued, would preserve and further strengthen Anglo-Turkish friendship, which was of great importance to Turkey.[51]

Meanwhile, the aged William Gladstone, now 85, resigned from the Office of Prime Minister and stepped down as the leader of the Liberal Party, passing on his portfolio to Rosebery. The Foreign Office papers show unequivocally that during Gladstone's last two years in office, his government had not come forward with any substantial initiative to press the Porte for implementation of reforms and improvement in the condition of the Armenian population. The only significant action during this period, the successful British intervention in the Marzvan incident, came as a result of public pressure and in response to American policy.

2. The Rosebery Cabinet's Reaction to the 1894 Massacre in Sasun and the May 1895 Reforms Program

On March 5, 1894, Lord Rosebery assumed the leadership of the shattered Liberal Party and therefore, also the Prime Minister's position. The Rosebery Government lasted until June 21, 1895, and is better known for its imperialist designs and policies. Rosebery, a wealthy scion of a prominent British family and son-in-law of banker Nathan Rothschild, had major business interests in South Africa and was a proponent of African colonization. It was during his term that the vested colonial interests began to affect the government's policy both in South Africa and the Near East.

Despite the personal popularity of the new Prime Minister, the political situation in Great Britain was far from stable. Assuming office at 10 Downing Street, Rosebery informed the Queen that Her Government was dependent on an unstable majority in the House and could fall at any moment. The European Powers and the Ottoman Empire likewise expected the new Government to change shortly, with ramifications for its foreign policy, and exploited the situation accordingly.[52]

Rosebery and his Foreign Secretary, John Kimberley[53] did not have a predetermined policy on the Ottoman Empire while the British Ambassador in Constantinople, Philip Currie, was appointed shortly before the change of government and was still navigating the vagaries of Constantinople politics. So, the Rosebery Government merely continued its predecessor's policy on Turkey and the Armenian Question, which was to resort to joint action with the European Powers if a crisis broke out again in the Ottoman Empire.[54]

The British Embassy and consular officers continued to report on the Armenian Question and the actions of Ottoman authorities, providing the Foreign Office with in-depth information on the local developments. In his March 23 report to Ambassador Currie, Consul Graves informed the Foreign Office of the recent events in Erzinjan where some 35 Armenians had been arrested and charged with sedition by the local authorities. The Consul noted that it was highly unlikely that the Armenian population, which comprised a small minority in the region, had arisen in rebellion, but the detained Armenians had been accused of carrying arms and of having links with the revolutionaries. Graves suggested that the most likely effect of the Armenian revolutionary agitation was to provoke the Turks to commit massacres, which would draw the attention of the European Powers.[55]

On March 28, Currie forwarded a confidential analysis of the Armenian movement to the Foreign Office. According to the document, the movement was not deeply rooted among the Armenian population and was spearheaded by the Russia-based Armenians who had penetrated the Ottoman Empire in 1892, following a decision made by a mass meeting in Kars. People from all walks of life and with different intellectual abilities comprised the movement, and the rank and file members usually did not know the identity of their leaders. The document claimed that the vast majority of the Armenian subjects were indifferent toward the movement. Most people had turned down offers to join those groups condemned the revolutionary methods; moreover, there was little hope or sympathy for the goals of the movement. The movement was comprised primarily of poorly informed people or those with an elementary education. Consequently, the Turkish authorities began to view with suspicion the American missionaries engaging in educational activities, charging them with responsibility for the increase in revolutionary activities. Government officials had frequently expressed the sentiment that the thoughtless spread of education had negatively affected the mentality of the Oriental people.

The document noted some troubling trends that could lead the conservative majority of the Armenian population to oppose the government and bring the Armenians to the brink of insurgency. The destabilizing trends had been caused by a number of factors, chief among them (1) tight control established by the Turkish Government over internal politics, based on Muslim standards; (2) inability of the authorities to differentiate between harmless criticism and active sedition; (3) random arrests and torture practiced by the authorities as investigation and prosecution tools; and (4) hiring informers and provoking conflicts among the Armenian religious communities, as for example, the analytical paper noted, the case in Marzvan where the Armenian protestant community had signed a memorandum agreeing to cooperate with the local authorities.[56]

In response to the analysis and another report by Currie about the death sentences passed on the 15 Armenians arrested in Yuzgat, Kimberley instructed the Ambassador to express to the Porte the concern of the British Government over these developments and draw the attention of the Sultan to the need for avoiding unnecessary reprisals and indiscriminate punishment.[57]

Meeting with Rustem Pasha on April 4 and April 18, Lord Kimberley cited numerous instances of the arrest of innocent Armenians by the local authorities in Turkey and urged the Turkish Government to observe legal procedure, refrain from summary punishment, and treat the Armenian subjects with greater fairness. The Turkish Ambassador said that the goal of the Armenian movement was an insurgency and denied that the Armenians were religiously persecuted.[58] On April 29, Currie told the Grand Vizier that carrying out death sentences against the Armenians arrested in Yuzgat would provoke a public outcry in England and urged the Turkish Government to take conciliatory steps to alleviate the Armenian concerns.[59]

On June 21, Currie reported to the Foreign Office that the Armenian revolutionary committee (that is, the Huntchak Party) had sent letters to all the Armenian churches in Constantinople threatening to punish the priests who mentioned the name of Patriarch Ashikian during the religions services. The Ambassador explained that Patriarch Ashikian had already stepped down but his resignation announcement had been put on hold pending nomination of the new Patriarch. According to the Ambassador, the gendarmerie promised to protect the parish priests and had urged Patriarch Ashikian to ignore the death threats.[60] The authorities consequently carried out mass arrests of Armenians in the capital. In a letter to Currie, Huntchak leader Aramyan claimed responsibility for the letter and asked the British Ambassador to intercede with the authorities to release the innocent detainees. The leader of the Huntchaks noted that only lawful measures and carrying out the just demands of the Armenian people would head off the threat of revolution in the Empire. A copy of the letter had been sent also to the Grand Vizier.[61]

On July 10, the Sultan's Chief Secretary met with British Dragoman Block to transmit to him the Sultan's views on the Egyptian, Balkan, and Armenian Questions, as well as on Turkish-Persian relations and asked for the British Government's comments. The Sultan's Secretary noted that the Armenians worked to create the image in Europe of Turkey as a barbaric country. The Armenians offended the Muslim faith, incited the people against the government and charged the authorities with having malicious goals, the Secretary complained. He added that the Armenians enlisted the support of the European media in their attempts to reach their final goals.[62]

The words and sentiments expressed by the Sultan's emissary were nothing but a final warning to the British Government before the Armenian massacres were to be carried out in an organized manner. It is obvious from the Sultan's request that he viewed with suspicion the Armenian people in general, not only revolutionary committees or individuals, and branded all Armenians 'criminals.' And he served notice that the punishment for those 'criminals' who offended Islam and incited people would be forthcoming.

Five days later, Kimberley instructed Currie to respond to the Sultan's proposal. He authorized the Ambassador to discuss with the Porte any proposal that would contribute to the final settlement of the Egyptian Question. As far as the Balkans were concerned, the Ambassador was told to assure the Sultan of the British Government's commitment to maintain amicable relations with Turkey and support the Sultan's determination to bring security and prosperity to his domains. The British Government offered the use of its good offices to establish the best possible relations between Persia and Turkey and resolve the border disputes.

As for the recent developments in Asiatic Turkey, the British Ambassador was instructed to tell the Porte that the only safe and successful method to prevent disturbances was to adopt a just and conciliatory approach toward the Armenian subjects of the Sultan. 'British sympathy and partnership with the Ottoman Empire would only expand' if the Porte adopted such policy, Kimberley noted. The Ambassador was also told to assure the Sultan that the British Government would never support a rebellion against his rule.[63]

Yet, the Turkish response was not what the Foreign Office hoped for. Having received British assurances of lack of support and encouragement for the Armenian movement and convinced that the Armenian population had increasingly become a threat to the security and integrity of the Ottoman Empire, the Sultan's government began to organize massacres of the Armenian population.

The local authorities organized a massacre of the Armenian population in Sasun, Bitlis Province, between August 12 and September 10. Kurdish Chief Hussein Bey's detachments had attacked the Armenian community in Sasun as far back as June 1893. Although the authorities had arrested Hussein Bey and exiled him to Erzurum for his role in the 1893 events, he had been quickly released and invited to Constantinople, presented with a medal by the Sultan, granted the title of Pasha and given the military rank of general.[64]

The pretext for the August 1894 massacre was created by the local authorities, which had assessed an additional tax on the Armenian population of Sasun. The Armenian community refused to pay, because of the damages caused by the constant attacks by the Kurdish irregulars. The Turkish authorities labeled the action as insurgency, and regular Turkish troops, gendarmerie, and Kurdish irregulars under the command of Bitlis Governor Tahsin Pasha besieged Sasun. The Turkish military attack was repulsed by the people of Sasun. Receiving reports of an Armenian uprising, the Sultan flew into a rage and ordered the brutal suppression of the Armenians.[65]

On September 3, Currie reported to Kimberley that the Grand Vizier had ordered 4th Army Commander Zeki Pasha to deploy to Sasun from Erzinjan to restore 'law and order.' Graves reported that three Kurdish cavalry regiments under Tahsin Pasha's command were to join the 4th Army at Mush.[66] Currie sent a demarche to the Grand Vizier protesting the use of Kurdish paramilitary units in putting down the uprising. He reminded the Vizier of the public outcry generated in Europe by the deployment of paramilitary units in Bulgaria, and 'the great misfortunes' it caused the Turkish Government. The

Ambassador urged the Grand Vizier to prevent a recurrence of similar events and forbid Tahsin Pasha's participation in the Sasun operation.[67]

The Grand Vizier replied that the Kurdish units had been deployed in Mush to strengthen the local garrison since the Armenian uprising had been expected to spread from Sasun to neighboring regions. He assured Currie that the Hamidiye units were not disorganized and were staffed by Turkish military officers, not unlike the Russian Cossacks. The Grand Vizier claimed to have issued an order to Zeki Pasha to prevent disturbances.[68]

The Sultan's government had successfully blocked the information about the Sasun uprising and subsequent military operations from reaching the outside world, and sealed off the entire region completely. Nevertheless, Vice Consul C. M. Hallward, referring to unofficial sources, reported from Van in early October that a massacre had taken place in Sasun the previous month.[69] Kimberley instructed Currie to request that Hallward be sent to Sasun to investigate,[70] but the Grand Vizier dismissed the British report as unreliable and refused to authorize his trip on the grounds that the presence of a British official in the rebellious region would be viewed as endorsement and rekindle the uprising that had been suppressed. He promised to permit Hallward to travel to Sasun in two months. Currie warned the Vizier that in the absence of an independent assessment, the British Government would not be able to take measures to dispel the wildest rumors circulating in Britain about the Sasun massacre. The Grand Vizier told him that according to Zeki Pasha's report, also forwarded to Rustem Pasha for dissemination, no massacre had taken place and women and children had been evacuated from the region. He added that the cattle and real estate would remain in the government's hands until claimed by rightful owners. If left unclaimed, the property of the massacred residents of Sasun would be sold and proceeds distributed as charity, the Turkish official stated.[71]

On October 15, Currie reported to Kimberley, referring to reports from Hallward, that according to credible reports the recent disturbances in Bitlis province had been suppressed by the government in savage fashion. Many residents had been killed and the rest evicted, leaving their property and land behind; the region had effectively been depopulated. According to Hallward, the authorities sealed off the region under the pretext of a cholera outbreak, and all travelers to Sasun had been quarantined.[72]

On November 2, Currie presented a memorandum on the massacre in Sasun, based on reports from the British Vice Consul.[73] The Ambassador was convinced that his report would be disputed or denied by the Porte, but decided to insist on an investigation. According to Currie, the persons responsible for the massacres were Tahsin Pasha, Army Commander Colonel Ismail Bey, and Mush battalion commander Major Salih. The Ambassador was convinced that the reports of an Armenian uprising had been untrue and urged an independent investigation of the results.[74]

The Sultan's reply to Currie was in a letter in which he rejected Hallward's report as not credible. The Sultan charged the British officials with supporting the actions of nihilists, socialists, and anarchists aimed against his government. The Sultan drew parallels with the Bulgarian situation wherein, he noted, the Bulgarians circulated similar stories of massacres, asked for support from the British Government, and achieved autonomous status for Bulgaria. The Sultan noted that it was not possible to establish Armenian autonomy since the Armenian population was not concentrated and was not in the majority in any locale. Abdul Hamid claimed that the Armenian hopes for autonomy were unrealistic and that the reports of persecution and oppression generating European sympathy were futile. He again complained of the British press publishing the massacre stories, although he did admit that the government had been forced to take tough measures against the 'insurgents' who took arms and resisted the government. Abdul Hamid referred to the British Government's suppression of the native insurgencies in India and Egypt as examples of similar actions.

In the conclusion of his letter, however, the Sultan, informed Currie that the Interior Minister had been ordered to conduct an investigation and should the British reports prove to be true, promised to hold the Governor of Bitlis responsible for the incident.[75]

Meeting with Lord Kimberley on November 7, Rustem Pasha accused the British Government of abetting the Armenian agitators, but the British Foreign Secretary told him the danger to the Turkish Government was posed by a corrupt and immoral administration, not Armenian agitators. Kimberley said that while the Sultan expressed his sincere desire to accord the Armenians fair treatment by the government, the local authorities carry out completely opposite policies, causing discontent and laying grounds for agitation.[76]

The Rosebery Government tried to prevent the news of the Sasun massacre from spreading in the country and refrained from publicizing the troubling consular reports about the destitute conditions prevalent in Western Armenia. The news of the massacre, however, reached the British press in early November and generated a wave of public sympathy for the Armenian cause. A rally held in London charged the government with indifference and complicity in the massacres. Dillon noted in his article that while the British consuls had sent exhaustive reports and the press had published heartrending details describing 'gruesome and nefarious' deeds, the Rosebery Cabinet characterized them as gross exaggerations and ignored the reality.[77] An article in the weekly *Spectator* charged the government with shelving the consular reports on the tragic events taking place in Turkey out of fear of provoking British public opinion.[78] *The Contemporary Review* stated that the British public owed this information to its enterprising press because the government had been determined to suppress the news.[79]

British public opinion charged its national government with greater responsibility for the conditions of the Armenian population in Turkey because while it was only one of the signatories of the Treaty of Berlin, the British Government was the Power most vocal in demanding reforms from the Porte. Also, the Turkish Government undertook a bilateral obligation, under the terms of the Anglo-Turkish Convention, to carry out reforms in the Armenian-populated provinces in exchange for protection from Russian territorial encroachment. Thus, the resurrection of the Armenian Question in the press presented a challenge to Rosebery although he was convinced naively that the crisis would go away on its own. As former Foreign Secretary Lord Derby noted, it became apparent to the government that it would be unable to intervene in Turkey's internal affairs unilaterally and would be therefore forced to cover up the excesses committed by the Sultan's government in order not to aggravate the Near Eastern Crisis.[80]

In November, the British Government publicly expressed its preference for acting in concert with the European Powers on the Armenian Question. Rosebery expressed his personal opposition to unilateral British actions on this issue, stating that joint intervention by the Powers would be the only reliable and safe method of achieving their goal, while any independent action would be futile and dangerous.[81]

During a traditional banquet at London Guild Hall on November 9, the Prime Minister delivered remarks calling for the improvement of relations with Russia and France and proposed joint action on the Armenian and Egyptian Questions as a mechanism to achieve his goal. He left the door open for the possibility of a Russian military intervention in Western Armenia although at that time the Russian Government was disinterested in such a possibility.[82] In return, he asked for Russian support vis-à-vis France on the issue of the British control of Egypt. The Russian Government rejected the proposal.[83] Russian Foreign Minister Prince Lobanov-Rostovski stated during the coronation of Czar Nicholas II that the Russian position on the Armenian Question had been caused by the Anglo-Turkish Convention. He said that Russia could not fail to appreciate the importance and significance of the Cyprus Convention that placed an obligation on Britain to obstruct Russia in case of serious danger to Turkey's territorial integrity. Despite assurances that the British Government had changed its attitude toward the Convention and wanted a rapprochement with Russia, Prince Lobanov pointed out that the Convention had not been annulled and even if it were, Russia would be hard pressed to alter its foreign policy.[84] Clearly, the Russian establishment carried a solid grudge against Britain. *The Contemporary Review* called the Prime Minister's attempt to forge closer ties with the Franco-Russian alliance without offering serious guarantees of friendship to Russia a tragic mistake.[85]

Having received no support from the Russian Government and having ruled out unilateral action, Lord Rosebery was forced to adopt a non-intervention approach to the developments in the Ottoman Empire, ostensibly to prevent a possible collision among the Powers against the British interests. During a public speech made in Edinburgh in 1896, Rosebery said he was convinced of an unequivocal determination of the Powers to stem by force any separate British intervention in Eastern affairs.[86]

The Prime Minister's decision was criticized by political and public figures, including Gladstone, who decried Rosebery's "self-delusion" about the Armenian Question.[87] Malcolm Maccoll[88] in his turn stated publicly that the Prime Minister's fears about encirclement and a counter reaction of the Powers in case of a unilateral British action were ungrounded.[89]

The British Ambassador clashed openly with the Porte in early November, when the Turkish Government accused Vice Consul Hallward of misinforming his government about the Sasun events and inciting the Armenian population in Mush and Bitlis against the Sultan's government. The Porte demanded to recall Hallward, but Currie informed Foreign Minister Said Pasha of his decision to send the British Embassy's Military Attaché, Colonel Chermside, to Sasun and Bitlis to investigate the reports of a massacre and Vice Consul Hallward's actions.[90] On November 11, the British Embassy sent a strongly worded note to the Porte demanding its acquiescence to Colonel Chermside's fact-finding mission.[91]

On November 15, Said Pasha told Currie of the Sultan's decision to dismiss the Governor of Bitlis, form a commission investigating the events in Sasun, and retract the charges leveled against Hallward. On the next day, Kimberley instructed the Ambassador to postpone Colonel Chermside's mission and expressed satisfaction with the Sultan's decisions.[92]

In his November 18 letter to Said Pasha, Currie urged the Porte to form the special fact-finding commission and send it to Sasun in timely fashion. He argued that the commission's existence was all the more important now that the European press had begun to publish articles about the Sasun events. The press reports pointed to the Sultan's Government as the main organizers of the massacres, Currie noted, and the Sultan and his administration could receive negative coverage, which he said had also happened during the Bulgarian events.[93]

Under pressure from the British Embassy, the Sultan's government announced on November 21 that a commission had been formed that included the Sultan's aides-de-camp Brigadier General Mehmed Ali Pasha (who was later replaced by General Staff officer, Brigadier General Hafviz Tewfik Pasha), Division General Abdoullah Pasha, Interior Ministry official Medjid Effendi and Constantinople Savings Bank Director Eymer Bey.[94] At the same time, the Porte announced officially that the commission had been instructed to investigate "cruel actions of the Armenian bandits" and denied the fact of massacre. The Turkish Ambassadors in European nations received a circular telegram with the official version of events, according to which regular Turkish troops had been sent to Sasun to stop the crimes committed by the Armenian insurgents and restore law and order. The telegram noted the unfriendly attitude of the European press and claimed that their reports of the Sasun events did not correspond to reality.[95]

The British Embassy was puzzled and irritated by the Porte's latest dose of double-dealing. Kimberley sent a dispatch to Currie expressing his "surprise and regret" over the position of the Porte and promised to provide him with instructions after he consulted with the foreign ministers of the European Powers.[96] On November 26, he summoned Rustem Pasha to read him the official protest of the British Government and told the Turkish Ambassador that the behavior of the Sultan's authorities would soon be discussed at a Cabinet session. The developments suggested consultations between the Foreign Ministries of the Powers, Kimberley said, and the events became a European issue.[97] The Russian Embassy in Constantinople reported that Rustem Pasha's report on his meeting with Kimberley had caused the concern of the Sultan.[98]

On November 26, Currie told Said Pasha that the only acceptable position of the Ottoman Government could be to allow the commission to conduct an honest and unbiased investigation of the events and mete out punishment to the guilty parties. If the British Government did not have confidence in the findings of the commission it would invoke Article 61 and delegate Colonel Chermside to Sasun to conduct an independent investigation and would publish the reports of the consular officers, Currie said. Said Pasha promised to apprise the Sultan of the British comments and expressed his belief in the impartiality of the commission.

In his report to Kimberley, Currie noted that in order to address the Armenian Question in a serious fashion and achieve significant results, the Government should invoke Article 61 and secure the support of other Powers on this issue. He added that the experience of the late 1870's and 1880's proved that Britain would be unable to achieve improvement in the administration of the Armenian-populated provinces if it acted alone. The Ambassador said he enjoyed the cooperation of his French and Russian colleagues in Constantinople while the German, Italian, and Austrian envoys avoided the subject. In Currie's assessment, if yet another effort to force reforms on the government failed, the plight of the Armenian population would deteriorate sharply while the Power associated with the latest initiative would lose credibility and authority in the East.[99]

On November 27, the British Cabinet decided to take an active stance on the Armenian Question and request the cooperation of the French and

Russian governments in an investigation of the Sasun events.[100] The Russian Foreign Ministry instructed its envoy in Constantinople to demand a comprehensive investigation of the events in Sasun and the bringing to justice of the main culprits; the Russian Ambassador was told to cooperate with the British efforts.[101]

The Sultan's government released another statement affirming its previously announced position on the objectives of the commission, and consequently Kimberley instructed the British Embassy to present a demarche to the Porte requesting the participation of the European Powers in the investigation. The demarche stated that under the circumstances, Article 61 allowed the Powers the liberty to intervene on the Armenian Question.[102]

On December 5, Currie met with French Ambassador Paul Cambon[103] and Russian Chargé M. Jadowsky and proposed that the British, French, and Russian Consuls in Erzurum conduct an independent inquiry into the Sasun events. The French and Russian envoys gave their preliminary approval and promised to inform their respective governments of the proposal.[104]

In an attempt to create friction among the European Powers, the Sultan's government offered the American Ambassador to take part in the investigation of the Sasun events. On December 3, the United States Senate passed a resolution expressing support for the U.S. Government's participation in the activities of the Turkish investigation commission, in concert with the European Powers.[105] American missionary Edwin Bliss claimed that the American President supposedly expressed a personal desire to travel to Turkey when the Sultan had invited the United States Government to take part in the investigation.[106]

The U.S. Government's involvement caused consternation in the British establishment, and Ambassador Currie's feeble reaction to the proposal was criticized not only in the House of Commons but also by Lord Kimberley who complained that Her Majesty's Ambassador always stood ready to alleviate the Porte's troubles.[107] Nevertheless, the European Powers rejected the proposal of the Porte. The Russian Foreign Ministry's cable of instructions to its Ambassador in Constantinople, stating that by giving a preliminary approval for the British plan to involve the Powers' consuls in Erzurum in the inquiry, Russia effectively turned down the proposal of the U.S. Government to appoint representatives in the commission.[108]

On December 7, Said Pasha informed Currie that the Porte concurred with the British proposal to include the British, French, and Russian consuls in Erzurum in the activities of the commission.[109] During the discussion at the British Embassy on December 13, the French and Russian Ambassadors insisted that the Consuls should not personally participate in the commission and should delegate a representative instead.[110] In an attempt to prevent derailment of the process, the Foreign Office concurred with the request although Kimberley noted that he believed the situation warranted the personal participation of the Consuls. Vice Consul H. S. Shipley was appointed as the British representative.[111] An agreement was reached with the Sultan's government to allow the representatives of the Powers to participate in all the functions of the commission, obtain the documents, question the witnesses with prior approval of the commission chairman, make comments and suggestions on the visits and the investigation procedure, report to Erzurum on a regular basis, and present a joint report on the activities and findings of the commission.[112]

On December 29, an Armenian delegation from Paris met with Gladstone at his home, Hawarden Castle, to congratulate him on his 85th anniversary. The former leader of the Liberal Party characteristically decried the Ottoman Empire as an enemy of mankind and civilization and said that Turkey should be 'expelled' from Europe by a joint action of European Powers.[113] The pro-Gladstone faction of the Liberal Party had in fact made the Armenian Question into an election issue during the parliamentary campaign to pave the way for Gladstone to resume the leadership role in the Party. Gladstone however chose not to contest the leadership of the Party but decided to act independently of his usual power base. During a meeting with U.S. citizens of Irish descent, Gladstone said it would be impossible to draw Britain and Turkey closer because of Turkey's actions.[114]

Provoked and irritated by Gladstone's public speeches, Abdul Hamid demanded an official explanation from the British Government.[115] On January 8, 1895, Kimberley instructed Currie to tell Sultan Abdul Hamid that the Government had no influence or carried no responsibility for Mr. Gladstone's statements, as he no longer headed a government department. At the same time, Kimberley noted that Gladstone had expressed the sentiments of the nation's public opinion, which would feel satisfied only after the Sultan's government carried out a complete investigation and brought the perpetrators to justice.[116] On January 9, Kimberley briefed Rustem Pasha on his position. Rustem Pasha pronounced himself dissatisfied with the British response and suggested that it could have catastrophic consequences for Anglo-Turkish relations. Kimberley reiterated that the Government could not be held responsible for statements by private citizens.[117]

On January 14, the London-based National Islamic Society appealed to Kimberley, on behalf of the British subjects of Muslim persuasion, to protest the anti-Ottoman agitation in Britain, which, according to the Society, was offending Islam and causing the indignation of the Muslim population. The Society claimed that the "grossly exaggerated" charges of complicity in the Armenian massacres were offensive to the Sultan who was the Muslim Caliph and an old friend of England. The appeal said the welfare of more than 60 million Muslim subjects was important for the British Empire, and the appeal demanded to contain what it termed as anti-Muslim propaganda, which it said could have catastrophic consequences for the peaceful coexistence of Christianity and Islam. The Society called on the Government to prevent possible Russian occupation of part of the Ottoman Empire.[118]

The Foreign Office rebutted the criticism in its January 17, response, reiterating that the Government was not responsible for the pronouncements and opinions of private citizens. The Foreign Office noted that the British efforts aimed to support an impartial investigation into the Sasun events, which would be in the interests of the Ottoman Empire as well as the Muslim and Christian subjects.[119]

The local authorities began to destroy evidence of massacres in advance of the commission's arrival and to resettle Kurds and Turks in the region to head off the possible demands for Armenian autonomy. British Consul Cumberbatch, in Angora, reported to Currie on January 10 that the authorities began to form clandestine 'committees for the defense of Turkey,' comprised primarily of government officials. According to the consul, he had credible information about the objective of these committees, which was to provoke the Armenian population to disturbances and anti-government activities. Cumberbatch noted that the local Turkish population had been convinced of the existence of Armenian revolutionary groups and was determined to crack down on them.[120]

On January 16, Currie reported to the Foreign Office that the Sasun Commission accompanied by the British, Russian, and French representatives—Erzurum Vice Consuls Shipley, Przhevalski, and Vilbert—departed for Mush from Erzurum three days before.[121] The following day Currie met with the newly consecrated Armenian Patriarch Izmirlyan, who told him the Commission's activities would be useless since the Armenian witnesses had been intimidated not to give testimony. The Patriarch added that he had received no information from the provinces since the correspondence had been censored by the government and many priests had been detained.[122] Currie recommended to the Patriarch to refrain from sending any appeals to the Porte that might be deemed irritating until after the commission completed its work.[123] Currie reported to the Foreign Office that Patriarch Izmirlyan referred to the suffering of the Armenian people during the official reception given by the Sultan to mark his consecration. The sovereign interrupted the Patriarch and urged him to contain his compatriots' rebellious and arrogant activities. The reception was cut short, and his audience with the Sultan lasted only two minutes; the Patriarch had been given to know that his presence was undesired by the Sultan.[124]

On January 19, Currie sent to the Foreign Office a new program for the reforms in the Armenian-populated provinces, which was based on the earlier plan by Wilson. This program had been re-drafted by Colonel Chermside, and called for (1) appointment of governors with approval of the Powers, for a five-year term; (2) an elected Council General of Delegates from districts, with control over finance, with each religious community represented proportionally in the Council; (3) provinces to be broken up into smaller districts, and the District Chiefs to be both Muslim and Christian in a ratio proportional to the respective numbers of these communities in the district; (4) districts to be divided into subunits, cazas, and the Kaymakams* to be chosen in the same manner; (5) Cazas to be divided into nahies, with the Mudirs to be chosen in the same manner; (6) the cazas to have Administrative Councils representing the community; (7) Vekils to be elected by the leaders of each community to represent its interests at the chief town of the vilayet; (8) a court of assizes for each province, composed of two Christians and two Muslims, who would

---

* *Kaymakam*, *Mudir*, and *Velik* are Turkish terms for officials in charge of the appropriate territorial subunits.

at fixed dates visit all places where justice is administered, would inspect the penitentiaries, review verdicts, and hear appeals; (9) a mixed gendarmerie to be established, in which the Muslims and Christians should be represented in proportion to their numbers, (10) special measures for the protection of Armenians against the Kurds.[125]

Ambassador Currie presented the Embassy's draft program to the Armenian Patriarch, also informing the Russian envoy of its main provisions.

While generally satisfied with the program, Patriarch Izmirlyan made some comments to the Ambassador. He said he was convinced the Powers should take part in the selection of a Governor and that the best possible arrangement would be a Christian or, even better, an Armenian governor. He also proposed that a portion of the locally collected revenue be used for the local administration. The Patriarch further proposed that the Mutessarifs, Kaymakams, and Mudirs should be named by the Governor rather than the Porte. With regard to local proportional representation and the ratio of Christian to Muslim population, he observed that the Kurdish nomads should not be taken into account. He stressed the importance of the last point in the program, noting that, compared to 1880, the situation had taken a turn for the worse as the chief persecutors of the Armenians, the Kurds, had now been armed by the authorities.

The Russian Ambassador, for his part, had expressed satisfaction with the idea of Christian officials, yet he thought that a practical difficulty existed in achieving total agreement among the Powers on candidacy. The Russian envoy had also proposed that immediate measures be taken to improve the discipline and control over the Hamidiye units.[126]

While the local authorities had tried to obstruct the meetings between the members of the commission and the local Armenians, the Armenian residents of Sasun succeeded in presenting a petition to the Commission describing the massacre. The investigation then ground to a halt after the local authorities arrested a number of Armenian activists in Bitlis and Mush. The European representatives appealed to the Porte, and Governor Tahsin Pasha was dismissed and replaced by Commissioner Eumer Bey. The representatives of the Powers noted that the Turkish Commissioners preferred to read government documents and hear the testimony of government officials, rather than of local residents.[127] On February 8, Shipley reported to Currie that the Commission had conducted twelve hearings to date but heard testimony from only one Armenian witness. According to the Vice Consul, the Turkish Commissioners had been instructed to prove that the Armenian population had been in open rebellion, that Armenians, not Kurds, were the aggressors, and that the Armenians had committed barbaric acts against the Muslim population. The European representatives had visited Armenian homes and institutions and interviewed numerous Armenians, which had irritated the Sultan's government.[128]

According to a March 13 report by the British Ambassador in St. Petersburg, Sir Frank Lascelles, Russian Foreign Minister Prince Lobanov-Rostovski had told him he had never expected 'satisfactory results' from the investigation and that the real perpetrators of the Sasun massacres would remain at large. He proposed asking the British Government to consider what was necessary to be done following the investigation, and expressed his satisfaction at the level of cooperation on the Armenian Question between the two Powers' Ambassadors in Turkey.[129]

The reports by the British Embassy and consular officers noted that the harassment of the Armenian population by the Sultan's government continued in earnest even while the Sasun Commission was functioning. Many Armenians were searched, detained and held without due process for alleged 'revolutionary activities.' On March 16, Kimberley informed Currie of intense interest in the Parliament and among the members of the public toward the events in Turkey. Kimberley referred to the reports of the arrest of some 80 Armenian activists in Constantinople for collecting donations for the victims of the Sasun massacre. The press continued to report on the abominable conditions of inmates in Turkish jails and the persecution of Armenians.

Kimberley noted that real-life evidence showed that the living conditions of the Christian population had not improved, contrary to the assurances given by the Sultan and his Government as well as the obligations under the Treaty of Berlin. The Ambassador was instructed to draw on this argument to demand that the Porte release the arrested Armenians, and allow the foreign consuls to be present at the trials of the Christian subjects. The Ambassador was instructed to hold consultations with the Powers on the subject of reforms.[130]

On March 19, Currie reported to Kimberley that the French and Russian

Ambassadors argued for presenting separate demarches to the Porte on the subject of detained Armenians, instead of a joint memorandum. They proposed that the joint memorandum be reserved for a later occasion, to press for a general amnesty or a reform program. According to the Ambassador, the German and Italian envoys agreed to cooperate on the issue but the Austrian Embassy refrained from taking action.[131]

On March 21, the Grand Vizier informed Currie of the Sultan's decision to hold trials of the arrested Armenian clergy in Constantinople and to release all detainees, with the exception of those charged with murder or other serious crimes. The Porte would also demand that the detained clergymen be barred from holding important church offices. The Vizier promised to persuade the Sultan to rescind arrest orders for the remaining prisoners as well, but Currie insisted that an additional order be sent to the provinces to stop arbitrary arrests and persecution.[132]

On March 21, Abdul Hamid invited Ambassador Currie to an Iftar dinner (the evening meal during the month of Ramadan) at his residence in Yeldiz Kiosk. During their discussion of the Armenian Question, the Sultan expressed surprise when Currie told him of more than 700 Armenian political prisoners throughout Turkey. The Sultan said that only 30 Armenian political prisoners—who had been arrested in Yuzgat, Kayseri, and Tokat following the disturbances—were being held. The Ambassador reiterated that all the jails in Turkey were filled with Armenians but Abdul Hamid said he did not believe that the local authorities held Armenian prisoners without due process. Currie cited almost daily reports by the consular officers about Armenians being arrested for political reasons or no reason at all.

The Sultan noted that he and his predecessors had always treated their Armenian subjects with mercy and justice, but the Armenians had recently begun to 'misbehave' and spread malicious and exaggerated reports that were received with total credulity in Europe. He warned the Ambassador that the moment was critical for the future of British-Turkish relations since the Sultan's Muslim subjects would not remain indifferent to the Armenian allegations that were encouraged and supported by Britain.

The Ambassador observed that the British public was concerned with the continuing arrests of the Armenian activists in Turkey and said he hoped the Sultan's order to release the detained clergymen would alleviate the concerns of the British people. The Ambassador used the occasion to ask the Sultan to release the other prisoners as well. The public indignation in Britain was sincere and strong, Currie noted, and the people demanded that their Government take more active measures to address their concerns; therefore, the Government demanded that the Porte carry out reforms and take measures to protect the Armenian population from Kurdish attacks.

According to Abdul Hamid, the laws passed by his predecessors were sufficient to secure good government. He added that it was only necessary to increase the number of troops and gendarmerie in the provinces where tensions existed between the Kurds and Armenians, appoint the best officials as judges, and appoint a few Armenians to government positions. The Sultan concluded that when comparable improvements were made, it would be unnecessary to carry out additional reforms.

The Ambassador expressed his conviction that the existing laws and the Sultan's best intentions alone could not address the situation in the distant provinces of the Empire, and exacted a promise from the Sultan to appoint a special commission after the Bayram holiday to hear the Armenian grievances and propose a reforms program.[133]

On March 28, Kimberley met with Rustem Pasha, who blamed the Armenian troubles on the activities of the revolutionary agents and organizations. Kimberley replied that while revolutionary Armenian groups did exist, the causes of the Armenian crisis were deeply rooted in the generally unhealthy internal administration mechanisms.

The Turkish Ambassador protested the unfounded accusations leveled by the British Government in connection with the Sasun events, inasmuch as the commission's work had not been completed. Kimberley replied that the British Government possessed credible information about the 'terrifying' massacres of helpless and defenseless Armenians in Sasun. Pending the completion of the commission's activities, the British Government would demand the implementation of serious administrative reforms in the Ottoman Empire, Kimberley said. The Foreign Secretary rebutted Rustem Pasha's protests about interference in Turkey's internal affairs, reminding him of the Porte's obligations under the Treaty of Berlin and the Cyprus Convention, as well as about the privileges of the British and other European governments. The Foreign Office believed that the situation in Asia Minor was getting out of control and the clashes between the Christians and Muslims could have serious ramifications.[134]

Russian Foreign Minister Prince Lobanov, meanwhile, told British Ambassador Lascelles that he was concerned with the recent developments in the Armenian Question and had been awaiting the results of consultations among the British, French, and Russian Ambassadors in Constantinople on the presentation of a joint memorandum on reforms. He noted that the Armenian communities were extended all over Asia Minor, and that the Armenian population was in the majority only in Angora, Alexandretta, and Bitlis, which were far removed from one another. As it was, the Armenian situation was different from Lebanon where it became possible to detach a region and appoint a Christian Governor to rule it, he added.[135]

Despite his advanced age, Gladstone engaged in an active anti-Turkish campaign in the spring of 1895. Unlike the real Liberal Leader, Lord Rosebery, and his supporters, the majority of the Liberals supported the idea of immediate and unilateral British action against Turkey. Gladstone presented a memorandum to the British Government in April, making the case for a British show of force since the Porte had always given in to the threat of British military intervention. He noted that the only appropriate measure, out of appreciation for the Armenian situation, was to threaten use of force against Turkey without concern for the 'Concert of Powers.'[136] On April 10, Said Pasha once again complained to Currie about the Sultan's irritation and frustration with Gladstone's remarks, requesting that the British Government either obstruct his public appearances or advise him to restrain his language. Lord Kimberley noted that he did not find Gladstone's remarks appropriate at the moment since the investigation of the Sasun events was under way and the Sultan had promised to form a commission on the preparation and implementation of the reforms.[137]

On April 10, Currie reported to the Foreign Office on his audience with Sultan Abdul Hamid. The Sultan said he appointed the former governor of Crete, Turkhan Pasha, to chair the Armenian Inquiry Commission, which would commence its activities in ten days. The Sultan added that he had reviewed the list of political prisoners and ordered many of them released from custody.

Currie thanked the Sultan for taking these steps, and informed him of the three Powers' intention to present a memorandum on reforms through their envoys. Abdul Hamid suggested that the European envoys discuss their proposals with the newly formed commission without the presentation of a formal document. The Ambassador promised to take the Sultan's view into account, saying he would discuss the venue for the memorandum with his colleagues once the work was finished. Currie assured the Sultan that the proposals were based on the dead letter of existing laws but would not divulge any details of the program.

When Abdul Hamid reverted to the subject of fair treatment of the Armenians by himself and his predecessors, and noted the large number of Armenians in the civil service, the Ambassador interjected that what the Armenian population wanted was not government positions but, rather, guarantees for protecting their lives, property, and human dignity. The Sultan noted cynically that the continued presence of the Armenian population in Turkey was the proof of the concern he and his predecessors had for the lives of the Armenian subjects, even as the Armenians grew richer and the Turks poorer.

Currie said he was sure of the Sultan's good intentions but added that the consular reports at his disposal showed that the local authorities supplied distorted information to the central government. The Ambassador assured Abdul Hamid that the British Government worked hard to improve its relations with Turkey and possessed no hostile intentions toward the Porte. The Turkish demands to restrain the press could not be addressed since the Government did not practice censorship, Currie noted, and inquired about the decision of the Porte to prevent visits by foreign journalists to Turkey. The Sultan assured him that it was a temporary measure, until the completion of the Sasun investigation.[138]

In March and April the British Embassy received reports from its consular agents in Erzurum, Trabzon, and Diyarbakir on continuing cases of persecution of the Armenian population by the local authorities and the deteriorating situation.[139] On April 16 Currie referred to this report during his meeting with Said Pasha, urging him to take reform measures before the crisis spun out of control, with a catastrophic outcome for the Ottoman Empire. He urged the government to warn the local authorities that every case of mistreatment of the Armenian population would be most severely addressed by the Porte.[140]

On April 22, Currie reported to Kimberley that the Porte had announced the establishment of a commission charged with inquiring into the state of affairs in the provinces; the commission was comprised of government officials.[141]

On April 27, Currie reported that the French and Russian envoys had informed him of their government's general approval of the British plan. The Russian and French Ambassadors proposed that the prepared memorandum be presented unofficially to the Sultan. Currie recommended to the Foreign Office that the reforms memorandum be presented to the Porte by the three Embassies in separate but identical notes.[142]

Although the Russian Government had approved the British reforms draft, it was convinced that British diplomacy intended to employ the Armenian Question for its own interests. The Russian Government believed that the primary objective of the British policies of promoting reforms in the Armenian-populated regions was to prevent possible Russian intervention in the internal affairs of the Ottoman Empire, acting in its role as protector of the Christian subjects. In particular, Russian Lt. Gen. Zelyoni sent a memorandum to the government arguing that the British policy on Armenia had been motivated not by humanity and concern for the Armenians but by British fears of the revival of the Russian Black Sea Fleet, Russia's advancement toward the borders of Afghanistan and India, and the amicable relations established between Turkey and Russia in the wake of the 1878 war. Zelyoni pointed out that England wanted to create a 'privileged province' populated by Armenians, countering the political interests of Russia and Turkey. He noted that Russia could not remain indifferent toward the establishment of a European political and military platform, "the Armenian Bulgaria," on its borders, which would prevent Russia from exercising its 'legitimate prevalent influence' over the region.[143]

The British Government's program was addressed to the Sultan's government and included proposals for the improved administration of the Armenian-populated provinces of Van, Erzurum, Sivas, Bitlis, Kharput, and Diyarbakir. The program provided for up to one-third of all local government positions in the provinces with predominant Armenian populations to be reserved for Christians. The gendarmerie had to be equally staffed by Muslim and Christian officers. The function of tax revenue collection had to be transferred from the gendarmerie to a special service established by local councils.

With prior approval of the Powers, a Christian Governor-General had to be appointed, who would report to a mixed Muslim-Christian commission in Constantinople. Finally, a European High Commissioner would be appointed to supervise the implementation of reforms.[144] Thus, under the British program Western Armenia would receive the status of de facto autonomy under the auspices of the European Powers.

The Russian Government did not agree with two principal points in the British draft. First, it did not want to limit the sovereignty of the Porte and force it to accept the proposals of the Powers. Second, it wanted to apply the reforms either toward the Christian population in general, or throughout the Empire. General Zelyoni's memorandum recommended that the Russian Government "would never agree to the idea of an Armenian 'privileged province,' even if it were to be comprised of only two districts instead of nine vilayets."[145]

The Russian position corresponded completely with the Ottoman Government's policies, which categorically rejected any European interference in its internal affairs. Zeki Pasha had told Russian Colonel Putyata that the implementation of the British proposals would lead to the establishment of a Greater Armenia and prepare ground for even tougher demands by the Armenian population.[146]

After the Russian and French Governments endorsed the British proposal and simultaneously expressed their opposition to any coercive measures to enforce it, on May 11 the substantially edited and reduced version of the British plan was presented to the Porte. The three Powers' Memorandum contained the following main points: (1) the number of provinces was to be reduced; (2) the Governors had to be selected and appointed with semi-official approval of the Powers; (3) a general amnesty had to be proclaimed releasing Armenian prisoners from custody and allowing exiled and displaced Armenians to return; (4) the judicial and penal systems had to be reformed; (5) a High Commissioner had to be appointed to oversee the reforms process, with the approval of the Powers; (6) a permanent commission of control had to be established, comprised of three Christian and three Muslim government officials; (7) the Armenian victims in Sasun, Talvorik, and other regions where massacres had been carried out had to be compensated; (8) the right to change religion had to be respected; (9) Armenians' land titles had to be respected;

(10) the conditions of the Armenian population in other parts of Asia Minor had to be improved; (11) the status of local administration officials, and members of the police, gendarmerie, Kurdish and Hamidiye paramilitary forces had to be reviewed; fiscal administration had to be reformed.[147]

Thus, under French and Russian pressure, the British Government removed important points from its reforms proposal, such as merging six provinces into one that would have established an Armenian administrative unit headed by a Christian Governor of the Powers' choosing.

Even then, many voices in London predicted that even in its abridged form, the reforms memorandum would be doomed to fail. *The Contemporary Review* wrote that before it presented the Memorandum, the Rosebery administration should have improved its relations with Russia and held a conference of signatories to the Treaty of Berlin.[148] *The Spectator*, in turn, recommended that the Government improve its relations and cooperate closely with France and Russia to make a real difference on the Armenian Question. The weekly noted that the Russian Government would find it unacceptable to place the Armenians under the influence of a Protestant Power, and that the French would have concerns about the British naval build-up in the Mediterranean as had existed since the British takeover of Egypt.[149] The weekly suggested that the reforms program presented to the Porte would not be carried out unless it had been approved by the Sultan in the form of a treaty.[150] Maccoll noted that the lack of control by the European Powers was the critical loophole in the reforms program.[151]

After the three Powers unveiled their proposal to the Sultan, the Triple Alliance expressed its dissatisfaction with the draft. On May 18, British Ambassador Mallet reported from Berlin that a personal appeal from Abdul Hamid to Kaiser Wilhelm was an important factor behind the German position. The Sultan asked that the German Kaiser restrain the joint actions of Britain, France, and Russia.[152] The Austro-Hungarian Foreign Minister, Count Agenor Goluchowski, criticized the proposal and suggested that a commission comprised of representatives of six Powers be formed instead to effectively oversee the reforms.[153]

Abdul Hamid closely followed the European diplomatic discussions and changes in the attitudes of the press and public opinion. If the press and public figures were indifferent to the developments in Turkey, which was usually the case, it was safe to ignore or obstruct foreign diplomats' recommendations. Conversely, if the press and public opinion were firmly behind the British Government in its attempts to force reforms in Turkey, the Sultan would take a conciliatory approach, issuing promises of reforms to delay them. As *The Spectator* noted, the Sultan was "fighting desperately against the proposals of the Powers, and trying by every diplomatic subterfuge—and the diplomatic subterfuges of the Turk are like the sands of the sea—to avoid the carrying out of reforms in Armenia."[154]

The position of the Triple Alliance became immediately known when Abdul Hamid issued his reply on June 3. Currie reported that the Sultan had rejected all the guarantees for implementation of the reforms, including the appointment of a High Commissioner, Commission of Supervision, and the vetting of gubernatorial appointments by the Powers. The Sultan further rejected the proposed reforms of the judiciary, gendarmerie, and the police, the demand to allow the displaced population to return to their original domiciles, to declare amnesty, compensate the victims, reform the penal system, and improve the condition of the Armenian population in other provinces.[155] The Sultan's Government rejected nearly all the proposals contained in the May Memorandum of the British, French, and Russian Governments.

The moment arrived for a European response to the arrogant position of the Sultan. The response never materialized. On June 4, the Russian Foreign told British Ambassador Lascelles that the Russian Government did not view the memorandum as an ultimatum to the Sultan and therefore was opposed to any show of force in response to its rejection or of the Sultan's counterproposals.[156]

The Rosebery Government proved to be indecisive as far as a unilateral action was concerned. The Mediterranean Fleet was deployed near Beirut, at a distance of 200–300 kilometers from Western Armenia. On June 19, the Cabinet discussed the possibility of a naval deployment against Turkey, but made no decision. Three days later the Cabinet resigned for domestic political reasons, and the following day, the Queen "invited" Lord Salisbury to form the new Government on behalf of his Conservative Party.[157]

3. The Armenian Question and the Salisbury Government in June–September 1895

The Salisbury government enjoyed rather high approval ratings in 1895, both domestically and internationally. Lord Salisbury, 65, wanted a successful term as the Prime Minister to crown his long career in public service. Due to ill health, he was already forced to spend the winter months in southern France. Salisbury had many wide-ranging interests, including classic literature, the French language, which he spoke flawlessly, and he liked to spend his free time in the chemical laboratory in his Hathfield estate. In the eyes of the British public, Lord Salisbury was the epitome of a Victorian statesman.[158]

The British public greeted the return of Salisbury's Cabinet to power with great hopes, and the overall consensus was that the Conservative government would be able to bring the Near Eastern crisis to an end and to stop the anti-Armenian policies of the Sultan. Even Lord Rosebery, now the leader of the loyal opposition, noted in August that Salisbury would have the support of not only his party, but also the British people as well.[159]

The Spectator weekly praised the Prime Minister's accomplishments and abilities, noting that his knowledge of Eastern affairs made him the only politician in England capable of ending the crisis and saving the Armenian population in Turkey that was then faced with extermination.[160] Another article in *The Spectator* noted that Salisbury was sincerely concerned with how to alleviate the predicament of the Armenian population and end the Turkish reprisals. According to *The Spectator*, the only flaw in Salisbury's position was his [unjustified, in the newspaper's opinion] concern that British intervention on behalf of the Armenian population of Turkey could lead to a European war.[161]

Nevertheless, members of the Liberal Party pointed out the inconsistency of Salisbury's perceived platform and his position during the Congress of Berlin, where British diplomacy succeeded in nullifying some of the provisions of the San Stefano Treaty. As a result, an area with a Christian population of more than a million people was returned to the Sultan's rule. George Russell[162] said that Salisbury was under the influence of Lord Beaconsfield and was like a prisoner "chained to the chariot of his triumphant leader." Russell noted that the situation at the end of the 19th century was markedly different from 1878, and Salisbury was no longer playing second fiddle to somebody. Despite having become the master of the British Empire, Salisbury's actions showed that history was merely repeating itself to the smallest detail, Russell concluded.[163]

Returning to power, Salisbury also assumed the Foreign Office portfolio. He granted the British Ambassador in Constantinople, Philip Currie, a personal friend of his, the rank of Under Secretary of State for Foreign Affairs, a privilege testifying to the importance of the Near East and the Armenian Question for British foreign policy. On the surface, Salisbury seemed to have distanced himself from the traditional conservative platform on the Eastern question by supporting the historical Russian mission of controlling the Black Sea Straits. In reality, Salisbury had concluded that the collapse of the Ottoman Empire was inevitable but he would not contribute to hastening that end. On the one hand, the interests of the British Empire required preservation of the territorial integrity of the Ottoman Empire and defending the Sultan's government from Russian encroachment, but on the other, any British action on Turkey would have been rendered useless and ineffective unless supported by Russia and the European Powers. Thus, Salisbury worked to secure British-Russian rapport on the Armenian Question, while simultaneously preparing the ground for the complete occupation of Egypt and restoring British influence in the Porte, which had been supplanted by closer ties between Russia and Turkey. This was the essence of the delicate maneuvering of British diplomacy on the Armenian Question. By proclaiming its intentions to cooperate closely with Germany and Russia on the Eastern issues, the British Government was attempting to bring Sultan Abdul Hamid's government back into its sphere of influence.

In June, the Foreign Office published a paper on its foreign policy. The main foreign policy objectives of the new government were: categorical rejection of Irish Home Rule, restoration of amicable and cooperative relations with the Russian and German governments, reconciliation of colonial disputes with Russia and France in Asia and Africa, and resolution of the Armenian Question. The policy of the new government on the Armenian Question was in fact a continuation of that of its predecessor. It demanded that the Sultan's government punish the perpetrators of the Sasun massacres and carry out the reforms under the Treaty of Berlin. Salisbury's instructions to Currie on the Armenian Question nearly repeated word for word the instructions of the previous Foreign Office Secretary.[164]

In his first dispatch to Currie, Salisbury instructed him to study the feasibility of deploying the British Navy against the Ottoman Empire to force the government to carry out reforms. In response, Ambassador Currie forwarded to the Foreign Office a letter from President Whittal of the British Board of Trade in Constantinople, who noted the impossibility of any British intervention to improve the conditions of the Christian population of the Ottoman Empire due to the increased fanaticism of the Muslims. Instead, he proposed that the Sultan be urged to carry out a general reform of his country. In his dispatch dated June 27, Currie reported on the meeting between French Ambassador Cambon and the Grand Vizier. The French Ambassador reportedly told the Grand Vizier that the British should have occupied Alexandretta instead of deploying the Navy, but the Grand Vizier dismissed the possibility of a unilateral British action since the European Powers would oppose it. The French envoy replied that the European Powers would endorse the British action if the British Government would announce the implementation of the reforms as its sole objective, would cooperate with other powers, and would agree to withdraw its forces immediately after a European conference were convened to discuss the situation.[165]

In Salisbury's assessment, occupying Alexandretta would be difficult to carry out in view of the small number of British troops and the scarcity of materiel in the region. On July 1, Currie received a self-described 'clever' proposal from Salisbury: the British troops would be transported to Armenia via the Tigris. The Ambassador replied that the proposed expedition would be impossible to carry out due to many shallow points in the river, which would damage the war boats.[166]

On July 10, Salisbury invited Rustem Pasha to discuss the British Government's position on the Armenian Question. He assured the Turkish Ambassador that it was his earnest desire to preserve the Ottoman Empire and that the Sultan's rightful prerogatives be protected but noted that the Sultan took no step to assuage and meet the demands of public opinion in Europe, and Britain in particular. He repudiated the idea of an Armenian autonomy as 'absurd,' urging instead to provide an impartial and fair administration for those provinces and stem the harassment by the Kurds. Salisbury suggested that the best solution would be to appoint a decisive, honest, and neutral Governor in whom Europe could have confidence.

Salisbury said he completely supported the policies inherited from the previous Government and would stand by the demands presented by the three European ambassadors to the Sultan. The British Government still demanded that Abdul Hamid carry out the reforms, Salisbury stressed, adding that Germany, Austria, and Italy would not oppose Great Britain on this issue while France and Russia acted together. He further noted that the only factor preserving the existence of the Ottoman Empire was the disagreements between Britain and Russia, and if those Powers should settle their differences, the Ottoman Empire would disappear. Salisbury urged the Ambassador to convey to the Porte that it was imperative to carry out reforms without losing time.

Sending the minutes of his conversation to Currie, Salisbury instructed him to continue to press for the implementation of the May program. Moreover, he noted that the British Government would be forced to consult with Russia should the Sultan prove unwilling to carry out reforms.[167]

On July 18, the Ottoman Foreign Minister informed the British, French, and Russian Embassies of the orders issued by the Sultan to the Porte to hasten the necessary reforms immediately put into force measures that would not be contrary to the existing laws, and take administrative and police measures to prevent conflicts and migration of the Kurds. Shakir Pasha was charged with the supervision of the reform effort.[168] The envoys of France and Russia in Constantinople presented notes to the Foreign Ministry expressing no reservations against the appointment of Shakir Pasha but asking for more scrutiny of the reform measures and the extent of Shakir Pasha's mandate.[169] The British Embassy's note, dated July 25, stated that if the reforms were adequate and satisfactory and Shakir Pasha's powers sufficient, Britain would not object to his appointment but would not accept any responsibility for it since it was not agreed upon with the Powers beforehand.[170] Receiving Ambassador Currie on July 26, Sultan Abdul Hamid assured him that the Council of Ministers would consider the reforms program shortly and take measures to carry out that it would be approved. The Ambassador asked that the reforms program adopted by the Cabinet be communicated to the three European Embassies at once.[171]

Meanwhile, the British Government wanted to assure Russia that a temporary deployment of the British Navy to Constantinople would not be detrimental to Russian interests. On July 26, Salisbury instructed the British

Ambassador in St. Petersburg, Frank Lascelles, to communicate to Prince Lobanov-Rostovski that the objective of the British proposals had been merely to secure justice and protection for the property and lives of the Armenian population, rather than bestowing exceptional privileges upon them.[172]

On July 16, the commission investigating the Sasun events concluded its work after hearing testimony from nearly 200 witnesses without making public its final recommendations. On July 20, the European commissioners presented their findings to their embassies, with the conclusion that a full-scale massacre of the Armenian population had taken place in Sasun with the participation of regular Turkish troops. The European commissioners' report did not confirm the reports of a serious insurgency by the Armenians preceding the events, but the complicity of the local authorities in the massacres could not be established since that was beyond the scope of the commission.[173] Thus, the British Government failed in its objectives to bring the perpetrators of the massacre to justice.

On August 1, the Turkish Government presented the reforms program to the three European Embassies. Having compared the program with the Memorandum presented to the Porte in May, Currie noted in his report to Salisbury that the new program contained no provisions for a five-year term for the governors or a fixed proportion of vice-governors and district administrators. The Sultan's government effectively refused the European demands for judicial reforms, election of Mudirs, improvement in tax collection, and granting of officer's commissions in the gendarmerie and rural police to the Christians. Meeting on August 3 to discuss the presented draft, the British, Russian, and French Ambassadors concluded that their May memorandum had been rejected almost entirely.[174]

Salisbury cabled Ambassador Lascelles, noting that the Turkish proposal had been neither satisfactory nor serious and instructed him to find out how far the Russian Government would be prepared to go to put pressure on the Porte. He said the British Government had concluded that further diplomacy would be of no avail, and proposed that France, Great Britain, and Russia work out more energetic measures to impress the Sultan since a mere withdrawal from the earlier position would be tantamount to a loss of face.[175] Meeting with the Russian Chargé d'affairés in London, Salisbury reiterated that Britain found it impossible to establish an Armenian state but suggested using the language contained in Article 61 of the Treaty of Berlin allowing for 'supervision' by the European Powers over the course of reforms. Such supervision need not be confined to monitoring by the diplomatic personnel and should involve a more active and effective form of vigilance, Salisbury noted.[176] On August 9, Prince Lobanov-Rostovski told Lascelles that the use of force by any of the Powers or by their combination to force reforms on the Porte was unacceptable to the Czar and objectionable to the Government. He proposed, instead, that the three Ambassadors continue to present a firm and united attitude, which might force the Sultan to yield.[177]

In his August 6 speech in Chester, Gladstone condemned the anti-Armenian policies of the Sultan, calling the Armenians the most ancient and peaceful race of Christian civilization. He advocated expelling the Turks from Armenia as a solution to the Armenian Question, and charged the European nations with indifference toward their fate.[178] Despite his seeming differences with Conservative Party leader Salisbury, Gladstone's pro-Armenian speeches and rhetoric had had the effect of defending the government's stance on Armenia. In fact, the rally at Chester had been held with the prior knowledge and approval of Salisbury and was presided over by a prominent Tory member, Duke of Westminster.[179] Concluding his speech, Gladstone said the meeting in Chester was not intended to protest the actions of the present Government but, rather, to uphold its position and provide national and moral support without which it could not speak for the whole nation.[180] The honorary leader of the Liberal Party wanted to rally public support for the Conservative government.[181]

The Chester rally passed a resolution in support of Armenia, declaring that the Government would have "the cordial support of the entire nation, without distinction of party," in providing effective guarantees for "the safety of life, honor, religion, and property" in Armenia.[182] Gladstone who had hitherto advocated unilateral and independent British action on the Armenian Question was now on record as advocating a coordinated European policy on this issue. Salisbury noted that not only his Party but also the British public itself was concerned with preserving the national honor.[183]

In the annual Queen's Speech on August 15, delivered by Queen Victoria, which opened the session of the Parliament, all references to the Armenian Question contained tough language. The Queen noted that the British

Government anxiously awaited the response of the Porte to the proposals presented by the British, French, and Russian Ambassadors in Constantinople. In his own remarks, Salisbury accused the Porte of openly carrying out anti-Armenian policies and threatened serious consequences if the Porte did not accept the Ambassadors' memorandum on the Armenian reforms. He also expressed disappointment with the reluctance of the French and Russian Governments to resort to force to press the issue on the Porte. Later that month, in a speech in Dover, Salisbury referred to Turkey as a 'center of destruction, a malignant tumor spreading disease to the healthy part of Europe bordering the Turkish dominions' and predicted an imminent collapse of the Ottoman Empire.[184]

Meeting with French Ambassador De Coursel on August 13, Salisbury noted that the three Powers had to adopt a tough position on the Armenian Question and invoke the right to supervise the Armenian reforms under Article 61. Since it was impossible to monitor reforms from Constantinople, the Prime Minister proposed that a Supervision Commission be formed and stationed in the Armenian-populated provinces, comprised of four Turkish officials and three European representatives. The European commissioners were to have equal rights, including the right to conduct investigations and present their findings to the Embassies. Approving the proposal, the French Ambassador said the Russian Government would probably endorse it as well since it did not constitute use of force but, rather, was an invocation of an existing treaty. He referred to France as a mediator, saying it would accept any decision agreeable to Great Britain and Russia.[185]

On August 14, Currie sent a dispatch to Salisbury noting a certain hardening and increasing fanaticism in the Sultan's position on the Armenian reforms. According to Currie, the instructions sent to Rustem Pasha from the Porte dismissed any new proposals on the reforms as affront to Islam. The Porte told the Turkish Ambassador that the Sultan had already approved a reform program and any attempt to adopt new measures would cause the Armenians to commit 'crimes' in the manner of the Bulgarians in Macedonia.[186]

Two days later, Russian Chargé Kroupensky met with Salisbury to brief him on his Government's position on the Armenian Question. While approving the proposal to establish a monitoring mechanism, the Russian envoy said Russia had never viewed the May memorandum as an ultimatum and would not therefore consent to forcing the Sultan to carry it out. Presenting his proposals on the composition and functioning of the Commission of Supervision to the Russian Government, Salisbury noted that the three Powers' Ambassadors should continue to pressure the Porte on a fixed term for the governors and the increase in proportion of Christians among appointed officials.[187] On August 19, Kroupensky presented to Salisbury the response from Lobanov-Rostovsky, who refused to press such demands since, in his opinion, they would be unacceptable to the Sultan. The Russian Foreign Minister presented no objections to the composition of the joint commission.[188]

However, on August 21 Rustem Pasha met with Salisbury and, on behalf of the Sultan, categorically rejected the idea of a joint Commission of Control. Rustem Pasha added that such a proposal would undermine the authority of the Sultan in the eyes of his Muslim subjects and lead to a serious shift in the foreign policy of Turkey, possibly driving it into the hands of Russia. Salisbury replied that the proposal to form a Control Commission was the least the Powers could demand under the terms of the Treaty of Berlin. If such a proposal was an encroachment on the Sultan's exclusive prerogatives then the encroachment had occurred eighteen years ago and had been endorsed by the Sultan, Salisbury argued. He said he was disappointed with the Sultan's position, which he said threatened Turkey's existence, and insisted that the Commission was an important guarantee of reforms for the European Powers.[189]

On August 24, Currie reported to Salisbury that the Commission charged with the implementation of the reforms was chaired by Shakir Pasha with Danish Bey, the head of the Consular division of the Porte, as deputy chair. The Sultan's aide-de-camp and members of the Imperial Court were the other members of the commission, and Currie had information that Shakir Pasha was to leave for Erzurum the following day.[190]

In his confidential dispatch, dated August 26, the Ambassador reported that some Imperial officials were convinced that the British position was a bluff since the Russian Government would not cooperate with Great Britain. They therefore urged the Sultan to withstand the British pressure. Another group of officials saw dangers in such an approach. According to Currie, the Sultan was concerned with Salisbury's latest public pronouncements, which Rustem Pasha had reported to him. Secret police sources reported widespread discontent among the Muslim population.[191]

Two days later Ambassador Currie met with former Foreign Minister Said Pasha who had been instructed by the Sultan to present the following proposal: if the British Government agreed that the Commission of Control should remain under the supervision of the Foreign Ministry, and the Dragomans from the embassies of all three Powers should communicate with the Commission through the Foreign Ministry, the Porte would accept the proposals of the three Powers on the following five points: institution of rural guards, reform of gendarmerie, proportion of Christians in the administration, nomination of mayors, and prison reforms.[192] Currie had barely forwarded the proposal to London when, the following morning, Said Pasha appeared at the British Embassy to withdraw the original proposal and transmit to the Ambassador the following changes: if the Powers accepted its position on the Commission, the Porte would 'agree to discuss' the above five points.[193] Several days later, the latter proposal was officially presented by Foreign Minister Turkhan Pasha to the envoys of the three Powers. Currie told the Foreign Minister that the Powers would insist on the inclusion of European members, but Turkhan Pasha categorically rejected the idea.[194]

On September 4, Lobanov-Rostovsky noted in his dispatch to Kroupensky that in his assessment, the Porte gave in to nearly all the significant demands of the three Powers and agreed to establish direct communications between the Dragomans and the Commission of Control to avoid the Commission of Supervision proposed by Lord Salisbury.[195]

Currie's assessment of the Sultan's proposal was different, and he did not think that the Porte essentially accepted all the proposals of the three Powers. He noted that missing from the Turkish proposal were: the appointment of a Christian deputy to the Commission Chairman, control over the appointment of governors, security measures for the Armenian population living outside of the six provinces, setting aside part of the tax revenues for local purposes, judicial reforms and many others. Currie recommended that Salisbury continue to press the Porte for acceptance of the May program in toto, and reject the formation of a joint commission. He noted that his French and Russian colleagues were tepid to the idea of a joint commission, being convinced that the Sultan would give in to such a demand only under threat of force and that the European commissioners would have no practical influence over their Turkish colleagues who took orders from the Porte. Currie also recommended that the Porte be forced to publicize the reforms program in a Sultan's Decree, and that military Vice Consuls be appointed in the eastern provinces so that the program not remain a dead letter. Currie noted his belief that the Russians would be hard-pressed to resist any British moves that could improve the conditions of the Armenian population, with the exception of a naval deployment in the Dardanelles. Nevertheless, he accepted that the Russians were generally concerned with the British intercessions on the Armenian Question as well as with the influence they now commanded among the Christian peoples in Asia Minor who, according to Currie, expected the assistance only of England to solve their problems.[196]

Salisbury concurred with the Ambassador's assessment, noting that he would accept the offer presented by the Porte in writing if it contained the reforms demanded by the Ambassadors and differed from the May proposals only in unimportant aspects. He added that he had no confidence in a commission comprised of Turkish subjects exclusively and feared they would prolong their work by several years. He also concurred with Currie's proposal for an Imperial Decree and the appointment of military Vice-Consuls.[197]

On September 9, Turkhan Pasha communicated to the foreign embassies the Sultan's decision to acquiesce to six additional reform measures. He expressed hope that Great Britain would be satisfied with the program, which he said would finally settle the Armenian Question and restore law and order in the eastern provinces. The Foreign Minister then insinuated that the three Powers would bear the whole responsibility for the possible harassment of the Muslim population by the 'Armenian revolutionary committees' working through the Christian members of the gendarmerie, police, and local administration. He referred to the massacres allegedly committed by the Armenian rebel bands in Erzinjan and Sivas, and suggested that the 'Armenian revolutionary committees' strove to provoke the Muslim population against the Armenians. He added that the Porte instructed the local authorities to prevent reciprocal massacres by the Muslim population. In conclusion, Turkhan Pasha noted that the Armenian population used to be peaceful but now, under the influence of England, it became 'discontent and unstable.' Hoping to put an end to the Armenian Question, the Foreign Minister said, the Porte passed the proposal for a reform program put forth by the Powers and requested that the Powers warn the Armenians that nothing more could be expected.[198]

Currie also met with Catholic Armenian Patriarch Monsignor Azarian and Armenian Patriarch of Constantinople Izmirlyan. Monsignor Azarian told the Ambassador he had not proselytized among the Armenian Apostolic Christians but offered his good offices for communications between the Armenian Apostolic Church and the Turkish authorities. This, however, incurred the wrath of the Armenian Church hierarchy, Azarian said, and the Armenian Patriarch refused to have any dealings with him. Azarian observed that he wanted a peaceful resolution to the dispute between the two Armenian churches, without recourse to a Turkish court, and asked the Ambassador to intercede with the Patriarch. Currie added to his report that Azarian had the reputation of a 'traitor,' and changed his position only after having received death threats from the Armenian revolutionary committees.[199]

During his meeting with the Patriarch, Currie assured him that the British Government would spare no effort to secure the life and property of the Christian population in the Ottoman Empire, but added that he had to act in concert with the Russian and French envoys. Currie asked the Patriarch to comment on the alleged activities of the Armenian revolutionary committees, but His Beatitude disclaimed any knowledge of existence thereof. He added that the living conditions of the Armenian population sharply deteriorated after the British and European show of support for their cause since it only served to enrage the Turkish Government. The Patriarch said that only under European pressure would the Porte carry out reforms capable of restoring peace in the Armenian-populated regions.[200]

On September 11, Salisbury told Rustem Pasha that the British Government was interested in a speedy resolution of the Armenian Question. Salisbury noted that it could be resolved only if the Sultan afforded guarantees for the lives and property of the Armenian-populated provinces, and proposed two methods by which it could be obtained. First, the government functionaries at all levels had to include a certain proportion of Christians, as set forth in the Ambassadors' May Memorandum, and the high-level Muslim government officials had to have a Christian deputy, and vice versa. Alternatively, the current Muslim-dominated administration could continue under the supervision of European commissioners empowered to report possible abuses to the European Ambassadors in Constantinople. Salisbury instructed Ambassador Lascelles to present his position to the Russian Government.[201]

On September 14, the Porte communicated its response through Ambassador Rustem Pasha. The proposal to establish a European Commission of Control was rejected out of hand on the grounds that it constituted intervention in the internal affairs of Turkey and would undermine the sovereign rights of the Sultan which the three Powers had promised to uphold. As for the proportional appointment of the Christians to government offices, the Porte referred to the second point in the additional reforms draft providing for Christian assistants to be appointed to the Governors and District Chiefs and for the enrollment of Christian officers in the gendarmerie and police. The Porte also claimed that Christian officials had already been enrolled in local administrations on a proportional basis, and thus this demand had been implemented.[202]

Dissatisfied with the Turkish offer, the Foreign Office held consultations with the French Ambassador and Russian Chargé in London on September 23–25 to coordinate the activities of the three Ambassadors in Constantinople. The British diplomats suggested that (1) appointments to the office of governor be open to Christians; (2) proportion of Christians among Deputy Governors be strictly observed; and (3) that Christian assistants be appointed to Muslim Governors and Deputy Governors. As a result of consultations, it was agreed that the three Powers' ambassadors should present a joint memorandum to the Porte urging addition of the latter demand to the six points in the Sultan's reforms draft, threatening to raise the issue of inclusion of European Commissioners again.[203]

The Chairman of the Turkish Governmental Commission, Shakir Pasha, arrived in Trabzon in early September. Consul Longworth reported to Currie that he found the commission's mandate to be restricted, especially in economic and financial matters, which meant that the commission's objective was hardly attainable if not futile.[204] On September 9, Shakir Pasha briefed British Consul in Erzurum Graves on his plans to build roads and add 210 Christians to the gendarmerie, and complained that this proposal had been stymied by, among other things, lack of funds and by the animosity between the Muslim and Christian communities that had been cultivated by some government officials.[205]

Throughout July–September, the British Consular officers in eastern Asia Minor (Consuls R. W. Graves in Erzurum, H. Z. Longworth in Trabzon, H.

A. Cumberbatch in Angora, Henry Barnham in Alexandretta, Vice Consuls C. M. Hallward in Van, Charles Hampson in Mush, and Thomas Boyadjian in Kharput) continued to submit reports on the difficult conditions of local Armenian population, clashes between the Muslims and Christians, Kurdish attacks, incitement of the Muslim mob against the Armenians by the local Turkish officials, and spread of the Armenian revolutionary movement.[206] On August 26, Vice Consul Hampson reported to Graves that he had reliable information about a clandestine society, comprised of the "worst characters" among the Muslim population, that had been established with the sole purpose of committing violence against the Christian population if the reforms were put forward.[207]

4. The British-German Negotiations of 1895 and the Armenian Question

The main objectives of German diplomacy in the Near East in the mid-1890's were the sharpening of Anglo-Russian dissension in that region and the prevention of collusion between the two Powers on partitioning of the Ottoman Empire, and consequently emerge as a genuine friend of the Sultan and the Porte. The rationale for the German position was a simple calculation that the British-Russian agreement on the fate of the Ottoman Empire would leave them with a lion's share of the spoils. In turn, Abdul Hamid wanted to have Germany as a counterbalance to the joint diplomatic actions of Britain, France, and Russia. When it became apparent in the summer of 1895 that the British and Russian Governments came close to agreement on the Armenian Question, German diplomacy went to work to derail such an agreement. It first approached London, and then, in November 1895, made overtures to the Czarist regime. The Germans offered to back the Russians' demands for the Straits and Constantinople in a scheme of the possible partition of the Ottoman Empire. Germany's outward professions of friendship with the Sultan and concern for the integrity of the Empire and the double-dealing with Russia were deceits to hide a young and hungry colonial appetite.

The British Government's disagreements with Russia on Persia and Tibet, and with France over Indochina, and its policy of maintaining the balance of power made it necessary to make overtures to Germany. British diplomacy skillfully engaged in double-dealing of its own: it used the prospect of a German-British alliance, so unnerving for the Russian Government, as a tool during the Russian-British negotiations, while simultaneously making proposals to Berlin for partitioning of the Turkish domains.

The British-German negotiations held in July–August 1895 are still among the darkest pages of recent modern history, since Lord Salisbury conducted them in utmost secrecy with the German Ambassador and Kaiser Wilhelm. The government papers on this issue have not yet been made public.[208]

Meeting with German Ambassador Count Paul von Hatzfeldt on July 9, Lord Salisbury noted the difficult conditions prevalent in Turkey and told him of his plans to reach an agreement with Russia on partitioning of the Ottoman Empire. The report of the German Ambassador convinced German Foreign Minister Baron Marschall von Bieberstein and Foreign Ministry State Counselor Friedrich Holstein that the British Government had already made plans for the division of Turkey. On July 27, Salisbury informed British Ambassador to Russia Lascelles, that the German envoy in London had been extremely concerned with the possibility of an Anglo-Russian agreement on the fate of Turkey. Salisbury added that Hatzfeldt proposed that such an agreement be signed by Britain and Germany, not Russia.[209]

The British historian James Grenville denies the possibility of German-British negotiations on the partitioning of the Ottoman Empire, since Russia was by far a better suitor for such a deal. According to him, Ambassador Hatzfeldt exaggerated the importance of possible discussions on the subject in an attempt to tout a major improvement in German-British relations.[210] In turn, Margaret Jefferson has also presented evidence that the British Government had never come forward with such a proposal. She refers to Salisbury's diary notes: having heard that interpretation of his conversation with the German Ambassador, he noted that he had never said that.[211]

In early August, German Kaiser Wilhelm II arrived in England in early August for joint naval maneuvers. During a dinner given by the Queen, he discussed the subject of Turkey with Lord Salisbury. Ambassador Hatzfeldt noted that the British Prime Minister had not raised the issue of partitioning but merely commented on the deplorable state of the Christian subjects of the Sultan. The Kaiser said he was optimistic about the improvement in Turkey's internal affairs and urged Salisbury to recommend to the Sultan that he get rid of corrupt officials. Salisbury's conclusion after his discussion with the German Kaiser was that Germany was apprehensive about the perceived pro-

Armenian tilt in British policy and the possible undermining of the Sultan's authority. In a telegram to Currie summarizing his discussions with the German and Austrian Ambassadors, he noted that the European governments were in opposition to the British position on the Armenian Question. Germany and Austria-Hungary, in particularly, were highly critical of the British stance, calling it quixotic and dangerous, Salisbury added. While France had no sympathy for the British position, it had to support the Russian regime, which had to uphold its status as defender of the Orthodox faith despite the concerns over its Armenian population. Therefore, Salisbury concluded that Russia and France would rather support Britain on this issue.[212]

On August 6, Lord Salisbury refused to call on Kaiser Wilhelm on board his yacht *Hohenzollern*. The ruling elites in both countries perceived this snub to be of historic significance, and the Kaiser was so upset that upon returning to Berlin, he authorized a series of articles critical of the British Prime Minister in the pro-government *Die Standart*.[213]

The Kaiser, nevertheless, did not give up his plans to derail a Russian-British understanding on the Ottoman Empire. Receiving the new British military attaché, Colonel Leopold Sweeney, the Kaiser presented to him a personally designed plan to partition the Ottoman Empire and promised to back the British show of force in Turkey, if the Triple Alliance countries were properly compensated. The Kaiser said he believed the political crisis in Turkey was nearing its peak and would result in a palace coup. He proposed awarding Egypt to England, Constantinople, Asia Minor and the eastern Balkans to Russia, Salonica to Austria-Hungary, and the Mediterranean islands and Sudan to Italy. In addition to this grandiose scheme, the German Kaiser recommended that the British Government promise to cede Syria to Russia to generate friction in Russian-French relations.[214]

Thus, the German Kaiser began to advocate partition of the Ottoman Empire. Lord Salisbury grew increasingly concerned about the possible isolation of the British Government, even a Crimean War–like scenario with Britain as the current-day Russia,[215] and rejected the German proposal out of hand. Having made a reference to possible cooperation in the partitioning plan to Germany, Salisbury only wanted to ascertain the German position and create an additional point of disagreement between Russia and Germany.

The Sultan's government had apparently never learned of the British-

German discussions on the subject of its future dismemberment, while the German Government continued to profess indifference to the internal affairs of the Ottoman Empire.

5. The Massacres of the Armenians in the Ottoman Empire and British Diplomacy, September 1895–August 1896

Despite the support and sympathy for the Armenian population expressed publicly by Salisbury, Gladstone and other prominent public figures, as well as overwhelmingly by the public, nothing influenced the implementation of reforms in the Armenian-populated provinces in the Ottoman Empire. Moreover, the Armenian political parties, buoyed by the pronouncements of British politicians and the media, rushed to condemn the Sultan's anti-Armenian policies. Despite the fact that the Armenian parties carried no real political weight and did not enjoy popular support among the Armenian population, the Sultan's government skillfully used the political activities of these groups as a pretext to launch large-scale massacres of the Armenian population.[216] The Armenian political parties that were headed and led by exiles from abroad had indeed increased their activities during that period, staging anti-government demonstrations and drawing the attention of the European public to the violations of the Treaty of Berlin and the excesses of the Ottoman regime. As American author Edwin Pears noted, any hopes of the Armenian revolutionary groups to secure European intervention on behalf of the Armenian people were 'mindless and dangerous.'[217]

On September 28, while the British, French, and Russian Embassies were holding consultations on the course of the proposed reforms program and finding common ground in negotiations with the Sultan, the three Ambassadors received identical letters from the Huntchak Armenian Revolutionary Committee. The Huntchaks notified the foreign envoys of their intention to spearhead a peaceful demonstration in Constantinople to demand that reforms be carried out in the Armenian-populated provinces. The organizers expressed hope that the Porte would not deploy the police and troops against the peaceful demonstration and disavowed any responsibility for regretful incidents should the authorities use force to disperse the rally.[218]

On September 30, some 2000 Armenians marched to the Sultan's residence Bab Ali, demanding an immediate implementation of reform measures. The demonstrators prepared a petition on administrative, economic, and judicial reforms, based largely on the May Memorandum. According to Currie's October 1 report to the Foreign Office, some 2000 [Author's note: the Armenian sources say 4000] demonstrators, who were mostly young middle-class men, were stopped by the gendarmerie and ordered to disperse. The demonstrators defied the ban, and a gunfight ensued during which Gendarmerie Chief Server Bey, 15 gendarmes, and 60 Armenian demonstrators were shot and killed. The gendarmerie and police dispersed the demonstration and arrested more than 500 participants, treating them with the utmost brutality. Then, the Muslim mob, armed with clubs, began to attack Armenians randomly on the streets, assaulting and killing without regard to the police, which did not intervene. More than 1,000 Armenian residents, including women and children, took refuge in the Patriarchal residence. Despite official assurances that law and order had been restored, the killings continued unabated, Currie reported.[219]

The firing of gunshots at the gendarmerie chief was used by the Turkish Government as a pretext for an Armenian massacre that claimed the lives of more than 6,000 Armenians.[220] Maccoll noted that the Armenian rally was lawful and peaceful but the Armenian community in Constantinople was subjected to a pogrom on account of a single gunshot. There was no evidence that the officer was killed by an Armenian demonstrator, and in fact, an Italian newspaper reported that it was a bodyguard of the Grand Vizier who fired the critical bullet so that there would be cause to crack down.[221]

The Spectator reported that while some Armenian demonstrators carried pistols, the city was flooded with regular troops and Osman Ghazi could have re-established order in the city within three hours. "There was no necessity for brutality. The decision to teach the Christians a lesson was made by the fanatical palace camarilla and local criminals and plainclothes police carried out a 24-hour massacre in the capital without the slightest interference from the police. Terror and violence reigned supreme," the weekly concluded.[222] Some British periodicals condemned the Armenian activists for staging a rally. The Standard Review blamed the organizers of the rally for the massacre. According to the newspaper, the lives and property of the Armenian community in Constantinople was protected and therefore there was no need to hold an anti-government rally.[223]

On the morning of October 2, the Ambassadors of six Powers met at the

Austrian Chancery to draft a joint statement on the Constantinople incident. The Ambassadors demanded that the Porte use only government troops to restore law and order, decried the inciting of the mob against the Armenians, and protested the police brutality toward the jailed Armenians.[224]

On October 2, Currie reported to the Foreign Office that the Turkish Foreign Minister ignored the demarche and told the Ambassadors that the government had already taken all measures to restore law and order and provide public safety. He dismissed the claims of massacres as hearsay and accused the Armenian Patriarch of provoking the anti-government demonstrations. Currie had information that the Sultan had personally ordered the War and Police Ministers to suppress the Armenian groups with brutality.[225] Currie forwarded the text of the Ambassadors' demarche to the Grand Vizier and demanded, on behalf of the British Government, to stop the massacres of the Armenian population in several districts of the capital.[226]

On October 4, Currie called on Grand Vizier Kiamil Pasha and presented evidence on the events that had taken place in the capital. The Ambassador urged the Vizier in strong terms to provide security to the Armenians who found refuge in the churches and to create conditions for them to return to their homes. Kiamil Pasha claimed to have been surprised by the facts and promised to conduct a fair investigation with the participation of a representative from the Embassy. The Vizier said it was necessary to find a settlement of the Armenian Question and noted that an agreement existed between the Porte and the Powers on the Armenian reforms. Currie retorted that there were some outstanding issues on the reforms program and requested that the program be announced in a decree by the Sultan.[227]

On October 4, Lord Salisbury received a letter from Queen Victoria who expressed her indignation over the Armenian massacres and suggested occupying the Turkish Straits as the only measure to prevent further massacres of the Armenian population in the Ottoman Empire.[228]

Currie reported on October 5 that Constantinople's Armenian population was gripped by panic and fear, as many residents fled to the sanctuary of local churches, and the arrests continued. The Patriarch told the British Embassy Dragoman that he could no longer restrain the community which was in despair. According to the Ambassador, medical examination of some 80 corpses in the Armenian hospital clearly showed the extent of the terrible brutality. The Embassy continued to receive reports of a large number of prominent Armenians who were murdered or missing, in addition to the many servants and working class people who met similar fates.

A decision was made at another meeting of the Ambassadors on October 5 to present a joint memorandum to the Porte, while the British Cabinet authorized deployment of six warships to Lemnos Island.[229] In the memorandum, dated October 6, the European diplomatic missions cited the evidence of the massacres and noted the continuing deterioration of public safety in the capital. The memorandum warned that the disturbances could spread to other parts of the Empire, if uncontained. The Embassies called on the Porte to take measures to check fanaticism in the Muslim and Christian communities, provide security to the Christian subjects and foreign nationals, and offered their assistance in the re-establishment of public order, collecting evidence and conducting an inquiry.[230]

The Sultan ordered Artin Dadyan Pasha, to visit the Patriarch and persuade the Armenians hiding in the church to leave, but the Armenians refused to go since the revolutionary committee had ordered them to stay in the church and close down shops and stores.[231] The British Embassy estimated that more than 2000 Armenians were hiding in the Patriarchal Church and the church in the Kum Kapu district, which was besieged by the gendarmerie.[232]

On October 7, Abdul Hamid instructed Zeki Pasha to call on Currie to tell him that the presence of a British fleet in the vicinity of the capital encouraged the Armenian revolutionary groups to continue resistance, and to request that the warships be deployed to Salonica instead. Zeki Pasha said that public order could not be restored as long as the British fleet was near Lemnos since the revolutionary committees hoped to provoke the Turkish population to commit acts of brutality to create a casus belli for the British naval deployment to Constantinople with subsequent demands for Armenian autonomy.

Currie replied that even if the disturbances had been provoked by the Armenians, it was the Muslim mob that continued the unrest without the least interference by the police. The Turkish authorities should restore public order and mutual confidence between the communities, he said. If the official response from the Porte satisfied the European Ambassadors, Currie said, he would forward to the Foreign Office the Sultan's request to have the warships moved from Lemnos.

In response to Zeki Pasha's claims that the events in Constantinople had been caused by the shots fired by the Armenian revolutionaries, Currie said that the widespread massacres of the Armenians could not be justified by the criminal actions of some activists.[233]

On October 8, Currie reported to Salisbury that an Armenian pogrom had taken place in Trabzon. The British consul reported a wave of murders and robberies that was waged for a day and took the lives of many victims. Order was restored overnight, he noted, but there were few government troops and the city was gripped by panic. 182 Armenians and 11 Turks were dead, while 19 Armenians, 26 Turks, and one Greek were wounded.[234] That the Army garrison took part in the massacres of the Armenians was confirmed by Russian Ambassador Nelidov. A Russian Consulate official testified that the Governor personally authorized distribution of arms to the Laz tribal elements and that the Armenian pogroms had been organized with 'exceptional premeditation.' Only members of the Armenian Apostolic Church had been killed while the Catholic Armenians and Russian subjects were spared, according to the Russian Consul.[235]

On October 9, the Porte responded to the Ambassadors' memorandum with a promise to take steps to prevent new disturbances from breaking out and to protect the Christians and foreign nationals. The Army and police would jointly patrol the streets day and night, and the authorities issued calls for calm through the newspapers and Sheikh-ul-Islam.[236]

On the same day, Said Pasha visited the French Chancery to meet with the European Powers' Ambassadors. He said that the Porte decided to allow free passage for all Armenians hiding in the churches, on the condition that they surrender their arms. The Ambassadors sent their Dragomans to deliver the news to the Armenian Churches to persuade the Armenian residents to return to their homes, and indeed, they began to do so the following day. According to the British Embassy Dragoman, out of 2414 Armenians hiding in the churches, only 12% were armed.[237]

On October 10, Currie reported to Salisbury that he had met with the French and Russian Ambassadors to discuss the upcoming program of reforms and the protection of the lives and property of the Armenians. The Ambassador's report proposed that the reforms program was to be formalized in the form of an agreement or treaty with the Powers and issued as an Imperial Decree.

This program included provisions for (1) a Christian assistant to Shakir Pasha, whose name should be unofficially submitted to the Powers for their approval; (2) the participation of Christians in the administration, and the posts of Governors and Deputy Governors to be open to Christians; (3) the Dragomans having the right of addressing to the Commission of Control any complaint, communication, or information; (4) the Commission of Control fixing the number of Christian functionaries in proportion to each vilayet; (5) Christian assistants being attached to the Muslim Governors and Vice Governors; (6) the Ambassadors reserving the right to remonstrate against the appointment of incapable, dishonest, or fanatical governors; (7) the number of rural guards being fixed by the Governor on the recommendation of the district police chief and in conformity with local requirements; (8) a note to be addressed by the Ambassadors to the Porte respecting prisons, arbitrary arrests, amnesty, reinstatement of emigrants, regulations for the Hamidiye cavalry, and insisting upon their complete and immediate execution; (9) a stipulation that the principles of the reform scheme would be applied to all the sanjaks and cazas of Asia Minor where the Christians form a palpable part of the population.[238]

On October 11, Ambassador Currie was received by Sultan Abdul Hamid who said that the British expressions of sympathy for the Armenians had had the effect of encouraging them in 'acts of violence' and complained of the attacks made on his person in the British press. The Ambassador said that the British Government carried responsibility neither for the press nor in the described acts of violence. The Ambassador assured the Sultan that the British interference in the Armenian Question had been directed to obtaining an amelioration of the condition of the Armenians in the Asiatic provinces.

The Ambassador further noted that it had been the Government's intention that the question of reforms should be brought to a speedy conclusion. Ambassador Currie, therefore, suggested that the Sultan authorize his Foreign Minister to confer with the British, French, and Russian Ambassadors to discuss, publicly proclaim, and implement the new proposals for the reforms. The Ambassador noted that the publication of reforms would be important in terms of satisfying public opinion in Europe, and it would calm the 'agitation' of the Armenians.

Currie said he had assured the Sultan that the British Government had no hostile feeling toward the Sultan or his Muslim subjects. "On the contrary," the Ambassador wrote, "they [the British Government] believed that a reform in the administration of the Asiatic provinces was essential to the very existence of the Empire... and should be carried out in such a manner as not to wound the susceptibilities of the Muslim population."[239]

Meanwhile, Austro-Hungarian Foreign Minister Goluchowski told British Ambassador Edmund Monson[240] that he was concerned with the latest developments in the Armenian Question and the Ottoman Empire, and expressed his support for the British actions following the Constantinople events. Buoyed by the unexpected expressions of support, Salisbury instructed Monson to request the Foreign Minister to instruct the Austrian Ambassador in Turkey to cooperate with his British, French, and Russian colleagues in pushing for a reforms program. Goluchowski, however, said Austria-Hungary could not explicitly support the three Ambassadors' proposal as long as Germany remained neutral on the subject. At the same time, Goluchowski instructed the Austro-Hungarian envoy in Constantinople to urge the Sultan to accept the three Ambassadors' plan.[241]

On October 13, the three Ambassadors met with Said Pasha and presented him with additional proposals for the reforms program. The Turkish Foreign Minister assured the Ambassadors that the program would be discussed at the Council of Ministers and on October 15 he said it would be released in the form of an Imperial Decree. Similar assurances had been received from the newly appointed Grand Vizier Kiamil Pasha.[242]

The Sultan's government passed different messages to Currie. The British Ambassador was told by Zeki Pasha that the program for reforms in the Armenian-populated provinces caused resentment among the Muslim subjects of the Sultan. Zeki Pasha added that the British demands on this subject could have ramifications on the future of bilateral relations, but Currie replied that the only safe policy for the Sultan was to unveil the promised reform program in his decree, without further delays. He said that British public opinion pressured the government to take a more active position, and there were calls for deployment of the British Navy. If the reforms were not carried out, nothing could save the Sultan or his Empire, the Ambassador noted.[243]

On October 17, Currie reported to Salisbury that the Sultan had signed a decision promulgating the reforms program negotiated by the three Ambassadors and the Turkish Foreign Ministry. Currie noted that the Sultan's decision was most likely to be released in the form of a decree or as an order to the Grand Vizier. Salisbury expressed his heartfelt congratulations to Currie. In turn, the Armenian Patriarch expressed the gratitude of the Armenian community to the British Embassy, promised to cooperate with the authorities in the implementation of the program and to restrain revolutionary agitation.

Abdul Hamid's mood was far from cheerful. He told the Russian Ambassador that although he had made a decision to carry out the reforms program, his Muslim subjects made the situation difficult with their demands. The Sultan expressed his displeasure with the Armenian Patriarch, accusing him of being the force behind the reforms agitation and unworthy of his position.[244]

On October 20, Currie received an official note from the Porte on the implementation of the reforms program, to which was attached an order from the Grand Vizier to Shakir Pasha.[245] The following day, the Grand Vizier told Currie that the resentment toward the program was widespread among the Muslims. At the same time, the information at the Ambassador's disposal testified to a generally positive reaction to the program among the Muslim population; in fact, there was widespread sentiment that the program should be carried out in the whole country.[246]

Meanwhile, Currie reported to Salisbury that a secret fort had been constructed not far from the Medjidie Castle on the Dardanelles with 12 cannons and mine launchers. Torpedoes had been installed at the Hamidiye and Sultanie Castles on the Asiatic side of the Strait and at the Namazie Castle on the European side.[247] This was proof of the Turkish Government's reluctance to carry out the promised program since it was clearly preparing to repulse a possible British or allied naval deployment in the Straits.

On October 22, Currie reported that the military and police commands in Trabzon and Akhisar had urged the local population to commit violence against the Armenians who had been accused of harboring secret plans to attack the Turks. The Grand Vizier told British Dragoman Marinitch that according to the Governor of Aleppo, the Armenians in the Andrin and

Zeytoun regions of Asia Minor had attacked the local Muslims. The Ambassador was convinced that the government was preparing to crack down on the Armenians in Zeytoun, who were well known for their fighting spirit. He recommended that the Mediterranean Fleet commander be ordered to deploy warships to Alexandretta if the crackdown began and that consultations be held with the other Powers to avert a disaster.[248]

British missionary Chambers testified that the primary targets of the pogrom in Akhisar were the Armenian storekeepers and merchants, whose property was looted. The perpetrators were the Turkish settlers from Bulgaria, Bosnia, and Rumelia, who were directed and encouraged by the local authorities, gendarmerie, and the Army. According to the missionary, there had been no trace of revolutionary activity in Akhisar, the Armenians had not been armed and had not resisted.[249] The Turkish Foreign Ministry circular sent to the Turkish Embassies presented a completely opposite picture, accusing the local Armenians of having attacked the Muslim population.[250]

On October 23, Currie reported to Salisbury, citing a report by Consul Cumberbatch in Erzurum, that riots broke out there, resulting in the deaths of several Muslims and more than 60 Armenians. The official report claimed that the melee started after a group of Armenians shot a mullah. The Consul reported that Kurdish and Las tribal gangs had robbed the Armenian residents of nearby villages.[251]

Confirming the British Ambassador's fears, the Grand Vizier summoned Dragoman Marinitch on October 23 and told him that the Armenian groups in Zeytoun had attacked the Turkish villages in Andrin and wounded 32 Muslims, including two police officers. The Armenian groups were supposedly gathering in Deredin. Acting on Currie's prior warning, Marinitch urged the Grand Vizier to avoid another bloodbath, and the Vizier said he had urged the Armenian Patriarch to issue calls for calm to the clergy in Zeytoun and Marash.[252]

On October 23, Salisbury instructed the British Ambassadors in France, Russia, Germany, Austria-Hungary, and Italy to hold consultations to prepare ground for pressuring the Porte and the local authorities in Zeytoun to prevent another massacre. He also informed them that the Admiralty would be given orders to deploy warships near the shore of Aleppo province.[253] The Foreign Office asked the Admiralty to draw up plans for a naval expedition to Alexandretta or nearby ports, in the expectation of a possible massacre of the Armenians in the wake of Armenian-Turkish clashes in Zeytoun. The letter noted Salisbury's preference for Ambassador Currie to give the go signal to the fleet commander if the crisis broke out. The Admiralty confirmed its readiness to do so.[254]

Accepting Salisbury's proposal, the Powers instructed their ambassadors in Constantinople to work together toward preventing another massacre of the Armenian population in Aleppo province and elsewhere. On October 24, the dragomans of six European Embassies met with the Grand Vizier and presented their governments' position. Kiamil Pasha replied that the efforts of the Porte and the Armenian Patriarch had paid off, and public order was restored nearly in all provinces. He mentioned that the city of Aintab had been illuminated to celebrate the passage of the reforms measure.[255]

On the same day, Currie made a courtesy call on Abdul Hamid before setting off for a two-week trip home. The Sultan expressed hope that the British Government had been satisfied with the reform measures and considered the matter closed. The Ambassador replied that all depended on the way the reforms would be carried out, as well as on the quality and abilities of the officials appointed to the provincial administration and the Commission of Control. The Sultan assured Currie of his honest intentions to carry out the reforms and requested that the British Government publicly state its approval with the reforms measure to head off criticism of the Sultan's government in the British press.[256]

On October 26, acting British Consul in Angora Fontana reported to Currie that upon receiving news from the capital, the Muslim population had begun to arm and threaten violent reprisals against the Christian communities. A committee of six Muslim fanatics was spearheading the movement and drafted plans for a simultaneous attack on the Christian quarter. According to Fontana, tensions were high in Yuzgat and Kayseri where the Armenians closed down their shops and made barricades. The situation in Yuzgat was aggravated by a group of 28 fanatical Muslims who had recently returned from a pilgrimage to Mecca and had been decorated by the Sultan.[257]

The following day, Currie received a report from the British Consul in Trabzon about the disturbances in Gümüshkaneh, which did not carry any details or the number of casualties.[258] Vice Consul Hampson reported from Mush that more than 630 Armenians had been killed in Bitlis. The Armenian community in Mush had been terrified by the news, and all the Armenian-owned shops were closed. Hampson noted that the Armenians in Mush or elsewhere had neither the desire nor the ability to attack the Muslims.[259]

On October 28, Said Pasha told British Chargé d'affairés Michael Herbert that the disturbances in Marash, Zeytoun, Bitlis, Gümüshkaneh, Baiburt, and Kharput had been caused by the Armenians. He declared that an Armenian mob attacked a mosque in Bitlis, and as a result, 173 Muslims and 179 Armenians had been killed. Said Pasha added that an Armenian paramilitary unit in Zeytoun numbering more than 2000 armed men had attacked a gendarmerie convoy killing five officers and their commander.[260]

Also on October 28, the Armenian Patriarch appealed to the British Government and other European Powers to intervene to prevent massacres in Asia Minor. Herbert informed the Patriarch that the Embassy had periodically made representations to the Porte and would hold consultations with the other embassies to chart a joint course of action.[261]

On October 29, Salisbury instructed Herbert not to make a tough statement to the Porte on the question of the Armenian massacres, lest it have negative results and further increase the tensions while the massacres continued, providing the Turkish Government with a pretext to request that the missionaries helping the destitute Armenians be recalled.[262]

Salisbury must have had a premonition about the Turkish Government's intentions. On the very next day, Herbert reported that the Porte had demanded the evacuation of the missionaries from Sasun, at the request of the Bitlis administration. Meeting with the Foreign Minister, Dragoman Marinitch condemned the decision and decried the lack of understanding for the missionaries' humanitarian objectives. The U.S. Embassy also protested the action since the majority of missionaries were American citizens.[263]

On October 30, Said Pasha asked Herbert if the British Government's would object to his concurrent appointment as the Chairman of the Commission of Control over the reforms in the Armenian-populated provinces. Herbert did object to such an appointment, arguing that the Commission should have administrative, not political functions and be independent of the Porte. He said that the British Government would welcome Said Pasha's appointment as Commission Chairman if he resigned from the Foreign Ministry, Herbert said. The Foreign Minister seemed to have concurred.[264]

On October 31, Hampson reported from Mush that the tensions in the province were at an all time high, and he was particularly worried about the situation in Sasun where the local authorities had proved unable to control the Kurdish tribes attacking, robbing, and killing Armenian villagers. Hampson suggested that the decision to remove the missionaries had been made because the local Muslim population had accused the missionaries of inciting the Armenians.[265] Herbert reported to Salisbury that the mood of the Muslims in Aleppo province was threatening and the situation grew worse daily. According to reports from the field, the Armenians had surrounded the Turkish troops between Zeytoun and Marash, and reserves were expected. Herbert noted he feared serious consequences if the Turkish troops were defeated.[266]

On November 1, Hampson cabled the Embassy that he had no reliable information about the events in Bitlis although reports indicated a large number of casualties and high tensions in the city. There were 400 corpses piled up near an Armenian church. The situation in Mush was also difficult; the Muslim mob calling for the expulsion of the missionaries and forcing the Armenian residents to sign a petition urging Hampson's recall.[267] The Acting Consul in Erzurum reported that the main target of riots in the city was the Armenian shops; some 60 people had been killed, most of them Armenians.[268]

The same day, Herbert met with Patriarch Izmirlyan and informed him of the Turkish claim that the Armenians had been the aggressors, causing disturbances and riots; he asked the Patriarch to do all in his power to calm the people. The Patriarch said he could not control the revolutionary movement, agreed on the magnitude of its activities, and suggested that it had been inspired by Russian agents and financed from Tiflis. Under pressure from Herbert, the Patriarch agreed to send a circular telegram exhorting the Armenians to be patient and remain quiet pending the publication and execution of the reforms.[269]

Also on November 1, Dragoman Block met with the Grand Vizier to discuss the situation in the eastern provinces. The Grand Vizier had assured the British diplomat that the Porte had done all in its power to restore public order throughout the Empire and had ordered the Muslim population not to resort to vengeance and to remain quiet. He admitted the potentially catastrophic consequences for the Empire if the disturbances continued, and blamed the situation on the Armenians. He gave the standard line: the Armenian societies provoked the Armenian population to commit aggression and clash with the Muslims to cause the intervention of the European Powers. The Grand Vizier said the Turkish Government was intending to uproot the movement which would be impossible with the gendarmerie and police forces alone. The Government therefore was calling up almost 40 battalions of reserves who would also restrain the Muslim populations.[270]

On November 2, Herbert reported to Salisbury that, according to a report from Consul Barnham in Aleppo, a Muslim mob sacked the Armenian Quarter in Urfa and killed an Armenian. After the Government made some arrests among the attackers, a larger mob comprised of Arabs, Kurds, and Turks launched another attack on the Armenian Quarter resulting in a greater number of casualties. Unable to control the situation, the municipal authorities resorted to the reserves that however sided with the mob.[271] Riots broke out in Aleppo on November 3. The Muslim mob armed with sticks began to attack the Armenian houses but the municipal authorities dispersed the attackers and prevented a massacre.[272] Reports flowed in from Diyarbakir about the massacres, which lasted for three days. Five hundred Christians found refuge in the French Consulate, and the French Embassy protested to the Porte. The Grand Vizier, as usual, explained the riots away by accusing the Armenians of having first attacked the Muslims in a mosque; Herbert was convinced that the Vizier's information was not true.[273] The Acting Consul in Erzurum reported that the Armenian settlements around Erzurum had been ransacked by a large number of gangs. Two hundred and sixty Armenians and a few Turks had been killed in Erzinjan, while the casualties in Bitlis included more than 120 Armenians and 39 Turks.[274]

Despite British objections, Shefik Bey was appointed President of the Commission of Control, the British Embassy observing his lack of necessary stature. The Muslim Commissioners were Agricultural Bank Director Djemal Bey, member of the Council of State Abdullah Bey, and Djemal Bey, President of the Criminal Section of the Court of Appeal. The Christian Commissioners were Greek Orthodox Constantine Karatheodori, member of the Council of State, Armenian Catholic Sarkis Ohannes Effendi, Public Prosecutor in

Accountant-General's office, and Armenian Apostolic Church member Dilber Effendi, a legal adviser to the Porte.[275]

On November 4, Herbert reported rumors of a Muslim coup in the capital but noted that it was obvious that such a movement was leaderless, if it existed at all. The Grand Vizier said he was aware of widespread discontent among the Muslim population but added that the Sultan had taken appropriate precautionary measures.

Meeting in Constantinople on the same day, the foreign embassies decided that the time was not appropriate for making a demand for the safety of foreign citizens in the Empire.[276]

The foreign envoys approved the text of an identical note to be presented to the Porte. The memorandum stated that the envoys of the European Powers held consultations to discuss their consular officers' reports about the serious situation in many provinces of the Empire. The memorandum expressed concern for the anarchy prevalent in several regions and threatening Christians of all ethnicities and dismissed links between the Armenian agitation and disturbances. The memorandum cited examples of massacres targeting all Christians. The Christians belonging to different sects were attacked in Diyarbakir without the slightest provocation from their side, the memorandum noted, while the situation in Mosul, Baghdad, and Syria—where no Armenians lived—was threatening. The memorandum noted that the Syrian events of 1860 should have proved to the Porte that the anarchy could not go unpunished. The memorandum promised a joint action of the Powers if the Porte failed to take effective measures to address the situation and asked the Foreign Minister to present the Porte's plans to stop the disturbances.[277]

On November 4, Herbert instructed Dragoman Block to call on the Sultan's principal secretary to warn him about the 'dangers of the present situation' and urged him to take appropriate measures. The Sultan replied on the evening of the same day that the next day's newspapers would carry the text of his decree on the reforms program. The Sultan said he ordered the local authorities to prevent the Muslim attacks on the Christians, and vice versa, and to bring the riot organizers to justice. The Sultan noted with regret that it became necessary to bring in regular troops to put down the disturbances but added that they had been issued orders to use arms sparingly. Abdul Hamid assured the envoy of his high regard for Salisbury, despite the British press reports attacking his person, and said he hoped Salisbury had similar sentiment for the Sultan and Turkey.[278]

Meanwhile, Herbert continued to send reports to Salisbury on the events in Zeytoun. The British Consul in Aleppo reported that the 8000-man-strong Armenian paramilitary units had repulsed the Turkish military attack on Zeytoun and Marash that had been led by an Army Corps of 25,000 troops, had seized the city citadel, and taken 420 prisoners and two cannons. According to the Consul, an additional 20 battalions had been sent to the region, and almost 60,000 troops had been amassed in Zeytoun.[279]

In connection with the events in Zeytoun and Marash, British Embassy official Eliott was sent to persuade the Patriarch to issue a fresh appeal for calm and peace to the Armenian-populated provinces. The Patriarch reiterated that he had no influence over the revolutionary movement since it had been financed and organized by Russian agents acting out of Tiflis. The 'poor and broken-spirited' Armenians were too timid to raise arms against their Turkish neighbors, the Patriarch stated. His Beatitude suggested that the Russian Government, disappointed by the European rejection of the San Stefano treaty, did nothing to ameliorate the plight of Christians in Turkey and awaited another opportunity when everyone would turn to Russia as the only Power capable of solving the crisis in Turkey. The Patriarch said he believed Russia had encouraged the massacres in the hope that it would be invited to occupy Armenia. He said he hated Russia's tyrannical and selfish government that desired to stamp out the Armenian language and religion but if the massacres continued, he would implore Russia to march to Erzurum to save the Armenians from slaughter. Drawing parallels between Bulgaria and Armenia, the Patriarch noted that Europe had cheered on as the Bulgarians had attacked and massacred Turks wholesale while it currently behaved as if the Armenians had forfeited their claim for assistance because a few Turks had been killed by the Armenians acting out of desperation.[280]

Abdul Hamid never honored his promise to publish his reforms program. When the British Embassy Dragoman called on the Sultan's First Secretary on November 7 to inquire about the status of the reforms program, the latter said the Sultan had postponed the announcement so as not to incite fresh attacks by the Muslims against the Christian population. He added that the press had already carried a general announcement of the program and since the Armenians were well aware of it there was no need to publish the details of the program. The Sultan's aide complained that while the Powers had expressed their satisfaction with the announced reforms, the Patriarch had never expressed a word of gratitude.[281]

On November 9, Salisbury gave the traditional Guild Hall banquet speech and noted that Abdul Hamid's reforms program could alleviate the grievances of the Armenian population of the Ottoman Empire if the Sultan's government carried out the reforms in a genuine and serious way. The Prime Minister said that the Powers were unanimous in their desire to uphold the integrity of the Ottoman Empire to allow a reformed Turkey to rise on its foundations. If it did not happen, the Powers would be forced to take matters into their own hands and establish new political entities out of pieces of the Empire. Lord Salisbury warned the Sultan to contain the brutality of his government to spare himself God's wrath.[282]

On November 10, Abdul Hamid passed a message to Herbert asking for the British support and assuring of the seriousness of his intentions to carry out reforms. He said the reforms had been granted and would be honestly implemented as they were in the interests of the country. The Sultan, however, noted that it would be necessary to reestablish public order first, as the reforms had to be carried out in peaceful conditions. It was the Armenians who by acts of aggression and rebellion caused delays in the reforms process, the Sultan argued, adding that a significant number of Reserves had been called up to restore public order. He urged the British Government to recommend to his own Armenian subjects to cease 'agitation and disturbances' because the reforms would not be carried out until it was calm. He again complained about the attacks on his person in the British press and asked for Lord Salisbury's personal support to stop such attacks.[283]

On November 11, Salisbury instructed Herbert to express regret and disappointment at the postponed publication of the reforms program. He expressed readiness to assist the Sultan's government on the conditions that it took measures to stop and prevent the Muslim attacks on the Christian population in several provinces of the Ottoman Empire. Salisbury noted that reports had reached him showing that the Sultan had been mistaken in his belief that the disturbances had been caused by the Armenian elements. In fact, there had been evidence of Turkish police and military forces encouraging and even taking part in the riots, he noted.[284]

Herbert forwarded a copy of Salisbury's message to the Grand Vizier who reiterated the Sultan's belief that it would be impossible to publish the reforms program in view of the present 'effervescence' in the Muslim community. The Grand Vizier asked for a show of British support for the Porte but Herbert complained that the Porte had continuously rejected solid and friendly advice from the British Government and, therefore, the current state of affairs had been caused solely by the Turkish policies.[285]

On November 11, Russian Ambassador Nelidov proposed at the meeting of the European Ambassadors that the Powers should dispatch gunboats or lightly armed vessels to the vicinity of Constantinople.[286] He said that the presence of the European gunboats would positively affect the positions of the Powers vis-à-vis the Sultan, stop the spreading of the crisis, and prevent recourse to measures involving political complications. Herbert informed Salisbury that the Powers' representatives had, surprisingly, expressed a generally positive attitude toward the Russian proposal.[287]

On November 15, the Governments of Austria-Hungary, France, and Italy accepted the Russian proposal and dispatched a gunboat with a crew of 100 each.[288] Salisbury informed Herbert on November 16 that the British Government agreed to do likewise.[289] The Admiralty dispatched HMS *Cockatrice* to join the Powers' naval expedition in the Straits.[290]

On November 16, the British Ambassador in Germany notified the Foreign Office that the German Government dispatched the *Moltke* warship in response to the Russian proposal.[291]

While the Powers were staging a largely useless naval demonstration of force near Constantinople, the Sultan announced that the British Government would be unable to support the Armenians in their quest. Abdul Hamid noted that all attempts to establish an Armenian autonomy, whether by means of a European conference or by show of force, should be stopped. He complained that the Armenians had boasted about the Powers' naval maneuvers as if the actions of the European nations had been intended to help them.[292] Abdul Hamid was convinced that the joint expedition would not take place because of constant disagreements between Britain and Russia.[293]

The British Embassy continued to receive reports from the provinces on

continuing massacres. On November 15, Herbert reported that according to
the British Vice Consul in Alexandretta, three days before the Turkish mob
had completely destroyed the Armenian village of Odjakhli with more than
300 Armenian households; all in all, almost 30 farms had been ransacked.
Odjakhlis's sad lot was shared by the Uzuli and Chokmarzvan villages on
the following day. The Vice Consul noted that the regular troops had not
intervened to restore public order while the authorities blamed the 'Armenian
aggressors.'[294]

According to another report from Herbert, nearly 4000 Armenians had
been killed in Gürün, 500–800 Armenians—in Kharput, 800 Armenians and
Muslims in Sivas,[295] 200 Armenians in Diyarbakir and 250 in Arabkir.[296]

On November 19, Salisbury addressed a gathering of the Conservative
Party at Brighton and showed a letter from the Sultan who had expressed disappointment with Salisbury's November 9 speech and requested that public
professions of the traditional British-Turkish friendship be made. The Sultan
again promised to carry out reforms and assured his personal attention to the
implementation of the program. He asked that no warships be deployed so as
not to provoke public opinion in Turkey and obstruct efforts to restore peace
and calm necessary for the reforms process. Salisbury, nevertheless, reiterated
his determination to act in concert with other Powers on the Armenian Question and not to change the current policies.[297]

The Sultan's government was bent on obstructing the European naval demonstration in the Straits. On November 19, he requested the foreign envoys to
change the decision on the warships pointing out to the efforts to stop disturbances and restore peace. The Embassies, in turn, requested that the Porte did
not obstruct the passage of the fleet and issue a decree authorizing the naval
deployment which, the envoys noted, would promote peace in the country and
prevent recourse to more stringent measures. Herbert noted that the Sultan
was not likely to give in without a fight.[298]

The newly appointed Foreign Minister, Tewfik Pasha met with Herbert to
offer fresh assurances of the determination of the Sultan's government to do
its best to restore the public order in the Empire. According to the Minister,
almost 120 battalions had been called up, all the governors had been issued
strict orders to prevent further Muslim attacks on the Christians, and central
government officials had been sent to the regions to ensure that the orders were

carried out. The Christians and Muslim victims of the disturbances would be compensated by the government, Tewfik Pasha said. The Hamidiye units had been ordered to protect the Armenians, he added.[299] Herbert reported, citing the Russian Ambassador, that the Sultan's orders to the provincial governors included a secret clause prohibiting troops from firing on Muslim crowds under any conditions.[300]

On November 20, British Dragoman Block handed the Sultan a message from Salisbury who asked for clemency for the Zeytoun rebels. The Sultan noted that he had always been merciful toward those asking for clemency but said he wanted to do it without prejudice in honor of the Sultan's government. Abdul Hamid suggested that the Zeytoun rebels appeal for clemency to the Government or the commandant of Marash. The Sultan said he had issued orders to restore public order peacefully and without vengeance toward those who would not offer resistance. He ordered the Army Commander in Marash to delay his advance on Zeytoun by two days to allow the Armenians to lay down arms and surrender the organizers of the disturbances. Abdul Hamid requested that Salisbury urge the Patriarch to issue a call to the Armenian community to remain calm and accept the reforms.[301]

Also on November 20, British Ambassador Goschen reported from Russia that Prince Lobanov had said that in view of the extremely agitated state of his subjects, the Sultan should be given more time to restore peace and public order in the country without damage to his moral authority. The threats of intervention by the Powers would undermine the authority of the Sultan without which his actions would be irrelevant, the Russian Minister argued. Ambassador Goschen agreed that the intervention should remain a last resort and undertaken only after it was established that the Sultan did not have the requisite authority to control the situation. Goschen added that if the events spun out of control and 'horrible scenes' continued to be enacted in Asia Minor, the Powers would be compelled to honor their duty and put an end to an intolerable situation. Lobanov argued that his experience showed that Oriental disturbances tended to 'die a natural death' unless some foreign Power, guided by its own interests, stirred up the opposition elements to continue action.[302] The foreign Power in the Russian Minister's scenario was, of course, Britain, while the Armenians thus became 'opposition elements.' The Russian

Government continued to suspect the British factor in the Armenian movement which would allow Britain to pressure both the Porte and the Russians.

Goschen clearly avoided the subject noting that the Minister's prior experience was not relevant in this case since all the Powers acted in concert on the question of reforms in Armenia. Lobanov, nevertheless, continued to discuss the political complications of a military intervention in Asia Minor, primarily because of the extent of the territory where the disturbances had occurred. When France had been given the Syrian mandate in 1860, the disturbances had taken place in one district and had been easily contained, Lobanov said, but the Armenian massacres were taking place in Zeytoun, Diyarbakir, and other remote regions. Therefore, the Powers would not be able to intervene without a significant force, and the more intervention was threatened, the more encouraged Armenians would be to continue disturbances in hopes of bringing it about and inviting more bloody reprisals by the Turks.[303]

On November 21, Herbert reported to the Foreign Office on the German Ambassador's meeting with Abdul Hamid. The German Ambassador urged the Sultan to heed the advice of the Powers and take effective measures to restore public order in the Empire because the alternative would be a joint action by the Powers and, possibly, the Sultan's dethronement. The Ambassador passed a message from his sovereign who had expressed solidarity with the actions of other European Powers on the Eastern Question. The Kaiser warned Abdul Hamid that he should follow the political line recommended by the Powers, and hinted at the possibility of dethronement if the situation continued. Apparently impressed by the strong language of the demarche, Sultan Abdul Hamid promised to consult with the European representatives and regain their confidence.[304]

Following the German demarche, the European Ambassadors drafted a series of recommendations that was presented to the Porte by Austro-Hungarian Ambassador Baron Calice, who was the Dean of the Diplomatic Corps. The draft urged the Sultan to remove or dismiss all government officials responsible for the Armenian massacres; launch an inquiry into cases of regular troops having taken part in violence and bringing them to justice; publish the order to the Governors and military commanders to restore law and order; publish an Imperial Decree urging the Sultan's subjects to restrain from creating disturbances; authorize the passage of the European naval group to the

Straits; and appoint military commanders to oversee various districts of the capital and ensure the safety of the Christian population of the city.[305]

On November 22, Abdul Hamid sent Ismail Kemal Pasha to meet with Herbert. Ismail Kemal Pasha, who was a supporter of Midhat Pasha and a proponent of further liberalization of the Ottoman Empire, told Herbert that the Sultan had been disappointed with Russia and wanted to rejuvenate relations with Britain and to pursue liberal reforms. In return, the Sultan asked Britain to cancel the naval demonstration that he said would target him personally. Herbert replied that a policy of liberalization would help the Porte regain the confidence of the European Powers but continued to insist on the passage of the warships. He said that the naval demonstration was not aimed against the Sultan, but would boost the confidence of the expatriate communities in the country. He warned that if the Sultan did not grant this 'small request,' new complications would arise for him because public opinion both in the Empire and in Europe would turn against him. Herbert suggested that the Sultan authorize the passage of the ships without delay, and recommended that Ismail Kemal Pasha call on all the ambassadors who had acted in unison.[306]

Herbert informed Salisbury on November 22 that Palace officials and the police were making surveys of Armenian homes in Pera and Constantinople in preparation for a general massacre. The Russian Embassy had received similar reports, and Herbert sent a message to the Sultan asking him to stop such measures since they constituted a danger to the public order. He reminded the Sultan of the agreement with the Powers that any provocations and disturbances in Constantinople could bring about a military intervention and endanger the existence of the Empire.[307]

Another round in their regular consultations was held by the European ambassadors on November 25 to discuss the delays in issuing an authorization for the passage of the warships through the Straits. The European envoys decided to invoke the provisions of their nations' treaties with the Porte and set a deadline for such an authorization.[308]

On November 26, Turkish Chargé in London Morel Bey asked Salisbury to cancel the British naval deployment near Constantinople, arguing that the foreign citizens in Turkey were not threatened. Morel Bey argued that the fanaticism of the Muslim population had been directed against the Armenians, while the foreigners and other Christians had been spared. Salisbury refused to change the Government's position on the issue.[309] Salisbury turned down a request from Russian Ambassador Yegor Staal[310] to postpone the naval deployment; after all, the proposal to deploy a naval detachment had been made originally by Russia.[311]

The Grand Vizier informed Currie, who had arrived back in Turkey, that the Porte had instructed the local authorities in Marash to form a commission comprised of prominent Armenians with the purpose of sending it to negotiate with the rebels in Zeytoun. The British Ambassador expressed his support for the decision.[312]

On November 27, the Sultan proposed to appoint former Governor of Diyarbakir Sirri Pasha as the new President of the Commission of Control; Shakir Pasha had been removed from the position. The Ambassador noted Sirri's good character to Salisbury and suggested giving assent to the appointment.[313]

Meeting with Currie on November 29, Abdul Hamid complained of the European perceptions that he had been insincere in his determination to carry out the promised reforms without delays. The reforms project demanded lengthy deliberation, the Sultan observed, but once approved it would be put into practice. Nevertheless, he added that it was important to restore public order as a condition for carrying out the reforms. The Sultan noted that the first steps had been made: candidates for inspectors, assistant governors and district chiefs had been selected while Shakir Pasha had begun to enroll Christians in the gendarmerie in six provinces who would have been active if not for the disturbances.

Currie admitted that while the British Government had expressed satisfaction with the decision to promulgate a reforms program, the recent developments in the Empire had shaken the Government's confidence. The acceptance of the reforms program had been followed by massacres in the Armenian-populated provinces, and thousands of people who lost their homes and property could starve during the winter season. The Ambassador cited reports of forced religious conversions as well as the report from the British Vice Consul in Mush about the action of the Bitlis authorities to force the Armenian population to send a telegram to the Porte admitting their guilt in having caused the disturbances. The Sultan promised to hold an inquiry into those reports and inform the Embassy of the proceedings.

The Ambassador then presented two issues of contention for the British Government. First, nobody had yet been punished for the massacres, and second, the Sultan had not yet signed a Decree on the reforms program.

Abdul Hamid said the publication of a Decree was meaningless since deeds were more important than words. Having made the decision to execute reforms, the Sultan would see to it that they would be carried out. Currie argued that publication of an Imperial Decree would serve several purposes. The Sultan would assure the Powers of his sincerity on the reforms program, the Armenian population would be assured that the reforms had indeed been granted, and the Muslim population would be convinced that the reforms contained nothing harmful to their interests. The Sultan disagreed with the latter two arguments but promised to review the decision with the Vizier and the Ministers.

Currie then deplored the Sultan's suspicions about the naval deployment, arguing that under the Treaty of Paris, each Power had the right to introduce two stationnaires, i.e., lightly armed warships, to the capital for the protection of foreign colonies. The Powers' intention to deploy naval personnel was caused by the loss of confidence following the disturbances and massacres, the Ambassador explained. The deployment was in the interests of the security of foreign subjects as well as in the interests of the Porte because if fresh disturbances broke out the Powers would be forced to deploy full fleets.

The Sultan disagreed, asking rhetorically if 'any foreigner's nose had been bled' during the disturbances. He said that the other Powers would follow Britain's lead in withdrawing their military vessels. Currie reiterated that the Powers' motivation in introducing the stationnaires was not a naval demonstration but a step toward restoration of confidence and a measure of assistance to the Porte in its efforts to restore public order. He made a plea to the Sultan to authorize the passage, saying that the ships would follow in procession one by one through the Dardanelles and would not attract much attention. Abdul Hamid promised to 'review the request.'[314]

On December 1, Foreign Minister Tewfik Pasha told Currie that the Sultan was hopeful that Britain would restore friendly ties with Turkey and reconsider its participation in the naval demonstration to force other Powers to cancel the deployment.[315] Currie recommended to Salisbury that, per the earlier decision of the foreign envoys, a deadline be set for the Porte to authorize the passage of the warships.[316] Meeting with the Austro-Hungarian Ambassador in London, Salisbury noted that in the view of the Russian rejection of any pressure on the Sultan, the Powers would be faced with two choices if the Porte did not authorize the passage of the naval deployment group: the Powers would either be forced to accept their defeat at the Sultan's hands or, alternatively, they could announce that any obstruction of the ships' passage would be viewed as a hostile act and lead to reprisals in other parts of his Empire.[317] On December 3, British Ambassador in Vienna Monson, met with Goluchowski who noted that the Porte could no longer afford to remain obstinate since Russia reiterated its support for the joint demand; the Sultan's authorization should be expected shortly. Goluchowski suggested that Russia's decision had been caused by its concern for deterioration of the Concert of Europe which would have given carte blanche to Britain.[318]

As the year 1895 drew to a close, British policies on the Eastern Question faced a crisis. Traditionally, the British demands for the reforms in the Ottoman provinces populated by the Christian subjects had been made primarily as a means of asserting Britain's influence and advancing its interests. The establishment of a protectorate and the implementation of reforms were the main elements of the political objectives of the Cyprus Convention. These objectives became irreconcilable by 1895, and this period surfaced the contradictions in the British position on the Eastern Question. The tragedy of the Armenian massacres had completely destroyed British hopes to control and direct the reforms measures. Sultan Abdul Hamid's delaying tactics, temporary suspension of the Armenian massacres, and the increasing difficulty of maintaining a common position with the European Powers effectively neutralized British diplomacy, preventing it from achieving any positive or practical results. Even the Sultan's acquiescence to the naval deployment in the Dardanelles did not bring about an effective change in the reforms issue and did not prevent the spread of disturbances. Salisbury blamed his predecessors, Rosebery and Kimberley, for their inability to envisage the real position of the French and Russian Governments on the issue of reforms.[319]

Salisbury was disappointed by the Russian Government's lack of support for Britain on the question of reforms. Russia continued to view the British initiatives on the Armenian Question with great suspicion and did not want to act in concert with Britain for fear of having to endorse the deployment of a British fleet to Constantinople and the Straits. Russia was also bent on preventing the establishment of Armenian autonomy which it believed would then become a British client state and endanger the Armenian-populated provinces of Russia.[320]

In turn, Salisbury made up his mind to prevent the deployment of the Russian Black Sea Fleet near Constantinople. Salisbury had no doubts about the inability of the Sultan's Government to maintain the status quo in the Ottoman Empire and the despotic nature of the Government, and readily admitted that the anti-Russian policy of the Crimean War was a mistake on the part of Britain. At the same time, he hoped that the traditional reputation and authority of the British Navy would prevent the loss of Constantinople to a third Power. The Prime Minister proposed that the Cabinet empower Currie to authorize deployment of the entire Mediterranean Fleet to the Straits to terrorize the Sultan and restore British influence. The Cabinet did not concur, while the Admiralty argued that the French-Russian alliance had unfavorably altered the naval balance in the Mediterranean.[321]

On December 3, Salisbury noted in his dispatch to Goschen that he did not support obstructing Russia's occupation of Constantinople and considered the British policies that had led to the Crimean War to be erroneous. At the same time, he noted that it had been 'a British credo for the previous 50 years, if not more, to prevent the Russian takeover of the Straits' and that 'British honor and its reputation had been staked on that proposition.' If Britain publicly adopted a different position it could lead to catastrophic results, he argued. The Cabinet's refusal to grant a carte blanche to Currie could only mean that the Russians would beat the British fleet to Constantinople, Salisbury complained. Having deployed first, the Russians would enforce the forts in the Dardanelles and make the Straits impregnable. If the British Fleet were deployed first it would strengthen Britain and make its voice more important, he concluded.[322]

Salisbury was facing an uphill battle in November–December 1895 as he was trying to explain and justify the British policy to a public greatly agitated by the continuing reports of massacres. The Foreign Office received an enormous number of letters, appeals, and protests from public, humanitarian, and religious groups. Motivated anew by the reports of the massacres, Gladstone began a fresh public campaign against the Sultan whom he had labeled the 'Great Assassin.'[323] Lack of support for the Government's policies from an anxious public and the apparent failure of British-French-Russian efforts to cooperate on the issue of reforms forced Salisbury to rethink his position on the Armenian Question. At the same time, he was concerned with the possibility of active cooperation among the five European Powers who supported the territorial integrity of the Ottoman Empire—cooperation that he feared would be aimed against British interests. The only specific proposal he made to the Powers was to depose Sultan Abdul Hamid. In mid-December, Salisbury refused to meet a delegation of the Armenian Society led by the Duke of Westminster and pressured the Duke and Gladstone to postpone a rally in support of the Armenian cause.[324] The British Government's indecisiveness and actions led to its international isolation and loss of public support at home.

Eventually, the Sultan granted an authorization for the passage of the stationnaires to Constantinople but only because of the Russian Government's intervention.[325] On December 12–16, a procession of British, French, Russian, Italian, and Austro-Hungarian warships passed through the Straits one by one.[326]

On December 10, Currie proposed to his fellow Ambassadors that joint action be taken to address the continuing reports of massacres and robberies throughout Asia Minor. He proposed establishing an international commission to visit the affected provinces, conduct an inquiry into the disturbances, and to address the issues of compensation and bringing the perpetrators to justice. The Austro-Hungarian and Italian ambassadors endorsed the idea, but Ambassador Nelidov balked at the proposal saying he had been instructed to cooperate with other Powers only as far as protection of foreign subjects was concerned. He proposed instead that the Embassies should forward the reports to the Porte demanding an explanation, and that they should ask their respective governments to review Currie's idea if it was officially endorsed by the British Cabinet. Currie recommended that the Cabinet approve the proposal, despite the disagreements among the Powers.

The Ambassador noted that the situation in the eastern provinces continued to be horrifying, and the provinces where the reforms were to take place had been especially devastated. The Armenians had been subjected to massacres in all the major cities, except for Van, Samsoun, and Erzurum; nearly all the Armenian settlements had been affected. Almost 300,000 Christians were in a state of extreme poverty and misery, Currie noted.[327]

The Sultan reshuffled his government in Constantinople, replacing Grand Vizier Said Pasha with Izgat Bey. Said Pasha called on Currie in an agitated state, saying the Sultan was insane and a lying murderer. He said he had discussed the situation in Sasun with Abdul Hamid prior to the massacres, and Abdul Hamid had supposedly told him that the Armenian Question had to be settled by blood, not reforms. Said Pasha noted that he had at first misunderstood the Sultan's words to be a reference to a possible war with a foreign Power, but it became clear to him what the Sultan had really meant when a massacre had been carried out in Sasun. On December 11, Currie noted that Said Pasha echoed the sentiment expressed by Gladstone earlier that Abdul Hamid was the scourge of Turkey.[328]

On December 16, Currie reported to Salisbury that he had information about the possible formation of a Commission of Inquiry into the disturbances that was to be headed by the Sultan himself. The measure had been meant to placate public opinion in Britain. The Ambassador expressed doubts about the ability of such a Commission to investigate the events effectively.[329]

Following instructions from Salisbury, the British Ambassadors held discussions with host governments in Europe to discuss the Armenian Question. Lascelles reported from Berlin on December 16 that the German Foreign Minister had told him he had had no doubt about the facts of mind-boggling massacres but suggested that they might have been provoked by Armenian groups in some instances. The Foreign Minister predicted that fresh disturbances and instability would break out in parts of the Ottoman Empire, especially Macedonia and Bulgaria, although he did not expect the troubles to start until spring.[330]

Ambassador Monson reported from Vienna that Goluchowski had told him that the Powers should refrain from further action and give the Sultan some time to carry out his promise to re-establish law and order in his domains. Goluchowski added that any intervention by the Powers could have had the same disastrous effect on the Armenians as the British-French-Russian attempt to force reforms on the Porte.[331]

On December 17, Russia's Foreign Minister Prince Lobanov told Goschen that, based on his experience during two years he had lived in England, the British were the most excitable race in the world, a quality that had been displayed in the British position on the Armenian Question. He claimed that the Englishmen's humanitarian inclinations encouraged Armenian revolutionary groups, provoked Armenians to rebel and incited Muslim fanaticism. Goschen took issue with Lobanov's statement and the widely held perception that the British Government had been acting out of self-interest as far as the Armenian Question was concerned.[332]

Russian Ambassador Nelidov told other Ambassadors in Constantinople that the Powers should only press for the re-establishment of public order.[333] He said he had learned in a cable from Foreign Minister Lobanov that on December 13 Abdul Hamid had sent precious gifts and tobacco to Czar Nicholas II. Nelidov commented that Salisbury had completely lost his authority and stature in Turkish Muslim circles.[334]

On December 18, Currie was told by the Turkish Foreign Minister that the Army had surrounded the Zeytoun rebels but the Sultan had ordered a halt to allow them to surrender. The Porte reported that the rebels attacked Muslim villages and killed the prisoners.[335]

On December 19, Currie noted that the situation in the Empire continued to remain tense and showed no signs of improvement. The Kurdish attacks continued unabated; the perpetrators of massacres remained at large; many innocent Armenians remained in custody; the called-up reserves were not paid and had resorted to robbing and looting the population; the Army had surrounded the Zeytoun rebels and was gearing up for a massacre, having already claimed alleged Armenian atrocities as a justification; disturbances had broken out in Crete and more were expected in Macedonia. The financial situation of the Sultan's government was hopeless, Currie noted, and would find itself unable to meet its needs as early as spring. He suggested using the Ottoman Government's default as an occasion to exact measures establishing public order and preventing further attacks on peace. He added that the foreign envoys in Constantinople, especially Nelidov, had been acting under orders to cooperate only in matters related to the protection of foreign citizens.[336]

On December 21, Currie reported to Salisbury that the military forces had apparently laid down conditions to the Zeytoun rebels, the most important of which was to surrender their weapons and hand over their leaders. Currie was convinced that the Armenians would turn down the offer and be massacred. He appealed to the Porte to use every means to prevent a massacre.[337]

The European embassies received letters from the Armenian Apostolic and Armenian Catholic Patriarchs, transmitting the request of the Zeytoun rebels to use the good offices of the foreign consuls for talks with the authorities. On December 23, Currie initiated a discussion with other Ambassadors, who decided to request their governments to authorize the consuls in Aleppo to travel to Zeytoun.[338] Before the Powers could take any action, the Turkish military advanced on Zeytoun, destroyed the citadel and captured the city; the remaining rebels escaped toward Killis. Official reports listed 21 Turkish casualties while no numbers were available for the rebel side. The British Consul in Aleppo reported that the Turkish military granted unarmed Armenians free passage to Marash but Kurdish and Circassian gangs terrorized the area.[339] The Porte announced that the military had captured the citadel and surrounded the city but the military commander had been ordered to advance slowly to allow the Armenians to surrender.[340] According to the next consular report, almost 5000 rebels retreated to the nearby strategic hills dominating the region.[341]

On December 28, the Powers' envoys decided to offer the Porte the use of the foreign consuls for mediation and, if the offer was accepted, to press for an immediate cease-fire.[342] The offer was made jointly through the Embassy dragomans.[343]

On December 29, Currie reported that he was convinced the Sultan would turn down the offer since he had the upper hand and would not hesitate to destroy the Zeytoun rebels in the same manner as had happened in Sasun. Given the position of the other Powers, especially Russia, Currie recommended that he be authorized to tell the Ambassadors he would send Colonel Chermside on a fact-finding trip to Zeytoun if the Sultan rejected or equivocated in his response. Currie noted that faced with British determination, the Ambassadors would be motivated to take practical measures and force the Sultan to accept their initiative.[344]

On December 31, Currie reported that the official response from the Porte on the Zeytoun mediation offer disappointed the Ambassadors who had decided to present a more strongly drafted memorandum to the authorities.[345] After another demarche, the Turkish Foreign Minister informed Currie that the Porte agreed to the proposal of negotiation by the consuls in Aleppo and issued appropriate orders to the authorities in the region.[346] On January 6, the Zeytoun rebels accepted the mediation offer from the consuls, the British Consul in Aleppo reported.[347]

On January 1, 1896, Salisbury met with the newly appointed Turkish Ambassador, Costaki Pasha. When Salisbury spoke of terrifying events that had taken place in Turkey in 1895, the Ambassador referred to clashes and unfortunate incidents that had been grossly exaggerated. He blamed the events on the dangerous and widespread Armenian conspiracy. The conspiracy, the Turkish Ambassador continued, aimed to establish an autonomous Armenian state which, he observed, was impossible to achieve given the ethnic composition of the provinces. The Sultan's Government was forced to suppress the movement that also aroused the resentment of the Muslim population and led to civil war, which was inevitably accompanied by 'horrifying violence,' just as in other countries. Costaki Pasha argued for giving the Sultan more time to establish law and order—a necessary condition for the reforms.

Salisbury concurred that before execution of the reforms it was important to restore the security of life and property that had disappeared throughout the Empire. England had been a close friend of Turkey in the past, Salisbury noted, and the Government was disposed to continue its relations. Nevertheless, he warned the Ambassador that as long as 'blood flowed' in Turkey and the dominant race continued to subject the weaker people to 'terrible oppressions,' the indignation of the British public would prevent any reconciliation with Turkey despite political expediency.[348]

On January 3, British consul Barnham reported from Aleppo that an Armenian massacre had been carried out in Urfa by the Hamidiye units. The official numbers claimed 900 Armenian deaths, but according to the Consul more than 2000 Armenians perished.[349] Salisbury instructed Currie to act in concert with the Russian and French ambassadors in urging the Sultan to engage the situation in the Empire and to form the Commission of Control for the Armenian-populated provinces.[350]

Salisbury was pessimistic about the prospects of a settlement of the Armenian Question and believed that the Armenian massacres would prevent Britain from re-asserting its former stature in the Ottoman Empire. In his January 15 letter to the Queen he noted that 'words were not enough to describe the horrors' but added that Britain would be unable to act alone against Turkey.[351]

The British Government wanted to show that it had lost political influence in Turkey over its position on the Armenian massacres. At the same time, it was concerned with the parallel rise in Russia's influence on the Sultan. Russia had continuously refused to go along with any proposed measures to pressure the Sultan over the Armenian Question and even conceded to a halt in payment of the reparations awarded to Russia after the Russo-Turkish war. In mid-January Currie sent a confidential message to Salisbury informing him of an alleged Turkish request to Czar Nicholas for protection in exchange for a ten-year occupation of the Ottoman Empire's six easternmost provinces. The report generated anxiety in the Foreign Office but Lobanov soon officially refuted the information. The rumors of Russian-Turkish collusion gained ground in the British press. Salisbury was reportedly concerned over a report in the January 25 issue of *Pall Mall Gazette* about the signing of a Russian-Turkish Treaty based on the premises of the Unkiar-Skelessi Treaty.[352]

British diplomacy began to strenuously fight the chimera of a Russian-Turkish alliance, arguing for a cooperative approach to improve the general welfare of the Ottoman Empire. In his response to a January 16 diplomatic note from the British Embassy, Prince Lobanov noted that the situation in the Ottoman Empire had begun to improve and therefore there was no need for the Powers to intervene. He argued against changing the status quo in the Ottoman Empire since the reforms promulgated by the Sultan would be enough to establish law and order in the country.[353]

The mediation effort in Zeytoun ended on January 30, with the signing of an agreement between the rebel leaders and the government delegates. The agreement provided for the Armenian rebels and the Muslims inhabiting the valleys to surrender their weapons. A general amnesty was proclaimed, and the Huntchaks who were foreign nationals were to be exiled from Turkey. The amount of 'mir' tax assessed on the people of Zeytoun was to be reduced and the previous indemnities were to be written off. The appointment of a Christian Kaymakam was to be made under the general program of reforms.[354] The agreement represented a major victory for the Zeytoun rebels and humiliated the Sultan's government which was forced to sign a treaty with its own subjects and to recognize their demands and rights. British Consul Barnham played a crucial role in the signing of the treaty. He had dispensed monetary grants to the people of Zeytoun and stayed there for a few months after the agreement was signed. In April 1896, the Sultan's government appointed a Muslim as Kaymakam of Zeytoun but retracted its decision under pressure from the British Embassy and appointed a Greek Christian instead.[355]

In early February Salisbury addressed the Nonconformist Union Association with a speech which was labeled by *The Spectator* as the final apology for the British inability to assist the Armenian population of the Ottoman Empire. In his speech, Salisbury ruled out any current or future British intervention on the Armenian Question and noted that the British Government had not undertaken any obligations on this issue. He argued that the provisions of the Treaty of Berlin were equally applicable to all the signatories, and Britain was not required to do more than other Powers. He noted that the Sultan had done all in his power to carry out reforms in Armenia.[356] He said that it was impossible to relieve the suffering of the Armenian population by a military intervention. Britain could defeat five or six sultans on the open seas, he said,[357] but on April 30, during a debate in the House of Lords, he remarked that 'our ships could not get over the mountains of Taurus."[358]

On February 10, Under Secretary of State for Foreign Affairs George Curzon[359] declared during parliamentary hearings that the Government's intentions and plans to force Abdul Hamid had been stymied by Russia together with other European Powers. MP Ashmed Bartlett called on the Government to adopt Disraeli's openly hostile stance on Russia. In reply, Liberal Party leader Lord Rosebery told his party's parliamentary caucus, the Britain that had always praised the heroes of the Treaty of Berlin had no right to assail Russia for failing to act on the Eastern Question in concert with the same person who had been the author of the Treaty.[360]

During the parliamentary debates, First Lord of the Admiralty George Goschen stated that as soon as the Sultan refused to carry out the necessary reforms, Britain would be free of its obligations to respect the territorial integrity of the Ottoman Empire, which would no longer be of importance to Britain. Other members of the Cabinet expressed similar sentiments; Colonial Secretary Joseph Chamberlain[361] expressed readiness to hand over Constantinople to Russia and cooperate with it on the dissolution of the Ottoman Empire.

Salisbury's position did not change after the debates. He agreed with Currie's view that the recent developments had strengthened Russian influence over the Porte and weakened Britain's stature there. Nevertheless, he never considered revoking the Cyprus Convention. He explained his decision not to engage in active efforts to address the Armenian Question by the need to avoid further complications. He noted during a debate in the House of Lords that he inherited the Armenian Question from the Liberals and said that forcing the Sultan to treat his Armenian subjects with greater fairness would bring Britain to the brink of war with Turkey as well as with Russia.[362] Curzon declared in March that the Government considered the British obligation to protect the territorial integrity of the Ottoman Empire to have lapsed. The contemporary accounts noted that Salisbury preferred to avoid the topic of the Armenian reforms altogether until the time when the 'Armenian affairs were frozen.'[363]

Thus, the British Government refrained from taking any action that could lead to a confrontation with Russia, unless Russia itself initiated an action against Turkey. Given the external developments, Abdul Hamid felt secure enough to organize another round of massacres aimed at the Armenian population in the Ottoman Empire.

The massacres that took place in the Ottoman Empire from September 1895 to January 1896[364] were planned in advance. Government agents had been sent to all the provinces with instructions to whip up the fanaticism of the Muslim mob. Government agents would meet with the Muslims gathering to pray at mosques and tell them that the Sultan believed all Armenians to be scheming to assault Islam and would call on the faithful to defend Islam and the Sultan from the seditious Armenians. The agents played to the greed of the mob by saying that the rules of the holy jihad allowed the property of the rebels to be taken by the faithful; any resistance from the Christians was punishable by death.[365] Single shots would be fired or trumpets would be sounded as a signal to launch the pogroms.[366] Before sacking the urban areas, the Kurdish tribes would attack and commit atrocities in the nearby Armenian villages. The mob comprised of Kurdish, Circassian or Las tribal elements would then enter the city and, joined by the Turkish mob, police and troops, would massacre and loot the Armenian population.[367] The local authorities issued orders to target males only. For example, the Muslim mob in Akhisar was told to kill off men as "the women and the children would be ours at the end."[368] Only Armenians were singled out for killing; the Greek and Jewish communities were rarely affected. The massacres of the Armenian population were well organized; regular troops and gendarmerie forces took part in killing and looting. The action would end as suddenly as it started; another signal would be sounded to call it off.[369] The local authorities in many locales would force the Armenian notables to sign a document acknowledging their role in beginning or provoking the disturbances.[370]

In 1896, the Sultan's government published inaccurate statistics on the casualties of 'the 1895 disturbances in Asia Minor.' According to the official paper, only 10,135 people were killed, including 1828 Muslims, 7863 Apostolic Armenians, 152 Armenian Catholics, and 292 Armenian Protestants[371]. Russian author L. Komarovski reported that at least 20,000 Armenians were killed in October-November alone.[372] The London *Times* reported that 12,500 Armenians had been killed between November 1 and November 22;[373] American missionary Bliss reported 40,000 casualties;[374] the U.S. press reported that nearly 50,000 Armenians had been killed.[375]

The following table lists an approximate number of victims of the massacres, based on European and U.S. sources:[376]

Locale	Date	Number of Victims
Trabzon	10/3–8/1895	1,100
Akhisar	10/09/1895	50
Gümüshkaneh	10/11/1895	350
Baiburt	10/13/1895	800
Erzinjan	10/21/1895	2,000
Bitlis	10/25/1895	3,000
Palu	10/25/1895	650
Diyarbakir	10/25/1895	3,000
Kara-Hisar	10/25/1895	800
Erzurum	10/30/1895	1,500
Boulanik and Khinus	10/30/1895	700
Urfa	10/27/1895 and 12/30/1895	10,000

Malatia	11/6/1895	5,000
Arabkir	11/6/1895	4,000
Gürün	11/10/1895	2,000
Sivas (Sivas)	11/12/1895	1,500
Kharput	11/11/1895	2,000
Mush	11/15/1895	350
Marzvan	11/15/1895	130
Aintab	11/15/1895	400
Marash	11/18/1895	1,000
Zilleh	11/26/1895	300
Kayseri	11/30/1895	400
Birejik	01/01/1896	900
TOTAL		41,930

The number of victims of the Armenian massacres in the Ottoman Empire in 1895 alone was equivalent to the number of military casualties in an average European war during the nineteenth century. Unlike a war, the casualties were inflicted on one party, the Armenian population. As the Russian *Vestnik Evropy* monthly noted, the Armenian Question was addressed in a typical Turkish fashion: actions had been taken to exterminate revolutionary or opposition-minded Armenians while, at the same time, an Imperial decree proclaimed the Sultan's good intentions and listing reform measures convincing enough to disarm any foreign diplomat.[377]

Relative calm prevailed in the Ottoman Empire in the spring and summer of 1896. British diplomacy markedly decreased its activities related to the Armenian Question. The Embassy no longer sent protest demarches to the Porte, while British political and public figures no longer addressed Armenian issues with the same frequency and fervor. However, the core problems in the Ottoman Empire had not been solved, and the Porte had no intention to carry out the reforms in the Armenian-populated provinces that it had announced the previous year.

On April 6, Salisbury noted that while the Turkish authorities had displayed their abilities in some instances, they had not made an 'exhaustive effort' to improve the administration, re-assert control over the Kurdish tribes, carry out reforms, organize the Commission of Control, or even to implement the existing laws. He noted that while no disturbances had been reported, the widespread fear and panic had paralyzed industry and trade. The Prime Minister instructed Currie to continue to inquire about the situation in the Armenian-populated provinces, and make occasional representations to the Porte on the need to address specific cases of bad governance and abuses. Salisbury noted that it was possible that the Ambassador's efforts would be futile and more serious complications could arise in the Ottoman Empire. In that event, the British Government would feel that it had done enough to avert the disaster by providing 'friendly advice and warnings,' and would not bear responsibility for any outcome.[378]

In June 1896, the three Armenian parties—Armenakan, Huntchak, and Armenian Revolutionary Federation—led the Armenian population in Van and nearby villages in a self-defense effort to fight off constant reprisals and atrocities committed by the Kurdish tribal elements and directed by the local authorities. On June 17 and 18 the Porte informed the British Embassy that while no disturbances had been registered in the province of Van in 1895, the situation had now gotten out of control because of the activities of the revolutionary groups. The Porte claimed that the Armenian revolutionaries had attacked the Muslim population; the Armenian population of the city and nearby villages had barricaded itself in one of the districts having driven out the local Muslim population. The local authorities would take measures to surround the city and isolate the rebels, the Porte reported.[379] It was already clear what the Porte meant. British Vice Consul Williams reported from Van on June 20 that the local state of affairs was critical: the Kurdish units had besieged the city, the Armenians resisted them successfully, and the local authorities had requested authorization from the Sultan to grant amnesty and safe passage to the Armenian rebels.[380] While the Armenian self-defense measures succeeded in repulsing the Kurdish attacks, lack of ammunition and arms forced the Armenians to accept the British offer of mediation. Due to Williams's mediation effort, some 1500 Armenians were granted safe passage to Persia but the Sultan's government did not honor its commitment to protect the lives of the rebels and the Armenian population. A Turkish force intercepted the Armenians on their way to Persia, and most of them perished. On June 23, the Hamidiye and Army forces attacked the Armenian Quarter of Van killing and looting with abandon. Williams estimated that nearly 400 Armenians were massacred on June 23, but his negotiations with the local authorities to end the crisis succeeded in saving more than 15,000 Armenians who had been afforded the protection of the British flag.[381]

The Armenian efforts to improve their living conditions and their just demands to end constant harassment and persecution by the Turkish authorities and nomadic Kurdish tribes, and the British policy of forcing the Sultan's government to carry out reforms in Western Armenia—a policy directed in part as response to public opinion in Europe and Britain—eventually culminated in an organized and determined effort by the Sultan's government to execute massacres of the Armenian subjects of the Ottoman Empire. The Sultan's government had successfully created and put to practice an extermination machine targeting the Armenian population in the provinces where they comprised a significant percentage of the population. The objective of the extermination campaign was to neutralize the European demands for reforms in the Armenian-populated provinces.

6. Massacre of the Armenians in Constantinople, 1896

On August 26, 1896, a group of 31 Armenian revolutionary activists, primarily from the Armenian Revolutionary Federation (the Dashnak Party), armed with pistols and grenades, took over the Ottoman Bank. The Dashnak activists threatened to blow up the building if the Sultan did not take active measures to carry out the announced reforms in the Armenian-populated provinces and prevent further massacres of the Armenian population. The foreign Ambassadors in Constantinople received official notices from the Party presenting the demands of the revolutionaries.[382]

The European diplomatic missions were extremely concerned about the seizure of the Bank and promised to fulfill the Armenians' demands and provide safe passage to the group holding the Bank building. The European Powers had a huge financial stake in the Bank, which was used as a clearing house for their loans to the Porte. In 1890–98 alone, more than 12 credits had been extended to the Bank totaling 12 billion francs.[383] Besides, the Porte had developed a plan to reform the Turkish Treasury through the Bank. The financial and Treasury reforms would have allowed the Porte to maintain relative financial independence from the Powers, especially Britain, by denying them the leverage of extending loans and credits to the Porte in exchange for concessions. The financial independence of the Porte would have allowed it to indefinitely postpone reforms in the Armenian-populated provinces.

The Turkish authorities had been warned in advance of the plot to seize the Bank but the Sultan had chosen not to prevent the attack so as to incite the anti-Armenian mood among the Muslim mob in the capital and score a point with European public opinion.[384] According to statements by Komarovski at the time, the Turkish secret police had in fact encouraged the Armenian revolutionary groups to carry out the plan while simultaneously taking measures to prepare a major massacre of the Armenian population.[385] Chalmers Roberts, a Foreign Service officer at the U.S. Embassy in Constantinople, noted that the Sultan's government had allowed the plans for occupying Bank Ottoman to proceed in order to justify the subsequent massacres.[386]

There had been indications that the Porte had laid the ground for another massacre of the Armenian population in Constantinople by August. There had been bread riots among the Muslim population of the city several weeks prior to the Bank Ottoman incident, and Muslim mobs had threatened to loot and sack the Armenian districts if their demands had not been met.[387] American missionary Pears testified that Abdul Hamid called on the faithful to punish the Armenians during a prayer.[388]

Interestingly enough, the massacre of the Armenian population of Constantinople had begun shortly before the publication of an Imperial Decree on negotiations with the European Powers on the fate of Crete; the Greek population of Crete had demanded to be reunited with Greece. As we have shown in the previous chapter, the Armenian massacres in 1895 had been sparked by the publication of the Sultan's decree on the Armenian reforms. The public announcement of reforms aimed to ameliorate the living conditions of a Christian minority in the Ottoman Empire had been aimed at the European Powers. Yet, the Sultan's government carefully manipulated such announcements to incite the Muslim population and to derail the very reforms it had proclaimed.

On August 27, armed groups of Muslim fanatics appeared in several districts of Constantinople and began to massacre Armenians without the least resistance or interference from the police, gendarmerie or regular troops.[389] Russian Ambassador Nelidov testified that "Muslim thugs" armed with knives and sticks began to attack anyone who looked Armenian; despite the widespread massacres of the 'defenseless and innocent' Christian population, he said, the police remained passive and in fact joined with the mob on several occasions to loot and kill with abandon. The troops who had been called up rather late did not interfere either. The massacres went on late into the night in Galata, Pera, and several other suburbs of Constantinople, and no measures had been taken to stop the pogrom.[390]

Only Armenians were singled out for killing; other Christian minorities were not affected. Roberts noted that the massacre had been carried out for political, not religious reasons. The Muslim population had been given to believe that the Armenians had conspired against the 'holy government of the Caliph,' and the Turkish authorities did not take active measures to stop the mass murder for fear of losing their authority with the crowd they had incited, Roberts believed.[391]

The group that had seized the Bank sent Deputy Director Obuano to negotiate with the palace. The revolutionaries demanded safe passage and implementation of their demands. Russian Embassy Dragoman Maksimov was also in the palace with instructions from Ambassador Nelidov to facilitate the negotiations, and the Sultan asked him to mediate, offering safe passage for the group if they left Turkey and refrained from destroying the Bank. Bank Director Vincent, Obuano and Maksimov went to the Bank to negotiate with the revolutionaries. The negotiators persuaded the Armenian group to voluntarily leave the bank and be transferred to an English ship taking them to safety in exile. The group was told that their exile would be in the best interests of the Armenian cause which had already gained the interest of Europe.[392]

The rebels departed Constantinople in Vincent's yacht. Although the main cause of the disturbances had been resolved, the situation did not stabilize. While the Bank was still held by the Armenian group, the Sultan's government transferred armed groups of Kurds, Albanians, and Lazes to the capital to assist the Muslim mob in carrying out reprisals against the Armenians.[393] The would-be perpetrators of the massacres had been issued sticks with sharpened brass caps, knives, and pistols. According to Alma Wittlin, Abdul Hamid personally suggested staging quiet but bloody reprisals.[394]

Measures had been taken to ensure that the perpetrators did not carry out massacres in their home districts so that the later police investigation, if the Powers would insist on carrying out one, could not find witnesses identifying the person. The gendarmerie and troops had been ordered to put down any attempts by the Armenians to resist, and were allowed to join with the mob if the resistance was serious. While the massacres continued unabated for three days, the police asserted control over the situation. Some districts, including Scutari and Kum Kapu, were well policed and seemed serene. The killings and looting were the worst along the Golden Horn, e.g., in the districts stretching from Dolmabahche Palace to Gategugh and from Cape of Saray Burnie to Ayvan Palace, as well as near Samatya, the Castle of Seven Towers, and the Adrianople Gate. The largest number of Armenian casualties was in Pera, with witness accounts of blood literally flowing in the streets. The massacres were targeted against Armenians without regard to social status or any other criteria. Most of the victims were laborers and working class Armenians, but a significant number of intellectuals, merchants, and wealthy Armenians had been killed in addition to nearly 100 Armenian women.[395]

A crewman of the British *Ramses* ship, William Johnson, noted that he 'had never before' encountered such brutality. 'The Armenians were killed like rats,' with stones and sticks. The crew prayed for the arrival of a British fleet which would have blown the whole place to pieces, Johnson added.[396]

Eyewitness accounts of the Armenian massacre appeared in *Contemporary Review*, including an editorial entitled "The Constantinople Massacre." According to the newspaper, Russian Dragoman Maksimov encountered two Turkish men who had beaten an Armenian half to death; with the help of his bodyguard, he apprehended one of the assailants and delivered him to the nearby police precinct. When the police refused to detain the person, the Russian diplomat delivered him to the Palace; it turned out the person was a Turkish military officer.[397]

Many diplomats had appealed to the military and gendarmerie officers to stop the killings, but were always told they "had orders" not to do so.[398] A witness recounted that the mob attacked an Armenian priest in front of the residence of a French diplomat. The residents protested to a Turkish military officer who told them that the Government had a right to punish the 'giaours,' i.e., the infidels.[399] In many instances, Muslim women joined in the orgy of violence; another eyewitness account told of a mob of women who had trampled an Armenian merchant to death and looted his store.[400]

The Armenians had made weak attempts to defend themselves in several districts of the capital but any resistance was suppressed by the Turkish military. U.S. Embassy Dragoman Lamlie testified that the Armenian parishioners in the Samatya district were besieged in a church, and after exhausting their ammunition, allowed the soldiers in and blew up the church.

The Turkish soldiers attacked the residence of the daughter of Sultan Abdul Mejid's private secretary, Mrs. Manelian. Her three sons resisted for a while. Running out of ammunition, all three of them committed suicide. After making sure the Armenians were dead, the soldiers were ordered by their officers to leave. 'Leave the old she-dog alone with her puppies,' the military officer ordered.[401]

Russian journalist Olga Kaydanova described the massacre in great detail. 'I have the scene before my eyes,' she wrote. The Armenians working in the ports were killed immediately; the mobs crashed their heads with sticks and stones. The mob dragged Armenians through the streets and trampled them to death. The police appeared only to oversee the removal of corpses. The looting was carried out all day long; when the property in a store had been completely stolen, it would be destroyed too. The looting and massacres went on at night as well; most Armenian-owned stores and kiosks had been looted. The Russian sailors testified that the corpses had been dumped into the sea. Kaydanova decried the widespread manhunt and mass murder.[402]

Wagons and carts had been procured in advance to remove the corpses, and special crews made the rounds of the streets of Constantinople after 10 p.m. to carry out their grim work. Witnesses recalled the carts filled with human bodies moving slowly on the streets after dark.[403] According to reliable estimates, 28 ox-driven and 136 regular carts had transported bodies from Galata and Pera, while 71 more carts had gone through the Gategugh road. Greek diplomat D. Kalopothakes recounted testimony from an Armenian porter employed by the main police precinct in Constantinople. According to the Armenian, who had found refuge at the Greek Embassy, the Chief of Police rounded up porters and sent them to the main cemetery which was the collection point for the victims of the massacres. The predominantly Armenian porters, whose work had been overseen by the police, separated the Armenian corpses from the Muslims. The porters recounted that among the human bodies, some were still alive, but they had been given no help.[404] A significant number of human bodies were dumped into the sea.[405]

The eyewitness testimonies largely agree on the number of victims of the Constantinople massacre. The Russian Military Attaché, Colonel Peshkov, testified that more than 5,500 Armenians had been killed in two days,[406] while other sources referred to 8,750 victims,[407] or more than 10,000,[408] or even 13,600 deaths.[409]

The six Powers made representations to the Porte in vain attempts to stop the massacres: notes of protest were sent on August 27 and 31, and September 15.[410] The Embassies refused to stage festivities to mark the anniversary of Sultan Abdul Hamid's birth, but their gestures did not have any effect. On September 5, *The Spectator* noted that the Powers had tried to prevent the massacres and horrors in Galata where Armenian men, women, and children had been killed by the mob while the Army and gendarmerie looked on. The Sultan was too smart to be frightened by the refusal of foreign embassies to light a candle on his birthday, the newspaper noted, since the Powers had already allowed him to do as he pleased in his dominions. Therefore, the Sultan no longer feared external pressure, concluded the weekly.[411]

The British Embassy took a largely passive stance during the massacres and did not come up with its own initiatives. Ambassador Currie was in London, and the Embassy was headed by Chargé Herbert. In his reports to Salisbury during the massacres, Herbert noted that the diplomatic effort to stop the massacres had been spearheaded by Russian Ambassador Nelidov, who had even warned the Sultan he would order the Russian ships to fire on Büyükdere if the massacres did not stop. Herbert noted that the Russian Ambassador's strong warning had made the Sultan issue orders to stop the massacres.[412]

The European diplomatic missions helped thousands of Armenians flee the massacres. Some 12,000 Armenians moved to Bulgaria, almost 1000 to Alexandria, another 1200 to Athens, and several hundred Armenians went to Marseilles.[413]

The Constantinople massacre was but another in the series of Armenian massacres in the Ottoman Empire organized by the government of Sultan Abdul Hamid. The Sultan's objective was to exterminate or displace the Armenian population from their native lands in Western Armenia, as well as in other parts of the Empire.

7. The British-Russian Negotiations of 1896 and the Armenian Question

In September 1896, *The Spectator* published an editorial expressing hope for an agreement between the Powers on the settlement of the Armenian Question, preferably by way of a partition of the Ottoman Empire. The newspaper noted that since Russia remained opposed to such a solution while other Powers considered the status quo in Turkey as essential to maintaining peace and stability in Europe, dethroning Sultan Abdul Hamid would be another alternative.[414]

On September 22, Czar Nicholas II and Czarina Alexandra visited Britain; Nicholas II was on his first tour of European capitals since his coronation in 1895. Russia was still, essentially, an autocracy, and the royal tour was an occasion for important Russian-British negotiations held in Queen Victoria's Balmoral Castle in Scotland. The main subject of negotiations was the situation in and the future of the Ottoman Empire.

The British public followed the negotiations with great interest. *The Spectator* hoped that the Russian monarch would be convinced that Britain had no ulterior motives in pressing for the dethronement of Abdul Hamid. The weekly noted that the questions of peace in Europe depended on Nicholas II's position on Turkey; a word from the Russian autocrat could save the Armenians—'the ancient Christian people'—from suffering and reprisals.[415] The Huntchaks, in turn, expressed their conviction that Salisbury's solid diplomatic skills would allow him to assure the young Russian monarch of Britain's impartiality on the Armenian Question.[416]

The only reliable account of the Balmoral Castle negotiations is the 1960 book by British historian Margaret Jefferson who published the minutes of negotiations between Lord Salisbury and Nicholas II taken by the Prime Minister himself. Salisbury later presented his records to the Cabinet for discussion.[417] The Russian archives do not contain the details of negotiations between Nicholas II and Queen Victoria and Lord Salisbury. It is a known fact that Russia's acting Foreign Minister Nikolai Shishkin took part in at least some negotiating sessions. Russian historian N. N. Bolkhovitinov noted that the personal participation of the Russian Czar and his Foreign Minister made filing a formal report unnecessary since the Russian autocrats usually saw no need to report their activities to the Government, even for archival purposes.[418] It is possible to deduce the substance of the negotiations from the confidential reports by Russian Ambassador Staal published by Bolkhovitinov. Ambassador Staal reported to the Foreign Ministry on his follow-up negotiations with Salisbury after the Balmoral meeting.[419]

While the two parties discussed other issues of international politics as well, the main subject was the Eastern Question. Salisbury noted that Nicholas II supported the status quo on Turkey's territorial integrity. The Russian monarch said that occupation of parts of the Ottoman Empire by any Power could lead to disagreement between the Powers and a potential cause of a European war. At the same time, he admitted that the current state of affairs in the Ottoman Empire was critical, and if left unattended, Turkey's serious political and financial problems could result in its Treasury's default and intervention by a European Power, in particular Austria-Hungary, which again could lead to a war. Both sides agreed that 'something must be done' to address the situation.[420] Fears of a general European war were the primary argument for preservation of Turkey's territorial integrity. Ambassador Staal noted that the defense of the status quo in Turkey was Russia's priority in that region and that such a policy was in the best interests of all Powers and would be supported by the concert of Europe.[421]

Salisbury proposed that instead of addressing the question of Turkey's territorial integrity, the European Powers should target the Sultan personally. Nicholas II accepted that the deposing of Abdul Hamid was a necessary step to improve the situation in the Ottoman Empire.[422] The British Prime Minister suggested instructing their Ambassadors in Constantinople that Abdul Hamid's dethronement was the best solution to the crisis. Salisbury noted that the Czar had originally agreed with his proposal on September 27,[423] but two days later—after consulting with his advisers—he had told Salisbury that the deposition would be a difficult task in view of the probable reaction from the Muslim population. Nicholas II said that the new Sultan could be viewed as a puppet of Christian Powers and that the Muslims would refuse to accept his authority or they might even murder him. Salisbury accepted that Nicholas II's point was not unfounded but argued that the alternative was deterioration of the crisis in Turkey and potentially devastating outcome of collapse and dismemberment of the Ottoman Empire.[424] Staal would later tell Salisbury that Russia could not accept the British proposal to place the Sultan under custodianship since nothing could prove that a change of monarch could alter the situation, while a change of government as a result of foreign intervention would only exacerbate Muslim fanaticism which was already formidable, Staal added.[425]

The Balmoral negotiations convinced Salisbury that Russia was primarily concerned about (and obsessed with) control of the Straits. Nicholas II told him that the Dardanelles and the Bosphorus must be controlled by Russia; he said that the Straits were 'the gates to Russia's room and Russia therefore should have the keys to the gate.' Despite defending the status quo in Turkey, Russia still asserted its age-old goal of dominating the Straits to secure unhindered access for its military and commercial fleet to the Mediterranean and the Suez Canal and to dominate the Ottoman Empire. The Czar told Salisbury repeatedly that Russia had no interest in Constantinople or in territories on both sides of the Straits.[426]

The British Prime Minister assured Nicholas II that Britain had no interest in controlling the Straits and even implied that it would welcome the Russian takeover. However, Salisbury told Staal later that Britain would not be interested in having the specter of a Sultan functioning in Constantinople under the protection of Russian military might in the Bosphorus.[427] Salisbury warned the Czar that unilateral Russian control of the Straits would affect the interests of the signatories of the Mediterranean Convention, including Romania, Italy, France, and Austria-Hungary.[428] The Austro-Hungarian Government was convinced that the Power controlling the Straits would also control the Ottoman regions from Bulgaria to the Aegean Sea. Russian control over the European dominions of the Ottoman Empire would threaten the stability and territorial integrity of the Austro-Hungarian Empire as it could upset the balance between Slavic and non-Slavic elements in its population. Salisbury noted that the British interests in the Mediterranean were limited to Malta and Egypt.[429] Salisbury effectively told the Czar that he would not oppose the Russian takeover of the Straits if Russia persuaded Germany, Austria-Hungary, and Italy to accept it.

Other questions addressed during the negotiations were Egypt and the Suez Canal. Since Far East remained an important priority to Russia, free passage of Russian military ships through the Suez Canal was of importance to the Czar. Even control of the Straits would be a moot question without guarantees of free passage through Suez. Nicholas II told Salisbury that while

Russia did not oppose the British occupation of Egypt, its ally France raised serious objections to it. Salisbury told the Czar that he bore no responsibility for the occupation of Egypt and said he hoped to withdraw British troops in the near future. He did note the humanitarian mission of the British presence in 'spreading civilization' to the people of Egypt who he said would only benefit from a temporary British administration of the country. Salisbury reminded the Czar that his grandfather and namesake Nicholas had proposed to Britain in 1851 to take over Egypt if the Ottoman Empire had been partitioned. The Russian monarch reiterated that Russia did not oppose a permanent British presence in Egypt as long as Russia was guaranteed free passage of ships through Suez. Salisbury said that France should be offered Syria as compensation for the British takeover of Egypt.[430]

The bottom line of the Balmoral negotiations was that the Russian Government was not interested in a dismemberment of the Ottoman Empire, although it retained its former ambitions for the Dardanelles and the Bosphorus. Russia remained deeply ambivalent toward the British policy and motivations on the Eastern Question. The British Government recognized this, and both Salisbury and, at his request, Queen Victoria tried to dispel the Russian concerns and persuade the Czar that the Russian and British interests did not clash in the Far or Near East. Salisbury expressed hopes for a Russian-British rapprochement, going as far as implying the possibility of a binding agreement.[431] Salisbury noted in his diary that he had told the Czar there were no disagreements between Russia and Britain, with the exception of the question of the Straits. Salisbury noted that the British interest in this issue was primarily naval while other Powers had a larger stake there. He said that the old maxim that Turkish rule in Constantinople was another bastion in the British domination of India was no longer applicable.[432]

No formal agreements were unveiled during the Balmoral negotiations. *The Spectator* noted on October 3 that it had no information on 'useful agreements' reached at Balmoral but added that the differences between Britain and Russia did not grow wider after several hours of negotiations.[433]

Throughout the nineteenth century, the Russian-British competition in the Near East remained the dominant dynamics of the international politics in the region, and the preservation of the territorial integrity of the Ottoman Empire was a by-product of that competition and balance-of-power politics. This did not prevent and in fact pre-determined the Turkish policies of annihilating or displacing the Armenian population of the Ottoman Empire. Neither side expressed regret or disappointment over the Armenian massacres of 1894–96. The only motivations of Salisbury and Nicholas II were the interests of their countries. The Russian Czar even disparaged some "English philanthropists" who had demanded that Russia be urged to occupy Western Armenia. The Czar said that occupation of Armenia would have been a costly adventure without any benefit to Russia; he added that it would be of no use to the Armenians living in other parts of the Empire.[434] The British Prime Minister said at the conclusion of talks that the Powers should take measures to prevent another massacre in Constantinople because it could threaten the lives of foreign citizens and diplomatic personnel.[435]

8. The Position of the Salisbury Cabinet on the Armenian Question During the Final Phase of the Near Eastern Crisis

Just as in the previous year, the massacres of the Armenian population in Constantinople in 1896 launched a series of similarly planned and executed pogroms throughout the Ottoman Empire on a bigger scale and in a more brutal fashion. Belgian writer Emil Antoine estimated that 186,655 Armenians perished in Asia Minor in the autumn of 1896.[436] Maccoll estimated that the 1896 massacres took a toll of 200,000 lives.[437] Almost 12,000 homes and kiosks had been burned, 47,000 homes were robbed, some 40,000 Armenians had been forcibly converted to Islam, while another 400,000 Armenians lost their homes and jobs as a result of pogroms.[438]

The total number of Armenian casualties in 1894–96 reached 300,000. Careful examination of various credible sources on the Armenian massacres shows that they were extensive, well planned, and executed. The perpetrators included not only the Muslim fanatics, but also the gendarmerie, police, and military forces. The prominent organizers were given government awards and promotions. The massacres in 1895 and 1896 began simultaneously in nearly all the provinces; a trumpet call or a single rifle shot would mark the beginning and end of the massacres.[439]

German public figure and historian Paul Rohrbach who visited the Armenian-populated provinces in 1898 noted that the horrors inflicted upon the Armenians would not have been as great if the Powers had not made the 'catastrophic gift' to the Armenians of Article 61 of the Treaty of Berlin in 1878.[440] Russian historian V. M. Khvostov noted that it was due to the provisions of Article 61 that Sultan Abdul Hamid preserved his 'rotten and autocratic' regime in 1890's and continued his policy of national and religious oppression.[441]

Despite its sponsorship of massacres that took the lives of nearly 300,000 Armenians in the Ottoman Empire, the Porte remained unpunished while European diplomacy remained indifferent to the suffering and oppression of an entire nation. The mutually exclusive interests of and mistrust among the Powers were the main factors preserving the corrupt Ottoman Empire. Abdul Hamid took advantage of these disagreements to get rid of the undesirable Christian elements that he believed threatened the stability and integrity of his Empire.

On September 24, 1896, a rally took place in Liverpool to protest the anti-Armenian policies of the Sultan. The main speaker at the rally that drew thousands of people was former Prime Minister Gladstone. Speaking for an hour and twenty minutes, he delivered what his biographer Philip Magnus called one of his best public speeches.[442] Gladstone said he spoke from heart and sought to stand above partisanship and politics and called on the Government to challenge the Sultan's denial of knowledge of the massacres the Porte had organized. Gladstone reminded his audience that the 1876 Bulgarian massacre had similarly been blamed on the Bulgarian agitators and rebels. He said that instead of exacting vengeance, the Government should have take measures to stop the killings and to prevent new massacres. Gladstone charged that the fabled 'Concert of Europe' had failed to assist the Christian population of the Ottoman Empire and prevent further carnage. He said that the British Government had acted in cooperation with other Powers and failed and asked the rally to adopt a resolution calling on the Foreign Office to take more active measures, including the use of force, to stop the Porte from carrying out further reprisals. Britain must assure other Powers of its impartiality on the Armenian Question, he said. He called the Sultan 'the Great Assassin' and urged the Government to invoke the existing international treaties and the Cyprus Convention to intervene in Turkey unilaterally.[443]

Despite his advanced age, Gladstone took an active part in trying to move the 'idle' British Government to take a policy stand more in compliance with norms of Christian morality. He even told his sons he prayed to the Almighty to give him the strength to lead a crusade against the inhuman Turks one day![444] On a different occasion he noted that he would run a parliamentary campaign if he were as young as he had been in 1876.[445]

Gladstone's stance on the Armenian Question was the final and one of the most important factors which compelled Lord Rosebery to resign as the leader of the Liberals. One of the Liberal activists, John Russell, noted that nobody in the party leadership dealt with foreign policy issues and Rosebery's policy of 'self-government' resulted in lack of direction.[446] Rosebery supported Gladstone in his assertion that the Armenian Question was above partisanship. He argued that Britain should have no conflict of interest on this issue; that this issue should not be an object of contention and tool of political struggle between the parties; and that the British people should have a stake in the final settlement. Rosebery, however, did not agree with Gladstone's point that Britain should act unilaterally against Turkey as if it had no conflict of interests. While the majority of party members supported Gladstone, Rosebery refused to support what he called pro-Armenian agitation. In his October 6 letter to the Liberal whip, he noted his deep disagreements with the majority of Liberal MP's on the Eastern Question but acknowledged that Gladstone's views gained serious ground among most Liberal members.[447]

The following day, Rosebery informed Gladstone of his decision to quit as Party leader and complained that he had never had a chance to effectively lead the Liberals. He accused Gladstone of having endorsed policies that he, as leader of the Loyal Opposition, could not encourage, allowing the Liberal activists to use Gladstone's authority to undermine Rosebery. In his reply, Gladstone asserted that he had always supported the policy of unilateral pressure on the Porte as the only means of achieving progress on the Eastern Question. He disputed Rosebery's views that such pressure could lead to a general war in Europe and noted that without active external pressure, the diplomatic representations in Constantinople were worthless.[448] This sentence sums up Gladstone's attitude toward Turkey, which however had not translated into real success in the nineteenth century.

On October 10, the Liberal Party conference convened in London to address the issue of the Armenian massacres in Turkey. Russell took note of Rosebery's resignation, which was announced during the meeting. Rosebery's

October 9 speech in Edinburgh had been read, in which he had urged the non-partisan approach to the Armenian Question. The speech lacked substance and was his final excuse for the indifference toward the Armenian massacres. Rosebery had noted that the British policy and interests had a thousand components and it would have been wrong to sacrifice 999 components for the sake of one, even if it required immediate attention. The former Prime Minister added that the extermination of the Armenian race was only one of a thousand British worries and largely irrelevant to its interests.[449] Rosebery announced his opposition to unilateral intervention saying he believed the Powers would oppose it by force.[450] Rosebery's views coincided with the official position of the Conservative party, and when the Gladstone faction assailed him for his position, he was forced to resign as party leader.

The Liberal Party conference adopted a resolution blaming the Conservative policies for the Eastern crisis. It went on to charge Lord Salisbury with personal responsibility for the present state of affairs in Armenia in view of his actions during the Treaty of Berlin. The Prime Minister could not be trusted with the Armenian Question, the Liberal Party stated.[451] Salisbury's position, however, encountered no serious domestic opposition. The leaderless Liberals were soon forced to backtrack on their position since the Armenian Question completely disappeared from the international agenda.

On October 20, Salisbury sent a circular note to the heads of governments in Europe, urging common and joint actions on the Armenian Question to avoid a clash of competing interests in the Ottoman Empire. He proposed convening a European conference to find a comprehensive settlement to the Eastern Question.[452] Salisbury was convinced that the Austro-Hungarian and French Governments would endorse the idea of the conference since they were concerned about the possibility of the Russian occupation of the Straits. Italy was expected to follow the British lead, but Salisbury was unsure about the German position, hoping however that it would agree with the proposal on account of its alliance with Austria-Hungary. The matter hinged on the support of Russia. Russian Foreign Minister Shishkin told the British Ambassador that Russia would agree to convene a conference in Constantinople on the condition that use of force against the Sultan was to be ruled out. The final decision was to be made by Czar Nicholas, Shishkin warned.[453]

Addressing the annual Guild Hall ceremony in London on October 29,

Salisbury said that Britain had enough resources to penalize the Sultan or cause him trouble, if the British people demanded so. At the same time, he said that a punitive expedition would not save the Christian and Muslim population of Turkey from the brutal regime; such an effort would require the consent of as many nations as possible. He said that the combined resources at the disposal of the Concert of Europe were far greater than any other nation's. Therefore, it was dangerous for Britain to act unilaterally as the other Powers could either refrain from joining or oppose the British action by force, leading to a general war. He said that the conflict of interests and disagreements among the European Powers were far too complicated to gamble on the issue of Armenia. He concluded that the amelioration of the state of affairs in the Muslim and Christian communities in Turkey was possible to achieve through the Sultan only.[454]

On November 23, Nicholas II chaired a session of the Council of Ministers in St. Petersburg to discuss Nelidov's plan of seizing the Straits. The Ambassador made a presentation on the grave crisis in Turkey and the subsequent need to occupy the Straits to prevent the crisis from developing further. While the War Minister and the Chief of the Army General Staff endorsed the idea, Finance Minister Count Sergei Witte categorically opposed it. He was concerned that this undertaking would lead in the direction of a European war that would undermine the excellent political and financial situation in which Alexander III had placed the Russian Empire. At the end of the discussion, the Czar concurred with Nelidov's proposal. A decision was made to provoke the Porte to such actions in Constantinople that would serve as cause for occupying the Bosphorus. The Sultan was then to be granted Russian protection if he requested such assistance. Nelidov departed for Turkey to prepare the ground, but the plans would eventually be scrapped under strong opposition from France and internal lobbying by Minister Witte and Chairman of the Holy Synod Pobedonostsev, who made the monarch change his mind.[455]

On November 25, Salisbury received the Russian endorsement of the idea to convene a conference of Ambassadors in Constantinople, on the condition that the foreign envoys did not 'offend the Sultan.'[456]

The conference of the Ambassadors representing the European Powers began on December 22. The mutual distrust and antagonism among the Powers increased after the Russian Ambassador insisted on discussing the question of Macedonia first. Currie was concerned that addressing the Macedonian Question would increase Russia's leverage and insisted on discussing the general state of affairs in the Ottoman Empire. He was supported by Austro-Hungarian Ambassador Calice who noted that any settlement in Macedonia would cause disturbances in the neighboring regions of Austria-Hungary, rekindle the Slavic peoples' national liberation movements, and inevitably lead to the collapse of the Ottoman Empire. When Currie mentioned the need for reforms in the European part of Turkey, Calice noted that reforms would only strengthen Russian influence in the region.[457] The British Government also concluded that deployment of the British Fleet in the Dardanelles would inevitably lead to reciprocal Russian action in the Bosphorus, seriously undermining Austro-Hungarian interests.[458]

The Armenian revolutionary groups were reinvigorated by the Ambassadors' conference. A day after the conference had begun, one of the groups threatened to blow up the Russian Embassy if the Porte did not guarantee implementation of reforms in Western Armenia within three months. The Armenian groups obviously concluded that the successful conclusion of the conference now depended on Russia.[459]

On January 6, 1897, Currie reported that he had not presented any initiatives out of fear that the envoys would then split into two opposing camps. He said he had preferred to hold bilateral and private discussions.[460] His consultations with the Russian and Austro-Hungarian envoys led to an approval of joint action to prevent further disturbances in Constantinople. The envoys agreed to deploy Austro-Hungarian and Russian warships in the Straits in the event that fresh disturbances and massacres broke out in the capital. The Austro-Hungarian and Russian gunboats were to be deployed in front of the Sultan's Palace and fire one shot each in its direction—the Austro-Hungarians first, the Russians second.[461]

On January 19, Currie reported that the Ambassadors had approved plans to form two international commissions to work on reform programs for the European and Asiatic parts of the Ottoman Empire.[462]

While the conference was underway, Abdul Hamid made several attempts to probe the intentions of the conferees. When the Turkish Ambassador in London asked Salisbury for information, the Prime Minister said all Powers had agreed that the only possible and necessary solution of the crisis was to curb the excessively authoritarian powers of the Sultan.[463]

An important dimension in the crisis that affected the Ottoman Empire was its dire financial situation. The financial difficulties of the Porte could result in the instigation of financial control by the Powers over the Ottoman Empire. Russia was repeatedly warning the Porte not to intervene too heavily in matters concerned with management of the national debt.[464]

It is possible that the Sultan misunderstood the Russian warnings because he published the country's 1897 budget while the conference was in progress. The published budget showed a surplus of 781,912 British pounds; in reality, the budget deficit was 2.5 million pounds. Such trickery could not increase Turkey's credit rating. The only sources of deficit financing were either by increasing the national debt or direct lending by the Powers. After long discussions, the foreign envoys agreed to provide funds for the salaries of civil servants and the military, a decision made at least partly so as to gain favor with Turkish public opinion. The Powers also decided on the establishment of an equally staffed Turkish-European commission to oversee the budgetary process and propose Treasury reforms.[465]

Salisbury noted in his January 25 dispatch to Currie that the loan to the Turkish Treasury might not save the Empire. He noted that many people in Britain openly questioned the necessity of preserving the Ottoman Empire and it would be impossible to persuade them to support the loan without guarantees of better government and administration in Turkey.[466]

On February 2, the European Ambassadors prepared a reform program that would provide for seven measures only: (1) establishment of a Supreme Council; (2) formation of a Control Commission to oversee the reforms process; (3) the Powers would establish controls over the Turkish Treasury; (4) reform of the judicial system; (5) reform of the police system; (6) establishment of municipalities; and (7) guarantees for the freedom of the press.[467] The reforms program was soon forgotten when the Turkish-Greek War broke out in 1897 and the European Powers sided with Turkey in its suppression of the rebels in Crete. The Ambassadors concluded that 'in this time of crisis, it would not be expedient to press for reforms.'[468]

Meeting with Abdul Hamid at that time, U.S. Ambassador Alexander Terrell told the Sultan that in his opinion the monarch had no cause to worry because the integrity of his dominions had been guaranteed by all the Powers. The Sultan was the only autocrat with such distinction, Terrell noted, as no Power guaranteed the integrity of the domain of France, England, Germany, Russia, Austria or Italy. The European Powers would go to such lengths to protect the Sultan, Terrell pointed out, that they even killed Greek Christians in Crete to assure the Sultan of their loyalties.[469]

The conference of European Ambassadors in Constantinople showed that the Powers were unwilling to risk deterioration in their relations with the Porte. By presenting demands diminishing the sovereign rights of the Sultan and threatening to reopen the Armenian Question, the Powers had intended to obtain fresh concessions from the Porte. Meanwhile, Abdul Hamid had organized the massacre of the Armenians, which had become an object of wrangling between the Powers and the Porte. When the Turks defeated Greece, the Muslim soul was buoyed and the Sultan's authority rose, and it became impossible for the Powers to press for implementation of reforms in the Armenian-populated provinces.

Thus, the last serious attempt of British diplomacy to secure reforms in the Ottoman Empire failed. This episode marked the end of the traditional British policies in the Near East. British diplomacy had also been unsuccessful in preventing a rapprochement between Russia and Turkey. Starting in 1897, Salisbury began to prepare ground for radical changes in British policy on the Eastern Question. As he wrote to Currie in October 1897, the British policy would be to strengthen its presence in the Nile region and to avoid any and all obligations in Constantinople.[470]

9. The Interaction of British Foreign Policy and Domestic Public Opinion on the Armenian Question

The influence of public opinion, domestic interest groups and the political process on the formation of the country's foreign policy and international relations in Britain rose steadily throughout the nineteenth century, parallel to the enfranchisement of the middle class and the liberalization of domestic politics. British public opinion was affected by the press reports of atrocities and disorders in the Ottoman Empire during the Eastern Crisis of 1895–97, and the British Government had to take domestic politics into account. Both Conservatives and Liberals engaged in criticism of the Sultan and his Government. Many prominent members of the British elite also sympathized with the Armenian population in the Ottoman Empire and demanded more forceful actions from their Government.

The existence of Armenian societies and émigré groups in Britain was a major factor in the development of pro-Armenian opinion in the country. The progressive Armenian groups advocated liberation and the establishment of self-government in Western Armenia, preferably under the auspices of Britain. Two Armenian periodicals were published in London, including *Hayastan* (in English and French) and *Huntchak*, the organ of the Social-Democratic Huntchak Party. Many Armenian groups and committees were based in London, including the Armenian Patriotic Union that was founded in 1888 by Karapet Hagopian. Another prominent group, the Armenian United Association of London, was founded in 1898 and published an English-language magazine, *Ararat: A Searchlight on Armenia.*[471]

Prominent British public figures, politicians, and clergymen were members of Anglo-Armenian societies in 1890's. Many of these groups lobbied the Government to take action on the Armenian Question, and engaged in charity work to assist the Armenian population in Turkey. One of the groups, The Anglo-Armenian Association, was founded by James Bryce in 1893 and was headed by MP Francis Stevenson and MP Edward Atkin, who later served as Chancellor of the Exchequer.

Another pro-Armenian group, Grosvenor House Association, was established with Salisbury's blessing and was headed by the Duke of Westminster (Earl of Grosvenor). One of the more prominent members of this group was Rev. Malcolm Maccoll, the Canon of Ripon, a notable clergyman and publicist who authored several books on the Armenian Question.

The two pro-Armenian groups were affiliated with, respectively, the Liberal and Conservative parties, and engaged in partisan politics. Nevertheless, their grassroots activities did much to educate the British public on the Armenian Question and bring to light evidence of atrocities and massacres organized in the Armenian-populated regions of Turkey.

Several groups and charities raised funds to alleviate the suffering of the Armenian population in Turkey; the funds were sent to the British and American missionary associations operating in Turkey.

The Armenian Mission of Religious Society of Friends, founded in Constantinople in 1881, was the first British group that carried out charity, medical, and educational activities in the Armenian-populated regions. The Mission was established as a medical charity and was initially headed by Mr. and Mrs. Dobrashian. In 1888, the Mission established a Sunday school, a vocational school and a Day school. The number of students in day school reached 150, while 400 students attended the Sunday school; new buildings had been built for the schools.[472]

The British missionaries were among the few private British citizens stationed in Turkey, and provided assistance and educational opportunities to the Armenian-populated provinces. Many Armenians converted to Protestantism and Catholicism to avoid persecution, although the local governments continued to harass the Protestant Armenians as much as they did the Armenian Gregorians.

Another group called Friends of Armenia was formed in London in 1897. Lady Cavendish was the President of the Society while Ms. Cantlow was the Executive Secretary. The society published a monthly called *Friends of Armenia,* with the self-declared objective of the revival of Armenia. In 1899 alone Friends of Armenia raised £509 from its members in Manchester, Edinburgh, Paisley, and Liverpool. Overall, the society raised nearly £60,000 in ten years to assist the victims of the Armenian massacres of 1894–96.[473]

In March 1897, the Friends of Armenia sent Cambridge University Professor of Paleontology Randall Harris and his wife, Helen Harris, on a fact-finding trip to Asia Minor. Upon their return to Britain, the Harrises published their correspondence with friends in Britain and missionaries in Asia Minor (Harris, R and Harris, H, *Letters From the Scenes of the Recent Massacres in Armenia,* London, 1897).[474]

Women's Relief Fund was another British group assisting the Armenian victims of massacres. The group brought together prominent British women and was headed by Madeleine Cole. The Women's Relief Fund sent funds to Van, Diyarbakir, Zeytoun, and Urmia; it raised and disbursed more than £16,000.[475]

The International Association of the Friends of Armenia was founded in 1896, and incorporated the Armenian Information Bureau. Its objectives were to disseminate information and literature on Armenia and educate the British public on the subject, as well as to facilitate interaction between various groups engaged in Armenian relief efforts. The Bishop of Rochester was the President of the Association while Lady Henry Somerset was the Honorary Secretary.[476]

Notes

1 "A Vanishing Treaty," p. 172.

2 Dillon, Emil, (1854–1933), Irish linguist and reporter, a specialist in Oriental languages and comparative linguistics. He worked in the St. Petersburg and Kharkov Universities and the Mekhitarian Order in Venice in 1880's, and studied Armenian language and literature. He is an author of several monographs on the Armenian language and translated several Armenian works. He visited the Ottoman Empire in 1895, working as correspondent for *The Daily Telegraph* of London, and made a trip to Western Armenia. Based on the information he collected, he published a series of articles on the Armenian Question.

3 E. B. Lanin, "Armenia and the Armenian People," *The Fortnightly Review* 54 (1890), p. 270.

4 Paul Knaplund, *Gladstone's Foreign Policy* (New York and London, 1935), p. 159.

5 M. Maccoll, "The Constantinople Massacre and its Lesson," *The Contemporary Review* 68 (1895), pp. 750–52.

6 Turkey, No. 3 (1896) , pp. 33–34.

7 Currie, Philip Henry Wodehouse, Sir (1834–1906), British diplomat. Currie served as Permanent Undersecretary of State for Foreign Affairs (1888–93), Ambassador to Turkey (1893–98), and Ambassador to Italy (1898–1903).

8 FO 424/172, No. 98, pp. 75–76.

9 FO 424/172, No. 103, pp. 77–78.

10 Turkey No. 3 (1896), pp. 42–43.

11 Ibid., p. 63.

12 E. M. Bliss, *Turkey and Armenian Atrocities* (Philadelphia, 1896), pp. 337–42; M. S. Gabrielian, *Armenia: A Martyr Nation: A Historical Sketch of the Armenian People from Tradition Times to the Present Tragic Days* (New York, 1918), pp. 225–30.

13 Turkey No. 3 (1896), pp. 63–64.

14 Ibid., pp.64–65.

15 Ibid., pp. 73–74.

16 Ibid., pp. 72–73.

17 Ibid., pp. 70–71.

18 Ibid., pp. 74–75.

19 FO 424/175, No. 32, p. 32.

20 Turkey No. 3 (1896), p. 80.

21 E. L. Godkin, "The Armenian Resolutions," *The Nation* 62 (January 30, 1896), p. 93.

22 U.S. missionary activities in the Near East began in 1819, during the presidency of James Madison, when the American Office of Overseas Missions delegated Rev. Pliny Fisk and Rev. Levy Parsons to the Ottoman Empire to study the opportunities for missionary work. The initial objective of the missionaries was to convert the Muslim population. However, faced with difficulties and legal challenges early on, the missionaries directed their proselytizing effort toward the Christian communities. J. De Novo, *American Interests and Policies in the Middle East, 1900–1939* (Mineapolis, 1963), pp. 8, 11–12.

23 As of 1900, some 162 American missionaries were working in the Ottoman Empire, assisted by local staff of 900. There were 40 boarding schools and 7 colleges run by the missionaries, with 2700 male and female students; 15,000 students were enrolled in elementary schools Ibid., p. 9.

24 R. Mirak, "Armenian Emigration to the United States to 1915," *Journal of Armenian Studies* 1 (Autumn 1975), pp. 33–34.

25 M. D. Gutor, *Noveyshaya istoriya Turtsii i Persii*, part 1 (Tiflis, 1913), p. 67–68.

26 De Novo, *American Interests*, p. 16.

27 U.S. Department of State, Papers Relating to the Foreign Relations of the United States, with the Annual Message of the President Transmitted to Congress, December 5, 1894, Washington, 1864, p. x.

28 FO 424/176, No. 53, p. 57.

29 FO 424/175, No. 51, p. 55.

30 Turkey No. 3 (1896), p. 107.

31 Ibid., p. 104.

32 Ibid., pp. 105–6.

33 Ibid., pp. 127–28.

34 Nicolson, Arthur, 1st Baron Carnock (1849–1928), British diplomat. He served as Minister at the British Embassy in Constantinople (1893–94), Minister to Morocco (1895–1904), Ambassador to Russia (1906–10), and Permanent Undersecretary of State for Foreign Affairs (1910–16).

35 Turkey No. 3 (1896), p. 129–30.

36 Ibid., pp. 135–36.

37 FO 424/175, No. 97, p. 108.

38 Turkey No. 3 (1896), p. 136.

39 Ibid., p. 137.

40 Ibid., pp. 145–46.

41 FO 424/175, No. 122, p. 123.

42 Turkey, No. 3 (1896), p. 149.

43 Ibid., p. 166.

44 Grey, Edward Sir (1862–1933), British Liberal politician and diplomat. He served as Undersecretary at the Foreign Office (1892–95) and Foreign Secretary (1905–16).

45 Gabrielian, *Armenia*, pp. 23–231.

46 Turkey, No. 3 (1896), pp. 184–85.

47 Ibid., pp. 201–2.

[48] FO 424/175, No. 227/1, p. 231; No. 229, p. 232; No. 250, p. 250; No. 252/1, p. 251; 424/178, No. 17/2, pp. 16–17; No. 17/3, pp. 17–18; No. 17/4, pp. 18–21; No. 34/1, p. 35.

[49] Nelidov, Alexander, Russian diplomat. He served as Ambassador to Turkey (1883–97), Italy (1897–1903), and Framce (1903–10).

[50] Turkey, No. 6 (1896), p. 36.

[51] Ibid., pp. 47–48.

[52] R. Douglas, "Britain and the Armenian Question, 1894–97," *The Historical Journal* 1976, no. 19, p. 115.

[53] Kimberley, John Wodehouse, 1st Earl of, (1826–1902), British politician. He served as Under Secretary of State for Foreign Affairs (1852–56, 1858–61), Ambassador to Russia (1856–58), Colonial Secretary (1870–74, 1880–82), Secretary of State for India (1882–86, 1892–94), and Foreign Secretary (1894–95).

[54] E. J. Dillon, "The Fiasco in Armenia," *The Fortnightly Review* 65 (March 1 1896), p. 348.

[55] Turkey, No. 6 (1896), p. 56.

[56] Ibid., pp. 57–58.

[57] Ibid., p. 64.

[58] Ibid., pp. 53, 65.

[59] Ibid., pp. 75–76.

[60] Ibid., p. 98.

[61] Ibid., p. 107; FO 424/178, No. 170/1, p. 167.

[62] Turkey, No. 6 (1896), p. 104.

[63] Ibid., p. 105.

[64] Turkey, No. 1 (1895). Correspondence Relative to the Armenian Question and Reports from Her Majesty's Concular Officers in Asiatic Turkey. London, 1896, Part 1, p. 2.

[65] Ibid., p. 10; S. Shahid Bey, *Islam, Turkey and Armenia and How They Happened* (St. Louis, 1898), pp. 198–99; Bliss, *Turkey and Armenian Atrocities*, pp. 368–73; Douglas, "Britain and the Armenian Question," p. 116; Lazarev, *Prichiny bedstviy armyan*, pp. 34–35; K. Z. Taroyan, "Narodnye dvizheniya v Sasune i drugikh rayonakh Zapadnoy Armenii v 90-kh godakh XIX v." (Abstract of Ph.D. diss. in history, Yerevan, 1966).

[66] Turkey, No. 1 (1895). Part 1, p. 2.

[67] Ibid., pp. 3–4.

[68] Ibid., p. 3.

[69] Ibid., p. 8.

[70] Ibid., p. 7.

[71] Ibid., pp. 7–8.

[72] Ibid., p. 10.

[73] According to a report sent by Zeki Pasha to the Porte, over 1,000 Armenians had been killed in Sasun as a result of operation in Sasun (R.

Davey, "Turkey and Armenia," *The Fortnightly Review* 63 (1895), p. 205), while more impartial sources set the casualties at 5–12 thousand Armenians (T. Peterson, "Turkey and Armenian Crisis," *The Catholic World* 61 (1895), p. 667; Douglas, "Britain and the Armenian Question," p. 116; Shahid Bey, *Islam, Turkey and Armenia*, p. 199): Zeki Pasha's report stated that "we have cleaned the country in such a way" so that no disturbances could occur again in the future. ("The Evil of the Turk," *The Outlook* 52 (August 24, 1895), p. 301): American publicist Theodore Peterson lists the Sasun massacre along with other atrocities committed by the Ottoman authorities against its subjects during the 19th century, including massacre of 50,000 Greeks in the Aegean Islands (1822), 10,000 Armenians in Mosul (1850), 11,000 Syrians in Lebanon (1860), 14,000 Bulgarians in Bulgaria (1876), 2,000 Yezidis in Mosul (1877), and 12,000 Armenians in Mosul (1894). (Peterson, "Turkey and Armenian Crisis," p. 667).

[74] Turkey, No. 1 (1895). Part 1, pp. 19–20.

[75] Ibid., p. 21.

[76] Ibid., p. 16.

[77] E. J. Dillon, "Armenia: An Appeal," *The Contemporary Review* 69 (1896), p. 5.

[78] "Mr. Gladstone on Armenia," *The Spectator* 75 (August 10, 1895), p. 164.

[79] "Armenia and the Powers: From Behind the Scenes," *The Contemporary Review* 69 (1896, pp. 628–43.

[80] Maccoll, "The Constantinople Massacre and its Lesson," p. 257.

[81] "Lord Rosebery's Deliverance," *The Spectator* 77 (October 17, 1896), p. 504.

[82] According to Fyodor Rotstein, the British Government pursued a different goal. "Proposing that Russia get closely involved in the Armenian Question and offering the perspective of Russian occupation of the Turkish Armenia was meant to prevent armed penetration of Russia in the Far East." (Rotshteyn, *Mezhdunarodnye otnosheniya*, p. 273).

[83] Georgiev, et al., *Vostochnyy vopros*, pp. 264–65.

[84] W. T. Stead, "The Eastern Ogre; or St. George to Rescue," *The Review of Reviews* 14 (1896), p. 578.

[85] "Armenia and the Powers," p. 636.

[86] M. Maccoll, *The Sultan and the Powers* (London, 1896), pp. 208–9.

[87] "Mr. Gladstone on Armenia," p. 164.

[88] Maccoll, Malcolm, (1838–1907), British publicist and clergyman who was appointed Canon

of Ripon in 1884. He was an active member of the British-Armenian "Grosvenor House" society, organized rallies in support of Western Armenia, and authored books and articles on the Armenian Question.

[89] Maccoll, *The Sultan and the Powers*, pp. 208–9.

[90] Turkey, No. 1 (1895). Part 1, pp. 17–18.

[91] Ibid., p. 24.

[92] Ibid., p. 22.

[93] Ibid., p. 32.

[94] Ibid., p. 26.

[95] Ibid., pp. 40–41.

[96] Ibid., pp. 29–30.

[97] Ibid.

[98] AVPR, F. Politicheskiy arkhiv, d. 3435, l. 97–98.

[99] Turkey, No. 1 (1895). Part 1, p. 41.

[100] Douglas, "Britain and the Armenian Question," p. 117.

[101] AVPR, F. Politicheskiy arkhiv, d. 3435.

[102] Turkey, No. 1 (1895). Part 1, pp. 39–40.

[103] Cambon, Paul (1843–1924), French diplomat. He served as Ambassador to Spain (1886–91), Turkey (1891–98), and Great Britain (1898–1920).

[104] Turkey, No. 1 (1895). Part 1, p. 42.

[105] L. J. Gordon, *American Relations with Turkey (1830–1930)* (Philadelphia, 1932), p. 26.

[106] Bliss, *Turkey and Armenian Atrocities*, pp. 384–85.

[107] Douglas, "Britain and the Armenian Question," p. 119.

[108] AVPR, F. Politicheskiy arkhiv, d. 3435, l. 10–11.

[109] Turkey, No. 1 (1895). Part 1, p. 44.

[110] Ibid., pp. 49–50.

[111] Ibid., pp. 51–52.

[112] Ibid., p. 64.

[113] P. Magnus, *Gladstone: A Biography* (London, 1954), p. 430.

[114] *Novoe vremya*, 9 January 1895; *Kavkaz*, 6 January 1895.

[115] FO 424/181, No. 2, p. 1.

[116] FO 424/181, No. 18, p. 12.

[117] FO 424/181, No. 25, pp. 16–17.

[118] FO 424/181, No. 50, pp. 37–38.

[119] FO 424/181, No. 59, pp. 40–41.

[120] Turkey, No. 6 (1896), p. 199.

[121] Turkey, No. 1 (1895). Part 1, p. 79.

[122] FO 424/181, No. 54, p. 39.

[123] FO 424/181, No. 57, p. 40.

[124] FO 424/181, No. 60, p. 41.

[125] FO 424/181, No. 88/1, p. 57.

[126] FO 424/181, No. 93, pp. 65–66.

[127] Turkey, No. 1 (1895). Part 1, pp. 74–75, 82; *Kavkaz*, 14 and 29 January 1895.

[128] Turkey, No. 1 (1895). Part 1, pp. 76–78.

[129] Ibid., pp. 92–93.

[130] Turkey, No. 1 (1896). Correspondence Relative to the Armenian Question and Reports from Her Majesty's Consular Officers in Asiatic Turkey. London, 1896, pp. 9–10.

[131] Ibid., p. 10.

[132] Ibid., p. 11.

[133] Ibid., pp. 12–15.

[134] Ibid., p. 12.

[135] Ibid., p. 16.

[136] Knaplund, *Gladstone's Foreign Policy*, pp. 267–68.

[137] FO 424/182, No. 35, p. 28.

[138] Turkey, No. 1 (1896), pp. 18–20.

[139] Turkey, No. 6 (1896), pp. 268–69, 271, 274, 276.

[140] Turkey, No. 1 (1896), p. 20.

[141] Ibid., p. 29.

[142] FO 424/182, No. 104, p. 175.

[143] AVPR, F. Politicheskiy arkhiv, d. 3440, l. 5–6, 9–10.

[144] "The Armenian Reforms," *The Spectator* 74 (May 18, 1895), p. 675.

[145] AVPR, F. Politicheskiy arkhiv, d. 3440, l. 22–23.

[146] Republic of Armenia, Central Historical Archive, "Collection of Excerpts of Documents," list 1, chapter 339, part 2, pp. 95–96.

[147] Kirakosyan, ed., *Hayastane mijazgayin divanagitutian*, pp. 130–47.

[148] "Armenia and the Powers," pp. 636–37.

[149] "The Armenian Meeting," *The Spectator* 74 (May 11, 1895), p. 643.

[150] "The Armenian Reforms," p. 674.

[151] Maccoll, *The Sultan and the Powers*, p. 11.

[152] Turkey, No. 1 (1895). Part 2, p. 66.

[153] "Armenia and the Powers," pp. 637.

[154] "Mr. Gladstone on Armenia," p. 164.

[155] Turkey, No. 1 (1895). Part 2, p. 66.

[156] Ibid., p. 73.

[157] Douglas, "Britain and the Armenian Question," pp. 121–22.

[158] J. A. S. Grenville, *Lord Salisbury and Foreign Policy* (London, 1964), pp. 4–6.

[159] G. W. E. Russell, "Armenia and the Forward Movement," *The Contemporary Review* 71 (1897), p. 21.

[160] "The Armenian Meeting," p. 643; "The Armenian Question," *The Spectator* 75 (July 27, 1895), p. 105; "Lord Salisbury in Turkey," *The Spectator* 75 (December 7, 1895), p. 808; "Our Failure in Turkey," *The Spectator* 75 (December 14, 1895), p. 884.

[161] "The Armenian Question," p. 105.

[162] Russell, George William (1853–1919), British

Liberal politician. He was elected to the House of Commons in 1880, and served as Under Secretary of State for India (1892–94), Under Secretary at the Home Office (1894–95), and as member of London City Council (1889–95) and Privy Council (from 1907).

163 Russell, "Armenia and the Forward Movement," p. 22.

164 Kennedy, A. L., *Salisbury, 1830–1903: Portrait of a Statesman* (London, 1953), pp. 256–57.

165 Douglas, "Britain and the Armenian Question," p. 122.

166 Ibid., p. 123.

167 FO 424/183, No. 57, p. 63.

168 FO 424/183, No. 78, pp. 89–90.

169 FO 424/183, No. 87, p. 96.

170 FO 424/183, No. 111, p. 115.

171 FO 424/183, No. 119, p. 118.

172 FO 424/183, No. 120, p. 118; Grenville, *Lord Salisbury and Foreign Policy*, p. 30.

173 Turkey, No. 1 (1895). Part 1, p. 134–46; "Americans and Armenians," *The Spectator* 76 (February 1, 1896), pp. 156–57.

174 Turkey, No. 1 (1896), p. 98–100.

175 FO 424/183, No. 151, pp. 154–55.

176 Turkey, No. 1 (1896), pp. 118–19.

177 Ibid., p. 121.

178 "Mr. Gladstone on Armenia," p. 164.

179 "Lord Salisbury and Armenia," *The Nation* 61 (August 15, 1895), pp. 110–11.

180 "Mr. Gladstone on Armenia," p. 164.

181 This is largely due to the fact that the Conservative Party emerged as clear victor in the July 12 Parliamentary elections.

182 "Lord Salisbury and Armenia," p. 110; "Mr. Gladstone on Armenia," p. 164.

183 Grenville, *Lord Salisbury and Foreign Policy*, p. 8.

184 *Novoe vremya*, 19 December 1912, 31 May 1913.

185 FO 424/183, No. 177, p. 187.

186 FO 424/183, No. 178, p. 182.

187 Turkey, No. 1 (1896), p. 120.

188 Ibid., p. 122.

189 FO 424/183, No. 198, p. 233.

190 Turkey, No. 1 (1896), p. 123.

191 FO 424/183, No. 216, p. 254.

192 FO 424/183, No. 224, p. 258.

193 FO 424/183, No. 230, p. 261.

194 FO 424/183, No. 239, p. 264.

195 FO 424/183, No. 262, p. 403.

196 FO 424/183, No. 263, pp. 403–4.

197 FO 424/183, No. 269, p. 405.

198 FO 424/183, No. 318, pp. 434–35.

199 FO 424/183, No. 316, p. 433.

200 FO 424/183, No. 317, p. 434.

201 Turkey, No. 1 (1896), pp. 142–43.

202 Ibid., pp. 143–45.

203 FO 424/183, No. 355, 356, pp. 463–65.

204 FO 424/183, No. 338/1, p. 450.

205 FO 424/183, No. 362/1, p. 469.

206 Turkey, No. 1 (1895). Part 1, pp. 198, 200–203; Turkey, No. 1 (1896), pp. 118–19; Turkey, No. 2 (1896). Correspondence Relative to the Armenian Question and Reports from Her Majesty's Concular Officers in Asiatic Provinces. London, 1896, pp. 2–4, 9–10, 14, 16–17, 21; FO 424/183, No. 208/2, p. 240; No. 219/2, pp. 255–56; No. 251/2, pp. 398–99; No. 280/1, p. 413.

207 FO 424/183, No. 339/2, p. 451.

208 A. S. Silin, *Ekspansiya Germanii na Blizhnem Vostoke v kontse xix v.* (Moscow, 1971), p. 209.

209 Grenville, *Lord Salisbury and Foreign Policy*, pp. 33–34.

210 Ibid., p. 25.

211 M. N. Jefferson, "Lord Salisbury and the Eastern Question, 1890–1898," *The Slavonic and Eastern European Review* 39, no. 92 (December 1960), p. 49.

212 Grenville, *Lord Salisbury and Foreign Policy*, p. 38.

213 Ibid., p. 39.

214 Ibid., pp. 40–41.

215 Silin, *Ekspansiya Germanii*, p. 215.

216 H. Hepworth, *Through Armenia on Horseback* (London, 1898), p. 282; E. Pears, *Turkey and its People* (London, 1911); G. H. Paelian, *Landmarks in Armenian History* (New York, 1942), p. 62.

217 Pears, *Life of Abdul Hamid* (New York, 1917), p. 232.

218 FO 424/183, No. 371, p. 476.

219 Turkey, No. 2 (1896), p. 22.

220 Shahid Bey, *Islam, Turkey and Armenia*, p. 201.

221 Maccoll, "The Constantinople Massacre and its Lesson," p. 756.

222 "The Suspense in Constantinople," *The Spectator* 75 (October 12 1895), p. 476.

223 *Saturday Review*, October 5, 1895.

224 Turkey, No. 2 (1896), pp. 22, 36.

225 FO 424/184, No. 6, p. 3.

226 Turkey, No. 2(1896), p. 23.

227 FO 424/184, No. 14, p. 5.

228 Douglas, "Britain and the Armenian Question," pp. 124–25.

229 Turkey, No. 2 (1896), p. 25.

230 Ibid., pp. 41–42.

231 Ibid., pp. 25–26.

232 Ibid., p. 37.

233 FO 424/184, No. 38, p. 26.

[234] Turkey, No. 2 (1896), p. 37.

[235] FO 424/184, No. 279, pp. 168–69.

[236] Turkey, No. 2(1896), p. 37.

[237] Ibid., pp. 38–39, 43.

[238] Turkey, No. 1(1896), p. 158.

[239] Turkey, No. 2(1896), p. 50.

[240] Monson, Sir Edmund John (1834–1909), British diplomat. He served as Ambassador to Austria-Hungary (1893–96) and France (1896–1905).

[241] Turkey, No. 2(1896), p. 43; FO 424/184, No. 81, p. 47.

[242] Turkey, No. 1(1896), p. 158; Turkey, No. 2 (1896), p. 57.

[243] FO 424/184, No. 135, p. 83.

[244] FO 424/184, No. 118, p. 68; No. 140, p. 95; No. 121, p. 68; No. 124, p 69; No. 126, p. 69.

[245] FO 424/184, No. 127, p. 70.

[246] FO 424/184, No. 143, p. 104.

[247] FO 424/184, No. 144, p. 104.

[248] Turkey, No. 2(1896), p. 57.

[249] FO 424/184, No. 195/1, pp. 126–28.

[250] FO 424/184, No. 153, p. 108.

[251] FO 424/184, No. 156, p. 109.

[252] FO 424/184, No. 155, pp. 108–9.

[253] FO 424/184, No. 157, p. 109.

[254] FO 424/184, No. 158, p. 109.

[255] FO 424/184, No. 160, p. 110.

[256] FO 424/184, No. 159, p. 110.

[257] FO 424/184, No. 301/1, p. 189.

[258] FO 424/184, No. 172, p. 115.

[259] FO 424/184, No. 179, p. 117.

[260] FO 424/184, No. 186, p. 119; No. 188, p. 120.

[261] FO 424/184, No. 190, p. 120.

[262] FO 424/184, No. 298, pp. 185–86.

[263] FO 424/184, No. 208, p. 142.

[264] FO 424/184, No. 297, pp. 184–85.

[265] FO 424/184, No. 213, p. 143.

[266] FO 424/184, No. 221, p. 146.

[267] FO 424/184, No. 224, p. 147.

[268] Turkey, No. 2(1896), p. 79.

[269] Ibid.

[270] FO 424/184, No. 237, p. 150.

[271] Turkey, No. 2(1896), p. 81.

[272] Ibid., p. 82.

[273] Ibid., p. 84.

[274] Ibid., p. 85.

[275] Ibid., pp. 85–86.

[276] Ibid., p. 85.

[277] FO 424/184, No. 311, p. 192.

[278] Turkey, No. 2(1896), p. 116.

[279] FO 424/184, No. 322, pp. 195–96.

[280] Turkey, No. 2(1896), pp. 104–5.

[281] FO 424/184, No. 376/1, pp. 217–18.

[282] Turkey, No. 2(1896), pp. 107–8.

[283] Bliss, *Turkey and Armenian Atrocities*, pp. 401–2; Russell, "Armenia and the Forward Movement," pp. 23–24; Grenville, *Lord Salisbury and Foreign Policy*, p. 47.

[284] Turkey, No. 2(1896), p. 127.

[285] Ibid., p. 122.

[286] Ibid., p. 124.

[287] It is symptomatic that Ambassador Nelidov was a passionate advocate of the Russian takeover of the Bosphorus and Dardanelles. He first raised the issue in 1892, justifying it by the threat of meddling in the Ottoman Empire's internal affairs by the Great Powers, especially Great Britain. The Ambassador again floated this proposal during the 1895 Massacre of the Armenians in Constantinople, which was then turned down by Foreign Minister Lobanov-Rostovski, who had been categorically against discussing the idea. V. M. Khvostov, "Problemy zakhvata Bosfora v 90-kh godakh XIX v." *Isto-rik-marksist* 20 (1930), pp. 109–10.

[288] Turkey, No. 2(1896), pp. 123–24.

[289] Ibid., p. 131.

[290] Ibid., p. 132.

[291] FO 424/184, No. 411, p. 231.

[292] Turkey, No. 2(1896), pp. 137–38.

[293] Ibid., p. 176.

[294] A. W. Williams and M. S. Gabrielian, *Bleeding Armenia: Its History and Horrors* (New York, 1896), p. 198.

[295] Turkey, No. 2(1896), p. 130.

[296] Ibid., p. 138.

[297] *Vestnik Yevropy*, 1895, vol. 6, bk. 12, pp. 862–63; Turkey, No. 2(1896), p. 140.

[298] Turkey, No. 2(1896), p. 141.

[299] FO 424/184, No. 554, pp. 198–299.

[300] FO 424/184, No. 520, p. 273.

[301] FO 424/184, No. 613/1, p. 328.

[302] FO 424/184, No. 570, p. 307.

[303] Ibid., p. 308.

[304] FO 424/184, No. 607, p. 323.

[305] FO 424/184, No. 556, pp. 299–300.

[306] FO 424/184, No. 617, p. 330.

[307] FO 424/184, No. 618, p. 331.

[308] FO 424/184, No. 567, p. 306.

[309] Turkey, No. 2(1896), p. 166.

[310] Staal, Yegor Yegorovich, Russian diplomat. He served as Ambassador to Great Britain in 1884–1903, and chaired the Hague Conference in 1889.

[311] Turkey, No. 2(1896), pp. 170–71.

[312] Ibid., p. 170.

[313] FO 424/184, No. 586, p. 314.

[314] Turkey, No. 2(1896), pp. 198–200.

[315] FO 424/184, No. 603, p. 322.

[316] FO 424/184, No. 643, p. 353.

[317] FO 424/184, No. 645, p. 354.

[318] FO 424/184, No. 655, p. 361.

[319] L. M. Penson, "The Principles and Methods of Lord Salisbury's Foreign Policy," *Cambridge Historical Journal* 87-106 (1935), p. 101; G. S. Papadopoulos, "England and the Near East, 1896-1898," *Thessalonica* 1969, pp. 45-47; Grenville, *Lord Salisbury and Foreign Policy*, p. 50.

[320] AVPR, F. Politicheskiy arkhiv, d. 3440 (year 1895), l. 5–23; d. 3448, l. 56–70.

[321] C. D. Clayton, *Britain and the Eastern Question: Missolonghi to Gallipoli* (London, 1971), pp. 185–86; R. Taylor, *Salisbury* (London, 1975), p. 169.

[322] Taylor, *Salisbury*, p. 170; Grenville, *Lord Salisbury and Foreign Policy*, p. 28.

[323] Grenville, *Lord Salisbury and Foreign Policy*, p. 47.

[324] *Kavkaz*, 12 December 1895.

[325] FO 424/184, No. 701, p. 385

[326] Turkey, No. 2(1896), pp. 208, 211, 224.

[327] FO 424/184, No. 703, p. 386; No. 750, pp. 424–25; Turkey, No. 2(1896), p. 210.

[328] Douglas, "Britain and the Armenian Question," p. 125.

[329] FO 424/184, No. 755, p. 427.

[330] FO 424/184, No. 813, p. 482.

[331] FO 424/184, No. 816, p. 454.

[332] FO 424/184, No. 815, pp. 483–84.

[333] Turkey, No. 2(1896), pp. 254–55.

[334] "Iz dnevnika V. N. Lamzdorfa," *Voprosy istorii* 1977, no. 6, pp. 103–4.

[335] Turkey, No. 2(1896), p. 226.

[336] Ibid., pp. 254–55.

[337] Ibid., p. 227.

[338] FO 424/184, No. 821, p. 487.

[339] FO 424/184, No. 828, p. 490.

[340] FO 424/184, No. 830, p. 491.

[341] FO 424/184, No. 831, p. 491.

[342] FO 424/184, No. 834, p. 492.

[343] Turkey, No. 2(1896), p. 285.

[344] FO 424/184, No. 836, p. 492.

[345] Turkey, No. 2(1896), p. 280.

[346] Ibid., p. 281.

[347] Ibid., pp. 289, 291.

[348] Ibid., pp. 280–81.

[349] Ibid., p. 282.

[350] Ibid.

[351] Taylor, *Salisbury*, p. 168.

[352] Papadopoulos, "England and the Near East," pp. 56–57.

[353] Turkey, No. 2(1896), pp. 292–93, 295–96.

[354] Turkey, No. 8 (1896). Further Correspondence Relating to the Asiatic Provinces of Turkey (In Continuation of Turkey No. 2 (1896)). London, 1896, pp. 51–54.

[355] Mkrtchyan, L. *Zeytuni apstambutiune, 1895–1896 tt.* (The Zeytoun Uprising, 1895–1896) (Yerevan, 1995), pp. 180, 182, 190–91.

[356] "Lord Salisbury and Armenia," p. 193; M. H. Gulesian, "England's Hand in Turkish Massacres," *The Arena* 17 (1897), p. 271; W. K. Stride, "The Immediate Future of Armenia; The Suggestion," *The Forum* 22 (1896), p. 311.

[357] "Lord Salisbury and Armenia," p. 193.

[358] Taylor, *Salisbury*, p. 168

[359] Curzon, George Nathaniel, 1st Baron Curzon of Kedleston (1859–1925), British politician and diplomat. He served as Under Secretary for India (1891–92) and for Foreign Affairs (1895–98), Viceroy of India (1898–1905), Aviation Secretary (1916), Lord Privy Council (1916–19), Foreign Secretary (1919–24), and Leader of the House of Lords (1916–24).

[360] *Kavkaz*, 28 February 1896.

[361] Chamberlain, Joseph, (1836–1914), British politician. Initially a member of Radical Liberals, he served as Chairman of Birmingham City Council (1873–76), entered the House of Commons (1876), and served in the Gladstone Cabinets of 1880–85 and 1886 before switching parties. He served as Colonial Secretary (1895–1903) in the Conservative Cabinet of Lord Salisbury.

[362] Papadopoulos, "England and the Near East," p. 48; P. Marsh, "Lord Salisbury and the Ottoman Massacres," *The Journal of British Studies* 11, no. 2 (May 1972), p. 81.

[363] Marsh, "Lord Salisbury and the Ottoman Massacres," p. 81.

[364] For a comparative review of the Armenian Massacres of 1894–96, see R. Melson "A Theoretical Inqiry into the Armenian Massacres of 1894–1896." *Comparative Studies in Society and History* 24, no. 3 (July 1982), pp. 481–505.

[365] Pears, *Life of Abdul Hamid*, pp. 232–34; Turkey, No. 2(1896), pp. 318–22.

[366] Russell, "Armenia and the Forward Movement," pp. 11–12; Bliss, *Turkey and Armenian Atrocities*, p. 463; Pears, *Life of Abdul Hamid*, pp. 234–35.

[367] Turkey, No. 2 (1896), p. 325; Bliss, *Turkey and Armenian Atrocities*, pp. 428–34, 475–76.

[368] Bliss, *Turkey and Armenian Atrocities*, p. 477.

[369] Turkey, No. 2 (1896), pp. 320–22; Bliss, *Turkey and Armenian Atrocities*, pp. 425, 451–66, 478.

[370] Turkey, No. 2 (1896), pp. 323–30.

[371] *Kavkaz*, 11 June 1896.

[372] *Novoe slovo*, December 1896, vol. 3, p. 176.

[373] *Vestnik Yevropy*, 1895, vol. 6, bk. 12, p. 854.

[374] Bliss, *Turkey and Armenian Atrocities*, p. 553.

[375] "Massacre in Turkey: From Oct. 1, 1895, to Jan. 1, 1896," *Review of Reviews* 13 (1896), p. 197; M. Mangasarian, "Armenia's Impending Doom," *The Forum* 21 (1896), p. 452.

[376] Bliss, *Turkey and Armenian Atrocities*, p. 553; Gabrielian, *Armenia*, pp. 257–58; Turkey, No. 2 (1896), pp. 318–37; Shahid Bey, *Islam, Turkey and Armenia*, p. 201; E. Antoine, *Les Massacres d'Armenie* (Bruxelles, 1897), pp. 72–79.

[377] *Vestnik Yevropy*, 1895, vol. 6, bk. 11, p. 409.

[378] Turkey, No. 8 (1896), pp. 118–19, 121.

[379] Ibid., p. 206.

[380] Ibid., pp. 206–7.

[381] Ibid., p. 222.

[382] Republic of Armenia, Central Historical Archive, "Collection of Excerpts of Documents," list 1, chapter 51, part 2, p. 10.

[383] M. G. Orudzhev, *Iz istorii proniknoveniya germanskogo imperializma v Turtsiyu* (Baku, 1961), p. 11.

[384] "The Constantinople Massacre," *The Contemporary Review* 70 (1896), p. 458; "The Massacres," *The Spectator* 77 (September 5, 1896), p. 292; V. M. Kurkjian, *A History of Armenia* (New York, 1958), p. 296.

[385] L. Kamarovskiy, "Vostochnyy vopros i ego zhertvy," *Novoe slovo*, Dec. 1896, p. 177.

[386] C. Roberts, "A Mother of Martyrs," *The Atlantic Monthly* 83 (1899), p. 95.

[387] *Huntchak*, 1 September 1896, p. 129.

[388] E. Pears, *Turkey and its People* (London, 1911), pp. 40–41.

[389] *Vestnik Yevropy*, October 1896, p. 835.

[390] Republic of Armenia, Central Historical Archive, "Collection of Excerpts of Documents," list 1, chapter 51, part 2, p. 10.

[391] Roberts, "A Mother of Martyrs," p. 92.

[392] Republic of Armenia, Central Historical Archive, "Collection of Excerpts of Documents," list 1, chapter 51, part 2, p. 11.

[393] *Istoriya diplomatii*, vol. 2, p. 336.

[394] A. Wittlin, *Abdul Hamid: The Shadow of God* (London, 1949), pp. 177–78.

[395] Republic of Armenia, Central Historical Archive, "Collection of Excerpts of Documents," list 1, chapter 51, part 2, p. 14.

[396] G. McDermot, "The Great Assassin and the Christians of Armenia," *The Catholic World* 64 (December 1896), pp. 295–305.

[397] "The Constantinople Massacre," *The Contemporary Review* 70 (1896), p. 460.

[398] Ibid., p. 461.

[399] D. Kalopothakes, "The Constantinople Massacres," *The Nation* (October 8, 1896), p. 266.

[400] "The Constantinople Massacre," p. 460.

[401] Roberts, "A Mother of Martyrs," pp. 92, 94–96.

[402] *Bratskaya pomoshch' postradavshim v Turtsii armyanam* (Moscow, 1898), pp. 75–80.

[403] A. Amfiteatrov, *Armyanskiy vopros* (Saint Petersburg, 1906), pp. 5–6.

[404] Kalopothakes, "The Constantinople Massacres," pp. 266–67.

[405] In autumn of 1896, the Russian periodical *Novoe Vremya* noted meaningfully that the Europeans refused to eat fish in Constantinople. The reported added that the fish caught in the Bosphorus was revolting to him since 'it was too well fattened.'

[406] Republic of Armenia, Central Historical Archive, "Collection of Excerpts of Documents," list 1, chapter 51, part 2, p. 14.

[407] L. Abbott, "Armenian Question," *The Outlook* 54 (1896), p. 1036; "The Constantinople Massacre," pp. 459–60; J. Bryce, *Transcaucasia and Ararat* (London, 1896), p. 516.

[408] A. Tyrkova, *Staraya Turtsiya i mladoturki* (Petrograd, 1916), p. 62; Roberts, "A Mother of Martyrs," p. 90.

[409] Antoine, *Les Massacres d'Armenie*, p. 90.

[410] Turkey, No. 1(1897). London, 1897, pp. 21, 29, 52.

[411] "The Massacres," *The Spectator* 77 (September 5, 1896), p. 292.

[412] Grenville, *Lord Salisbury and Foreign Policy*, pp. 75–76.

[413] M. H. Gulesian, "Armenian Refugees," *The Arena* 17 (1897), p. 652; Kalopothakes, "The Constantinople Massacres," pp. 265–66.

[414] "The Massacres," p. 292.

[415] "Czar's Visit," *The Spectator* 77 (September 26, 1896), p. 389.

[416] *Huntchak*, 1896, No. 17.

[417] "Lord Salisbury's Conversations with the Tzar at Balmoral, 27 and 29 September, 1896," *The Slavonic and East European Review* 34, no. 92 (December 1960), pp. 216–18.

[418] N. N. Bolkhovitinov, "O pozitsii Solsberi v Vostochnom voprose osen'yu 1896 g.," in *Problemy britanskoy istorii* (Moscow, 1973), p. 267.

[419] "Sekretnaya zapiska russkogo posla v Londone Ye. Ye. Staalya o besede s lordom Solsberi," in *Problemy britanskoy istorii* (Moscow, 1973), p. 272.

[420] "Lord Salisbury's Conversations," p. 216.

[421] "Sekretnaya zapiska," p. 273.

[422] "Lord Salisbury's Conversations," p. 216.

[423] Ibid., p. 217.

[424] Ibid., p. 221.

[425] "Sekretnaya zapiska," p. 272.

[426] "Lord Salisbury's Conversations," pp. 218–21.

[427] "Sekretnaya zapiska," p. 273.

[428] The Mediterranean Convention was signed on February 12, 1887, by Great Britain, France, Romania, and Italy; Austria-Hungary acceded to the Convention on March 24, 1887. The signatories undertook to preserve *status quo* in the Black, Aegean, Adriatic, and Mediterranean Seas.

[429] "Lord Salisbury's Conversations," p. 219.

[430] Ibid., p. 217.

[431] Grenville, *Lord Salisbury and Foreign Policy*, pp. 78–79.

[432] "Lord Salisbury's Conversations," p. 218.

[433] Grenville, *Lord Salisbury and Foreign Policy*, pp. 78–79.

[434] "Lord Salisbury's Conversations," p. 220.

[435] "The Situation of To-day," *The Spectator* 77 (October 3, 1896), p. 426.

[436] Antoine, *Les Massacres d'Armenie*, p. 79.

[437] Maccoll, *The Sultan and the Powers*, p. 53.

[438] Gabrielian, *Armenia*, pp. 257–58.

[439] Melson "A Theoretical Inqiry," pp. 481–505.

[440] Rohrbach, P., "The Contribution of the Armenian Question," *The Forum* 29, no. 4 (1900), pp. 488–89.

[441] *Istoriya diplomatii*, vol. 2, pp. 344–45.

[442] Magnus, *Gladstone*, p. 430.

[443] Knaplund, *Gladstone's Foreign Policy*, pp. 267–68; Magnus, *Gladstone*, p. 430.

[444] Magnus, *Gladstone*, p. 431.

[445] Knaplund, *Gladstone's Foreign Policy*, p. 268.

[446] Russell, "Armenia and the Forward Movement," pp. 27–28.

[447] "At Colchester," *Liberal Magazine* (October 20, 1896), p. 483.

[448] Magnus, *Gladstone*, p. 431; Douglas, "Britain and the Armenian Question," p. 131.

[449] "Lord Rosebery's Deliverance," p. 504.

[450] E. Galevi, *Istoriya Anglii v epokhu imperializma*, vol. 1 (Moscow, 1957), p. 34; "At Colchester," p. 483.

[451] Russell, "Armenia and the Forward Movement," pp. 25–26.

[452] W. L. Langer, *Diplomacy of Imperialism, 1890–1902*, vol. 1 (New York, 1935), pp. 333–34.

[453] Grenville, *Lord Salisbury and Foreign Policy*, p. 85.

[454] *Kavkaz*, 8 November 1896.

[455] S. Yu. Vitte, *Vospominaniya*, vol. 2 (Moscow, 1960), pp. 100–102; Grenville, *Lord Salisbury and Foreign Policy*, pp. 87–89.

[456] Douglas, "Britain and the Armenian Question," p. 132.

[457] Papadopoulos, "England and the Near East," p. 103.

[458] Ibid., p. 107.

[459] Grenville, *Lord Salisbury and Foreign Policy*, p. 89.

[460] Papadopoulos, "England and the Near East," p. 103.

[461] Ibid., p. 111.

[462] Ibid., p. 103.

[463] Ibid., pp. 103–4.

[464] D. C. Blaisdell, *European Financial Control in the Ottoman Empire* (New York, 1929), pp. 100–101.

[465] Papadopoulos, "England and the Near East," p. 104.

[466] Ibid., p. 106.

[467] Ibid., p. 111.

[468] Ibid., p. 112.

[469] A. W. Terrell, "An Interview with Sultan Abdul Hamid," *The Century Magazine* 55 (1897), p. 136.

[470] Clayton, *Britain and the Eastern Question*, p. 187.

[471] A. Nassibian, *Britain and the Armenian Question. 1915–1923* (London and New York, 1984), pp. 45–46.

[472] Ibid., p. 59.

[473] Ibid., p. 44.

[474] "Armenia's Desolation and Woe," *The Review of Reviews*, 1897, vol. 15, p. 626; J. R. Harris and H. B. Harris, *Letters from the Scenes of the Recent Massacres in Armenia* (London, 1897).

[475] *Nor Kyank*, 1 November 1898, no. 98, pp. 333–34.

[476] Nassibian, *Britain and the Armenian Question*, p. 45.

Chapter 5. The Policy of Great Britain and the Armenian Question on the Eve of the World War I

1. British Diplomacy and the Ottoman Empire, 1900–1914

The infighting among the European Powers over domination of the Near East reached new levels in the early twentieth century. As the major Powers divided the world into colonial dominions and the disputes multiplied, the Ottoman Empire remained an important source of natural resources and an important market for European products, trade, and investment. It was only natural that the competition among the European Powers over control of parts of the Ottoman Empire became fiercer. By 1900, Turkey had become a semi-colony of the European Powers which obtained commercial and financial concessions while foreign capital controlled important sectors of the Turkish economy. The gradual reduction of the Ottoman Empire and loss of the central government's control over its far-fetched dominions exacerbated tensions between the Powers that vied for domination of the detached parts of the Empire. At the same time, the situation in the Balkans continued to remain highly volatile as the newly independent Balkan states competed with one another and their ethnic brethren in the Austro-Hungarian and Ottoman Empires who aspired to self-government or independence. The authority of the Porte continued to be undermined by insurgencies, disturbances, and open dissent in many regions of the Empire, which gave rise to the Young Turk movement and more interventions by foreign Powers.

A new factor in the Powers' struggles in the Near East was the activation of German policy in the region. Germany's obtaining the concession to build the Constantinople-Baghdad Railroad strengthened German-Turkish relations while the investment of German capital into the Turkish economy made the German Government sensitive to any actions that could affect the territorial integrity of the Ottoman Empire. The Sultan's Government found a new ally in its quest to deny self-determination to the many ethnic and religious minorities under its domination. Abdul Hamid enlisted the support of the German Government and private capital to secure his rule, stifle domestic dissent and national liberation movements.

The occupation of Bosnia and Herzegovina in 1878 allowed Austria-Hungary to gain a solid foothold in the Balkans and project its interests in the East. Denied access to overseas colonies, Austrian capital could only be invested in the Balkan states and European Turkey, which Austria-Hungary began to view as its natural sphere of political and economic influence. Therefore, at the turn of the century Austro-Hungarian diplomacy sought to neutralize Serbia and prevent the emergence of a Serb-dominated South Slav union that could jeopardize the very existence of Austria-Hungary. Italy, the least influential among the Powers, also began to assert its influence in the Balkans using Albania as a launching pad for its plans.

At the same time, Britain and France continued their influential and serious presence in the commercial and financial sectors of the Ottoman Empire. The share of French capital in financing Turkey's foreign debt rose from 46% in 1895 to 60% in 1914.[1] In turn, Britain continued to dominate Turkey's commerce, accounting for 35% of the Turkish foreign trade turnover in 1899–1901.[2]

Dependent on financial support from its allies, Russia could not compete openly with Western European nations for the economic markets in Turkey. Russian trade with the Balkans and Asia Minor continued to remain insignificant; the Ottoman Empire ranked fifth in Russian imports, and eighth as destination for Russian exports. Russian capital was virtually absent in the Ottoman Empire.[3] Russia did continue to follow closely the developments in the Balkans, and many elements in Russia actively supported the national aspirations of the Slav population in the European part of the Ottoman Empire. Although the Russian establishment and foreign policy elite continued to view the occupation of the Straits and Constantinople as an important foreign policy objective, the rise in revolutionary movements, domestic instability, and the weakness of Russia's international position early in the twentieth century effectively rendered that issue moot. Russian diplomacy addressed the more limited issue of free passage of Russian military ships through the Straits. The assertion of Austro-Hungarian and German influence in the Balkans and the Near East increased tensions in Russia's relations with those two nations and drew it closer to Britain. The growing British-German tensions in the Near East, in turn, were an impetus to the British Government to settle its long-running differences with Russia in Persia, Tibet, and Afghanistan. This process culminated in the Anglo-Russian Convention of 1907, which was the final formal step in the establishment of the Entente, a process that began with the British-French understanding of 1904. The Entente squared off against the Austro-German alliance.

The displacement of Britain by Germany as the pre-eminent Power in the Porte dramatically altered the balance of power in the Ottoman Empire and forced British diplomacy to reconsider its position vis-à-vis the national aspirations of the Armenian and Balkan Slav peoples. The main policy of the British Government, dating back to the Congress of Berlin, had been to press for the implementation of reforms to preserve its influence over, and the territorial integrity of, the Ottoman Empire. Although this policy had failed to secure the necessary reforms and led to the deterioration of British-Turkish relations, the Foreign Office did not completely abandon this approach. The British insistence on reforms and calls to institute a Constitution and a Parliament in Turkey were viewed with deep suspicion by the Sultan's authorities.

The refusal of the Sultan's government to deal with the issue of reforms and the memory of the Bulgarian massacres in 1876 as well as the Armenians massacres of 1894–96 gradually convinced the foreign policy elite in Britain that the only possible solution to the problems facing the Christian subjects of the Sultan was 'by cutting the Gordian knot, that is, the subsequent dismemberment of the Ottoman Empire.'[4] In January 1908, British Ambassador to Turkey Nicholas O'Connor[5] reported to Foreign Secretary Edward Grey that British-Turkish relations would continue to remain tense as long as they depended on the Sultan. His government's policies in Macedonia, Armenia, and against other oppressed peoples were deplorable and appalling, O'Connor noted.[6] President of the British Board of Trade in Turkey Adam Block, formerly the British Embassy Dragoman, noted in his March 1908 letter to Permanent Undersecretary Charles Hardinge[7] that no improvements and reforms could be expected as long as Abdul Hamid remained in power.[8] In May, Foreign Secretary Grey noted in his dispatch to British Chargé d'affaires George Barclay that 'no matter what, Britain has no ill feelings toward Turkey, but the Porte does not provide the possibility of improving our bilateral relations.'[9]

On the issue of Macedonia, British diplomacy began to cooperate more actively with Russia. While Russia was overwhelmed with the conduct and consequences of the war with Japan, the British Government acted in concert with all Powers on the issue of implementing reforms in Macedonia. However, in the second phase of the Macedonian crisis, the British Government went further in its demands, coordinating its approach with Russia. In March 1908, the British Government proposed to carry out reforms in Macedonia that would have established de facto independence while preserving the nominal rule of the Sultan. The coordination of their positions on the Macedonian Question became the main subject of discussions between King Edward VII and Czar Nicholas II in Revel in June 1908. Although Russia lobbied the British Government to weaken some elements in its reforms program for Macedonia, the German and Austro-Hungarian Governments rejected the British proposal as detrimental to their interests and to the territorial integrity of the Ottoman Empire. The failure to carry out another reforms program signaled for the British Government the demise of nineteenth century's 'Concert of Europe' and the need to regroup forces on the Eastern Question.[10]

Thousands of Armenians left their ancestral homeland as a result of Abdul Hamid's anti-Armenian policies and deteriorating living conditions in Western Armenia and found refuge in Persia, Russia, European nations, and the United States. Despite the ideological differences between the main Armenian parties—Dashnaks and Huntchaks—they shared the determination to liberate Western Armenia and establish an independent Armenian state. The Armenian parties and groups, however, did not manage to resolve their differences and work in unison to advance their objective of an independent homeland. Consequently, they failed to generate a mass following and lead the national liberation movement, as happened among other peoples oppressed by Turkey. The Armenian groups also attempted, unsuccessfully, to cooperate with non-Christian minorities in Turkey, including Kurds who had been used by the Turkish Government to oppress Armenians. The rise of the Armenian national movement at the turn of the century was noted by the nascent Young Turk movement that would strike an alliance with the Armenian parties, most notably the ARF. The Young Turks hoped to use the Armenian groups against the Sultan although they shared the Sultan's views on Turkey's national policies. The Armenian political parties contributed to the domestic revolutionary movement that culminated in the Young Turk revolution of 1908.[11]

The peak of the Armenian national liberation movement in 1898–1907 was the uprising in Sasun in 1903–4. The revolutionary activities that were taking place in Western Armenia were not viewed favorably on the international scene , with the Armenian Question completely removed from the agenda of European nations. While British diplomacy did not intervene or make new proposals on the Armenian Question, the British Embassy continued to follow the situation closely and occasionally intervene in developments in Western Armenia.

In March 1904, the British Embassy received reports of tensions and instability in the Sasun region and the Turkish Government's plans to suppress the 'revolutionary movement' there. British Ambassador O'Connor met with Abdul Hamid II on March 11 and urged him to peacefully resolve the differences with the Armenian leaders by granting them amnesty and safe passage abroad. The Ambassador had earlier urged the Patriarch to petition the Porte for the same. The Patriarch had proposed to use the Armenian clergy in Mush to persuade the revolutionaries to lay down arms on the condition that they be amnestied and exiled abroad.

If the negotiations failed, O'Connor proposed using the good offices of the Russian and British Consuls for mediation. The French Embassy endorsed the proposal and offered the services of its Consul as well. When the revolutionaries turned down the offer passed by the clergymen, the Consuls of the three countries were instructed to contact them for negotiations. They reported that the Armenian revolutionaries 'arrogantly' turned down the mediation offer and repulsed a Turkish military attack. Consequently, the local administration provoked the Kurdish tribes to commit atrocities in several Armenian-populated villages.[12]

On May 24, O'Connor urged the Grand Vizier to punish several Kurds for their attacks on the Armenian villages to show that the central Government was in control and disapproved of such reprisals. The Grand Vizier assured the envoy that the Kurds had been forbidden to enter the insurgent areas and that a large military force had been sent to the region to prevent bloodshed. He noted that the fact of an Armenian conspiracy had been established and that a group of 600 Armenian rebels had crossed the frontier from Kars and penetrated to Sasun. On June 13, O'Connor warned again of the awesome responsibility borne by the Porte if the participation of Kurds in the latest disturbances were proven. The British Embassy had reports of the Armenian population being forced to relocate to the valleys where they would become easy targets for the Kurdish reprisals. O'Connor asked the Porte to issue orders to the Governor of Bitlis to allow the Armenian refugees to return to their homes and provide security.[13]

On June 21, the Grand Vizier informed O'Connor that the Porte had decided to allow the Armenian refugees in Mush and neighboring provinces to return to Sasun, and to allocate 5000 Turkish gold pieces to the Governor of Bitlis to rebuild the destroyed houses of the refugees. A garrison was to be established in the Sasun region to prevent the Kurdish attacks and suppress potential revolutionary activities. A general amnesty was issued for those rebels who would surrender, with the exception of the organizers. The gendarmerie in Bitlis and neighboring regions would be reorganized and an inquiry would be launched to root out abuses by the local government.[14]

On July 6, the British Vice Consul in Mush reported that the situation had markedly improved owing to the Turkish authorities providing basic assistance to the refugees returning home and the Governor's promise to prevent Kurdish attacks. On August 12, the Foreign Office Permanent Undersecretary replied in response to parliamentary inquiries that, according to British consular agents in the field, the Turkish authorities had taken measures in June to improve the situation. The mixed commission that included prominent Armenians had worked to assist the returning refugees, help rebuild their houses and restore livestock. The Foreign Office noted that the participation of the Kurdish tribes in the latest disturbances had not been independently confirmed, but the local administration had taken measures to protect the Armenian population. While acknowledging reports of clashes between the Turkish military and Armenian revolutionary groups near the Turkish-Persian border, the Foreign Office pronounced the situation in Asia Minor as 'normal.'

On September 27, the Grand Vizier informed O'Connor of the establishment of a special mixed commission to coordinate the government's efforts to assist the returning refugees and oversee the expenditure of funds allocated for rebuilding their houses and other relevant assistance. British Vice Consul

Captain Taylor reported in January 1905 that the local administration had worked hard to improve the situation in Sasun.[15]

O'Connor reported in August that the police had discovered a significant amount of grenades and explosives in Smyrna and had made arrests among the Armenian activists. About 100 to 200 Armenians had been arrested daily, and one Armenian had been executed. On September 19, the Ambassador reported that according to rumors circulating among the Muslim population of Constantinople, the Armenian activists had planned to attack the government offices using explosives and weapons. The rumors had been circulated so widely, O'Connor noted, that the Muslim community had been put on high alert and was prepared to carry out 'bloody reprisals.'

O'Connor reported that the recent assassination attempt against the Sultan had contributed to the general environment of anxiety and suspicion, while the Sultan himself told O'Connor on September 26 that the Armenian groups had been responsible for the attempt. The Sultan claimed that 12 powerful bombs had been discovered in various districts of Constantinople. Abdul Hamid told O'Connor that the 'Armenians imagine they enjoy the protection of the Powers,' but if they angered the Sultan, they would 'all be slaughtered' before the Powers even began to intervene. 'After that, what could the Powers do?' asked the Sultan rhetorically. "I am an old man already."[16]

British diplomacy had largely ignored the developments leading to the Young Turk revolution of 1908 but the Foreign Office had been forced to change its position when the Sultan was stripped of his absolute powers on July 24. British Chargé d'affaires George Barclay[17] reported to Grey that significant changes had taken place in Constantinople: the newly appointed Grand Vizier Said Pasha had announced the amnesty of the political prisoners and the abolition of censorship; the people had been shocked and staged demonstrations in front of government buildings, and there had been episodes of fraternization between the Muslims and Armenian Christians.[18]

On July 27, Grey instructed Barclay to congratulate Said Pasha on his appointment and on the promulgation of the Ottoman Constitution by the Sultan. Barclay was to assure the new government of Britain's friendly intentions and support. He considered the revolution to be an important step toward the moderation of the Ottoman Empire, and instructed Barclay to tell Said Pasha that Britain's actions and demarches on the Armenian and Macedonian Questions had been necessitated by its obligations under previous treaties and agreements to improve the administration of those regions, and not meant to be an affront to the Porte. Grey noted that the Macedonian and Armenian Questions would be settled only when a general reform of government throughout the country achieved better administration in all regions of the Empire, and pledged the support of the British Government toward reaching that objective.[19]

Addressing the parliament on that issue, Grey said that if the new Turkish authorities were ready to improve the whole government structure of their country and to ensure that the Muslim and Christian communities benefited equally from the reforms, it would be better for the Macedonian question to be resolved as part of the general reforms, rather than by pressing partial reforms on 'reluctant, unwilling and obstructing' local authorities. Grey noted that the British Government would continue to promote improvement in Macedonia while preserving 'an expectant and sympathetic attitude' toward the new Government.[20]

Not everyone in the Foreign Office shared Grey's enthusiasm. Barclay, in particular, was skeptical about the success of the new Government while Hardinge decried the uncertainty in the British position on the Macedonian Question in view of unexpected turn of events in Turkey. He believed that if the Young Turks established a stable government and improved the administration of the country, they 'would have been playing our game entirely.' The Foreign Office concluded that the revolution had delivered a blow to German influence in Constantinople.[21] Grey noted that British diplomacy had to be sensitive so as not to offend the Russian Government by establishing closer relations with Turkey. He ruled out the return to Disraeli's old policies; even if British diplomacy became pro-Turkish again it would do so without giving rise to suspicions of an anti-Russian tilt.[22]

On July 30, Sir Gerard Lowther[23] who had just been appointed British Ambassador to Turkey arrived in Constantinople. (Lowther would later be held responsible for the deterioration in Turkish-British relations.) On July 31, Grey sent him a dispatch on his discussions with the Turkish Ambassador in London. Asked to comment on the British Government's position vis-à-vis the new Government in Turkey, Grey had noted that Great Britain welcomed the new Turkish Government, adding that the sole objective of Britain had been a secure administration in Turkey. Therefore, the British Government would be satisfied and content if the new authorities achieved that goal. He noted that the British Government had only taken issue with the Turkish rulers for the abuses that were now challenged by the Turks themselves.[24]

On August 3, British Consul Shipley reported from Erzurum that 92 political prisoners, including 60 Armenians, had been released from custody. The Armenians had been held on charges of revolutionary agitation, illegal crossing of the Turkish-Russian border, and carrying arms. The Consul noted the enthusiasm of the Armenian population following the change of the Turkish Government.[25] On August 4, Lowther reported that a large crowd of Armenians and Turks led by the Christian and Muslim clergy had jointly commemorated the victims of the Armenian massacres of 1895 and 1896 at Constantinople's Sisli Cemetery.[26] On August 12, Consul Stevens reported from Batum that the local Turkish Consulate had published a statement addressed primarily to the Armenian refugees living in the South Caucasus, informing them of the general amnesty and urging them to return home.[27] On September 1, British Consul Safrastian reported on the tremendous enthusiasm prevalent among the Armenian population of Mush and Bitlis, and multiple instances of fraternization between the Turkish and Armenian communities.[28]

At the same time, Lowther reported on September 20 that despite the general improvement since the Revolution, there had been numerous instances of Kurdish attacks and robberies in the Armenian-populated areas of Mush and Bitlis.[29]

The Foreign Office continued to view the reforming of government as its main objective in Turkey and pledged assistance to the new authorities. Grey noted that the Young Turk movement should not act hastily as it was important to appoint able and honest individuals to the government positions in Turkey. He also had hoped for greater opportunities for British capital and commerce in Turkey but was disappointed when a French specialist had been selected to reform the Treasury.[30]

Lowther made his first contacts with the Young Turk movement on September 2, when he met with Mehmed Talaat and Behaeddin Shakir. The Ambassador reported that he had been impressed with their progressive views and realistic assessment of challenges facing Turkey. The two officials had proclaimed their pro-British leanings.[31]

The dynamics of international politics, however, would force Britain to adopt a different policy. The situation changed in early October when Bulgaria proclaimed its full independence and Austria-Hungary annexed Bosnia. The British Government sided with Russia on the question of Bulgaria's independence but rejected the French proposal to call a European conference in response to the annexation of Bosnia. Grey advised the Turkish Ambassador in London to quietly accept Bulgarian independence and the loss of Bosnia as Turkey needed 'time and finances' more than it needed war. He promised loans and assurances of support from the British Government. On October 5, Turkish Foreign Minister Tewfik Pasha asked Lowther to reconsider the British policies.[32]

The declaration of independence in Bulgaria, Austria's annexation of Bosnia and Herzogovnia, and the Greek annexation of Crete were heavy blows to the prestige of the nascent constitutional government in Turkey and led to serious protests in the country. To compensate for the territorial losses, the Foreign Office offered its assistances through the removal of Articles 23 and 61 of the Treaty of Berlin, providing for reforms in the European and Armenian-populated provinces of Turkey. If the Turkish authorities succeeded in reforming administration in the country, Britain promised to scrap the system of capitulations and concessions that characterized the Porte's treaties with the European nations, and to replace it with bilateral treaties on the basis of equality of parties. In return, the Turkish Government was asked to recognize the independence of Bulgaria and the loss of Bosnia. When new Grand Vizier Kiamil Pasha rejected the British proposal, Lowther recommended adopting a rigid position. Grey told the Turkish Ambassador in London that Turkey had no room for argument on its political interest, while Hardinge noted that the opposition from Britain and Russia would prevent Turkey from reclaiming Eastern Rumelia even if it defeated Bulgaria militarily. The British attempt to foster an alliance of convenience between the Balkan Slav states and Turkey to oppose the Austro-Hungarian actions in the Balkans also failed.[33]

Following these developments, the relative influence of Germany consequently continued to increase in Turkey, Lowther reported in 1908. The British diplomatic reports began to question and challenge the Young Turk Government's nationalist policies and rhetoric. The British Ambassador noted that the new authorities sought to represent the interests of Turkey, rather than those of the Ottoman Empire. Hardinge noted in his letter to Lowther that it would be good if the Young Turk Committee disappeared in the near future, before it became corrupted and adopted policies pursued by the court coterie in the past. Former Military Attaché in Constantinople Lt. Col. Maunsell noted that it was hopeless to expect reforms from the new Government since the differences between the Old and Young Turks were only in their costumes. The British Government avoided discussions of the Turkish offer of an alliance between the two countries. Hardinge noted that a friendly Turkey was preferable to an allied Turkey.[34]

In the spring of 1909, the supporters of Abdul Hamid and Kiamil Pasha attempted to stage a coup to overthrow the Young Turk Government, not without the secret assurances of British support. The Young Turks easily suppressed the coup and deposed the Sultan in favor of his brother, the detached Mehmet V. The new Grand Vizier was Hilmi Pasha, who had a pro-German reputation. The British diplomats chose to excise from memory their support for the restoration of 'the constitutional monarchy of Abdul Hamid.' Grey noted that the British Government had underestimated the powers of the Committee (Author's note: Committee of Union and Progress was the official name of the Young Turk movement.) As the best elements in Turkey now sided with the Committee it was best for Britain to support them as well, Grey noted. He added that the Foreign Office should dispense less criticism and more encouragement in its dealings with the Committee.[35] At the same time, Lowther's reporting continued to remain overtly critical of the new administration that he accused of resorting to Abdul Hamid's tactics on the national policy. There had been no improvement in the conditions of the Christian population of the Empire, Lowther noted.[36] The Ambassador's fears and concerns were realized when bloody events took place in Adana in April 1909.

On April 13, the British Dragoman in Adana, Athanasios Tripanis, informed British Vice Consul Doughty-Wiley in Mersin that disturbances had broken out in the city. The British Vice Consul arrived in Adana in time to witness the Armenian massacres that lasted three days; the pogrom had been carried out by the Muslim mob without interference by the local authorities. Despite Doughty-Wiley's warnings and demands, the local administration did nothing to stop the massacres.[37] He estimated that nearly 2000 Armenians perished in

304 BRITISH DIPLOMACY AND THE ARMENIAN QUESTION

the city of Adana on April 13–16, and between 15 and 25 thousand Armenians perished in the nearby villages.[38]

In his report to Lowther, Vice Consul Doughty-Wiley categorically rejected the charges of Armenian aggression, noting that the massacres had started simultaneously in several districts of the city. He was convinced that the local authorities were at least aware of the preparations for the massacre.[39] When the Young Turks returned to power on April 24, one of the first governmental actions was to deploy the Rumelian regiments from Damascus and Beirut to Adana to restore public order, which, however, only prolonged the massacres as the troops gladly joined in the pogrom. A British eyewitness testified that the Turkish soldiers attacked the Armenian district, targeting the Mushegh School and Armenian Church where thousands of Armenian residents gathered. As a result of the 'restoration of public order' by the military and local authorities, 4,437 Armenian houses were destroyed, and the massacres spread to all the regions in Adana Province, as well as to the Armenian-populated areas of Aleppo Province. More than 30,000 Armenians perished as a result of the 1909 massacres in Adana.[40]

The Foreign Office rejected the idea of a European intervention to address the consequences of the Adana massacres. Grey considered a limited diplomatic intervention to be useless and provocative, since the Armenians might be encouraged to take actions inciting the Muslims to stage massacres on a massive scale and necessitating a full-scale military intervention by the Powers.[41]

The Foreign Office continued to remain skeptical about the motives and actions of the Turkish authorities in 1909 and 1910. According to Lowther, the political situation was hopeless in the wake of the assassination of the popular editor of the Sedai Millet newspaper. The Government was controlled by 'military dictator' Shevket Pasha, whose orders were absolute law in the country.[42] On June 28, Hardinge noted in his dispatch to British Ambassador in Germany Goschen that the situation in Turkey was bad and that British influence had waned, while German Ambassador in Constantinople Marschall had restored Germany's former influence over the Turkish Government. The Committee for Union and Progress (CUP) had established a dictatorship that was more brutal and rigid than Abdul Hamid's rule, Hardinge noted.[43]

Germany had indeed emerged as the winner in its competition with Britain in asserting influence over the new Turkish authorities. The major factor in this political shift had been the British policies in Macedonia, Mesopotamia, the Persian Gulf, and Crete—actions that had alienated and irritated the Turkish Government.

The British diplomats detected a shift in the Young Turk's ideological platform from the idea of Ottomanism to Pan-Islamism, a shift intended to exploit the religious feelings of the predominantly Muslim population of the Ottoman Empire for the nationalistic policies of the Young Turk movement. Following the reports that the CUP Conference in Monastir had rejected the program granting equality and liberties to the Christian population of Macedonia, Grey noted with shock that 'playing off one nationality against another was Abdul-Hamid's old policy and would lead to similar results.'[44] The Foreign Office backed the Serbian and Bulgarian rejection of the Young Turk Government's Turkification program for Macedonia and Albania. The new Foreign Office Permanent Undersecretary, Sir Arthur Nicolson, commented that he remained skeptical about the new Turkish regime and doubted that any Turk, 'young, old or middle-aged,' would accept the equality of Christian and Muslim elements.[45]

The Foreign Office elite's opinion of the Turkish regime was not shared by every member of the British Cabinet. One prominent member, Home Secretary Winston Churchill,[46] who had visited Constantinople in 1910 and met with Talaat Pasha and Djavid Pasha, proclaimed himself to be impressed with the 'quality, vigor, and practical character' of the Turkish Government. He even concluded that the Turkish ministers' views and methods, as well as their manner in relation with the domestic and external political partners, reminded him of the usual British 'way of doing business.'[47]

The November 1910 CUP Conference in Salonica confirmed the worst fears in the Foreign Office about the Turkic and pan-Islamic tilt in the new regime. The Foreign Office concluded that the Turkish regime was distinctly pro-German and neutral toward the Entente Powers. The analysis noted the continuing policies of harassment and, wherever possible, extermination of the Christian elements in the Empire.

The Turkish regime was also accused of fanning pan-Islamic propaganda beyond Turkey's borders.[48] Nicolson wrote that "...it would be interesting if in the 20th century we would be witness to a revival of the 17th century Ottoman Empire. I think that the pan-Islamic movement would be a much greater threat to the British Empire than the 'Yellow Peril.'"[49] Lowther, however, dismissed the threat of pan-Islamism as irrelevant, noting that it could produce a community of interests but not a community of religion. The British Ambassador noted that the Persian Shiites abhorred the Ottoman Sunnis, that the Arab Muslims viewed the Turkish Muslims with disdain and believed that the Caliphate should be in Arab hands, and that the Indian Sunnis viewed the Young Turks as 'sacrilegious revolutionaries' for having dethroned the Caliph.[50]

The British Embassy's Chief Dragoman, Gerald Fitzmaurice,[51] believed that the general discontent with the Young Turk regime in Macedonia, Albania, Yemen, and Arabia would eventually lead to the collapse of the Ottoman Empire. He decried the Young Turks' lack of respect for the use of moral authority in domestic politics, noting that they preferred to employ brutal methods that would only hasten their collapse.[52]

The policies of Great Britain toward the Ottoman Empire on the eve of World War I were determined in part by its economic and commercial interests. British diplomacy fought with great intensity to obtain concessions for the Baghdad Railroad, oil wells in Mosul and Baghdad, and the reforms of trade and irrigation in Mesopotamia. The Young Turk regime and the German Government resisted the British attempts to reassert influence and authority in Mesopotamia and Persian Gulf. The Young Turk regime harbored suspicions that the British would use the railroad concession to further their plans for dismemberment of the Ottoman Empire while the Germans sought to prevent the construction of a British-controlled railroad linking the Persian Gulf with Mesopotamia.

When Hakki Pasha became head of the Turkish Government in the spring of 1910 and adopted a more anti-British position, Grey offered assurances of Britain's impartiality and lack of conflict of interests in Mesopotamia. Lowther was instructed to propose conditionally to the Porte that the Tigris section of the railroad be constructed by a Turkish company.[53] The Turkish Government's plan for the Baghdad-Gulf railroad, which had been submitted to the British Government in March, provided for a British share of 20% in the railroad and demanded Turkish control over the terminus in Kuwait.[54] Further negotiations yielded no results.

The British Committee of Imperial Defense (CID) addressed the present state of British-Turkish relations. The Chief of the Imperial General Staff, General Nicholson, noted that the Turkish Army was large and rapidly improving and cautioned that any British military or naval deployment would have to be temporary. He noted that the Turkish military could create trouble in Egypt. Field Marshal Kitchener said that if Britain allowed the Porte to take over Kuwait, it would 'have consequences in India.' Hardinge, who had by that time been vested with vice-regal powers in India, noted that there was no danger from the Indian Muslims in the event of a British-Turkish war since the Young Turk's espousal of pan-Islamic policies was a 'fallacy.' Grey made the most bellicose presentation, arguing for interruption of the flow of Turkish reinforcements to Yemen. The CID concluded that the Porte could not be coerced.[55]

On July 14, a standing sub-committee of the CID made the following decision on the British policy: Basra, and not Kuwait, was to be the terminus of the railroad. Britain was ready to accept Ottoman suzerainty over Kuwait if the Sheikh was accepted as an Ottoman Kaymakam. Britain, Russia, and France were to be allotted a 20% share each in the Baghdad-Basra railroad. The remaining 40% were to be allocated to Germany and Austria-Hungary.[56]

The Turkish Government eventually rejected the British proposal in April 1912, demanding instead the principle of a fourfold division of shares, excluding Russia. Essentially giving up the fight for the Russian share, the British Government submitted a counterproposal that would have withdrawn the British claims on the Baghdad-Basra Railroad in exchange for applying the principle of the fourfold division of shares in all railroads in Asiatic provinces and appointment of two Britons to the board of the future Baghdad-Basra Railroad. The Porte was to provide guarantees that the line would not be extended beyond Basra and would allow three additional British steamers to sail between Baghdad and Basra. Britain also insisted on the exclusive right to patrol and control the Gulf waters.[57]

The British Government hoped that the recent change of Government[58] in Constantinople would be favorable to the acceptance of the British plan. After realizing that no progress would be made on the railroads, British diplomacy turned its attention to the oil concessions in Mosul and Baghdad. The Foreign Office concluded that the oil concessions would be potentially more important than the Basra Railroad. The British-German negotiations on the oil concessions ended in March 1914 with the signing of an agreement establishing a joint venture between the British D'Arcy and Anglo-Persian Petroleum (75% of shares) companies and the Deutsche Bank (25%).[59]

British diplomacy adopted a neutral stance during the Italian-Turkish war over the control of Tripoli from September 1911 to October 1912. Despite the Turkish requests for assistance, Grey's diplomacy ensured that the British and French navies would not obstruct Italy. As a result, Italy gravitated closer to Britain, and tensions suddenly came to the surface in the Triple Alliance. The war also undermined Turkish morale and sapped its military strength. Britain conditioned its assistance to Turkey on three points: ceasing hostilities with Italy; reduction of German influence in Turkey; and effective reforms of internal administration. In October 1911, the British diplomats argued to the Porte that Tripoli had been lost and further resistance would be futile. However, the escalation of hostilities, including the naval bombardment of the Dardanelles and the occupation of Rhodes and the Dodecanese by Italian forces, was of serious concern to Britain which did not want to allow a member of the Triple Alliance to occupy strategic positions in the Eastern Mediterranean and the Aegean Sea. Hostile bases in that area would have threatened the British control of Egypt and the flow of commerce toward the Near East and the Black Sea.[60] The Turkish-Italian War concluded on October 18, 1912, with the Treaty of Lausanne that established Italian control over Tripoli.

While the Turkish-Italian war was underway, another round of instability affected the Balkans. Serbia and Bulgaria signed a secret treaty of alliance in March 1912. The Foreign Office initially ignored the intelligence reports of the treaty, erroneously assuming that it was yet another Slav conspiracy against the Austro-Hungarian Empire. It soon became obvious that the alliance was aimed against Turkey and had been clandestinely supported by the Russian Government. British diplomacy faced another dilemma—it could not jeopardize its relations with Russia but its support of the anti-Turkish alliance would have resulted in the loss of Britain's influence in Turkey. The fears of the consequences that a pan-Islamic movement could have on Britain's Muslim subjects began to gain currency in the Foreign Office.[61]

The situation in Macedonia further deteriorated in August, when the Turkish authorities organized a massacre of Christian residents in Kochana after a revolutionary group had attacked the local Turkish Government's offices; more than 700 Christians perished. As Serbia and Bulgaria demanded self-government for the Slavic nationalities in Macedonia and Thrace, British diplomacy sought to avert a Balkan war. The British Embassy urged the Porte to immediately begin implementation of reforms in the European provinces and to punish the perpetrators of the massacre in Kochana.[62] When Turkey did not respond, Bulgaria, Serbia, Montenegro, and Greece declared war on the Ottoman Empire in October.

The Foreign Office was skeptical about the Balkan states' chances vis-à-vis Turkey, but its opinion began to change as the Ottoman Army suffered major reverses. Britain fully endorsed the Russian position of open support for the Balkan states, and concluded that the European provinces would be lost to Turkey forever. The only differences between Russia and Britain were on the issue of Constantinople. Russia proposed to establish international control over the city and the Straits, while Britain insisted on its status as a neutral free port.[63] Preservation of the British-Russian and British-French alliances were of greater importance to Britain than the occupation of Constantinople and a potential negative reaction among the Muslim subjects of the British Empire.

Foreseeing the Turkish military defeat and its consequences, the Turkish Foreign Minister, Gabriel Effendi and Grand Vizier Kiamil Pasha asked the British Government to secure the mediation of the Powers in this conflict. Following recommendations of the British Embassy, the Turkish Government signed an armistice agreement on December 3. Grey noted that if Turkey wanted to avoid further defeats and complications, it should allow the European Powers to decide the terms of the peaceful settlement.[64] Lowther urged the Young Turk government to be moderate and reasonable during the negotiations in London. The British Government was prepared to intervene militarily to break any deadlock in negotiations.[65]

The Turkish delegation in London was presented with highly unfavorable terms as Britain openly sided with the Balkan states. It demanded that Adrianople be ceded to Bulgaria and the Aegean Islands to Greece and that self-government be granted to Albania. Near Eastern specialist in the Foreign Office, Alvin Parker, predicted that the breakdown of peace talks and resumption of hostilities would inevitably result in the collapse of the Ottoman

Empire, as the disturbances in the Asiatic provinces would lead to Russian intervention in Armenia, the French occupation of Syria, and the German takeover of Anatolia.[66] The British Foreign Office urged Turkey to consolidate its forces to become a solid Asiatic Power. Fitzmaurice was convinced that the Young Turk Government faced stiff opposition from the Arab and Armenian elements.[67] Lowther warned the Foreign Office that open support of the Balkan states by Britain would restore the radical wing of the Young Turks to power and deliver the Ottoman Empire to the Central Powers.[68]

On January 22, 1913, Kiamil Pasha gave in to British pressure and agreed to surrender Adrianople to Bulgaria. The Young Turks regained power the following day and immediately resumed hostilities on the Bulgarian front. The Turkish military suffered further reverses, culminating in the loss of Adrianople after a 155-day siege. Under the terms of the Treaty of London signed in May, Turkey lost practically all its territory in Europe to the Balkan states while predominantly Muslim Albania was placed under international control.

In June 1913, the Foreign Office debated the possibility of a defense alliance with Turkey, but the idea was rejected by all senior diplomats. Grey argued for a neutral 'Concert of Europe' approach to the Turkish problem since a violation by any Power would lead to unpredictable consequences. Lewis Mallet,[69] who would be appointed British Ambassador to Turkey in October, noted that a British-Turkish defense treaty would unite the whole of Europe against Britain. He suggested that all Powers should adopt a neutral position on Turkey, guarantee the territorial integrity and independence of its current possessions, and establish control over its finances and the process of reforms.[70]

The Treaty of London did not put an end to the instability in the Balkans, and the second Balkan War broke out soon. Three of Bulgaria's former allies and the Ottoman Empire attacked Bulgaria to deprive it of its territorial gains. Turkey recaptured Adrianople. Despite his reputation as a Turkophobe, British Prime Minister Herbert Asquith[71] turned down the Russian proposal to open a second front in the Caucasus, fearing a complete disintegration of the Ottoman Empire. The Foreign Office warned the Young Turk Government that if the Turkish military advanced beyond the Enos-Midia line, it would lead to a European intervention and threaten Constantinople. Even when the Turkish troops crossed the Maritza River, the British Government refused to accept the Russian proposal of severing ties with the Porte. The Foreign Office insisted on a joint European military deployment against the Porte.[72]

As noted above, Ambassador Mallet replaced Lowther in October 1913; the Foreign Office held Lowther responsible for the deterioration of Turkish-British relations. In fact, all senior diplomats in the British Embassy in Constantinople were recalled. Mallet accepted the offer of ambassadorship despite realizing the near impossibility of serious improvements in bilateral relations. He noted that he would share the fate of all British Ambassadors in Turkey since the time of Canning, i.e., being classified as failures. Mallet was a supporter of Turkey's territorial integrity, explaining that the occupation of six Armenian-populated provinces by Russia, of Anatolia by Germany and Syria by France would threaten the British presence in India.[73] Mallet's sympathetic attitude toward the Young Turk regime became obvious in the first days of his tenure. He reported that the present government of Turkey was the ablest and most effective regime that had ever ruled the Ottoman Empire. Convinced that the relations with the Porte were progressively improving, Mallet sent reports seeking to dispel the views prevalent in the Foreign Office that the Young Turk regime had been permeated with animosity toward Britain. Mallet also denied that the Young Turk Government was an ally of Germany.[74]

The British Government did not react appropriately when the German Military Attaché in Turkey, General Liman von Sanders, was appointed Commander of the First Turkish Army stationed near Constantinople. Although Russian Foreign Minister Sergei Sazonov[75] demanded that the British Government announce its readiness to deploy the Navy, Grey rejected such an action, suggesting instead that the Entente's Ambassadors in Turkey send identical demarches to the Porte to protest Germany's receiving an exclusive privilege. The Foreign Office had concluded that the best possible action under the circumstances was to downplay von Sanders' appointment and leave the matter to be resolved between Germany and Russia.[76] The Foreign Office ignored the warnings of the British Military Attaché that 47 officers attached to the German Military Mission in Constantinople had been given ranking appointments in the Turkish Army's command structure in the capital and provinces.[77]

Although the British Cabinet, lobbied by the Admiralty, looked favorably at the possibility of a Greek occupation of the Aegean Islands, Mallet worked hard to neutralize the British position on this issue. He argued that the Greek occupation of the islands would antagonize the Young Turk regime, threaten the territorial integrity of Turkey's Asiatic provinces, and force Turkey to ally itself with the Central Powers. He recommended that the Foreign Office work with the British press to change the critical coverage of the Young Turk regime and to persuade British capital to invest in Turkey.[78]

Throughout 1914, the British Government suppressed any action or move that would have been overtly hostile toward the Ottoman Empire or the Young Turk regime. The Foreign Office had announced its opposition to any policies that would threaten British economic interests in Mesopotamia, i.e., the Arab separatist movements threatening to sever Arabia from the Ottoman Empire. Mallet recommended that Britain should continue to implement its 'traditional policies' in the Ottoman Empire without the least regard for the Arab movement. The British Government's position on the much less important Jewish Question and the Zionist Movement were also included in this recommendation.[79]

Despite the friendly overtures, the British Government never succeeded in restoring the former rapport in its relations with the Porte and in securing Turkey's neutrality in the Great World War. Britain's allied relations with Russia and France had dictated its position on the Balkan question and predetermined the course of British-Turkish relations. When Talaat Pasha and Djemal Pasha failed to secure an alliance with Russia or France, Enver Pasha's pro-German faction gained sufficient strength to determine the fate of Turkey in World War I. The German-Turkish negotiations concluded in August 1914 with the signing of a treaty of alliance and mutual assistance, which was followed by the deployment of the German battleships *Breslau* and *Goeben* near Constantinople.

Regardless of the obvious deterioration in bilateral relations, the British Government did not abandon its efforts to reach an understanding with Turkey's leaders. On August 15, First Lord of Admiralty Churchill sent a letter to Enver Pasha, urging him not to conclude an alliance with Germany in the view of the overwhelming naval dominance of the Entente. Churchill promised that the Entente Powers would preserve the territorial integrity of the Ottoman Empire.[80] In turn, Mallet spared no effort to persuade the Young Turk leaders to renounce the alliance with Germany, negotiating with the

Porte even as the Foreign Office instructed him to draft plans for the evacuation of British diplomatic, military, and civilian personnel from Turkey, and for directing the Arab revolt against Turkish and German military forces in the event of a formal declaration of war. Grey requested the U.S. Government to represent its interests in Turkey during the war.[81]

British efforts to secure Turkey's neutrality were futile, and the Porte announced on October 3 that the Dardanelles, which had been mined by German engineers, would be closed to navigation by Entente naval ships. On August 25, Enver Pasha authorized Admiral Wilhelm Souchon, the German Commander of the *Breslau* battleship group, to attack the Russian Navy. On November 1, Mallet departed Constantinople, and Britain declared war on the Ottoman Empire on November 5.

2. British Diplomacy and the Issue of the Armenian Reforms, 1912–14

In 1910–12, the British consular agents continued to report on the difficult conditions in the Armenian-populated provinces in Anatolia. Consular reports suggested that the Young Turk regime had not improved the situation in those regions and, in fact, the Young Turk ideology of Turkish nationalism and pan-Islamism had only aggravated the tensions between the Christian and Muslim communities. The local government continued the old practice of abuse of power, which had only grown worse in the absence of Sultan's central authority. In many provinces, land plots owned by the Armenians were being seized by the Muslim refugees from the Balkans while the Kurdish tribal leaders continued to mount attacks on the Armenian settlements. The Foreign Office was well aware of the developments, but continued to pin its hopes on the internal reforms promised by the new regime. British diplomacy was also wary of interventions and demarches that would have strained relations between the European Powers and the two groupings—the Triple Alliance and the Entente.

The Porte realized the potential dangers of allowing the Armenian groups to petition the Powers, and developed a program of reforms on its own. In December 1912, Interior Minister Reshid Pasha presented the program for reforms to the special commission headed by the Grand Vizier himself. The program provided for the appointment of an Inspector General of the eastern provinces for a six-year term; the Inspector General would have jurisdiction over the governors, military commanders, and gendarmerie and police chiefs. A special commission would be formed, comprised of three Christians and three Muslims and headed by a foreign national in the employ of the Ottoman Government familiar with the laws and customs of Turkey. The Special Commission would oversee the restoration and preservation of public order, resolution of land disputes between the Armenians and Kurds, reform of the gendarmerie, construction of the roads, and so on. The President of the Commission would concurrently serve as a Counselor to the Inspector General. The program did not provide for amendments in the existing laws and legislation, and would only cover the provinces of Van, Bitlis, Kharput, and Diyarbakir.[82] The Armenian community had lobbied for some changes in the draft, including the division of the six Armenian-populated provinces into two sectors, each headed by a Turkish Inspector General. The Special Commissions would be created in each sector and be comprised of two Turks, two Christians, and two foreign nationals. The Presidents of the Commissions would be selected from foreign nationals and serve concurrently as Counselors to the Inspectors General.[83] The Porte, however, delayed the implementation of this program.

Russia's increasing interest in the Armenian Question, which became pronounced in late 1912, gave rise to concerns from the Foreign Office. In January 1913, Lowther noted that the Armenian population had tired of half-measures and looked forward to radical changes in their status, preferably by achieving self-government under a Russian protectorate. Mallet believed that the re-emergence of the Armenian Question would lead to partition of Asia Minor among the Powers, while Nicolson considered the Russian occupation of the Armenian-populated provinces to be a matter of time.[84]

German diplomacy also calculated the consequences of the re-emergence of the Armenian Question on the agenda of international politics, inciting British suspicion of Russia's intentions. Germany hoped to neutralize Russia by reaching an understanding with Britain on guarantees for the territorial integrity of Turkey's Asiatic provinces against possible encroachment by Russia. The Cyprus Convention was to serve as a model for the British-German understanding.[85] The German Government began to lobby the Porte to carry out reforms in the Armenian-populated provinces. When the Committee returned to power in January 1913, a new reforms draft was circulated that would have divided the Armenian-populated provinces into the Northern

Anatolian (Erzurum, Sivas, Trabzon) and Eastern Anatolian (Van, Bitlis, Kharput, and Diyarbakir) sectors.[86] The new draft not only did not take into account the geographic, demographic, and economic peculiarities of the eastern provinces, but intended also to dissolve the Armenians among the Muslims.

Grey realized the opportunities lost if Germany and Russia achieved success in addressing the Armenian Question, and urged the Entente Powers to refrain from raising the Armenian issue to allow the Young Turk regime to carry out reforms in Anatolia. On January 23, Grey wrote to British Ambassador in Paris Francis Bertie[87] that it was inopportune to raise the Armenian Question until the Balkan States and Turkey signed a peace agreement.[88]

Germany also expressed its concern about Russia's 'Armenian policy'. On January 27, the German Ambassador to Britain told Grey that Germany attached great importance to preservation of Asiatic Turkey's territorial integrity and had been concerned with the concentration of Russian troops in the Caucasus and Russia's attachment to the Armenian Question. Germany would not remain on the sidelines while Russia occupied Armenia and France took over Syria, the German Ambassador noted.[89] At the same time, the German Government urged the Porte to hasten the reforms in Anatolia. On April 24, Lowther reported to Grey that German diplomats had been telling the Armenian activists that the reforms promised by the Young Turk regime would be in accordance with the Treaty of Berlin and the Cyprus Convention. According to Lowther, the German diplomatic maneuvering had aimed to undermine Russian authority among the Armenians who, however, had remained greatly skeptical about the German motives.[90]

In April 1913, after the Russian Embassy had received drafts of the reforms programs from the Armenian Patriarchate and the Dashnak Party, it began to work on a program of its own. The British Ambassador was instructed by the Foreign Office to urge the Porte to carry out reforms immediately, as the matter could not be postponed. Dragoman Fitzmaurice told Grand Vizier Shevket Pasha that Britain sought no benefit and rejected coercive measures in pressing for reforms, and urged him to take practical measures to initiate the reforms process and to order the governors to protect the Armenian population. Mallet noted that Britain wanted Turkey to remain a Power in Asia while also wanting reforms for the Armenian population. If the reforms did not materialize, the situation in those provinces would deteriorate and lead to massacres and disturbances, he noted. He added that Britain was the only Power that could either assume the responsibility for the reforms or allow another Power to do so, since Britain had no territorial or political ambitions in Asia Minor. Otherwise, Britain's influence and authority would be diminished and come under severe domestic criticism.[91]

In early May, the Turkish Ambassador in London delivered the proposal of the Young Turk regime to the British Government for British participation in the Porte's reforms program in the Armenian-populated provinces. The British Government had been asked to supply inspectors for the gendarmerie, agriculture, and public works, with seven gendarmerie officers in each province, and a counselor to the Inspector General.[92] Grey and Nicolson were not excited about the Turkish proposal, which could have been viewed by the other Powers, especially Russia, with dissatisfaction. Mallet warned that the rejection of the proposal would turn the Young Turk regime toward Berlin.[93] On May 15, Grey told the Turkish Ambassador that while Britain would be more than willing to provide officials and assistance to Turkey, he recommended that Russia, France and Germany be fully informed so as to reduce dissension and speculation.[94]

Russian Foreign Minister Sazonov was apprehensive about the Turkish proposal. On May 21, British Embassy official O'Bierne reported from St. Petersburg that the Russian Government did not want to separate the issues of reorganization of the gendarmerie from the general reforms in the government. The Russian Government asked that the Turkish request be put on hold pending an arrangement for the reforms to be worked out by the Entente's ambassadors in Constantinople. Grey agreed with the Russian counterproposal but was loath to reject the Turkish request for assistance for fear that it would force the Porte to turn to Germany for assistance. Grey noted that reorganization of the gendarmerie was an important objective, independent of any program of reforms.[95] On May 23, Grey instructed O'Bierne to tell Sazonov that the British Government would consent to the Turkish request and assign British officers to the gendarmerie in the Armenian-populated provinces only, while continuing to work with Russia on the general program of reforms.[96] The following day, Grey communicated this decision to Turkish Ambassador Tewfik Pasha, promising to supply a list of British candidates for the position of Inspector General at the Interior Ministry, as well as for the officers and inspectors of gendarmerie. Grey noted that the Interior Ministry Inspector General should be the liaison between the gendarmerie inspectors in the Armenian-populated provinces and the Interior Ministry.[97]

On May 26, Sazonov told O'Bierne that he still disagreed with the British decision and insisted on holding discussions between the Entente's envoys in Turkey to decide the general program of reforms. He told the British diplomat that a delegation of prominent Armenians had recently asked the Russian Government to annex Turkish Armenia. The Armenian committees realized the impossibility of establishing self-government in the eastern provinces where the Armenians comprised only 30% of the population, Sazonov opined. He said he had rejected the petition but promised to take measures to promote reforms in the Armenian-populated provinces. Sazonov said Russia 'would not play second fiddle' on this issue in view of its special obligations to the Armenians. He added that Russia would not commit the mistake of 1894–96 when it had remained indifferent to Armenian suffering during the massacres. He noted that the Armenians could no longer live under the present conditions and suggested that the Entente's envoys regularly consult with the Armenian leaders who, he said, were well aware of the real state of affairs in Turkish-controlled Armenia.[98]

Grey consented to discuss the general program of reforms, allowing the Russian Government to take initiative on this issue. He proposed accepting the 1895 Memorandum as a basis for the draft, and to circulate it later to other Powers as well.[99]

At the same time, French Ambassador Cambon told Nicolson that the French government believed the time was not ripe for practical measures to carry out reforms. He proposed raising the issue of reforms after the conclusion of the Paris Conference, the purpose of which was to examine aspects of Turkey's financial situation. Cambon agreed that the reforms in Asiatic Turkey would be of interest not only to the Entente, but also to other Powers.[100]

On June 2, the German Ambassador told Grey that Germany was opposed to the Armenian Question. He said that Germany would present territorial claims of its own if the other Powers presented any to the Porte; otherwise, it would support Turkey's territorial integrity. Grey assured the Ambassador that the Entente Powers had made no plans for partitioning Asiatic Turkey, but rather wanted to resort to the 1895 model of a joint preparation of the reforms program by all the Powers. Grey said that the program should address the whole territory of Asia Minor, with special provisions for the Armenian-populated provinces.[101]

On June 4, O'Bierne reported that the Russian Foreign Ministry had suggested amending the 1895 Memorandum, and Grey replied the following day that he would instruct the British Ambassador to hold informal consultations with his Russian and French counterparts.[102]

Lowther, in turn, proposed to carve up Asia Minor into spheres of influence among the Powers. He noted that the experience of the previous 35 years and the peaceful existence of the two-million strong Armenian community in the Russian-controlled Caucasus had convinced the Armenians that implementation of the reforms was possible only with the patronage of Russia, and Anglo-Russian agreement. Lowther viewed the Turkish request to appoint 17 British officers in the Kurdish-Armenian provinces as an attempt to create tensions between Russia and Britain and to preclude the implementation of reforms in these provinces which he said were largely devoid of the Turkish element. Lowther noted that the Young Turk regime had hoped to address the issue of reforms under the joint auspices of Germany and Britain, leaving Russia out altogether. Lowther, therefore, proposed to divide Turkey's Asiatic provinces into four areas of responsibility: the Armenian-populated provinces would be assigned to Russia, Mesopotamia to Britain, Syria to France, and Western Asia Minor and Adana to Germany.[103] Fitzmaurice was less constrained than the Ambassador in expressing bolder and clearer, and proposed to allow Russia to assert its control over the Armenian-populated provinces as Austria-Hungary had done over Bosnia in 1878 and Britain over Egypt in 1882.[104]

Immediately after the end of the first Balkan War, the Russian Embassy submitted a proposal to an ad hoc commission of the Entente Powers' representatives. The draft, based on the program prepared by Russian Embassy Dragoman Andrei Mandelstam, had earlier received preliminary approval from the French and British Governments. Mandelstam, Fitzmaurice, and French Embassy official Saint-Cantine were members of the ad hoc commission. The draft provided for merging the six Armenian-populated provinces of Erzurum, Van, Bitlis, Diyarbakir, Sivas, and Kharput into one unit to be administered by a foreign national or a Christian subject of the Empire. The

Governor General was to be appointed by the Sultan and approved by the Powers. The Christian and Muslim subjects would be equally represented in the new entity's council, administration, and gendarmerie. The draft would help found national schools, provide for equality of languages, dissolve the Hamidiye units, and return the land plots that had been seized illegally from the Armenian peasants.[105]

After the draft had been approved by the French and British representatives, it was presented to the other Powers. The German Embassy was unhappy about the Russian initiative and complained that it would allot a greater role to the Russian Government. The Germans suggested holding another conference on the Armenian reforms in London to countermand the pro-Armenian and pro-Russian bias of the Constantinople consultations, and solicit a Turkish proposal for the reforms.[106] Grey proposed a compromise measure through the British Ambassador to Russia, Sir George Buchanan: [107] Russia would call another meeting of Ambassadors in Constantinople and accept a Turkish draft before presenting the final version of the program to the Porte.[108] On June 16, Buchanan reported that the Russians were opposed to such a compromise because it would disappoint the Armenian community and allow Germany to insist on accepting the Turkish draft.[109] Grey defended his proposal, noting that Turkey and Germany would eventually insist on discussion of their proposals as well. Therefore, it was better to begin working on the Russian proposal and accommodate the Turkish suggestions in the final draft.[110]

On June 17, Lowther reported that the Entente's ambassadors had agreed on a draft and recommended presenting it to the ambassadors of the Triple Alliance. According to Lowther, the 1895 Memorandum, Turkish laws of 1880 and 1913, as well as Cretan and Lebanese charters had been used in preparation of the program. When a preliminary draft was presented to the German and Austro-Hungarian Embassies, the German envoy told Russian Ambassador Mikhail Giers that the proposal would be acceptable to Germany if two conditions were met: the Sultan's sovereignty over the provinces had to be preserved and the Turkish representatives had to be included in preparing the program. Lowther suggested that the involvement of Turkish officials in the deliberations would complicate the process, but Ambassador Giers said he hoped the Germans would drop the condition.[111] Although Sazonov categorically rejected the German proposal, Giers argued that consultations with the Porte would be necessary at some point in the process.[112]

On June 30, the five Powers' representatives met for the first time to discuss the Russian draft of the reforms program. German and Austrian envoys told their colleagues that the Porte had already prepared a program of reforms of its own, which they said should be submitted to the foreign envoys as well.[113]

On July 2, British Ambassador in Berlin William Goschen[114] reported to Grey that the German Foreign Ministry had been concerned about the Russian-proposed reforms, regarding them as the beginning of Turkey's dismemberment. Goschen noted that while Germany nominally defended the territorial integrity of what was left of the Ottoman Empire, it would certainly demand a fair share if the Empire was partitioned.[115]

British Chargé in Constantinople, Charles Marling reported to Grey that the Young Turk regime had submitted its draft of reforms in early July. Marling noted that the German and Austro-Hungarian envoys almost certainly would insist on accepting the Turkish draft as the basis for discussion. Both envoys had told Marling privately that their governments would not accept Russian control over northeastern Anatolia, and promised to back a British candidate for Governor General in those provinces. Marling was convinced that this was another trick to create tensions between Britain and Russia.[116]

Buchanan reported that Sazonov had told the Turkish envoy in Russia that he believed the Turkish regime had submitted a draft as a device to delay reforms and sow discord among the Powers. Sazonov said that the Powers would present to the Young Turk regime a program of reforms prepared by them. When the German envoy had told Sazonov that the Russian plan would result in other provinces and regions demanding the same status as the Armenian-populated provinces, Sazonov had assured him that Russia would defend the principle of Turkey's territorial integrity to the degree possible. That said, Russia would not accept half-measures in the Turkish regions bordering Russia, Sazonov implied. Russia would continue to insist on its own proposal while accepting any recommendations and suggestions from the German Government, Sazonov had said.[117]

The Foreign Office was as always gripped by indecision and opposing positions. An official of the Eastern Department, Herman Norman, believed the Turkish draft to be more comprehensive than the Russian proposal, and recommended accepting it as the basis for negotiations. He noted that the Armenian community in Turkey would not favor autonomy under Russia's auspices or a Russian protectorate, inasmuch as the Armenian population in Russia had not been fully content with their situation. Norman believed that the majority of Turkey's Armenian population would choose Turkish rule if they were provided specific guarantees.[118] The same sentiment was expressed by Eastern Department Chief Mallet, who expressed the belief that Russia would use the Armenian Question to divide Europe. He noted that the Armenian Question was of vital importance to all Powers, and above all for Britain, and was convinced that the dismemberment of the Ottoman Empire would affect British interests in the Mediterranean and India.

Conversely, the British Embassy in Turkey became a hotbed of anti-German and pro-Russian sentiment. Marling believed that the Armenians would totally reject the Turkish proposal and provoke a Russian military intervention.

Nicolson was more cautious and moderate. While accepting that Russia had direct interests in the Armenian-populated provinces of the Ottoman Empire, he recommended a cautious approach to the Russian-sponsored program. In the end, the Cabinet took Nicolson's line: announcing British support for the Russian program, the British Government insisted that the program be harmonized with other Powers and that coercive measures against the Porte be ruled out.[119]

Grey did not want to upset Britain's relations with both Russia and Germany and decided to mediate a compromise between the Russian and German-Turkish proposals[120] even though he remained personally opposed to the Russian plan. He had earlier predicted to the Cabinet that the Russian reform plan would in reality enfeeble an autonomous Armenia, which would then be occupied by Russia at an opportune moment.[121]

On July 12, Marling reported that Baron Wangenheim, the German Ambassador to the Porte, had said that the Russian plan would establish a de facto Russian sphere of influence and eventually result in the Russian occupation of Armenia, as well as of Constantinople. Wangenheim said that there were Armenians in other parts of Turkey as well, including Cilicia, and Germany would demand to establish a sphere of influence over Cilicia if Russia had done the same over northeastern Anatolia.[122] Marling noted that the German position was unfounded since it was obvious that the six Armenian provinces needed urgent reforms to address the lack of public order and miserable living conditions that the Turkish authorities had been unable to correct for the previous three decades. Marling added that the problems facing the Armenians in other provinces of the Ottoman Empire should be addressed by general administrative reforms in Turkey, as provided in the 1895 Memorandum, and the current Turkish and Russian plans. Marling dismissed the German fears of Russia's domination over Armenia since there was no linguistic and religious affinity between the two peoples as was the case in Bulgaria; a prosperous Armenia would never submit to the Russian control, he added. Marling believed that the Russians would intervene only if the Armenian population was massacred again, and noted that the German and Turkish governments should have a vested interest in implementing real reforms, rather than half-measures that would provoke disorder and massacres.[123]

On July 22, German Ambassador Lichnowski presented to Grey in London a memorandum on Armenian reforms. The memorandum noted that the establishment of a united Armenian administrative unit out of six provinces in Anatolia would begin the process of ethnic and geographic partition of Turkey since Syria and Arabia would demand self-government as well. Germany insisted that the Turkish plan that it had endorsed be considered first, since the concurrence of the Young Turk regime was necessary for establishment of administrative self-government. The German Government suggested a few changes in the Turkish program, proposing establishment of a Commission of Control with Turkish and European members.[124]

A discussion held at the Austro-Hungarian Embassy between the European Dragomans ended without results as the Russian, Austrian, and German representatives clashed openly. The Central Powers categorically refused to accept two points in the Russian plan: creation of a united Armenian province and appointment of a Governor General by the Powers, although all other marginal points, such as dissolution of the Hamidiye, establishment of national schools and equality of languages had been approved.[125] The British and French diplomats walked a thin line since they realized that the opposing groups would almost certainly not arrive at a compromise. Finally, on July 10 the German representative demanded approval of the Turkish plan based on the reforms with some modifications drawn from the Russian proposal.

Russian Embassy official Mandelstam rejected the German proposal, and the negotiations of the Powers broke down.[126]

Russia's diplomatic defeat on the issue of reforms and in the aftermath of the Second Balkan War undermined Russian international prestige in the Balkans and Asia Minor at a time when it really needed it. Even concentration of Russian troops near the Turkish border and threats of occupation of Western Armenia did not change the situation in Russia's favor. The German Government announced that it would view the Russian occupation of Western Armenia as a casus belli, and Britain and France both declared the Russian plan to be unacceptable.[127]

The Russian Government decided instead to negotiate directly with Germany, and talks began in Constantinople at the end of August. After long and arduous sessions, an agreement was reached in mid-September between the Russian and German Ambassadors. Marling reported on September 26 that the Russian-German agreement would divide eastern Anatolia into a northern sector (provinces of Erzurum, Trabzon, and Sivas) and southern sector (Van, Bitlis, Kharput, and Diyarbakir), to be headed by European Inspectors General. The Inspectors General would sign a five-year contract with the Porte and could present to the Porte nominations for judges and high-ranking local government officials in their sectors. The Inspectors would be empowered to dismiss other low-ranking government officials. An elected council would be created in every sector; both council members and local administrations would be proportionally representative of Christian and Muslim elements. The Porte would cooperate with the foreign ambassadors and allow them to oversee the reform process on behalf of their national governments.[128]

The British Government immediately endorsed the agreement and hailed it as the only mechanism to avoid unnecessary complications.[129] Sir Eyre Crowe, the head of the Eastern Department at the Foreign Office, told the Russian Chargé that Grey had been enthusiastic about the agreement since he had recognized the urgency of the reforms measures.[130]

Russian Ambassador Giers and German Ambassador Wangenheim presented the program to the Porte and negotiated with the Young Turk regime throughout the autumn and winter months of 1913–14. However, the negotiations, well documented in historiography, stalled over the issues of European control over the sectors and the appointments of foreign officials there.

Suspecting yet another foreign scheme to partition Turkey, the Young Turk regime viewed the joint Russian-German proposal with anxiety and resorted to the tactics of delay and playing off one Power against the other. Interior Minister Talaat Pasha proposed to the British Embassy that it authorize the appointment of two British advisers in the Turkish civil service, Richard Crawford at Treasury and Robert Graves at the Interior Ministry, as Inspectors General of the eastern Anatolian sectors. The British Embassy rejected the offer after concluding that it was an attempt to generate discord among the Powers.[131] British Ambassador Mallet similarly dismissed the offer to appoint Crawford as President of an unofficial advisory commission on the Ottoman Reforms program.[132]

On November 4, Grey wrote to British Ambassador Goschen in Berlin that the Turkish authorities had made several offers to appoint British officials to high-ranking positions in the Turkish civil service in the Armenian-populated provinces. Grey noted that he did not want to create an impression of an independent British action on the reforms in Anatolia, and would turn down all offers of appointments from the Young Turk regime. Admitting that the reforms were overdue, Grey said he hoped that the German and Russian Governments would use the occasion to press the reforms that they had earlier presented to the Grand Vizier.[133] Goschen met with Germany's Acting Foreign Minister, who assured him of the German Government's resolve to press forward with reforms despite the Turkish objections. The German official noted that the Porte was sensitive about the appointment of Inspectors General by foreign Powers, viewing it as an encroachment on its sovereign rights and interference in its internal affairs. During his visit to Berlin, Sazonov had told the German officials that Russia would respect Asiatic Turkey's territorial integrity, and Goschen had been told that the Germans would report Russia's assurances to the Porte.[134]

While the British Consular agents in Western Armenia continued to report troubling signs of disorder and discontent in their provinces, newly appointed British Ambassador Mallet, who had arrived in Constantinople in October, expressed optimism about the Young Turk regime's intentions of reform. He held a high opinion of Talaat and Djemal who, he claimed, had shown extraordinary sensitivity about the Armenians. Mallet cited their participation in the celebrations marking the 1500th anniversary of the Armenian alphabet, and their statements pledging cooperation with the Armenians in the constitutional revival of the Ottoman Empire. At the same time, Mallet admitted that the Young Turks' statements and public position might have had something to do with their hopes of defeating the European calls for reforms, to which they were obligated.[135]

Grey instructed Mallet to follow the Young Turk regime's negotiations with Russia and Germany and to make separate representations to the Porte urging it to accept and carry out the European program. On November 11, Mallet told the Grand Vizier that Britain was deeply interested in the successful implementation of the reforms which Mallet said was of vital importance for the preservation of the Ottoman Empire. Mallet assured the Grand Vizier that the Turkish fears of Russian encroachment on the Armenian-populated territories had been unfounded. He added that Russia's acceptance of joint European control over the reforms process would rule out the possibility of a unilateral intervention by any Power.[136]

Mallet reported to the Foreign Office that the Young Turk regime was determined to carry out serious reforms in the country and Talaat personally announced his intention to visit the eastern provinces. The Ambassador was convinced that Talaat's visit would have a positive influence on the implementation of the reforms, although he expressed deep suspicion about their continuity. Therefore, he urged following a cautious policy and the avoidance of provocative steps that could worsen the situation.[137] Mallet urged his German and Russian colleagues to avoid any action that would be interpreted by the Porte as a threat. He was genuinely convinced of the Young Turk regime's goodwill on the issue of reforms and improvement in relations between the Armenian and Turkish communities. He also took seriously the Turkish warnings of a "volcano" of instability that would follow the European control of the eastern provinces.[138]

On December 1, Mallet told the Grand Vizier of Great Britain's disappointment at the lack of progress in the negotiations, but the Turkish official said the Porte would not agree to allow the representatives of foreign governments to be stationed in the provinces and report to their ambassadors because it would constitute interference in Turkey's internal affairs. It would insult Turkish sensibilities and dignity, the Grand Vizier said. Quoting the Armenian Patriarch, Mallet assured the Grand Vizier that the Armenians did not seek independence and would be content to live under Turkish rule and be loyal subjects if their lives and property were properly protected. Mallet said the British Government would be disappointed if the Porte rejected its assistance to the reforms process. The British Government had ruled out coercive measures in its sincere intention to help the Porte, but would view the Turkish rejection of 'friendly advice' as a 'counter-attack.' Mallet noted that the success of reforms in Armenia would render moot the Armenian Question and the need for European control, adding that the Armenian-populated provinces would become a 'source of strength' for the Ottoman Government.[139]

The positive tone and optimism of Mallet's reports to the Foreign Office soon began to fade. He reported in December that there existed much sensitivity to European intervention on the reform issue from fanatical nationalist circles, which could endanger implementation of the reforms. He noted that the Armenian Patriarch had received death threats from a self-styled "Young Muslims" committee; an Armenian clergyman had been harassed by Muslim provocateurs, and an Armenian church had been coated with red paint.[140]

During the winter months of 1913–14, Mallet continued to justify the Young Turk regime's internal policies, describing them as 'normal survival tactics.' Mallet noted that the Turkish element was in the minority, and commercially and intellectually 'inferior' to the Armenian, Jewish, Arab and Greek elements. At the same time, the British Ambassador expressed his satisfaction, when on December 24, 1913, the Porte acceded to the nominations of two foreign Inspectors General in the eastern Armenian provinces. Mallet noted that the Powers would appreciate the gesture although he was skeptical of the Inspectors' ability to rule over their far-spread sectors without effective help. He was convinced that much depended on their ability to punish criminal violators of the law. It is interesting that Mallet totally agreed with British Vice Consul Smith in Van, that the Armenian demands had been more of an economic rather than political nature since the Armenians were a 'nation of shopkeepers.' If the Porte built roads, railroads, established ferry transportation in Lake Van, and provided corresponding conditions for the economic revival of eastern Anatolia, Smith had written to Mallet, the Armenian Question would cease to exist.[141]

The Russian Government, however, remained dissatisfied with the Turkish offer, responding on December 24 that important points were absent: the provinces to be assigned to each sector had not been selected; the Porte had not agreed to empower the Inspectors to appoint low-ranking officials in local administration and to nominate high-level officials for the approval of the Porte; there were no provisions for judicial reforms or for allowing conscripts from the Armenian-populated provinces to serve within two sectors only. On December 26, Sazonov instructed Giers to continue to negotiate with the Porte over the remaining issues.[142] German diplomacy went to work to prevent further negotiations, arguing that the Turkish concessions would allow continuing the reforms process through the office of Inspectors General. The German Embassy in London protested the Russian action to the Foreign Office, pointing out that Russia's eleventh-hour objections could not be addressed by the Porte.[143] The Foreign Office did not want to be seen as supporting Germany over Russia on any issue and Mallet was instructed to oppose the German position. On January 25, 1914, Mallet reported that the German Embassy's points, in reality, did not correspond to the Russian objections to the Turkish plan and sought to create 'wrong impressions' concerning the workings of the Russian Embassy in Constantinople and to obstruct negotiations between Russia and Turkey.[144]

Despite German obstruction and Turkish resistance, the negotiations between the Porte and the Russian Embassy resulted in the signing of an agreement on January 26. The Russian-Turkish agreement on reforms in Armenia was signed in Constantinople by Russian Chargé Gulkevich and Turkish Foreign Minister Said Halim Pasha. The agreement established two sectors out of the seven Armenian-populated provinces of Erzurum, Trabzon, Sivas, Van, Bitlis, Kharput, and Diyarbakir, to be headed by two foreign Inspectors General appointed by the Porte with the approval of the Powers. The Inspectors would have authority over administration, justice, police, and the gendarmerie in their sectors, and could have authority over military forces in case of emergency. The Inspectors would have authority to dismiss 'incompetent' officials and appoint lower-level bureaucrats, resolve land disputes, and dismiss judges in certain cases; they would also present nominations for high-level officials to the Porte. Laws, decrees, and government dispatches would be published in the local languages while the Central Government would not obstruct the local communities' efforts to fund their schools. In times of peace, each Ottoman subject eligible for conscription would serve in his own province. The Hamidiye paramilitary units would be transformed into Reserves. Prior to the census held under the auspices of Inspectors to determine the exact demographics of the two sectors in terms of religious and ethnic affiliation, general councils and committees in Bitlis and Van would have an equal number of Christian and Muslim members. If a census was not held in Erzurum within a year, its general council would also have equal representation of Christians and Muslims, while the councils in other provinces would be elected on a proportional basis. The Inspectors would be empowered to enforce the equality principle in the police and gendarmerie forces, as well as in the local administration.[145]

The Russian-Turkish Agreement of 1914 was of huge importance for the future of the Armenian population of the Ottoman Empire. It represented a triumph of European, and particularly Russian, diplomacy because for the first time since 1878, the issue of reforms in the Armenian-populated provinces emerged as an integral part of a bilateral treaty. Although the agreement would not grant self-government to the Armenians and represented a step back from the original Russian proposal, nevertheless, its implementation would undoubtedly address the most pressing challenges facing the Armenian population in eastern Asia Minor. For the first time, the administration of Western Armenia would be in the hands of European officials, and the ground would be laid for the subsequent self-determination of Western Armenia.

The Russian-Turkish agreement was met with great enthusiasm and optimism in London, since it was an important opportunity to address the problems of Western Armenia and, no less important, favored neither Germany nor Russia in the reforms process. With neither Power being able to exercise exclusive influence over eastern Anatolia, the British interests in the region would not be affected either. Nicolson was optimistic about the chances of the reforms program since it had all the prerequisites for success; he noted, however, that all previous schemes for reforms had failed completely.[146]

The consultations on the nominations for Inspectors General began immediately. On January 30, Sazonov proposed that the Powers should agree on candidates before they approached the Porte, and Grey endorsed the Russian approach.[147]

The Russian Government submitted a list of candidates from neutral European nations, which included Assistant High Commissioner with the

Dutch East Indian Administration Westenenk and the War Ministry's Secretary General Doormann from the Netherlands, Major-General De Guise and Vice Governor of the Congo Henri from Belgium, and Norway's War Ministry Secretary General Hoff. Although the Foreign Office was unhappy about Russia's highly active participation in the matter,[148] Grey told Sazonov on March 10 that the British and French Governments would endorse the Russian candidates. After the Triple Alliance Powers had endorsed the list, the Dean of the Diplomatic Corps in Constantinople, Austro-Hungarian Ambassador Pallavicini, presented the list to the Porte on March 24.[149] In early February, Mallet reported that the Armenian Patriarchate questioned the impartiality of the Belgian candidates since Belgium had certain economic interests in Turkey.[150] Interestingly enough, the Porte was opposed to the Belgian candidates as well, albeit for a different reason. The Turkish Foreign Ministry complained that Turkey's Muslim population was being place on a par with 'black people of the Congo.'[151]

On April 15, Mallet reported that the Porte had selected Hoff and Westenenk for the positions of Inspectors.[152] The contracts were signed in May, and the Inspectors were ready to take up their duties by July. Westenenk was appointed Inspector General in the sector comprising Erzurum, Trabzon, and Sivas, with residence in Sivas, while Hoff was to be stationed in Van with responsibility over Van, Bitlis, Kharput, and Diyarbakir. The Inspectors had arduous negotiations with the Porte about their duties and logistics. Grand Vizier Halim Pasha spoke dismissively of 'the foreign inspectors' greed,' while Mallet noted that they would almost certainly not receive cooperation from the Porte.[153]

This program of reforms in the Armenian-populated provinces met the same fate as its predecessors. As soon as World War I began, the Young Turk regime abrogated the Russian-Turkish agreement and the Inspectors' contracts. Westenenk never reached Sivas, while Hoff was recalled from Van in August.

While Britain maintained diplomatic relations with Turkey from August until November 1914, it received almost no information on conditions in the eastern provinces. In late September, Mallet reported that significant tensions surfaced between the Young Turk leaders and the Armenian community.[154] On September 18, noted British political activist Anevrin Williams wrote to

Notes

1 *Vneshneekonomicheskie svyazi*, p. 123.

2 Ibid., p. 149.

3 Georgiev, et al., *Vostochnyy vopros*, p. 287.

4 J. Heller, *British Policy Towards the Ottoman Empire, 1908–1914* (London, 1983), p. 2.

5 O'Connor, Nicholas, (1843–1908), British diplomat. He served as Minister to China (1892–95), Ambassador to Russia (1895–96), and Ambassador to Turkey (1896–1908).

6 Heller, *British Policy*, p. 2.

7 Hardinge, Charles (1858–1944), British diplomat. He served as Permanent Under Secretary (1906–10, 1916–20), Viceroy of India (1910–16), and Ambassador to France (1920–22).

8 Heller, *British Policy*, p. 4.

9 Ibid., p. 5.

10 Ibid., pp. 5–6; *Istoriya diplomatii*, vol. 2, pp. 638–45; Georgiev, et al., *Vostochnyy vopros*, pp. 307–8.

11 John Kirakossian, *Yeritturkere patmutian datastani araj (19-rd dari 90-akan tt.–1914)* (The Young Turks before the judgment of history, 1890s–1914) (Yerevan, 1982); M. Kochar, *Armyano-turetskie obshchestvenno-politicheskie otnosheniya i Armyanskiy vopros v kontse xix–nachale xx v.* (Yerevan, 1988).

12 FO 881/8556, No. 1262, T.R. Memorandum respecting the Armenians, December 11, 1905, pp. 1–2.

13 Ibid., p. 2.

14 Ibid., pp. 2–3.

15 Ibid., pp. 3–4.

16 Ibid., pp. 4–5.

17 Barclay, George (1862–1921), British diplomat. He served as Minister to Thailand (1906–8), to Persia (1908–12), and Romania (1912–18).

18 Turkey, No. 1 (1909). Correspondence Respecting the Constitutional Movement in Turkey. 1908. London, 1909, p. 11.

19 Ibid., p. 14.

20 Heller, *British Policy*, p. 10.

21 Ibid., pp. 10–11.

22 Ibid., p. 11.

23 Lowther, Sir Gerard (1858–1916), British diplomat. He served as Ambassador to Turkey in 1908–13.

24 Turkey, No. 1 (1909), p. 18.

25 Ibid., pp. 61–62.

26 Walker, *Armenia*, p. 181.

27 Turkey, No. 1(1909), p. 61.

28 Ibid., p. 89.

29 Ibid., p. 80, 88.

30 FO 371/545, No. 235.

31 FO 371/549, No. 541.

32 FO 371/550, No. 294.

33 Heller, *British Policy*, p. 18–19.

34 Ibid., pp. 24–25.

35 Ibid., p. 30.

36 Ibid., p. 31.

37 FO 424/219, pp. 80–85.

38 Ibid., p. 84.

39 M. Somakian, *Empires in Conflict: Armenia and the Great Powers, 1895–1920* (London and New York, 1995), p. 42.

40 Ibid., pp. 92–93; C. Woods, *The Danger Zone of Europe* (London, 1911), pp. 136–38, 155–61; G. Abbott, *Turkey in Transition* (London, 1909), p. 304–5; Walker, *Armenia*, pp. 182–86; *Turkish Atrocities: The Young Turks and the Truth about the Holocaust at Adana in Asia Minor , during April, 1909* (London, 1913).

41 Heller, *British Policy*, p. 82.

42 FO 371/1007, No. 268.

43 Heller, *British Policy*, p. 33.

44 FO 371/1012, No. 512.

45 Heller, *British Policy*, pp. 34–35.

46 Churchill, Sir Winston Leonard Spencer (1874–1965), British statesman and politician, leader of the Conservative Party. He served a member of parliament in 1900–1922 and 1924–64. His public service included appointments as Under Secretary for Colonies (1906–8), Home Secretary (1910–11), First Lord of the Admiralty (1911–15, 1939–40), Minister of Munitions (1917), Secretary for War and Air Force (1919–21), Colonial Secretary (1921–22), Chancellor of the Exchequer (1924–29), Prime Minister and Defense Secretary (1940–45, 1951–55).

47 M. Gilbert, *Winston S. Churchill*, vol. 3, *1914–1916* (London, 1971), pp. 188–89.

48 FO 371/1000, No. 158.

49 Heller, *British Policy*, p. 39.

50 FO 371/1017, No. 93.

51 Fitzmaurice, Gerald, (1865–1939), British diplomat. He served as Vice Consul in Van (1891–92), Erzurum (1892–93), Trabzon (1893), as Third Dragoman at the British Embassy (1894–95), Vice Consul in Smyrna (1895–96), Adana (1896), Consul in Salonica (1900–1901), Dardanelle (1902), as Second Dragoman at the Embassy (1906), Chief Dragoman (1907–14).

52 Heller, *British Policy*, p. 40.

53 Ibid., p. 47.

54 Ibid., p. 50.

55 FO 371/1245/18946.

56 FO 371/1234/29868.

57 FO 371/1484/16000.

58 In July 1912, the "Liberty and Accord" move-

ment, which had been formed in November 1911, took advantage of the discontent with the Young Turk regime and forced the government to resign, then dissolved the parliament that had been under the control of the Young Turks.

[59] Heller, *British Policy*, pp. 90–92.

[60] FO 371/1535/2334, No. 425; FO 371/1491, No. 133; Heller, *British Policy*, pp.53–56, 64.

[61] FO 371/1492, No. 129.

[62] Heller, *British Policy*, pp. 67.

[63] Ibid., p. 74.

[64] FO 371/1502, No. 524.

[65] Heller, *British Policy*, pp. 75–76.

[66] FO 371/1507, No. 177.

[67] Heller, *British Policy*, p. 77.

[68] FO 371/1798, No. 120; 371/1757, No. 521.

[69] Mallet, Lewis (1864–1936), British diplomat. He served as Assistant Under Secretary for Foreign Affairs and Chief of Asian Department (1907–13), and was Ambassador to Turkey (October 1913–November 1914).

[70] Heller, *British Policy*, p. 80.

[71] Asquith, Sir Herbert (1852–1928), British politician and Liberal leader. He served as Home Secretary (1892–95), Chancellor of the Exchequer (1905–8), and Prime Minister (1908–16).

[72] Heller, *British Policy*, pp. 81–82.

[73] Ibid., pp. 101–2.

[74] Ibid., pp. 104, 106.

[75] Sazonov, Sergei (1860–1927), Russian statesman and diplomat. He served as Counselor at Russian Embassies to Great Britain, the U.S., and the Holy See (1883–1909), Deputy Foreign Minister (1909–10), and Foreign Minister (1910–16).

[76] FO 371/1847, No. 385.

[77] U. Trumpener, "Liman von Sanders and the German-Ottoman Alliance," *Journal of Contemporary History* 1966, pp. 179–92.

[78] FO 371/2114, No. 1512.

[79] Heller, *British Policy*, pp. 129–30.

[80] Ibid., p. 136.

[81] Ibid., pp. 139–40, 149.

[82] AVPR, F. Politicheskiy arkhiv, d. 1044, l. 319.

[83] Central History Archive of the Republic of Armenia, , fund 57, List 5, Ch. 55, p. 13.

[84] FO 371/1773, No. 1229.

[85] L. G. Istyagin, "Ekspantsiya germanskogo imperializma v Turtsii i russko-germanskie protivorechiya po Armyanskomu voprosu, 1912–1914 gg.," in *Iz istorii agressivnoy vneshney politiki germanskogo imperializma* (Moscow, 1959), p. 27.

[86] Djemal Pasha, *Memories of a Turkish Statesman, 1913–1919* (London, 1922), p. 226.

[87] Bertie, Francis (1844–1919), British diplomat. He served as Ambassador to Italy (1903–4) and France (1905–18).

[88] *British Documents on the Origins of the War. 1898–1914*, vol. 10 (London, 1936), p. 424

[89] Ibid.

[90] Ibid., p. 426.

[91] Heller, *British Policy*, pp. 84–85.

[92] *British Documents*, pp. 430.

[93] Heller, *British Policy*, p. 85.

[94] *British Documents*, pp. 431–32.

[95] Ibid., pp. 433–34.

[96] Ibid., p. 436.

[97] Ibid., pp. 437–38.

[98] Ibid., pp. 438, 441–42.

[99] Ibid., p. 442.

[100] Ibid., p. 443.

[101] Ibid., pp. 444–45.

[102] Ibid., p. 446.

[103] Ibid., p. 448; Heller, *British Policy*, p. 86.

[104] Heller, *British Policy*, p. 86.

[105] *Sbornik diplomaticheskikh dokumentov. Reformy v Armenii. 26 noyabrya 1912–10 maya 1914 gg. (Oranzhevaya kniga)* (Petrograd, 1915), p. 61–69.

[106] R. Davison, *The Armenian Crisis, 1912–1914* (New York, 1948), p. 15.

[107] Buchanan, George (1854–1924), British diplomat. He served as Consul General and Minister in Sofia, Bulgaria, and Ambassador to Russia (1910–18).

[108] *British Documents*, p. 450.

[109] Ibid., p. 452.

[110] Ibid., p. 453.

[111] Ibid., pp. 454–55.

[112] Ibid., p. 463.

[113] Ibid., p. 468.

[114] Goschen, William (1847–1924), British diplomat. He served as Ambassador to Austria-Hungary (1905–8), and Germany (1908–14).

[115] *British Documents*, p. 470.

[116] Ibid., p. 471.

[117] Ibid., p. 472.

[118] Ibid., p. 473.

[119] Heller, *British Policy*, p. 87.

[120] Davison, *The Armenian Crisis*, p. 15.

[121] Heller, *British Policy*, p. 89.

[122] *British Documents*, p. 493.

[123] Ibid., pp. 495–96.

[124] Ibid., pp. 501–2.

[125] AVPR, F. Politicheskiy arkhiv, d. 3465, l. 147.

[126] Davison, *The Armenian Crisis*, p. 18; Georgiev, et al., *Vostochnyy vopros*, p. 370; R. Kodzhoyan,

"Russkaya diplomatiya i problema reform v Zapadnoy Armenii nakanune pervoy mirovoy voyny" (Ph.D. diss. in history. Yerevan, 1989), p. 122.

[127] H. Howard, *The Partition of Turkey: A Diplomatic History, 1913–1923* (University of Oklahoma Press, 1931), pp. 49–50.

[128] *British Documents*, pp. 515–16.

[129] *Sbornik diplomaticheskikh dokumentov*, p. 95.

[130] Central History Archive of the Republic of Armenia, "Collection of Excerpts from Documents," List 1, Chapter 37, p. 35.

[131] Heller, *British Policy*, p. 90.

[132] Ibid., pp. 107–8; Davison, *The Armenian Crisis*, p. 21.

[133] *British Documents*, p. 523.

[134] Ibid., pp. 524–25.

[135] Heller, *British Policy*, p. 107.

[136] *British Documents*, p. 528.

[137] Ibid., p. 529.

[138] Heller, *British Policy*, p. 108.

[139] *British Documents*, p. 534–35.

[140] Ibid., p. 535.

[141] Heller, *British Policy*, p. 110.

[142] S. Sazonov, *Fateful Years* (New York, 1928).

[143] FO 371/2116/426, No. 37.

[144] FO 371/2116/426, No. 41.

[145] For full text of the treaty, see *Armenia in International Diplomacy*, pp. 339–42; *Sbornik dogovorov Rossii*, pp. 421–24; *Sbornik diplomaticheskikh dokumentov*, p. 162–65

[146] Heller, *British Policy*, p. 110.

[147] *Armenia in International Diplomacy*, p. 354.

[148] Heller, *British Policy*, p. 111.

[149] *Sbornik diplomaticheskikh dokumentov*, p. 177.

[150] FO 371/2116/426, No. 34, 73, 82.

[151] W. Van der Dussen, "The Question of Armenian Reforms in 1913–1914," *Armenian Review* 39, no. 1 (1986), p. 26.

[152] *British Documents*, p. 548.

[153] Heller, *British Policy*, p. 111.

[154] Ibid.

[155] Nassibian, *Britain and the Armenian Question*, p. 31.

[156] Heller, *British Policy*, p. 111.

Conclusion

In the early nineteenth century, Britain became the world's leading industrial, commercial, and colonial Power. Having overtaken the rest of Europe in terms of economic growth, Britain sought to strengthen and increase its commercial and industrial supremacy. Achieving that objective had been the aim of its relations with other Powers.

The balance-of-power politics practiced by Britain throughout the nineteenth century was the reflection of its intentions to frustrate plans by other nations to increase their share of relative power on the continent and in the competition for colonies.

The importance of the Near East and the Balkans in international (i.e., European) politics grew significantly, beginning in 1830's, as the European countries sought to assert political and economic influence over the Ottoman dominions. The Ottoman Empire occupied an important geographic niche giving it control over the strategic and commercial crossroads of Europe and Asia. Control of the strategic crossroads became the goal of all major powers. Since the balance-of-power system was designed to avoid conflicts, the Ottoman Empire became an important component of the international practice of this system.

With Napoleonic France firmly defeated, in the 1830's Russia emerged as the major challenger to Britain's dominant position in Europe. A series of Russo-Turkish wars that began late in the 18th century had augmented the territory occupied by Russia, which now emerged as a military force to be reckoned with. Russia's military successes against Persia in 1828 and in the Russo-Turkish war of 1828–29 were of serious concern to Britain which viewed Russia's ascendance as a threat to the balance of power in Europe. The British Government was especially alarmed after the conclusion of the Russian-Turkish Treaty of Unkiar-Skelessi in 1833, which provided for permanent consultations on issues of security and for a mutual defense arrangement.

The development and implementation of the new British position regarding the Ottoman Empire coincided with the era of Lord Palmerston, who was Foreign Secretary and, later, the Prime Minister of Britain. Palmerston viewed the Near East to be a top priority of British foreign policy, and the preservation of the territorial integrity of Turkey became an important component of British policy in the 1830's. Parlmerston's Near East policies pursued the following objectives: to deny Russia the right to intervene in and assert its protectorate over the Ottoman Empire; to strengthen the British political and economic presence in the Ottoman Empire and make the Sultan dependent on Britain's support; and to secure implementation of military, administrative, and legal reforms in the country and equal rights for the Christian subjects of the Sultan. The Turkish Government of the day accepted the alliance with the leading world power, believing that reforms were a first step for the survival and Europeanization of the Empire.

The Ottoman Empire remained a multi-ethnic state with over 60 ethnic, religious, and tribal groups at different levels of social and political development. The hitherto practiced Ottoman policies of pro-Islamic discrimination and benign oppression of the Christian element became untenable in view of the growth of economic power and revival of national movements among the Christian communities, and the increasing role of the European powers in the region. The first period of Tanzimat brought forward new ideas and approaches to the challenges facing the Christian subjects of the Sultan. The author of Tanzimat reforms, Reshid Pasha, advocated equality and guarantees for life, property, and human dignity of all subjects of the Sultan. The idea of unity of all the ethnic and religious elements in the Empire gained ground before the Crimean War, and was used as a tool against external enemies, primarily Russia.

British diplomacy encouraged and supported the Ottoman elite in implementing these reforms, especially for the ethnic groups. Palmerston believed that internal reforms and liberalization of the Ottoman Empire would check the growth of national movements and prevent the Christian peoples' from resorting to help from other Powers to overthrow the Sultan's yoke. In the late 1840's the British Government, acting in agreement with other Western European countries, presented a program of reforms to the Porte that would take away initiative from Russia in espousing the cause of the oppressed Christian peoples in the Ottoman Empire.

The Eastern Question—the complex web of economic and political rivalries between the Powers, national liberation movements in the Ottoman Empire, and the crisis in relations between the Porte and the European Powers and Russia—had become a major factor of instability in Europe immediately before the Crimean War. While Britain, France, and Austria pursued their national interests vis-à-vis the Ottoman Empire, what brought them together was the recognition of the need to achieve, through internal reforms, the economic and military revival of the Ottoman Empire and to prevent the national movements from undermining the country.

Between 1850 and 1853, the Porte and the British Government cooperated in suppressing several rebellions and the resurgence of national movements in various parts of the Empire. British diplomacy demanded that the Porte suppress anti-Turkish revolts to prevent Russian intervention. It was in this period that Britain began to post consular and military agents throughout the Ottoman Empire to monitor local developments and the reforms process. Usually representing the most competent and respected element of British diplomatic personnel, the British consuls would, in the years to come, develop solid reputations and work arduously to press for reforms, documenting the abuses and oppression by the Ottoman authorities.

In 1853, Russia and Britain began talks on the situation in the Ottoman Empire and improving the conditions of its Christian subjects. Britain rejected the Russian proposals for dismemberment of the Ottoman Empire and the use of coercive measures to force reforms on the Sultan.

While the Crimean War was underway, British diplomacy worked industriously to produce a program of reforms for the Christians, and the Porte published the Sultan's Decree (Gülhane-Hatte-Hümayun) granting equality to the Christian population and promulgating financial, fiscal, legal, and police reforms in the Empire. Since the Decree had been published before the Paris Conference in 1856, British diplomacy pushed for a clause prohibiting Powers from individually interfering in the internal affairs of the Ottoman Empire.

The Treaty of Paris did not make a specific reference to Western Armenia but nevertheless directly affected the subsequent fate of Western Armenians. Although the Russian Army was defeated on the Caucasian front, it occupied Kars and Armenian-populated areas in eastern Anatolia. The Russian territorial gains in the Caucasus were reversed at the conference, at the behest of

Britain, which emerged in a dominant position with the Ottoman Empire, and diminished the influence in the Near East of its chief antagonist—Russia. While the Ottoman Empire was among the victors, the mounting political and economic challenges prevented it from claiming its share of victory. Even as Turkey's dependence on the European countries now rose, its oppression of the Christian minorities increased, and gave new hopes to the national liberation movements throughout the Empire.

Between 1850 and 1860, Britain continued to press the Porte to carry out the Hatte Humayun reforms, improve the lot of non-Turkish peoples, and achieve equality between the Christian and Muslim subjects. In the British view, the alternative was the gradual dismemberment and eventual collapse of the Empire, resulting in the emergence of several independent states bound to fall within Russia's sphere of influence. British diplomacy encouraged reformist Ottoman activists such as Ali Pasha and Fuad Pasha, who developed the ideology of Ottomanism that would give equal treatment to all subjects of the Sultan, independent of their religious and ethnic affiliation, and not deprive the non-Turkic peoples of their national identities.

The British Government continued to support the efforts of the Porte to suppress national movements and insurgencies. Britain provided financial and moral support to the Porte as it quashed rebellions in Herzegovina and Zeytoun, suppressed the activities of the Italian revolutionaries in the Balkans, and defeated Montenegro. British diplomats were concerned about the persecution of the Armenian population in Zeytoun and Diyarbakir in the wake of the Zeytoun insurgency, viewing the Armenian discontent as a possible cause for Russian intervention.

The first Gladstone Ministry (1868–74) had sought to establish control over Egypt and the Suez Canal, which contravened the British policy of preserving the territorial integrity of the Ottoman Empire. Consequently, the British Government also relaxed its concerns about the reforms in the Ottoman Empire, ignoring consular reports of growing mismanagement, oppression, and abuses of the local authorities, which were increasingly directed against the Armenians and other Christian peoples.

The June 1875 revolt in Bosnia and Herzegovina, which had been caused by the continuous political, economic, and national oppression practiced by the Sultan's government, resulted in a serious international crisis. The specter of

Ottoman collapse and the emergence of new independent states and statelets on its ruins that would be dominated by Russia, aggravated the international situation and upset the European balance of power. The many promises of reforms issued by the Porte remained unfulfilled. The clause in the Treaty of Paris that would have allowed for collective action of the Powers on behalf of the Christian population had always been invoked to prevent a Russian unilateral intervention, rather than for improvement of the conditions in Turkey.

From 1874 to 1880, the British Cabinet was headed by Disraeli, the leader of the Conservative Party. In the initial phase of the Balkan crisis, Disraeli believed that the Porte would easily crush the uprising in the Balkans. When the German, Austrian, and Russian Governments agreed on a course of action, Britain decided to join in, but without tying itself to any specific obligations. The Disraeli Government was essentially indifferent to the fate of Balkan Slavs, but the increasing importance of public opinion in Britain and other European countries forced him to intervene. Disraeli also faced stiff opposition from the Liberal Party which turned the Balkans into an issue of domestic politics.

In late 1876, Disraeli proposed to convene a conference of European nations in Constantinople to address the Eastern Question while working diligently to make sure the Porte would reject the representations from other Powers. British diplomacy employed the same British policies to draw the Ottoman and Russian Empires into a war, which would result in territorial acquisitions by Russia and Britain and establish a strong British economic and military presence in the Near East and eastern Mediterranean.

Parallel to the increasing oppression of the Western Armenian population in the Ottoman Empire in 1875–78, British diplomacy began to monitor developments in Western Armenia. While the British diplomatic agents had primarily been interested in the Christian population in Lebanon or Balkans and the actions of the local authorities in those regions, British interest in the Armenian-populated regions of Asia Minor began to grow in early 1870's. The British consular reports began to detail the oppressive policies of local Turkish authorities and Kurdish tribal leaders toward the Armenians, with reports of robberies, murders, and arson flowing in constantly. The growing interest in Western Armenia was the result of the increasing realization of an outstanding level of government-induced corruption, oppression and mismanagement in this region, which, in the opinion of the Foreign Office, could result in a Russian takeover with consequences for British interests in the Near East and India.

The news of Russian military victories and the Russian-Turkish Peace Treaty of San Stefano spurred the British Foreign Office into action to reverse the Russian advances in Asia Minor. Disraeli threatened to use coercive measures, declared partial mobilization and deployed the navy to the Marmara Sea. Russia was forced to give up Bayazid and Alashkert regions in Western Armenia. The control over reforms in Armenia would be shared by all powers, not just Russia. The British Government forced a secret treaty on the Porte that ceded Cyprus to Britain in exchange for the return of Russian territorial gains in Armenia and defense against future Russian encroachment on Turkey's territorial integrity and interests.

The British delegation at the Congress of Berlin used the Armenian Question exclusively to pressure Russia and replaced the comprehensive approach of Article 16 in the San Stefano Treaty with the limited scope of reforms under Article 61 of the Treaty of Berlin. Article 16 would allow the presence of Russian military forces in Western Armenia to oversee the reforms process; Article 61 did not include an effective enforcement mechanism for reforms. The San Stefano Treaty referred to 'Armenia' as a sole entity, while the Treaty of Berlin referred to the 'Armenian-populated provinces.' British diplomacy avoided using the geographic term 'Armenia' to prevent the future establishment of autonomy, and created the unclear and weak language of Article 61, which was also perceived as such by the Porte. The Government of Abdul Hamid increased the level of oppression against its Armenian subjects and modified the administrative divisions of Anatolia to alter demographics and lay the ground for eventual displacement and extermination of the Armenian population.

Domestic pressure forced the British Government to take issue with the Sultan's anti-Armenian policies in the early 1880's. The British Government spearheaded an active effort by the European nations to demand the implementation of reforms promised under the Treaty of Berlin. The British position on the Armenian Question was motivated by the need to prevent Western Armenia from falling under Russian influence, and prepared the ground for forcing the Porte to accept the British takeover of Egypt in 1882.

Having secured control of the Eastern Mediterranean and Egypt, the British Government's involvement in the Armenian Question began to wane in the 1880's, although extensive diplomatic correspondence shows continuing high-level British interest in the Armenian-populated areas.

The next phase of Britain's active involvement in the Armenian Question started in the 1890's, parallel to the rise in Turkish oppression of the Armenian population and the mounting challenges in Western Armenia. The British Government's actions and public indignation in Britain failed to prevent the massacres of the Armenian population in the Ottoman Empire in 1894–96. The 1894 massacre in Sasun led to public protests in Britain, and the Government had to face charges of indifference and even complicity in the actions of the Porte. The Rosebery Government reluctantly joined the European nations in demanding an inquiry into the Sasun events and urging safety guarantees for the Armenian population. The Liberal Party turned the Armenian reforms and liberation of Armenia into campaign issues in 1895, while Gladstone went on a spree of passionate speeches decrying the Sultan's inhuman policies and demanding unilateral British intervention.

In April 1895, the British Government prepared a reforms program that would have established self-government under European auspices in the Armenian-populated provinces. The British, French, and Russian envoys presented a somewhat modified proposal to the Sultan in May 1895; the program, however, was not carried out. In June, the British Government briefly discussed the possibility of deploying warships to force the Sultan to accept reforms, but came to no decision. The Rosebery Cabinet's vacillation in the Armenian Question led to its resignation.

The return of Lord Salisbury's Conservative Party to power in 1895 gave cause to hope that the British Government would be able to address the Near Eastern crisis and stop the anti-Armenian policies of the Ottoman Government. On the one hand, traditional British policy and interests in the region demanded the preservation of Turkey's territorial integrity; on the other, without the assistance of Russia and the consent of the European Powers, the British Government could not achieve success. Salisbury did his best to achieve a rapprochement with Russia to advance reforms in Armenia while keeping a channel of communications open with Germany to preserve the traditional balance of power.

In the wake of the Armenian massacres in September 1895 in Constanti-nople, British diplomacy sought to prevent the spread of the carnage. Despite numerous demarches from the British Embassy and passionate anti-Turkish speeches in Parliament, the massacres soon spread to other Armenian-populated areas. By the end of 1895, the British Government absolved itself of responsibility to enforce reforms in the Armenian-populated provinces, attributing it to disagreements among the Powers. The tragedy of the West Armenians signified the end of British hopes to control internal reforms in Turkey.

Another round of massacres in Turkey in the autumn of 1896 caused the British Government to rally the support of the Powers for joint action on the Armenian Question. The Powers endorsed Salisbury's proposal for a European conference on reforms, but the draft prepared by European envoys in Con-stantinople was shelved after a war broke out between Greece and Turkey.

Faced with the complex dynamics of international politics in the early 20th century, the British Government did not raise the Armenian Question fearing that another wave of disorders would result in dismemberment of the Otto-man Empire, and that instability in the Near East that would be detrimental to British interests. But the Young Turk Government not only had no intention of implementing any reforms in the eastern provinces, it revived intra-national enmity, encouraged and helped official lawlessness, the seizure of Armenian lands, the resettlement of refugees from the Balkans, and the destructive attacks of Kurd detachments on Armenian settlements and people

The Turkish defeat in the First Balkan War did not seriously affect British interests. The greatest danger to Britain lay in Russia's success in Western Armenia which threatened Britain's political and economic endeavors in the Near and Middle East. The existence of equilibrium among the Powers in Europe to preserve the integrity of Turkey's eastern provinces corresponded to the interests of Great Britain. It was from these considerations that the Brit-ish approached the Russian proposals for the examination of the Armenian reforms, seeking the best advantage in serving its interests.

The 1914 Russian-Turkish agreement was received enthusiastically in Brit-ain inasmuch as it provided for real reforms in internal administration and did not accord special privileges to either Russia or Germany; in other words, the British interests were not seriously affected. This program of Armenian

reforms shared the fate of its predecessors although it came closest to fruition. World War I put an end to the Russian-Turkish agreement; Britain was
unable to secure Turkish neutrality and declared war on Turkey in November.

From 1830 to 1914, British diplomacy successfully carried out the British
Government's policy of preventing the Russian takeover of the Straits, Con-
stantinople, and Western Armenia, but proved unable to force the Ottoman
authorities to carry out reforms in Armenia or provide guarantees for the
Armenian population in Turkey. In 1915, under the cover of World War I, the
Young Turk regime began the deportation and annihilation of the Armenian
population of the Ottoman Empire, thus "solving" the question of reforms in
Armenia and, generally, the Armenian Question.

Bibliography

1. Archives

Republic of Armenia. Central Historical Archive. "Collection of Excerpts of Documents," fund 57.

Russian Federation. Arkhiv vneshney politiki Rossii (AVPR): F. Politicheskiy arkhiv, Kantselyariya.

United Kingdom. Public Record Office. Foreign Office 424: Confidential Print, Turkey; FO 371: Foreign Office Political Correspondence; FO 881: Confidential Papers Relating to Foreign Affairs; Cabinet Office 37: Cabinet Papers, 1880–1914.

2. Official Documents

British Documents on the Origin of War, 1898–1914. Vol. x. London, 1936.

German Diplomatic Documents. 1871–1914. Vol. 1. London, 1928.

Great Britain. *Hansard Parliamentary Debates*, 3d ser., vol. 97 (1848); 3d ser., vol. 79 (1853); 3d ser., vol. 240 (1878)

———. House of Commons, "Opinions and Policy of Palmerston." 11 July 1833 (London, 1852).

Great Britain. Foreign Office. *Correspondence Respecting Protestant Missionaries and Converts in Turkey.* London, 1865.

———. *Correspondence Respecting the Condition of Protestants in Turkey, 1853–1854 (In Continuation of Papers presented to both Houses of Parliament in 1851).* London, 1854.

———. Eastern Papers. Part IX. *Protocol Signed at Vienna on the 23rd of May, 1854 by the Representatives of Austria, France, Great Britain and Prussia.* London, 1854.

———. Eastern Papers. Part LXVII (1875–1876). London, 1883.

———. Eastern Papers. Part LXVIII (1876–1877). London, 1884.

———. Eastern Papers. Part V. *Communications Respecting Turkey made to Her Majesty's Government by the Emperor of Russia, with the Answers returned to them, January to April 1853.* London, 1854.

———. Eastern Papers. Part VIII. *Protocol Signed at Vienna on the 8th of April, 1854, by the Representatives of Austria, France, Great Britain and Prussia.* London, 1854.

———. Eastern Papers. Part XIII. *Papers Relating to the Negotiations at Vienna on the Eastern Question.* London, 1855.

———. Eastern Papers. Part xv. *Communications with the Austrian Government.* London, 1855.

———. Eastern Papers. Part xvi. *Instructions to Lord John Russell on Proceeding to Vienna.* London, 1855.

———. Eastern Papers. Part xvii. *Firman and Hatti-Sherif by the Sultan, Relative to Privileges and Reforms in Turkey.* London, 1856.

———. Eastern Papers. Part xviii. *Correspondence Respecting Christian Privileges in Turkey.* London, 1856.

———. *Papers Relating to Administrative and Financial Reforms in Turkey. 1858–1861.* London, 1861.

———. *Protocol of Conferences Held at Paris Relative to the General Treaty of Peace.* London, 1856.

———. *Reports received from Her Majesty's Ambassador and Consuls Relating to the Condition of Christians in Turkey, 1867.* London, 1867.

———. *Reports received from Her Majesty's Consuls Relating to the Condition of Christians in Turkey, 1860.* London, 1861.

Great Britain. Foreign Office. Russia, No. 2 (1877). *Correspondence Respecting the War between Russia and Turkey.* London, 1877.

———. Turkey, No. 1 (1876–1877). *Correspondence Respecting the Conference in Constantinople and the Affairs in Turkey.* London, 1877.

———. Turkey, No. 1 (1878). *Further Correspondence Respecting the Affairs of Turkey.* London, 1878.

———. Turkey, No. 1 (1880). *Correspondence Respecting the Commission sent by the Porte to Inquire into the Condition of the Vilayet of Aleppo.* London, 1880.

———. Turkey, No. 1 (1889). *Correspondence Respecting the Condition of the Populations in Asiatic Turkey. 1888–1889.* London, 1889.

———. Turkey, No. 1 (1890). *Correspondence Respecting the Condition of the Populations in Asiatic Turkey and the Trial of Moussa Bey.* London.

———. Turkey, No. 1 (1890–1891). *Correspondence Respecting the Condition of the Population in Asiatic Turkey and the Proceedings in the Case of Moussa Bey.* London, 1891.

———. Turkey, No. 1 (1892). *Further Correspondence Respecting the Condition of the Populations in Asiatic Turkey.* London, 1892.

———. Turkey, No. 1 (1896). *Correspondence Relative to the Armenian Question and Reports from Her Majesty's Consular Officers in Asiatic Turkey.* London, 1896.

———. Turkey, No. 1 (1897). London, 1897.

———. Turkey, No. 1 (1909). *Correspondence Respecting the Constitutional Movement in Turkey. 1908.* London, 1909.

———. Turkey, No. 10 (1879). *Correspondence Respecting the Condition of the Population in Asia Minor and Syria.* London, 1879.

———. Turkey, No. 15 (1877). *Further Correspondence Respecting the Affairs of Turkey.* London, 1877.

———. Turkey, No. 16 (1877). *Reports by Her Majesty's Diplomatic and Consular Agents in Turkey Respecting the Condition of the Christian Subjects of the Porte. 1868–1875.* London, 1877.

———. Turkey, No. 16 (1877). *Reports by Her Majesty's Diplomatic and Consular Agents in Turkey Respecting the Condition of the Christian Subjects of the Porte. 1865–1875.* London, 1877.

———. Turkey, No. 17 (1877). *Instructions Addressed to Her Majesty's Embassy at Constantinople Respecting Financial and Administrative Reforms and the Protection of Christians in Turkey, 1856–1875.* London, 1877, Part 1.

———. Turkey, No. 2 (1896). *Correspondence Relative to the Armenian Question and Reports from Her Majesty's Consular Officers in Asiatic Provinces.* London, 1896.

———. Turkey, No. 2. (1876). *Correspondence Respecting Affairs in Bosnia and Herzegovina (1875–1876).* London, 1876.

———. Turkey, No. 23 (1880). *Further Correspondence Respecting the Condition of the Populations in Asia Minor and Syria.* London, 1880.

———. Turkey, No. 27 (1878). *Further Correspondence Respecting the Preliminary Treaty of Peace between Russia and Turkey signed at San-Stefano.* London, 1878.

———. Turkey, No. 3 (1896). *Correspondence Relating to the Asiatic Provinces of Turkey. 1892–1893.* London, 1896.

———. Turkey, No. 36 (1878). *Correspondence Respecting the Convention between Great Britain and Turkey of June 4, 1878.* London, 1878.

———. Turkey, No. 39 (1878). *Correspondence Relating to the Congress of Berlin with the Protocol of the Congress.* London, 1878.

———. Turkey, No. 4 (1880). *Correspondence Respecting the Condition of the Populations in Asia Minor and Syria.* London, 1880.

———. Turkey, No. 51 (1878). *Correspondence Respecting Reforms in Asiatic Turkey.* London, 1878.

———. Turkey, No. 53 (1878). *Further Correspondence Respecting the Affairs of Turkey.* London, 1878.

———. Turkey, No. 54 (1878). *Further Correspondence Respecting the Affairs of Turkey.* London, 1878.

———. Turkey, No. 6 (1881). *Further Correspondence Respecting the Condition of the Populations in Asia Minor and Syria.* London, 1881.

———. Turkey, No. 7 (1880). *Correspondence Respecting the Affairs of Turkey.* London, 1880.

———. Turkey, No. 8 (1896). *Further Correspondence Relating to the Asiatic Provinces of Turkey (In Continuation of Turkey No. 2 (1896)).* London, 1896.

————. Turkey, No. 1 (1895). *Correspondence Relative to the Armenian Question and Reports from Her Majesty's Consular Officers in Asiatic Turkey.* London, 1896, Part 1.

Kirakosyan, J. S., ed. *Hayastane mijazgayin divanagitutian yev sovetakan artakin kaghakakanutian pastatghterum (1828–1923)* (Armenia in the documents of international diplomacy and Soviet foreign policy, 1828–1923) (Yerevan, 1972).

"Lord Salisbury's Conversations with the Tzar at Balmoral, 27 and 29 September, 1896." *The Slavonic and East European Review* 34, no. 92 (December 1960).

Nersisyan, M. G., ed. *Genotsid armyan v Osmanskoy imperii. Sbornik dokumentov i materialov.* Yerevan, 1982.

Sbornik diplomaticheskikh dokumentov. Reformy v Armenii. 26 noyabrya 1912–10 maya 1914 gg. (Oranzhevaya kniga). Petrograd, 1915.

Sbornik dogovorov Rossii s drugimi gosudarstvami. 1856–1917. Moscow, 1952.

"Sekretnaya zapiska russkogo posla v Londone Ye. Ye. Staalya o besede s lordom Solsberi." In *Problemy britanskoy istorii.* Moscow, 1973.

Simsir, Bilal, ed. *British Documents on Ottoman Armenians.* Vol. 2 (1880–1890), Ankara, 1983; vol. 3 (1891–1895), Ankara, 1989; vol. 4 (1895), Ankara, 1990.

3. Memoirs and Biographies

Cecil, G. *Life of Robert Marquis of Salisbury.* London, 1921.

Djemal Pasha. *Memories of a Turkish Statesman, 1913–1919.* London, 1922.

Gilbert, M. *Winston S. Churchill,* vol. 3: *1914-1916.* London, 1971.

"Iz dnevnika V. N. Lamzdorfa." *Voprosy istorii* 1977, no. 6.

Jenkins, R. *Gladstone.* London, 1996.

Kennedy, A. L. *Salisbury, 1830–1903: Portrait of a Statesman.* London, 1953.

Knaplund, Paul. *Gladstone's Foreign Policy.* New York and London, 1935.

Magnus, P. *Gladstone: A Biography.* London, 1954.

Malcolm-Smith, E. F. *The Life of Stratford Canning.* London, 1933.

Monypenny, W. F. and G. Buckle. *The Life of Disraeli.* Vol. 6.

Pears, E. *Forty Years in Constantinople: The Recollections of Sir Edwin Pears (1873–1915).* London, 1915.

————. *Life of Abdul Hamid.* New York, 1917.

Sazonov, S. *Fateful Years.* New York, 1928.

Taylor, R. *Salisbury.* London, 1975.

The Memoirs of Ismail Kemal. London, 1920.

Victoria, Queen. *Letters.* Vol. 2. London, 1926.

Vinogradov, K. B. and O. A. Naumenkov. "Na sluzhbe britanskogo kolonializma (Stranitsy politicheskoy biografii lorda Solsberi)." *Novaya i noveyshaya istoriya* 1981, no. 1.

Vitte, S. Yu. *Vospominaniya.* Vol. 2. Moscow, 1960.

4. Monographs, Books, Articles

"A Vanishing Treaty." *The Spectator,* 9 August 1890 (vol. 65).

Abbott, G. *Turkey in Transition.* London, 1909.

Abbott, L. "Armenian Question." *The Outlook,* 1896, vol. 54.

"Americans and Armenians." *The Spectator,* 1 February 1896 (vol. 76).

Amfiteatrov, A. *Armyanskiy vopros.* Saint Petersburg, 1906.

Antoine, E. *Les Massacres d'Armenie.* Bruxelles, 1897.

"Armenia and the Powers: From Behind the Scenes." *The Contemporary Review,* 1896, vol. 69.

Arutyunyan, G. M. "Angliya i Armyanskiy vopros v seredine 90-kh godov XIX veka." *Novaya i noveyshaya istoriya* 1959, no. 6.

———. "Politika Anglii v Armyanskom voprose v 90-kh godakh XIX veka i pozitsiya velikikh derzhav (problematika, istochnikovedcheskiy i istoriograficheskiy obzor)." *Vestnik Yerevanskogo universiteta. Obshchestvennye nauki* 1988, no. 2-3.

"At Colchester." *Liberal Magazine,* 20 October 1896.

Bayramian, L. "Haykakan hartse yev Anglian 1890-akan tt.," (The Armenian Question and England in the 1890s). *Patmabanasirakan Handes* 1979, no. 1.

Beales, D. *From Castlereagh to Gladstone. 1815–1885.* London, 1971.

Blaisdell, D. C. *European Financial Control in the Ottoman Empire.* New York, 1929.

Bliss, E. M. *Turkey and Armenian Atrocities.* Philadelphia, 1896.

Bolkhovitinov, N. N. "O pozitsii Solsberi v Vostochnom voprose osen'yu 1896 g." In *Problemy britanskoy istorii.* Moscow, 1973.

Bondarevskiy, G. A. *Angliyskaya politika i mezhdunarodnye otnosheniya v basseyne Persidskogo zaliva (konets xix–nachalo xx vv.).* Moscow, 1968.

Bor'yan, B. A. *Armeniya, mezhdunarodnaya diplomatiya i SSSR.* Part 1. Moscow and Leningrad, 1928.

Bourne, K. *The Foreign Policy of Victorian England. 1830–1902.* Oxford, 1970.

Bratskaya pomoshch' postradavshim v Turtsii armyanam. Moscow, 1898.

Bryce, J. *Transcaucasia and Ararat.* London, 1896.

Chikhachev, P. A. *Velikie derzhavy i Vostochnyy vopros.* Moscow, 1970.

Clayton, C. D. *Britain and the Eastern Question: Missolonghi to Gallipoli.* London, 1971.

Cunningham, A. *Stratford Canning and the Tanzimat. Beginnings of Modernization in the Middle East.* Chicago, 1968.

"Czar's Visit." *The Spectator,* 26 September 1896 (vol. 77).

Davey, R. "Turkey and Armenia." *The Fortnightly Review,* 1895, vol. 63.

Davison, R. *The Armenian Crisis, 1912–1914.* New York, 1948.

Dawson, W. H. *Richard Cobden and Foreign Policy.* London, 1926.

De Novo, J. *American Interests and Policies in the Middle East. 1900–1939.* Minneapolis, 1963.

Dillon, E. J. "Armenia: An Appeal." *The Contemporary Review,* 1896, vol. 69.

————. "The Fiasco in Armenia." *The Fortnightly Review*, 1896, vol. 65.

Douglas, R. "Britain and the Armenian Question, 1894–97." *The Historical Journal*, 1976, no. 19.

Fadeeva, I. L. *Osmanskaya imperiya i anglo-turetskie otnosheniya v seredine xix v.* Moscow, 1982.

Gabrielian, M. S. *Armenia: A Martyr Nation. A Historical Sketch of the Armenian People from Tradition Times to the Present Tragic Days.* New York, 1918.

Galevi, E. *Istoriya Anglii v epokhu imperializma.* Vol. 1. Moscow, 1957.

Galoyan, G. *Patmutian karughinerum* (At the crossroads of history). Yerevan, 1982.

Gasratyan, M. A., S. F. Oreshkova, Yu. A. Petrosyan. *Ocherki istorii Turtsii.* Moscow, 1983.

Georgiev, V. A., N. S. Kinyapina, M. T. Panchenkova, et al. *Vostochnyy vopros vo vneshney politike Rossii (konets xviii–nachalo xx veka).* Moscow, 1978.

Gladstone, W. E. *Bulgarian Horrors and the Question of the East.* London, 1876.

Gleason, J. H. *The Genesis of Russophobia in Great Britain.* London, 1950.

Godkin, E. L. "The Armenian Resolutions." *The Nation,* 30 January 1896, vol. 62.

Gordon, L. J. *American Relations with Turkey (1830–1930).* Philadelphia, 1932.

Grenville, J. A. S. *Lord Salisbury and Foreign Policy.* London, 1964.

Grinval'd, M. "Angliyskaya diplomatiya za 25 let (1892-1916)." *Morskoy sbornik,* 1926, no. 8-9.

Gulesian, M. H. "Armenian Refugees." *The Arena,* 1897, vol. 17.

————. "England's Hand in Turkish Massacres." *The Arena,* 1897, vol. 17.

Gutor, M. D. *Noveyshaya istoriya Turtsii i Persii.* Part 1. Tiflis, 1913. Pp. 67–68.

Haykakan Harts. Hanragitaran (Encyclopedia of the Armenian Question). Yerevan, 1996.

Heller, J. *British Policy Towards the Ottoman Empire. 1908–1914.* London, 1983.

Hepworth, H. *Through Armenia on Horseback.* London, 1898.

Hovannisian, R. *Armenia on the Road to Independence, 1918.* Berkeley and Los Angeles, 1967.

————. *The Armenian Holocaust.* Cambridge, Mass., 1978.

Howard, H. *The Partition of Turkey: A Diplomatic History, 1913–1923.* University of Oklahoma Press, 1931.

Intchikian, H. G. *Osmanian kaysrutian ankume* (The fall of the Ottoman Empire). Yerevan, 1984.

Istoriya diplomatii. Vols. 1 and 2. Moscow, 1959–63.

Istyagin, L. G. "Ekspantsiya germanskogo imperializma v Turtsii i russko-germanskie protivorechiya po Armyanskomu voprosu, 1912–1914 gg." In *Iz istorii agressivnoy vneshney politiki germanskogo imperializma.* Moscow, 1959.

Jefferson, M. M. "Lord Salisbury and the Eastern Question, 1890–1898." *The Slavonic and Eastern European Review* 39, no. 92 (December 1960).

Kalopothakes, D. "The Constantinople Massacres." *The Nation,* 8 October 1896.

Kamarovskiy, L. "Vostochnyy vopros i ego zhertvy." *Novoe slovo,* Dec. 1896.

———. "Young Turks, Freemasons and Jews." *Middle Eastern Studies,* 1971, no. 1.

Kedourie, E. *England and the Middle East: The Destruction of the Ottoman Empire, 1914–1921.* London, 1956.

———. "Blizhnevostochnyy krizis 1895–1897 gg. xix v." *Istorik-marksist* 1929, vol. 13.

Khvostov, V. M. "Problemy zakhvata Bosfora v 90-kh godakh xix v." *Istorik-marksist* 1930, vol. 20.

Kirakossian, A. "Anglo-russkie peregovory 1896 goda i Armyanskiy vopros." *Vestnik obshchestvennykh nauk AN Armyanskoy SSR* 1989, no. 5.

———. "Anglo-turetskie otnosheniya i vopros o reformakh v Zapadnoy Armenii (1895 g.)." *Vestnik arkhivov Armenii* 1987, no. 3.

———. "Armyanskiy vopros na stranitsakh zhurnalov Velikobritanii (seredina 90-kh gg. xix v.). *TsNION AN.* Yerevan, 1980.

———. "Avstro-Hungariayi kaghakakanutiune Haykakan hartsum (1895–1897) (The policy of Austro-Hungaria on the Armenian Question, 1895–1897). *HKhSH GA Lraber Hasarakakan Gitutiunneri* 1984, no. 1.

———. "Haykakan hartse AMN-i amsagreri ejerum (19-rd dari 90-akan tt.)" (The Armenian Question in the pages of U.S. Periodicals, 1890s). *HKhSH GA Lraber Hasarakakan Gitutiunneri* 1984, no. 1.

———. "K voprosu o konstantinopol'skoy rezne 1896 goda." *Literaturnaya Armeniya* 1989, no. 4.

———. "Politika Anglii v Armyanskom voprose po materialam ezhenedel'nika *Spekteytor* (90-e gg. xix v.)." *TsNION AN.* Yerevan, 1982.

———. [Kirakosyan, A.] *Velikobritaniya i Armyanskiy vopros (90-e gody xix veka).* Yerevan, 1990.

Kirakossian, J. *The Armenian Genocide: The Young Turks Before the Judgment of History.* Madison, 1992.

———. *Burzhuakan divanagitutiune yev Hayastane (19-rd dari 70-akan tt.)* (Bourgeois diplomacy and Armenia, 1870s). Yerevan, 1978.

———. *Burzhuakan divanagitutiune yev Hayastane (19-rd dari 80-akan tt.)* (Bourgeois diplomacy and Armenia, 1880s). Yerevan, 1982.

———. "San-Stefanoyi hashtutian paymanagire yev angliakan divanagitutiune" (The San Stefano peace treaty and English diplomacy). *Banber Yerevani Hamalsarani,* 1978, no. 1.

———. *Yeritturkere patmutian datastani araj (19-rd dari 90-akan tt.–1914)* (The Young Turks before the judgment of history, 1890s–1914). Yerevan, 1982.

Kochar, M. *Armyano-turetskie obshchestvenno-politicheskie otnosheniya i Armyanskiy vopros v kontse xix–nachale xx v.* Yerevan, 1988.

Kodzhoyan, R. "Russkaya diplomatiya i problema reform v Zapadnoy Armenii nakanune pervoy mirovoy voyny." Ph.D. diss. in history. Yerevan, 1989.

Kurginyan, Ye. A. "Yevropeyskaya diplomatiya i Armyanskiy vopros v 90-kh godakh XIX v." *Uchenye zapiski Moskovskogo oblastnogo pedinstituta*, 1968, Vol. 191, no. 9.

Kurkjan, V. M. *A History of Armenia*. New York, 1958.

Langer, W. L. *The Diplomacy of Imperialism, 1890–1902*. Vol. 1, New York, 1935.

Lanin, E. B. "Armenia and the Armenian People." *The Fortnightly Review*, 1890, vol. 54.

Lazarev, Ya. D. *Prichiny bedstviy armyan v Turtsii i otvetstvennost' za razorenie Sasuna*. Tiflis, 1895.

Lee, Dwight E. *Great Britain and the Cyprus Convention Policy of 1878*. Cambridge, 1934.

"Lord Rosebery`s Deliverance." *The Spectator*, 17 October 1896 (vol. 77).

"Lord Salisbury and Armenia." *The Nation*, 15 August 1895 (vol. 61).

"Lord Salisbury in Turkey." *The Spectator*, 7 December 1895 (vol. 75).

Maccoll, M. "The Constantinople Massacre and its Lesson." *The Contemporary Review*, 1895, vol. 68.

Mangasarian, M. "Armenia's Impending Doom." *The Forum*, 1896, vol. 21, p. 452.

Markosyan, S. M. *Arevmtahayutian vichake 19-rd dari verjerin* (The conditions of Western Armenians at the end of 19th century). Yerevan, 1968.

Marsh, P. "Lord Salisbury and the Ottoman Massacres." *The Journal of British Studies* 11, no. 2 (May 1972).

"Massacre in Turkey. From Oct. 1, 1895, to Jan. 1, 1896." *Review of Reviews*, 1896, vol. 13.

McDermot, G. "The Great Assassin and the Christians of Armenia." *The Catholic World*, December 1896, vol. 64.

Melson, R. "A Theoretical Inquiry into the Armenian Massacres of 1894–1896." *Comparative Studies in Society and History* 24, no. 3 (July 1982).

Mirak, R. "Armenian Emigration to the United States to 1915." *Journal of Armenian Studies* 1 (Autumn 1975).

Mkrtchyan, L. *Zeytuni apstambutiune, 1895–1896 tt.* (The Zeytoun Uprising, 1895–1896). Yerevan, 1995.

"Mr. Gladstone on Armenia." *The Spectator*, 10 August 1895 (vol. 75).

Nassibian, A. *Britain and the Armenian Question*. London, 1984.

Orudzhev, M. G. *Iz istorii proniknoveniya germanskogo imperializma v Turtsiyu*. Baku, 1961.

"Our Failure in Turkey." *The Spectator*, 14 December 1895 (vol. 75).

Paelian, G. H. *Landmarks in Armenian History*. New York, 1942.

Papadopoulos, G. S. *England and the Near East, 1896–1898*. Thessalonika, 1969.

Park, J. H. *British Prime Ministers of the Nineteenth Century: Policies and Speeches*. New York and London, 1950.

Pears, E. *Turkey and its People*. London, 1911.

Penson, L. M. "The Principles and Methods of Lord Salisbury`s Foreign Policy." *Cambridge Historical Journal*, 1935, vol. 87-106.

Peterson, T. "Turkey and Armenian Crisis." *The Catholic World*, 1895, vol. 61.

Petrosyan, Yu. A. "Turtsiya." In *Zarozhdenie ideologii natsional'no-osvoboditel'nogo dvizheniya (xix–nachalo xx vv.)*. Moscow, 1973.

Polozhenie armyan do vmeshatel'stva derzhav v 1895 godu. Moscow, 1896.

Roberts, Ch. "A Mother of Martyrs." *The Atlantic Monthly*, 1899, vol. 83.

Rohrbach, P. "The Contribution of the Armenian Question." *The Forum*, 1900, vol. 29, No. 4.

Rotshteyn, F. A. *Mezhdunarodnye otnosheniya v kontse xix veka*. Moscow and Leningrad, 1960.

Russell, G. W. E. "Armenia and the Forward Movement." *The Contemporary Review*, 1897, vol. 71.

Safrastyan, R. A. *Doktrina osmanizma v politicheskoy zhizni Osmanskoy imperii (50–70 gg. xix v.)*. Yerevan, 1985.

Sarkissian, A. O. *History of the Armenian Question to 1885*. Urbana, 1938.

Sarkisyan, Ye. K. *Politika Osmanskogo pravitel'stva v Zapadnoy Armenii i derzhavy v posledney chetverti xix i nachale xx vv*. Yerevan, 1972.

Seton-Watson, R. W. *Disraeli, Gladstone and the Eastern Question: A Study in Diplomacy and Party Politics*. New York, 1962.

Shahid Bey, S. *Islam, Turkey and Armenia and How They Happened*. St. Louis, 1898.

Sheremet, V. I. *Osmanskaya imperiya i Zapadnaya Yevropa. Vtoraya tret' xix v*. Moscow, 1986.

Shparo, O. B. *Zakhvat Kipra Angliey*. Moscow, 1974.

Shpil'kova, V. I. "Iz istorii proniknoveniya amerikanskogo kapitala v Turtsiyu v xix i nachale xx veka." *Uchenye zapiski MGPI im. Lenina* 1957, vol. 109, no. 6.

Silin, A. S. "Iz istorii politiki Bismarka v vostochnom voprose v 1870–1890 godakh." In *Voprosy istorii vneshney politiki SSSR i mezhdunarodnykh otnosheniy*. Moscow, 1976.

———. *Ekspansiya Germanii na Blizhnem Vostoke v kontse xix v*. Moscow, 1971.

Simonyan, H. R. *Turk azgayin burzhuaziayi gaghaparabanutiune yev kaghakakanutiune* (The ideology and policy of the Turkish national bourgeoisie). Yerevan, 1986.

Skazkin, S. *Konets avstro-russko-germanskogo soyuza*. Vol. 1. Moscow, 1928.

Somakian, M. J. *Empires in Conflict: Armenia and the Great Powers, 1895–1920*. London, 1995.

Stead, W. T. "The Eastern Ogre; or St. George to Rescue." *The Review of Reviews*, 1896, vol. 14.

Stepanyan, S. *Armeniya v politike imperialisticheskoy Germanii (konets xix–nachalo xx veka).* Yerevan, 1975.

Stride, W. K. "The Immediate Future of Armenia; The Suggestion." *The Forum,* 1896, vol. 22.

Tarle, Ye. V. "Angliya i Turtsiya. Istoricheskie korni i razvitie konflikta." *Annaly* 1923, no. 3.

Taroyan, K. Z. "Narodnye dvizheniya v Sasune i drugikh rayonakh Zapadnoy Armenii v 90-kh godakh xix v." Abstract of Ph.D. diss. in history. Yerevan, 1966.

———. *The Victorian Age in Politics, War and Diplomacy.* Cambridge, 1928.

Temperley, H. W. V. *England and the Near East. The Crimea.* London, 1936.

Temperley, H. W. V. and L. M. Penson. *Foundations of British Foreign Policy from Pitt (1792) to Salisbury (1902).* Cambridge, 1938.

Terrell, A. W. "An Interview with Sultan Abdul Hamid." *The Century Magazine,* 1897, vol. 55.

"The Armenian Question." *The Spectator,* 27 July 1895 (vol. 75).

"The Armenian Reforms." *The Spectator,* 18 May 1895 (vol. 74).

"The Constantinople Massacre." *The Contemporary Review,* 1896, vol. 70.

"The Evil of the Turk." *The Outlook,* 24 August 1895 (vol. 52).

"The Massacres." *The Spectator,* 5 September 1896 (vol. 77).

"The Situation of To-day." *The Spectator,* 3 October 1896 (vol. 77).

"The Suspense in Constantinople." *The Spectator,* 12 October 1895 (vol. 75).

Tigranyan, T. *Anglian yev hayere* (England and the Armenians). Yerevan, 1994.

Todorova, M. N. *Angliya, Rossiya i Tanzimat.* Moscow, 1983.

Trumpener, U. "Liman von Sanders and the German-Ottoman Alliance." *Journal of Contemporary History,* 1966.

Turkish Atrocities: The Young Turks and the Truth about the Holocaust at Adana in Asia Minor, during April, 1909, London, 1913.

Tyrkova, A. *Staraya Turtsiya i mladoturki.* Petrograd, 1916.

Van der Dussen, W. "The Question of Armenian Reforms in 1913–1914." *Armenian Review* 39, no. 1 (1986).

Vandal', A. *Armyane i turetskie reformy.* Saint Petersburg, 1908.

Vardanyan, H. G. *Arevmtahayeri azatagrutian hartse yev hay hasarakakan-kaghakakan hosanknere 19-rd dari verjin karordum* (The question of the liberation of Western Armenians and Armenian social-political currents in the last quarter of the 19th century). Yerevan, 1967.

Vneshneekonomicheskie svyazi Osmanskoy imperii v novoe vremya (konets xviii–nachalo xx v.). Moscow, 1989.

Walker, Christopher J. *Armenia: The Survival of a Nation.* New York, 1980.

Webster, C. K. *The Foreign Policy Of Palmerston: Britain, the Liberal Movement and the Eastern Question.* Vol. 2, London, 1951.

Williams, A. W. and M. S. Gabrielian. *Bleeding Armenia: Its History and Horrors.* New York, 1896.

Williams, Ch. *The Armenian Campaign: A Diary of the Campaign of 1878 in Armenia and Koordistan.* London, 1878.

Wittlin, A. *Abdul Hamid: The Shadow of God.* London, 1949.

Woods, Ch. *The Danger Zone of Europe.* London, 1911.

Zeidner, Robert F. "Britain and the Launching of the Armenian Question." *International Journal of Middle East Studies,* 1976, no 7.

5. Periodicals

Annaly, 1923, Moscow.

Arena, 1895–97, Boston.

Armenian Review, 1986, Watertown, Mass.

Atlantic Monthly, 1899, Boston.

Banber Hayastani arkhivneri, 1971, Yerevan.

Cambridge Historical Journal, 1935.

Catholic World, 1895–97, New York.

Century Magazine, 1895–97, New York.

Contemporary Review, 1894–97, London.

Fortnightly Review, 1890, 1895, 1896, London.

Forum, 1896, 1900, New York.

Hayastan (in Armenian), 1891, London.

Hayk (in Armenian), 1893-1895, New York.

Historical Journal, 1976, London.

Huntchak (in Armenian), 1894-1896, London.

Istorik-marksist, 1929–34, Moscow.

Journal of Armenian Studies, 1975, Cambridge, Mass.

Journal of British Studies, 1972, London.

Journal of Contemporary History, 1966, London.

Kavkaz, 1895–97, Tiflis.

Liberal Magazine, 1896, London.

Lraber hasarakakan gitutiunneri, 1980, 1984, Yerevan.

Middle Eastern Studies, 1971, London.

Morskoy sbornik, 1926, Leningrad.

Nation, 1895–99, New York.

Nor Kyank, 1898, London.

Novaya i noveyshaya istoriya, 1959, 1978, 1981, Moscow.

Novoe slovo, 1895–96, Saint Petersburg.

Novoe vremya, 1895, 1912–14, Saint Petersburg.

Outlook, 1895–97, New York.

Patmabanasirakan handes, 1979, Yerevan.
Review of Reviews, 1895–97, New York.
Saturday Review, 1895, London.
Slavonic and East European Review, 1960, London.
Spectator, 1890, 1891, 1895, 1896, London.
Uchenye zapiski MGPI im. Lenina, 1957, Moscow.
Vestnik Yerevanskogo universiteta. Obshchestvennye nauki, 1988.
Vestnik Yevropy, 1895–97, Saint Petersburg.

Index